WESTERNS

Lee Clark Mitchell

WESTERNS

MAKING THE MAN IN FICTION AND FILM

THE UNIVERSITY OF CHICAGO PRESS Chicago & London

LEE CLARK MITCHELL is Holmes Professor of Belles-Lettres and Chair of the Department of English at Princeton University. Among his books are *Witnesses to a Vanishing America* (1981), *Determined Fictions* (1989), and *The Photograph and the American Indian* (with A. Bush, 1994).

Frontispiece: photograph of Charles Schreyvogel, courtesy The National Cowboy Hall of Fame and Western Heritage Center, Oklahoma City, Oklahoma.

The University of Chicago Press, Chicago 60637
The University of Chicago Press, Ltd., London
© 1996 by The University of Chicago
All rights reserved. Published 1996
Printed in the United States of America
05 04 03 02 01 00 99 98 97 96   1 2 3 4 5

ISBN: 0-226-53234-8 (cloth)

Library of Congress Cataloging-in-Publication Data

Mitchell, Lee Clark, 1947–
    Westerns: making the man in fiction and film / Lee Clark Mitchell.
        p.   cm.
    Includes bibliographical references and index.
    1. Western stories—History and criticism.   2. American fiction—20th century—History and criticism.   3. Masculinity (Psychology)—United States—History.   4. Literature and motion pictures—West (U.S.)   5. Masculinity (Psychology) in literature. 6. Western films—History and criticism.   7. West (U.S.)—In literature.   8. Men in motion pictures.   9. Men in literature. I. Title.
PS374.W4M55   1996
813'.087409353—dc20   96-13216
                                                             CIP

For Carolyn

I think nowadays, while literary men seem to have neglected their epic duties, the epic has been saved for us, strangely enough, by the Westerns, . . . has been saved for the world by of all places, Hollywood.

Jorge Luis Borges (1967)[1]

The Old West is not a certain place in a certain time, it's a state of mind. It's whatever you want it to be.

Tom Mix (ca. 1938)[2]

The more a system is specifically defined in its forms, the more amenable it is to historical criticism. To parody a well-known saying, I shall say that a little formalism turns one away from History, but that a lot brings one back to it.

Roland Barthes (1957)[3]

contents

illustrations

acknowledgments

Writing a serious book about a form which appeals precisely because it does not seem serious can create problems.

Rick Altman (1987)[1]

I have been blessed with friends who, dubious as they may be about popular culture, indulge me—an indulgence that nonetheless rarely extends to simply accepting what I have to say. In the process of trying to convince them—or better yet, listening to their hesitations—I have incurred a debt only those writing books can take pleasure in detailing.

James McPherson inadvertently started it all in a seminar we taught a decade ago by getting me to read *The Virginian,* then encouraging me to articulate my misgivings. Since then, many colleagues and friends have generously critiqued separate chapters: Brian Dippie, Gordon Hutner, Gail Jardine, Michael Kowaleski, Jules Law, David Leverenz, Jim Longenbach, Deak Naybors, Patrick O'Kelley, Elaine Showalter, and David Wyatt. Others just as generously shaped my thinking in other forms and forums, including Christine Bold, Karin Esders, Shelley Fischer Fishkin, Winfried Fluck, and Daniel Rodgers. P. Adams Sitney provided timely assistance with film illustrations, and without the assistance of Mark Erwin the Index would be far less effective. Under pressure, Beth Harrison and Kathy DiMeglio performed with their usual grace and efficiency in getting the book to press. And at the University of Chicago Press, Alan Thomas has been exemplary in support of the project, as have Randy Petilos and Lila Weinberg.

For invitations to lecture (and hospitality that accompanied the visits), I am grateful to John Atherton (Université de Paris VIII), Emily Budick (Hebrew University), Marc Chénetier (Ecole Normale Supérieure), Winfried Fluck and Heinz Ickstadt (Freie Universität, Berlin), Barbara Hochman and Hana Wirth-Nesher (University of Tel Aviv), Linda Ferber (Brooklyn Museum), Pierre Lagayette (Université de Paris X), Patricia Limerick (NEH Summer Institute, Boulder, Colorado), Townsend Luddington (Reynolda House Museum of American Art, Winston-Salem, North Carolina), and Richard Martin (Technische Hochschule, Aachen). More than a quarter century ago in a Sussex theater, Doug Gordon and I first stumbled upon Sergio Leone, and my ongoing encounter with questions left lingering then is much at the heart of this book. Even earlier, as a boy in the 1950s, I learned the delights of film Westerns from a father who inspired me to choose for my first written essay in grade school the subject of John Wayne. My only regret is that his death came just as this book was going to press.

Five good friends exceeded the bounds of friendship in rigorously reading the entire manuscript, and they—Martha Banta, Frank Bergon, Alfred Bush, Howard Horsford, and Garrett Stewart—spurred me to take greater risks by warning of pedestrian arguments and tame conclusions (whether they saved me from such hazards is another matter). Likewise, the readers for the University of Chicago Press—Edward Buscombe and particularly David Leverenz—offered detailed critiques that were invaluable in the final stages of revision.

More than anyone, Carolyn Abbate is the reader for whom this book was intended, and not simply because she has read and watched more Westerns than a spouse should be asked to endure, nor even that she has regularly turned from her projects on German Romantic opera to improve the draft of yet another chapter on horse operas. More important than her indulgence has been her engagement with issues addressed here, her playfully imaginative way of joining the conversation, getting me to see what I wanted to say often simply by saying it better. As loving partner throughout, she has listened, challenged, inspired, comforted. May there be many more books together (though preferably not on Westerns), and may they be as much fun to write knowing she is there to read them.

For financial support I am grateful to the Fulbright Commission for fellowships awarded in 1990 and 1994 at both the Freie Universität and the Humboldt Universität in Berlin. The Princeton University Committee on Research in the Humanities has been generous with moneys to help in completing the manuscript. Earlier versions of three chapters have appeared in *American Literary History, PMLA,* and *Reading the West: New Essays on the Literature of the American West* (Cambridge University Press, 1996).

WESTERNS

introduction

I've always acted alone. Americans admire that immensely. Americans like the cowboy who leads the wagon train by riding ahead alone on his horse, the cowboy who rides all alone into the town, the village, with his horse and nothing else. Maybe even without a pistol, since he doesn't shoot. He acts, that's all, by being in the right place at the right time. In short, a Western.

Henry Kissinger (1972)[1]

The Western is a great grab-bag, a hungry cuckoo of a genre, a voracious bastard of a form, open equally to visionaries and opportunists, ready to seize anything that's in the air from juvenile delinquency to ecology.

Philip French (1973)[2]

The image remains unaltered in countless versions from the genre's beginning—a lone man packing a gun, astride a horse, hat pulled close to the eyes, emerging as if by magic out of a landscape from which he seems ineluctably a part. And the stark simplicity of the Western appears as obvious as that image—one that generations of Americans have come to admire (as Kissinger effuses) "immensely." As setting for this masculine prize, the Western relies on an assortment of visual props: of colorful garb (from ten-gallon hats to high-heeled boots), photogenic terrain (high plains ranch-land, desert Southwest), and a stock cast of characters (ranchers and farm-ers, sheriffs and desperados, boys in blue surrounded by red men in paint). Alone among genres, moreover, the Western has recast mythical icons out of drab historical figures: lawmen (Wyatt Earp, Pat Garrett), outlaws (Billy the Kid, Jesse James), Indian leaders (Geronimo, Cochise), even tubercular dentists (Doc Holliday).[3]

These familiar materials, however, are only so many unwoven raw strands. What actually brings them together into the narrative we recognize as a Western are a set of problems recurring in endless combination: the problem of progress, envisioned as a passing of frontiers; the problem of honor, defined in a context of social expediency; the problem of law or justice, enacted in a conflict of vengeance and social control; the problem of violence, in acknowledging its value yet honoring occasions when it can be controlled; and subsuming all, the problem of what it means to be a man, as aging victim of progress, embodiment of honor, champion of jus-tice in an unjust world.

More than anything else, this persistent obsession with masculinity marks the Western, even though to put the matter so simply seems either inaccurate or banal. After all, other genres have confronted the problem of "making the man," making it hard to see how so many different solutions   3 to that problem over a century could grant a characteristic single shape to "the" Western. Isn't it easier to assume instead that readily identifiable raw materials (hats, Indians, horses) lend the genre its characteristic tenor? Easier, perhaps, but less interesting than the versatile Western itself, which has repeatedly transformed itself for different audiences and different ideals of manhood.

One of this book's two premises, in fact, is that any popular text engages immediately pressing issues—issues that become less pressing in time. With each generation, a genre's plots, narrative emphases, stylistic pressures, even scenic values have less in common with earlier versions of that genre than with competing genres, all striving to resolve the same contemporary anxieties. Yet the second premise is just as crucial and controverts the first: that from the beginning the Western has fretted over the construction of masculinity, whether in terms of gender (women), maturation (sons), honor (restraint), or self-transformation (the West itself). The Western may be "a hungry cuckoo of a genre" (in Philip French's words), "ready to seize anything that's in the air from juvenile delinquency to ecology," but it is also deeply haunted by the problem of becoming a man. Each of these two aspects of the genre lies at the heart of the following chapters, which identify habitual gestures evoked by the ongoing dilemma of masculinity on the one hand, and on the other address the ephemeral contexts that lend particular Westerns their urgency. Yet what are the limits of a form so often *trans*formed yet still recognizable? What are the general coordinates of the Western—and of the West as the Western presents it—that have continued to make the genre such a resonant vehicle?

The West and the Western

The Western may be unmistakable, with a conspicuous set of characters, settings, and props, but these provide little by way of generic guarantee. In fact, the landscape naming the genre, that signals it *as* a Western (and in the process as the sole popular genre marked in geographical terms), turns out to be uncommonly diverse, resistant to any straightforward reading. More generally, the central terms "West" and "Western," which have forged American cultural identity, are less self-evident than initial impressions might lead one to believe. Actual landscapes are everywhere recast in the Western, which conceives of setting not as authentic locale but as escapist fantasy. The West in the Western matters less as verifiable topography than as space removed from cultural coercion, lying beyond ideology (and therefore, of course, the most ideological of terrains).

4

The one aspect of the landscape celebrated consistently in the Western is the opportunity for renewal, for self-transformation, for release from constraints associated with an urbanized East. Whatever else the West may be, in whatever form it is represented, it always signals freedom to achieve some truer state of humanity. Or as Frederick Jackson Turner declared shortly before the birth of the genre, the West's "significance" lay in the utopian expectations it aroused. Regardless of quite different topographies embraced by the region, Turner's West matched Americans' aspirations—economic and social, political and personal. And though historians have repudiated Turner's slighting of actual history, his depiction matches the singular landscape found in countless horse operas.

The very persistence of this utopian view of the West has meant that the Western has been a peculiarly flexible form, available to an array of ideological issues. Because the landscape remains the same despite change of scene (site of transformation, place of free speaking), the paradox of Western plots is that they can alter with altering winds of cultural anxiety and popular ideals. The *West* is stable, the *Western* labile: the distinction is apparent in commonplaces associated with each. As sheer scenery, the American West is indistinguishable from parts of Australia, Paraguay, Spain, and New Jersey (as directors from Edwin S. Porter to Sergio Leone have known to their profit). But phrases like "Far West," "El Dorado," "Big Sky Country," or "Virgin Land" all resonate with semantic excess, imposing on that terrain the blankness of an uninscribed page, implying a freedom to alter it at will.

And just as scenery in Westerns need not match Far Western topography, so Western plots have had only the vaguest basis in actual conditions—conditions that in any event were marginal to the consciousness of most Americans. Cowboys, cattle towns, and long drives north formed a minor chapter in western history; range wars were simply labor strikes on horseback, and the "lone gunman" a rare psychopath, regarded as such and with contempt. It is not unfair to say that few Americans attached more than passing significance to Indian wars, railroad extensions, mining and lumber operations—certainly vis-à-vis more pressing eastern considerations. And yet this negligible history was seized upon by writers, who transmuted facts, figures, and movements beyond recognition, projecting mythic possibilities out of prosaic events (Pat Garrett's capture of Billy the Kid, Custer's last stand, the Earp-Clanton shoot-out at Tombstone's O.K. Corral). In fact, a reason western history could be transmuted into art so readily was because it was viewed by Americans as pleasantly varied but inconsequential.

5

When factual accuracy comes to seem inconsequential, novels emerge to do the narrative work that history refuses. Viewers and readers of the Western lacked (still lack) a conviction that western history mattered—just the conviction to steel one against literary suasions. Instead of attempting to modify belief with historical truths, then, the Western's public accommodates itself to the self-referential dictates of a flexible genre. Like other escapist narratives, Westerns map out anxieties about conditions from which people want to escape—anxieties that change with time as do their imaginative solutions. Countless Westerns have appeared for nearly a century now, supposedly fixed by generic code but actually responsive to crises and fears that earlier Westerns failed to anticipate. If the genre is our fullest "objectified mass dream," as Henry Nash Smith once claimed, we need then to acknowledge how fluently that dream has always mutated.[4]

The West of "free speaking" was thus never an actual place, first discovered, then explored, but has always been instead an ideological terrain reinvented with each generation of fears and hopes. Western authors have responded to current issues through narrative transformations so severe that even the ongoing obsession with "making the man" has taken distinctive shapes at different moments in American history. The most successful examples win their audiences not by replaying that obsession as simply "another Western" but rather by reshaping it, weaving it together with other problems and issues, in the process offering resolutions that seem satisfyingly unique. As Tony Bennett and Janet Woolacott have written of James Bond's appeal, "it is not the popularity of *Bond* that has to be accounted for so much as the popularity of *different Bonds,* popular in different ways and for different reasons at different points in time."[5]

Those who speak of "the" Western as all of a piece, formulaically fixed, fail to realize how fully it endures as entertainment because it *has* changed, inventively altering both its materials and narrative shape. Westerns are always written from the East on behalf of values signaling the West's demise. After all, one might well ask, who else would be so in touch with issues that appeal to consumers of popular culture if not one of their own, immersed in more clearly national rather than regional contexts? The most popular writers and directors have never been westerners affirming some version of their own story. Quite the contrary: the Western has so little to do with an actual West that it might better be thought of as its own epitaph, written by an exuberant East encroaching on possibilities already foreclosed because represented in terms of a West that "no longer exists," never did, never could.

Constancy and Change

While no formula binds such varied texts together, the Western has none-theless persisted as what might be called a mode through a long history of changing formats: from "penny dreadfuls" and dime novels through "pulp" and "slick" magazines; from silent, black-and-white one-reelers through the sound era of Technicolor film; from half-hour weekly television programs through blockbuster miniseries. Despite advances in production technique and evolutions in aesthetic form, despite flagrant accommodations to less local concerns (in anti-Nazi and anti-Communist Westerns, in singing cowboy and film noir Westerns, in spaghetti and hippie and anti-Western Westerns), the mode never seems to lose what Wittgenstein referred to as a "family resemblance"—a resemblance due to its preoccupation with the problem of manhood.[6]

Other factors have also lent a hand, including the paradoxical fact that pressure to reshape conventions according to contemporary criteria has had the effect of augmenting family resemblances. The dime novel of the 1860s, for instance, relaxed James Fenimore Cooper's rigid structures to suit current needs, collapsing class and regional distinctions into the person of a youthful hero.[7] At the same time, Erasmus Beadle's pulp fiction borrowed a plot unchanged from Cooper (and by Cooper from an earlier tradition) of capture, flight, and pursuit. Ironically, this captivity pattern emulates the problem of the Western itself, regularly escaping Cooper's influence through ever more updated forms even as that influence keeps reinscribing itself in narrative structures themselves. The same can be said of every other strong practitioner—Owen Wister notably, but also Zane Grey and Louis L'Amour—who seized material from predecessors in order to give it a distinctive stamp only to find that earlier emphases lingered on.

The following chapters clarify some of the forms of that persistence, and not only thematically, as expression of irresolvable questions about masculinity. Just as important has been an aspect often ignored in popular genres: recurrent formal properties and abstract design, the characteristic claim they make for aesthetic delight. In the case of Westerns, a notable instance of this form of generic persistence emerges in the contrast of novelistic and cinematic examples: the emphasis on landscape (unmatched in any other popular genre) into which violence intrudes confirms an inborn predisposition to scenic representation. That may be why written Westerns aspire to a dramatic, even theatrical status attained by the genre only with the advent of film.[8] In this regard, it is worth recalling that Cooper inspired American painters as no other novelist before or since, and that an imaginative engagement with the optical continues so vigorously in the legacy he left that one of the questions raised by Western novels is whether they actively foster a mental process of covert dramatization. Is it true that the reader is visually compelled to shift between narrative and descriptive modes in a process associated more often with drama or cinema than with novels? The question dominates much that follows, and it directs us to aesthetic innovations that lend to certain texts a surprising appeal despite their reliance on well-worked themes.

For the moment, such innovations are less important than the acknowledgment that popular Westerns succeed in engaging even audiences ill-disposed to the West, combining an attention to "making the man" with other equally compelling issues in an exhilarating narrative mix. That combination cannot be satisfactorily explained in terms of political allegory or social fable, of straightforward mutation of current anxieties into plots that stage and assuage them—the way, for instance, Bruno Bettelheim viewed fairy tales, as parables guiding children through adolescence. After all, we are not children; literature and film are rarely fables; reading and viewing are more complex than studies of fictional plot as a culture's "talking cure" allow. The most popular texts are also always a culture's most powerful, most fragily balanced, and require attention commensurate to their capacity to move and assuage.

Formal Selection

The sustaining premise behind the choice of Westerns discussed in this book is twofold: they reveal a contemporary self-consciousness about ideals of masculine behavior, and they define a history of otherwise contested moments in popular culture (a history far from apparent on their narrative surfaces). The fact that these are among the most popular texts in American history ought to tell us something about the Americans who avidly read and watched them. Yet it is not simply the fact of popularity itself that should command interest—or, at least, not popularity in the narrow sense of best-seller lists and first-run ticket sales. For if these books and films exerted an extraordinary hold on contemporaries, they also had a transformative effect on the genre itself, altering our ongoing sense of what the Western ought to be. I would go even further to claim that their popularity was allied to this transformative flexibility, seeming at once familiar and new, comforting yet freshly up-to-date, all the while appearing to resolve a series of widespread misgivings less through story line than other means.

After an introductory chapter that explores more fully the implications of popularity, I turn to an author who cleared the ground for the genre in his celebration of frontier landscape, feats of violence, and masculine self-construction. Fenimore Cooper's descriptive technique, moreover, nicely coincides with his ideal of moral restraint, seeming to paralyze action in novels that otherwise stress an action-adventure format. In a period of social dislocation, the allure of Natty Bumppo lay in the capacity to read him as a mediating figure, poised yet still, responsible yet detached, at last no more socially or politically involved than the landscape itself. He is the model on which all other attempts to "make the man" will be practiced. And here a caveat is in order: the fact that none of the Leatherstocking series were actually set in the Far West is irrelevant to their influence on a genre that relies on landscape as an essential constituent. More important than the choice of upstate New York (or the trans-Missouri prairie) was Cooper's investment of wilderness scenes with a rejuvenative, highly moral ambience. His descriptions allowed "nature's nation" finally to relish how fully its identity was tied up with the continent's native scenes, and more significantly how those scenes could be made to incarnate social aspirations.[9] The actual Far West being explored and settled as Cooper wrote would become the site of the Western not simply for geographical reasons, then, but because authors adapted the arresting techniques he first devised to imagine how masculinity might be constructed.

Chapter 3 focuses on two figures—Albert Bierstadt and Bret Harte—who transformed possibilities introduced by Cooper to become the most popular artists of the 1860s. Bierstadt set out a mythic landscape, Harte the stereotypical characters, for a Western novel yet to be invented. The mood of nationalistic self-congratulation they engaged, however, demanded a marriage of separate triumphs (landscape *with* character) that neither artist was able to provide. Not until Owen Wister's *The Virginian* (1902) does the Western reach its acknowledged embodiment, the first in a line of narratives that stretch through this century. Yet as Chapter 4 reveals, that novel fails to fulfill the functions usually attributed to the Western, which makes its influence an intriguing question of literary history. Part of the answer lies in *The Virginian's* adroit engagement of gender issues at a time of intense concern about "woman's place," helping to explain how readers of differing convictions about male and female roles could find it so appealing. Wister's ambivalence strongly influenced Zane Grey, whose *Riders of the Purple Sage* (1912) is the subject of Chapter 5. At a time of even greater concern about the independent New Woman, his novel introduces the idea of a conspiracy against women, who are presented as at once self-sufficient yet nonetheless dependent on men for their safety. Like Wister, Grey offers male bodies and masculine self-construction (if also female

9

bodies self-constructed) to define an even more erotically charged field of gender relations.

Chapter 6 turns from individual texts to the genre's admiration for the male body, assessing scenes from fiction and film to see why so many Westerns punish men as a pretext to allow them to recover, restoring them once more to manhood. Westerns repeatedly insist that continuous effort is required to remain a man, to achieve paradoxically through cultural forms a state that is supposedly biological. The question is why that achievement must be negotiated through scenes depicting the body's destruction. Chapter 7 turns from violence to juxtapose three films that share a pattern common from the beginning, if never so glaringly emphasized: initiation, education, sons and fathers. *High Noon* (1952), *Shane* (1952), and *Hondo* (1953) succeeded in a period distressed about adolescence by seeming to resolve the problem of "growing up" in mutually exclusive ways, offering parental (indeed paternalistic) models that never quite secure our belief. And while the Westerns of the following decade are sometimes termed "anti-Westerns," Chapter 8 explores Sergio Leone's *A Fistful of Dollars* (1964) and Sam Peckinpah's *The Wild Bunch* (1969) as films suggesting the West can be anywhere and that the western code has never been more than a form of ruthless capitalism. The increased violence of these films disguises a disagreement over liberal social policy, of state subventions and economic distress, even though one film's environmentalism differs little from the other's Hobbesian vision.

Though arbitrary, this sequence can be faulted less for texts it includes (among the genre's most popular and influential) than those it ignores. Few novelists have been as successful as Karl May and Frederick Faust (otherwise known as "Max Brand"), and were this book longer they would both have required ample space. The history of cinema is likewise filled with important examples: the first Western, Edwin S. Porter's popular, innovative, and influential twelve-minute *The Great Train Robbery* (1903);[10] the most lucrative Western ever filmed (based on production costs), David O. Selznick's *Duel in the Sun* (1946); and Mel Brooks' *Blazing Saddles* (1974), still cinema's top-grossing Western.[11] Almost single-handedly, *Broken Arrow* (1950) was responsible for transforming cinematic attitudes toward the Indian at the moment when sentiments for black integration were first given a national hearing. Again, such examples call out for rigorous analysis to explain not only their appeal but their transformation of generic conventions.

On the other hand, one reason for slighting a film like John Ford's *The Searchers* (1955), at once commercially successful and among the most influential Westerns, is that it has already served as locus classicus in so

10

many other accounts. There is, more generally, a history of intelligent commentary on Westerns that extends back to Robert Warshow's groundbreaking essay, "Movie Chronicle: The Westerner" (1954). Taking for granted the seriousness of a genre that until the 1950s was dismissed out of hand, Warshow offered a compelling defense of the Western's concern with violence and pointed the way for many of the more detailed examinations that followed.[12] A decade later, John G. Cawelti advanced discussion by proposing attention to popular texts across genre lines (including examples from sports, politics, even social manners), believing that such an approach would give a more historical sense of the Western's structure and meaning.[13] If the very ambitiousness of his scope condemned him to "being neither adequately structural nor adequately historical" (as Fredric Jameson ruefully observed), the seriousness of his approach nonetheless inspired others.[14]

Not all succeeded equally. By contrast with Cawelti, Will Wright's study is more strictly defined (top-grossing films between 1931 and 1972), his critical take more exacting (literary structuralism), and his interpretation of stages in cultural contradiction more historically specific. Yet while *Six Guns and Society* (1975) is the most ambitious investigation of the film Western to date, it suffers from theoretical incoherence, collapsing Vladimir Propp's diachronic sequence of undeviating plot functions together with Claude Lévi-Strauss's synchronic pairing of thematic oppositions, as if the two antithetical methods could be combined.[15] Even more important, Wright's exchange of isolated texts for a master plot ends up confirming instead how much individual details always do matter—the non-sequential minutia of scenery and cinematography, the evocations of music and sound track, the idiosyncrasies of casting, that also make for successful films.

A prominent recent example at once more incisive and less suasive than Wright is Jane Tompkins, whose *West of Everything* (1992) makes the generic claim that "the Western *answers* the domestic novel."[16] Her totalizing theory extends over a century of Westerns in fiction and film to argue that similar partial descriptions "all describe the same man" (72)—a man in flight from the domestic constraints of Victorian culture, afraid of losing mastery, at the center of an endlessly repeated drama of death, inarticulateness, emotional numbness in a genre whose pattern of violence "never varies" (228). As ambitious as Cawelti, if less theoretically constrained than Wright, Tompkins moves through a broad swath of Westerns to prompt provocative observations she can neither prove nor disprove, more interesting in themselves than for what they say about her thesis of a twentieth-century Western and a nineteenth-century domestic novel.

Resisting the temptation of grand master narratives, some critics have begun to attend more closely to local features of novelistic language and cinematic imagery. Following their lead, I want to address the question of how it is that unlikely, even eccentric, structural materials and aesthetic gestures can have such immense appeal, how narratives so distant from the lives of most Americans nonetheless captured their imaginations. My point is that loudly significant plots do not explain such appeal. Obvious stories divert attention instead away from the impact of verbal ploys and camera angles, rhetorical tropes and inspired acting, unusual descriptive maneuvers and film editing. Indeed, plot—as simple parable or obvious allegory—plays a relatively minimal part in the force exerted by Westerns.[17]

The approach adopted in the following chapters, summarized best by Barthes's injunction in the epigraph to this book, is a series of historical readings that ensue from an intense regard for aesthetic form. The question driving the whole is: What can be learned by attending to formal considerations about contested ideals and persistent anxieties that transformed some Westerns into such monsters of popularity? More important, how are an era's inadmissible disparities, its covert social contradictions, perhaps particularly its deepest concerns about gender, erased by fictional and cinematic dynamics? How, in short, is the pain of "what hurts" (to borrow Jameson's terse characterization of "history") so often relieved by strange rhythms incompatible with that pain?[18]

Two final caveats are in order. The first is that the contextualizations offered in the following chapters are sketchy and suggestive, unapologetically so. This book begins and ends as a formalist analysis of popular texts, not a historical study of the moments in which they appeared. Those interested in more exacting explanations of these moments are encouraged to turn to scholarly accounts listed in the notes. The second caveat ensues from the first: historical explanations suggested for the appeal of these Westerns are hardly meant as exclusive, if only because my central premise is that these Westerns won favor by sustaining *multiple* interpretations. Success is always overdetermined, the result of a constellation of enthusiasms and causes, and popular texts do more than assuage anxieties about "sexual anarchy," or adolescence, or social policy. In short, Westerns "make the man" in forms varied enough to appeal to a broad spectrum of contemporary audiences. My claim is only that the crises about gender construction adduced in the following chapters help explain part of these Westerns' broad-based appeal, an appeal that requires in turn more broadly ranging explanations. What seems hardest for those no longer in the thrall of a given cultural moment to grasp is the capacity of art to resolve ideological issues far removed from its fictive terrain. To gain a sense for that historically specific response, we need to explore not only the blunt plots so characteristic of such texts but rather all the strange textures, the contours and grains, the idiosyncrasies that draw our eyes away from the center to unlit places where their power resides.

1 POPULAR APPEAL

*[Magua] so blended the warlike with the artful, the obvious with the
obscure, as to flatter the propensities of both parties, and to leave to
each subject of hope, while neither could say, it clearly comprehended
his intentions.*

*The orator, or the politician, who can produce such a state of
things, is commonly popular with his contemporaries, however he
may be treated by posterity. All perceived that more was meant than
was uttered, and each one believed that the hidden meaning was precisely such as his own faculties enabled him to understand, or his own
wishes led him to anticipate.*

James Fenimore Cooper (1827)[1]

*"Home on the Range," one of President [Theodore] Roosevelt's favor-
ites, in which the Pollyanna sentiment is contradicted by the doleful
music, is an instance of the larger paradox of horse opera itself.*

Marshall McLuhan (1951)[2]

A curious sense of disproportion is evoked by any listing of luminaries who loved Westerns, as if that were the sole common denominator among such different lives: Richard Nixon, Jorge Luis Borges, Joseph Stalin, Ludwig Wittgenstein, Jean Cocteau, Sherwood Anderson, Dwight D. Eisenhower, Simone de Beauvoir, Douglas MacArthur, Akira Kurosawa. Self-made men (mostly men) find Westerns appealing for their accent on masculine self construction, captured perfectly by F. Scott Fitzgerald in the forlorn gesture of Mr. Gatz after the death of his son, pulling "from his pocket a ragged old copy of a book called *Hopalong Cassidy*" in which Jay Gatsby had copied out a schedule of daily resolutions.[3] But this obsessive attention to "making the man" cannot alone account for the appeal of what for much of this century has proved America's most popular fiction and film. As Henry Kissinger has admitted, the attributes championed by the genre (of conviction, independence, action) are part of the common coin of American social and political sensibility, whether in "Marlboro Country," John F. Kennedy's "New Frontier," the ubiquity of blue jeans, Ronald Reagan's "cowboy presidency," or countless other cultural locales.

Still, broad claims for the popularity of any genre end by seeming tautological, failing to explain why individual texts are more compelling than others at given historical moments. There is nothing obvious about the fact that certain Western novels and films have appealed with a particular intensity, especially when neither the cowboy, the West, nor the shoot-out have had much to do with the lives of most Americans. While the following chapters take for granted the popularity of texts they examine, then, a larger question needs to be addressed at the outset: What does popularity mean in general, and how is it that particular Westerns have engaged such a broad audience? Part of the answer lies in the capacity of any really popular text to fulfill yet alter expectations, giving its audience a sense of novelty

15

tinged by familiarity. As well, part lies in appearing to resolve cultural dilemmas in a way that satisfies disparate groups with opposed interests. After exploring implications of this theory of popular texts, I turn in this chapter to two of the Western's most theoretically self-conscious practitioners (Stephen Crane and John Ford), before briefly describing the emergence of the cowboy hero at the turn of the century.

Multivalent Possibilities

This book is premised on the assumption that popular culture is never univocal, even in defiance of stated intentions. Books and films that appeal overpoweringly at a given time resist a straightforward reading—indeed, attract disparate audiences because they *do* so effectively satisfy different constituencies. Readers and viewers simply respond to the same materials in differing ways, reconstructing texts to suit views that are often diametrically opposed. In short, popular texts only seem to resolve the issues they engage. When looked at more methodically, they achieve something more complex: negotiating a threatened middle terrain, offering narrative forms that avoid inherent contradictions in the ideological premises they celebrate. And by so doing, they provide appealing patterns of allegedly good behavior, attractive models for mediating conflict *in a certain way.*

Nowhere else are such models of behavior so clearly delineated, and the reason is that any more logical discussion of the ideals Americans share—of equality, say, or the right to life, or privacy and the pursuit of happiness—leads immediately to contradiction and conflict. In American society, the burden of having to decide what it is that constitutes equality, life, and privacy is left to judges and legislators. But the conflict is not thereby relieved. And to these most basic of premises can be added a host of other contested beliefs that shape our lives without being resolved: gendered difference or biological similarity, class distinctions or character traits, immediate (if illegal) justice or the unfair delays of the law, innate evil or social conditioning. The hard-won attraction of popular novels and films lies in their capacity not simply to give both possibilities a hearing but to make each seem convincing (if only to those already convinced).

A striking embodiment of this view of popular culture is the Iroquois Magua of Cooper's *The Last of the Mohicans,* who leads a divided tribe by cultivating an ability (as the epigraph states) "to flatter the propensities of both parties," allowing each to believe "that the hidden meaning was precisely such as his own faculties enabled him to understand, or his own wishes led him to anticipate." Where Magua stoops to oratorical vagueness, however, popular texts on the contrary display a crystalline clarity—

whether hard-boiled detective novels or Cold War spy films, the 1940s "woman's picture" or science fiction space odysseys. And the Western's ability to maintain its hold as the most popular of genres may have been partly due to the starkness of its materials—of familiar characters, settings, and situations that allow contested agendas to be defined simply yet suggestively. This narrative economy encourages a semantic resonance in which alternative readings with mutually exclusive "resolutions" of social issues are seen as equally possible, equally persuasive. Even more to the point, the Western's multivalent structure is matched by an array of aesthetic ornaments, stylistic and formal features that reinforce those tensions. Marshall McLuhan's observation on "the larger paradox of horse opera itself," as akin to the contradiction between the sentimental lyrics and doleful music in "Home on the Range," forms a notable example of this contrapuntal strain.[4]

If nothing is so obvious about the Western as its persistent popularity, nothing seems at the same time so inexplicable. Certainly, the constitution of its audience remains peculiarly obscure for a genre dominant so long in so many media (hardcover novels, slick magazines, technicolor film extravaganzas, and television series, among others)—and this despite some attention to identifying the specific consumers of Westerns.[5] The larger question of the relation between a popular text, its consumers, and any larger historical analysis continues therefore to be a particularly vexed one. What can safely be deduced, with or without empirical research, about a text that appeals to millions—or more to the point, about those millions themselves? Among others, Geoffrey O'Brien has simply denied there is much to say:

In looking at old movies, historicism is indispensable, but it has its limits. By watching *Foolish Wives* do we come to understand anything about 1922 and the mentality of its spectators, or do we construct a fiction from the haunting shapes and moods of *Foolish Wives,* and call it 1922? Must we, in fact, linger unduly over the fact that *Foolish Wives* was made in 1922?[6]

The answer to this last is "yes," and for two reasons, one textual, the other historical: textually, because the context we construct for any film or book is as important (and complexly interrelated) a part of its present meaning as anything else we may see in it—indeed, forms the basis of its intertextual meaning. Texts never come unaccompanied. And historically, because those who lived in the past are available to us (as we are to each other) through the evidence of their preference in cultural forms. Those enthusiasms evoke what others thought and believed. Meanings in this sense are not parsed out as we will—here to context, there to formal structure—but come tumbling in as fully in our aesthetic considerations as in our historicist claims.[7]

Still, the issue of gross popularity prompts a number of questions at the outset: If purely a matter of sales, does that mean only books sold on first publication or movies seen on initial release? Are volumes that sell well for a number of years as popular as those that shoot to the top of best-seller lists only to fade from view? And how should one consider the matter of textual influence—of lesser-known films, say, that have a decisive impact on subsequent productions? In short, what confers the pedigree of popularity on a text?[8] Even when answers are unambiguous, the meaning of popularity itself remains. Mario Puzo's *The Godfather* and D. H. Lawrence's *Lady Chatterley's Lover* are, for instance, "the bestselling novels ever in the US and UK respectively." John Sutherland goes on to claim that "until the great 10 million blockbusters of the 1970s, Spillane was the all-time fiction bestseller."[9] Indisputable as these facts are, their significance remains enigmatic, allowing us to assume at once too little and too much about what such popularity can reveal of an audience or a culture.

Theorizing the Popular

Part of the difficulty posed by the question of popularity is simply that reading and viewing themselves are such complex activities, making it hard to determine what actually appeals in a text at a particular moment or why that appeal is so ephemeral. Ever since the 1930s, when F. R. and Q. D. Leavis polarized a distinction between art as creative moral enrichment and mass culture as escapist consumption, critics have disdained popular culture as a debased version of folk culture in an industrial age. "Kitsch," as Clement Greenberg defined the product, "is mechanical and operates by formulas. Kitsch is vicarious experience and faked sensations. Kitsch changes according to style but remains always the same."[10] In lamenting the leveling effect of this "mass product of Western industrialism," Greenberg and other New York intellectuals of the 1940s and 1950s clearly had the Western in mind.

As did the Frankfurt School critics of the same period (most prominently Adorno, Horkheimer, and Marcuse), who emigrated to America and declaimed against the manipulative means through which a homogenized mass culture had been imposed upon a passive public. The most popular products (Hollywood films) were constructed to appeal to the least common denominator of interest, in order not only to turn a profit but to shape popular thought. A so-called culture industry was envisioned in essentially fascist terms, as a regimenting of compliant consumers in what Marcuse described as "the systematic moronization of children and adults alike by publicity and propaganda." Much in the manner of Greenberg's analysis, those of the Frankfurt School were pitched so starkly on the high moral ground of modernism (in contempt of all capitalist productions) that any significance to be gleaned from popular music, literature, dance, sports, or film was reduced to little more than an opiate for a depoliticized, inert population.[11]

During the same period, popular culture was investigated less gloomily, more evenhandedly by American theorists, prominently by Henry Nash Smith, who transformed American Studies in his attention to the dime novels and penny dreadfuls of the nineteenth century. Churned out at amazing speed by anonymous hacks, this "automatic writing" reflected Americans' deepest assumptions and beliefs, or so Smith believed, as if cultural anxieties were speaking through the comatose body of the writer, inscribing themselves ventriloquistically in a series of widely read, formulaic texts. Indeed, Smith believed that simple content analysis would reveal the significance of these texts for their original readers. All one needed was New Critical reading techniques to retrieve from dime novels their meaning for an entire culture.[12]

Peter Burke has indirectly critiqued Smith's method in his study of the eighteenthth-century *Bibliothèque Bleue* (anonymous French chapbooks distributed by peddlers). "*Who* is speaking through these chapbooks?" he pointedly asks. "To *whom* were these messages addressed?" And he admits that "we are left with the most difficult questions, those of intentions and effects." Though Burke offers few specific answers, he argues forcefully against treating chapbooks as evidence of popular belief, as if one could assume that people (usually a class below us) simply "passively absorb what is fed to them."[13] The implication of his cautious approach is that social meanings are always contested, far more than any thematic appraisal of popular texts allows.

Two of the most brilliant readers of popular culture emerged in the 1950s: Marshall McLuhan with *The Mechanical Bride* (1951), and Roland Barthes with *Mythologies* (1957). Affected by the Frankfurt School, both viewed popular culture (in Anthony Hilfer's words) "as a structure of reassurances, a gigantic pacifier operating to mark and narcotize the pain caused by an exploitative and dehumanizing social and economic order."[14] Yet the energy, wit, and ingenuity with which McLuhan and Barthes unmasked an array of cultural texts—including comic books, popular advertising, television wrestling, Charlie McCarthy, and Superman—undermined the pessimistic vision they expressed of cultural conditioning. And their willingness to read such popular documents with an intensity usually   19 reserved for avant-garde and "high" cultural icons meant that the conventional distinction between these supposedly disparate realms began to dissolve despite their efforts to preserve the distinction.

In the early 1970s, the Birmingham School built on such work to theorize a position on behalf of the complexity, even the revolutionary potential, of mass culture. Anxious not to reduce whole populations to the role of placid consumers, Stuart Hall explicitly positioned himself against Adorno's view of "mass manipulation and deception." He started with the idea that there is a "double-stake in popular culture, the double movement of containment and resistance," and then depicted a situation in which film, music, fiction, and journalism all offer occasions for struggles of meaning, ongoing engagements ever contested and partial. Instead of falling into the trap of thinking of cultural forms as somehow coherent or self-sufficient, Hall cautioned a judicious wariness about the contradictions in any popular text—contradictions that were the very source of its appeal. Turning Smith's and Burke's idea around, Hall argued for "a highly complex species of linguistic *ventriloquism*" in which ideas supposedly imposed by a culture industry—presumably to some narcotic or reassuring purpose—are transformed in turn by their audiences. It was as if the dummy were now allowed to speak back, at cross-purposes.[15]

This position has since been developed by Fredric Jameson into a sophisticated reading of resistances offered to all kinds of cultural forms, and of opposition to the manipulations and diversions they impose. Mass culture need not be seen "as empty distraction or 'mere' false consciousness, but rather as a transformational work on social and political anxieties and fantasies which must then have some effective presence in the mass cultural text in order subsequently to be 'managed' or repressed."[16] In other words, popular culture is not simply escapist but embodies critiques of issues that cultural czars had blithely assumed were invisible to a diverted mass audience. Mass dreams, like individual dreams, trace a return of the repressed, but in them as well repressed material is never either obvious or unambiguous. And in the most dominant and persistent of these mass dreams, the potential for structural complexity matches their capacity to at once reassure and subvert.

Even comic books have this transformative power, as Ariel Dorfmann and Armand Mattelart have shown through a politically impassioned reading of the Donald Duck comics distributed in Chile in the 1960s. Disseminating capitalist and racist ideas in the guise of a wacky duck, Walt Disney effected American foreign policy through innocuous popular forms. As Dorfman and Mattelart go on to claim, Disney's penny comics also exposed the exploitative bureaucratic control, corporate irresponsibility, class oppression, and widescale social alienation that allegedly lies at the heart of the American system.[17] Studies of Edgar Rice Burroughs' classic Tarzan novels have taken a similar tack, revealing their conjoint support yet critique of imperialist and sexist ideals.[18] And even Arthur Conan Doyle's ratiocinative tales of Sherlock Holmes, "whose overt project is total explicitness," have been shown to purvey an irrational, mysterious, even magical view of Victorian gender relations.[19]

While these inquiries into mass culture each adopts a distinctive approach, all share the assumption that popular texts covertly question values overtly proclaimed. Audiences from diverse classes and biases can thereby enjoy different degrees of recognition and resistance.[20] Such a formal tension between the self-confirming and self-contradictory animates Westerns most of all, if only because the genre presumes to represent a past it invents, imposing stereotypes at once incorrect yet all-determining, molding responses to history in ways that actually create that history. The assertion is an ambitious one in need of fuller demonstration, and at this point we might best turn to two self-conscious artists whose fascination with this aspect of the genre (its self-authenticating relationship to history) led to Westerns in which the form itself is held up for wry inspection.

Legend or History?

Of all who wrote Westerns, the most incisive analysts of the genre's capacity to alter history have been Stephen Crane and John Ford, both of whom adapted self-conscious historical attitudes in creating their works. So prescient is Crane, in fact, about directions the Western would take that he parodies expectations even before they can be said to coalesce into standardization (with Wister's *The Virginian*). Crane borrowed a mix of clichés and stereotypes from Bret Harte and Mark Twain, yet unlike them his stories confront the intersection of history and fiction, fact and legend, without in the end appealing to either at the expense of the other. Refusing to acknowledge that legends are more interesting than history (art, that is, surpassing life), his stories at the same time resist any simple equation of the legendary with fact itself (art matching life). Instead, he reveals how tenaciously life imitates art and how historical facts therefore always need interpretation according to the conventions, clichés, and expectations established by legends that people believe. "The Blue Hotel" (1898), "A Bride Comes to Yellow Sky" (1898), and "One Dash—Horses" (1896) all celebrate even as they puncture commonplace Western ideals, drawing attention to their transformative power most dramatically through verbal style   21 itself—an idiosyncratic verbal technique that consistently breaks with readers' expectations.

As few others since, Crane inquired into the conventionalized violence at the heart of the genre through the unexpectedly violent prose style *of* his Westerns, whether in abrupt descriptions of surreal landscapes or in wrenching analogies and eccentric comparisons. The opening of "One Dash—Horses" is exemplary:

> Richardson pulled up his horse and looked back over the trail where the crimson serape of his servant flamed amid the dusk of the mesquite. The hills in the west were carved into peaks, and were painted the most profound blue. Above them, the sky was of that marvelous tone of green—like still, sun-shot water—which people denounce in pictures.[21]

The oddness of the description lies in part in its self-ironic inversion: of an artfully painted opening that establishes a sense of conventional realism by acknowledging its terms as too artful. And the Western that then ensues (itself an ironic variation on an actual experience Crane had had in Mexico) continues to register an unusual stylistic self-consciousness through a series of bizarre images: "José entered, staggering under two Mexican saddles, large enough for building sites" (733); "A 44-caliber revolver can make a hole large enough for little boys to shoot marbles through" (736); "Their valor would grow like weeds in the spring" (740); and (to describe the sudden back-peddling of a band of pursuing Mexican bandits), "If toboggans half way down a hill should suddenly make up their minds to turn around and go back" (743). In this defamiliarized world, it is as if almost anything can happen—and in fact, at the level of narrative description, does—making the stereotypical plot of chase and last-minute rescue somehow newly fresh. The surrealistic conceits evoke not only the characters' astonishment but the reader's as well, reopening plot possibilities in such a way that every crisis is unexpected, every dénoument unprecedented.

For Crane, the western experience is not simply a matter of biased interpretation on the one hand (myths, legends, Westerns) and neutral observation on the other (statistics, documents, historical accounts), but of the two combined. After all, West and East are not all that different: the boosterism of western towns is the same as civic aspirations in the East, and the pattern of cowboy life varies little from that of other agricultural (or industrial) laborers. Shoot-outs and lynchings, nighttime ambushes and knifings by gamblers occur (so Crane suggests) at least as often on one side of the Mississippi as on the other. The strength of Western belief lies not simply in baldly asserting the contrary but in inducing characters as well as readers to act as if it were so, thus creating a history that actually begins to correspond with the belief that first inspired the behavior. "Why don't he wait till he gits *out* West," young Johnny asks of the headstrong Swede in "The Blue Hotel," who believes he is "in the middle of it—the shootin' and stabbin' and all." As the "traveled Easterner" laughingly responds, "It isn't different there even—not in these days. But he thinks he's right in the middle of hell" (809). Crane reveals how conventions fashion their own brand of truth to the extent that they *are* believed, and in the belief make events happen (in this sense, Henry Kissinger seems little more than a character invented by Crane). If that brand of truth is not of a first-order historical variety, depending on only the loosest of correspondences to documented experience, it is still no less powerful *as* belief, with consequences as dangerous and deadly.

John Ford's illustrious career of cinematic Westerns only further confirms this insight, one pursued in his trilogy of "7th Cavalry" films (especially *Fort Apache* [1948]), but subjected to his most compelling scrutiny in *The Man Who Shot Liberty Valance* (1962). The film's ironic tone works at every level to complicate the relation between history and myth that lies at the heart of the Western—at once confirming yet subverting the assertion by the newspaper editor, Maxwell Scott: "When the legend becomes fact, print the legend." As critics have observed, Ford's film does the opposite, printing the unsavory fact about Liberty Valance's death against a sentimental legend that we as viewers have been persuaded against all odds to believe (that Jimmy Stewart's clumsy Ranse Stoddard, wearing an apron, shooting nervously with an uninjured left hand, might actually have won a shoot-out against Lee Marvin's gunslinger Valance).[22]

The double perspective offered by Ford reveals how we are already inside the history we supposedly only see or read, actively constructing it in the process of trying to understand. And that goes as much for characters as for viewers. After all, John Wayne's Tom Doniphon is saved by the "legend" from having to face the consequences of his immoral act: as he says, "cold-blooded murder, but I can live with it," so long as it remains unknown. Similarly, the legend insidiously belies Ransom Stoddard's self-righteous touting of law over brute force, in an irony that draws attention to the incoherence of the Western's customary resolution (with masculine violence forced to establish the terms by which violence can be declared illegitimate). Yet Ford, like Crane, delights in how such lies not simply misrepresent but actively comprise history, and refuses in *Liberty Valance* to allow the fact instead to stand in for the legend. The historical record, after all, embodies a legacy of powerful lies more than of countless irrelevant truths.

Ford, in short, insists upon both the "fact" *and* the "legend," viewing   23 them as mutually sustaining interpretive gestures rather than one as a misreading of the other. So fully has the legend of Ransom Stoddard's victory become a social fact that the film's central flashback appears to be less a neutral representation of things as they once were than the wish-fulfillment reconstruction on the part of a later generation. Tag Gallagher's remark of the film, that "everything speaks of age," thus tells only half the story, as confirmed in Ford's presentation of his mature actors—John Wayne, James Stewart, and Sara Miles—each decades older (and allowed to look it) than the youthful characters they play in the flashback.[23] Token gestures, makeup, and coiffure do far more than merely draw attention to the oddness of aging actors playing twenty-year-olds. Such gestures quietly generate an eery sense that what we see before us are introspective elderly figures, continuing to play out myth, perform it in the present, prompted to this theater of memory by their very attempt to recall the past.

Everything in the film speaks not simply of age, then, but of age's reconstruction of its own youth—of the past's continuing grip on the present, which reshapes that past to present needs. Thus if Westerns are always stage settings for the enactment of solutions to cultural problems, then here we literally detect the stage mechanism revealed within the work (as if Ford were exposing the dynamic common to all Westerns). For this trick to work, we cannot witness events "as they occurred" (with Wayne, Stewart, and Miles filmed as if actually young, or with younger actors cast in the flashback). Rather, we must be made to see distinctly older figures imagining themselves *as* young, trying dimly to put a past to rest that has not yet been resolved, and doing so according to strategies that Westerns have invoked from the beginning. The foregrounding of conventions achieved by Crane stylistically through pressure on narrative clichés, then, Ford accomplishes with a play of shifted temporal perspectives.

Cowboys

Part of the reason Westerns are so invested in historical authenticity (far more than musicals, detective stories, soap operas, or other popular forms) is paradoxically because they aspire to mythic resolution of crises. Crane and Ford both saw through the deceptive allure of this dialectic even as they delighted in its recapitulation. Yet while the following chapters investigate the pressure of narrative form on audience expectations, one of the central *historical* issues involves the choice of cowboys as heroes—a choice far from obvious on its surface. After all, few Americans were affected by western history, and under any circumstances the actual working cowboy was an odd choice for national hero, someone to be endowed with dramatic élan, then avidly pursued by readers and viewers intent on narrative escape. Among a constellation of other suitable types, how did the cowboy prevail?

A hired hand on horseback—in effect, a shepherd with a gun—cowboys were overworked, underfed, poorly paid, ill-educated laborers. When ranchers invented the cattle industry in the post–Civil-War period, cowboys were hired to accompany boring drives north from Texas to the railroad stockyards in Kansas. And during the twenty-odd years in which the industry boomed and collapsed, their daily routine continued to be monotonous and uneventful, more so than most occupations. Even in the cowboys' own vocational world, it was ranchers and cattlemen who were regarded as the industry's heroes—shrewd mercantile-capitalists like Richard King, Charles Goodnight, Nelson Story, and John Iliff, who made sharp speculative ventures to earn windfall profits.[24] If anyone warranted the distinction, these were the Western individualists, who moved fast, risked fortunes, and ended by transforming the West through innovative ideas and marketing practices. By contrast, cowboys in the peak years of the 1880s were essentially seasonal laborers whose modest skills earned them barely more than the average industrial worker. And like other laborers, they protected their interests through union membership in the newly emergent Knights of Labor—a membership that, far from confirming a touted individualist ethos, speaks of Rotarian aspirations.

Despite such logic, the romanticized image of rugged individualism that would fuel countless cigarette advertisements, beer commercials, and cologne promotionals was already falling into place in these years.[25] In 1882, Richard Irving Dodge averred: "For fidelity to duty, for promptness and vigor of action, for resources in difficulty, and unshaken courage in danger, the cow-boy has no superior among men." For Dodge, the cowboy was "the most reckless of all the reckless desperadoes developed on the frontier."[26] Only a half-dozen years later, Teddy Roosevelt embellished this portrait, relying on firsthand experience ranching in Montana: "The whole existence is patriarchal in character: it is the life of men who live in the open, who tend their herds on horseback, who go armed and ready to guard their lives by their own prowess, whose wants are very simple and who call no man master."[27] And Roosevelt's lifelong lionizing coincided with a national fascination with rough-rider exploits—a fascination fed by the western paintings of, most famously, Frederic Remington and Charles Russell. By 1902, when Alfred Henry Lewis cashed in on his reminiscences of cowboy life, it was possible to keep an entirely straight face in elaborating the cowboy's unlicensed wildness, even in the most unbridled prose: "His religion of fatalism, his courage, his rides at full swing in midnight darkness to head and turn and hold a herd stampeded . . . his troubles, his joys, his

25

soberness in camp, his drunkenness in town, and his feuds and occasional 'gun-plays' are not to be disposed of in a preface."[28] As it happened, of course, this prefatory comment itself served as "preface" to the following century's fascination with the figure.

To wonder why cowboys were translated into such mythic status ("the Cowboy") or to ask why the Western emerged when it did is to enter into vexed historical terrain. The simplest explanation involves the collective response to industrial capitalism: the West once again as escape valve for eastern tensions and psychological pressures. Or as Theodore Roosevelt expressed it: "Ranching is an occupation like those of vigorous, primitive pastoral peoples, having little in common with the humdrum, workaday business world of the nineteenth century."[29] With the transition to an urban economy and the pressures of a newly modernized society, the allure of a more stable, agrarian working culture is not hard to imagine, perhaps especially since the frontier had come to seem irrevocably closed. In an era of massive immigration, urbanization, and production-line labor, the West could be imagined as "the premodern world that [Americans] had lost."[30]

A growing middle-class veneration of efficiency, bureaucracy, and professionalization, accompanied by rising levels of union solidarity and labor resistance, could only have contributed to the enthusiasm with which Wister's *The Virginian* (1902) and Porter's *The Great Train Robbery* (1903) were received. Frederick R. Taylor's efficiency experts were introducing more elaborate techniques of worker supervision just as cowboys appeared to show that work need not be closely monitored. Offering a stark contrast to the situation most Americans knew, the cowboy represented a throwback to the idea of precorporate capitalist structure, when journeyman apprentices felt primary loyalty to shop and supervisor, and work space intersected with family and living space as well.

In the actual cowboy's everyday world, work and play, rest and activity, sleeping and eating were activities not easily demarcated nor assigned fixed settings. The variable rhythm of his day (as opposed to industrial or domestic labor) meant that long periods of monotony were punctuated unexpectedly by moments of excitement, whether a stampede erupted, or the crew hit town, or tribal delegates appeared to exact a toll for crossing Indian lands. The additional fact that cowboys wore guns—the only laborers to do so for nonpolicing duties—lent them an independent, even sovereign air of self-confidence. More generally, the figure of the principled drifter compels an insistent fascination that extends back to *The Odyssey*, in part by defining the freedoms that others have sacrificed for the security of civilized life. In a period of increasing pressure on the nuclear family, the cowboy represented a nostalgic dream of escape from middle-class obligations, and in particular from family ties (a basic theme elaborated in the frequency of the phrase "just passin' through" or in the popularity of western songs like "Don't Fence Me In" and "Wayfarin' Stranger"). Compounding that footloose status was the thinly veiled sexual liberty associated with figures who lived in an environment that encouraged, indeed prized, intense male bonding without the conventional justification of military need. As Marshall McLuhan has observed, the cowboy's appeal is part of "the deep nostalgia of an industrial society"—a character so perfectly posed against modern culture that if he had not existed he would have been invented.[31]

In fact, of course, the figure adopted by the Western *was* invented, transformed from actual cowboys who wandered onto the historical stage at the moment their presence seemed required. Later chapters will detail assumptions that reinforced the cowboy's appeal, especially as they became appropriate for different generations, different Westerns. Yet critically, the cowboy became the instrument-body upon which Westerns practiced their favorite tune—the construction of masculinity, the making of men, a process never straightforward or consistent. As Martin Pumphrey notes, deep "unresolvable tensions" persist in the Western's representations of that process, as its most familiar narrative moments suggest:

> When examined, those moments—the refusal to draw first, the gentlemanly kindnesses, the glass of milk or soda pop in the saloon—reveal an ideal of masculinity founded on fundamental contradictions. Heroes must be *both* dominant and deferential, gentle and violent, self-contained yet sensitive, practical yet idealistic, individualist but conformist, rational but intuitive, peace-loving yet ready to fight without "quitting" when honor demands. They must bridge, that is, not simply the division between savagery and civilization but the anxiously guarded (ambiguously experienced) frontier between the two worlds usually coded as masculine and feminine.[32]

Yet the Western is a form not committed to *resolving* these incompatible worlds but to *narrating* all those contradictions involved in what it means to be a man, in a way that makes them seem less troubling than they are. While the particular shape of those contradictions alters in the decades covered by the following chapters, in each case the Western is committed to revealing how contemporary versions of manhood are achieved. Why the terrain of gender identification needs to be made secure is a question only to be answered for particular historical moments, only in characteristic forms that the most popular Westerns devise. No other pastime, however, continues to be so popular as the ongoing worry about how to attain, then maintain one's proper gender.

2 STILL LANDSCAPES AND MORAL RESTRAINT

*[The] rules governing literary art in the domain of romantic fiction
. . . require that the personages in a tale shall be alive, except in the
case of corpses, and that always the reader shall be able to tell the
corpses from the others. But this detail has often been overlooked in
the* Deerslayer *tale.*

Mark Twain (1887)[1]

*The American landscape has never been at one with the white man.
Never. And white men have probably never felt so bitter anywhere, as
here in America, where the very landscape, in its very beauty, seems a
bit devilish and grinning, opposed to us.*

*Cooper, however, glosses over this resistance, which in actuality
can never quite be glossed over. He wants the landscape to be at one
with him. So he goes away to Europe and sees it as such. It is a sort of
vision.*

And, nevertheless, the oneing will surely take place—some day.

D. H. Lawrence (1923)[2]

*It's a terrible pity you can't make time stand still. There are moments
that you want to relive over and over, very slowly, moments that you
never want to end.*

Sergio Leone (1973)[3]

Early in Clint Eastwood's *Unforgiven* (1992), Ned Logan (Morgan Freeman) meets the Schofield Kid (Jaimz Woolvett), who seems oddly indifferent to the threat of an approaching storm. Ned asks whether he has noted the distant lowering skies, and when the Kid assures him he has, an unconvinced Ned directs his attention above to a circling hawk. After squinting at an empty sky, the Kid sullenly concurs, only to be informed by Ned that no hawk is there, confirming what we have suspected: that the Kid is acutely nearsighted. Angered, the Kid hurls Ned's canteen to the ground and blows it full of holes. The scene establishes a (negative) conjunction of ocular sight and moral insight, played out through the film in the Kid's adolescent braggadacio, empty taunts, and blind dependence on others, until at last reduced to sobbing hysteria by his first killing (of a man whose complete defenselessness is accentuated by being caught in an outhouse, pants at his ankles). The moral myopia displayed by the Kid throughout has been anticipated in his lack of 20–20 vision.

Yet the striking aspect of the scene in which Ned slyly points to a hawk is its reference back through countless Westerns to a moment in Fenimore Cooper's *The Pathfinder* (1840), when Natty Bumppo directs attention to two gulls crossing overhead and "quick as thought" shoots them both with one bullet.[4] Long before, he had earned the sobriquet "Hawkeye" by "aiming almost without sighting" to kill an unseen enemy (*Deerslayer*, 2:598). And repeatedly through the series, the hunter's "true eye" is featured as his most distinctive trait, confirmed by his everready ability to shoot all but invisible objects. Even when aged sight fails in *The Prairie* (1827), such moments weigh heavily through a reiteration of their present impossibility. The capacity to see clearly, to hit the most distant of targets, to discover all but invisible signs of an enemy becomes at last a moral injunction, equated with the capacity to draw sharp ethical distinctions. Natty, in short, is   29 formed "in a moral sense" (*Deerslayer*, 2:759) by his hawkeyed perusal of the natural world—a strangely ethical view of landscape that is among Cooper's strongest legacies to the Western, where moral discernment is always signaled by a visual knowledge of surroundings.[5]

Given the sheer weight of landscape description in the Leatherstocking series, however, the question arises of what function beyond that of moral barometer is served by such scenes. In the following, I want to pursue related answers—one narratological, the other ideological—that help explain Cooper's contemporary appeal. The first involves the peculiar effect of landscape description on reading itself. For improbable as Cooper's narratives were, the seductive lure that first hooked his readers was less a matter of plot than technique: a combination of frozen *tableaux vivants* and brisk cinematic action, of descriptive *longeurs* and narrative flashes. And that combination was seductive not only as readerly trick but as ideological tempo, playing out assumptions about masculinity that first took hold in the Jacksonian era.

The second answer, then, involves the role of landscape *within* the novels to define the moral stature of different characters. Natty Bumppo exemplifies for Cooper's readers an eminently moral figure because of a hawk-eyed vision that allows him to perform in a certain laudable fashion. By contrast, the historical figure of Montcalm lacks such a vision and for all his worldly success is essentially a failed man, "deficient in that moral courage, without which no man can be truly great" (1:677). The issue comes down for Cooper to a moral distinction between seeing and not seeing. That this distinction should lead to an empty morality consisting in little more than the performance of restraint is as important to understand as the fact that that repeated performance is itself so appealing, to become one of the Western's most resonant leitmotifs.

Pictures!

The Pioneers created a popular audience not only for the rest of the series but for fiction itself in America, dispelling endemic resistance to the novel as a cultural form even as it altered that form's potential.[6] Three years later, *The Last of the Mohicans* swept all competition aside as "the most popular and—for a century after its publication in 1826—internationally famous of American novels."[7] While the last three novels of the series could hardly exceed this unique feat, each was highly successful on first publication. And through the century, all five books won enormous popularity, were translated into dozens of languages, sold millions of copies, and generated countless imitators.[8] This unprecedented appeal has intrigued generations of scholars, whose explanations range from the formal to the historical to the sociological.[9]

All agree, however, that Cooper appropriated the American continent for fiction at a moment when that landscape was newly being celebrated—creating "pictures!" as D. H. Lawrence would exclaim, "some of the loveliest, most glamorous pictures in all literature."[10] A thirst for native scenes had intensified by the 1820s as a consequence of several developments: a burst of nationalism following the War of 1812, growing antipathy to insistent urban conditions, curiosity about a continent barely explored and little known, even incipient fears about the sacrifice of wilderness to westward expansion and therefore a need to memorialize it. This enthusiasm had initially been fed by Charles Brockden Brown and Washington Irving, but it was Cooper's elaborate depictions that pricked desire for views of a continent still unsettled, still remarkable for panoramas of grassland prairies, sea-sized lakes, and the "wild luxuriance of a virgin American forest" (*Deerslayer*, 2:543). In the effort to quench that taste, painters borrowed directly from Cooper, transposing moments from the series into such prominent oils as Thomas Cole's *Scene from The Last of the Mohicans, Cora Kneeling at the Feet of Tamemund* (1827), and Asher Durand's *The Indian's Vespers: Last of the Mohicans* (1847).[11]

The reason Hudson River School painters found inspiration in Cooper was because he wrote in a mode painterly enough to constitute a new literary technique. So much descriptive detail distinguishes his tableaux that action is precluded for pages on end, making his novels seem to aspire at times to the condition of leisurely drawing. In 1849, having finished *The Pathfinder* (1840), Balzac expressed his enchantment with its

succession of marvellous tableaux, which in this work as in those that preceded it are quite inimitable. Never did typographed language approach so closely to painting. This is the school that literary landscape-painters ought to study; all the secrets of the art are here. This magic prose not only shows to the mind the river, its banks, the forests and their trees, but it succeeds in giving us a sense of both the slightest circumstances and the combined whole.[12]

Striking to the heart of Cooper's achievement, Balzac relishes how sequential details build to a "combined whole" that resembles nothing so much as the stark immediacy of painting. Yet what Balzac fails to note about this "magic prose"—in which the sharpest detail coexists easily with a panoramic view—is that landscape itself is made to *live*, resembling a huge animal or a god incarnate. The question of what message is communicated by this uncanny being, "at once animated and still" (*Last of the Mohicans*, 1:640), will need to be asked below.

For the moment, it is worth pausing instead over Sainte-Beuve's more   31 straightforward characterization twenty-one years earlier, of *The Pioneers* as "principally a descriptive work" in which "a small number of events, which make up an engaging plot, seem placed in the novel for the purpose of introducing the descriptive passages."[13] The very subtitle of the novel (*A Descriptive Tale*) suggests how often activity originates in stillness: the opening sleigh ride, the night-fishing scene, the slaughter of passenger pigeons. And this pattern is characteristic throughout the series, with each of the novels opening in a panorama, an eagle-eye view of native scenes that invokes the sublime before diving into more picturesque terrain. Thereafter, landscapes are offered as self-sufficient set pieces—indeed, as stage sets that draw attention to their own theatricality, or as self-consciously painted canvases. "The whole scene formed a striking picture," the narrator of Cooper's *The Last of the Mohicans* claims, "whose frame was composed of the dark and tall border of pines" (1:744). That "frame" itself conjures up the appearance of characters so captivated by what they see that they are often described as "transfixed" or "rapt." Emerging out of the landscape to stand like statues in a garden, they function simply to stare—stiff, silent, intent on surroundings. Duncan Heyward is rooted to the ground in the dramatic aftermath of the massacre at Fort Henry, "for many minutes, a rapt observor" stunned by the "deserted charnel-house" before him (1:691). And what brings the nighttime prospect alive is his own awed perusal, as if the scene's "embodied gloom" were animated by Heyward's impaired vitality.

Prior to the massacre, Natty Bumppo had led Heyward's fugitive party to a mountain overlooking Fort Henry, Lake George, and Montcalm's troops—each scene already earlier described in some detail. Once again, however, three long paragraphs describe the silent "spectacle," tacitly prodding one to memorize the "scene, which lay like a map beneath their feet" (1:632–33). More pointedly, the reader is enjoined to recognize that Montcalm's "contempt for eminences" has contributed to the horror enacted below (1:638). His aversion to taking a larger descriptive view of his situation signals not only the "weakness" of his military logic, then, but a moral deficiency that renders him partially responsible for the ensuing Iroquois massacre (1:638). Here, an insufficient man has refused to enact the calm, motionless gazing so typical of the narrator himself—a refusal of stillness and silence that is the origin of his flawed manhood.

Whatever this scene hints about an ethics of stillness, however, it also serves as stage setting for action par excellence, the most frenzied such episode in the novel. The very excessiveness of the violence unleashed by Montcalm's Indian allies—a narrative ferocity corroborated by historical records—sharply contrasts with the motionlessness of the panorama that precedes it. Yet stark as is the discrepancy between landscape and action—

between static description and the explosive narration that immediately follows—our attention is hardly alerted. It almost seems that the reader is lulled into assenting to outrageous events *because* they are described as accurately and painstakingly as the terrain itself. How is it that Cooper elicits this striking sensation of assent through an economy established between descriptive and narrative modes?

Aimless Glances

Let me begin a narratological explanation through an implausible juxtaposition: Umberto Eco's study of James Bond. According to Eco, Ian Fleming's novels (1953–64) appealed so broadly because of a style that resorted to irrelevant description in order to authenticate narrative improbabilities: "What is surprising in Fleming is the minute and leisurely concentration with which he pursues for page after page descriptions of articles, landscapes, and events apparently inessential to the course of the story and, conversely, the feverish brevity with which he covers in a few paragraphs the most unexpected and improbable actions." A description of Player's cigarettes extends for five pages, an explanation of golf goes on for fifteen, fully one-quarter of *Thunderball* is given over to naturalist cures, and other novels likewise devote numerous pages to a wide array of actions and objects: "a game of canasta, an ordinary motor car, the control panel of an airplane, a railway carriage, the menu of a restaurant."[14]

Eco identifies this formulaic pattern as the "technique of the aimless glance," a stylistic convention that compels the reader to alternate between two modal registers: protracted *depictions* of inessential items on the one hand, and brief spurts of *narrative* action on the other. Invariably, long descriptive digressions are devoted to what is "already known," thus accustoming the reader to highly improbable, often unbelievably brutal activity. Through an apparently realistic style, "our credulity is solicited" so that when plot breaks in and "rejects" these interludes through outbursts of violence, they have already been reduced to "trifling acts seen with disillusioned eyes." The clincher in Eco's stylistic analysis is his observation that Fleming's style is akin to Bond's, with both men gaining an edge on hapless victims and readers through seemingly aimless activity: "the language performs the same function as do the plots."[15]

Compellingly as Fleming mastered the "aimless glance," the technique was hardly unique to Cold War spy thrillers. On the contrary, it is a standard convention for countless popular genres (Westerns most obviously), lashing together sometimes interminable descriptive passages that are interrupted by spurts of impossibly brutal action. The effect of these varied registers (as Eco intimates about Bond) is to reinforce the Western hero's stature as a supremely laconic figure, able to cast "disillusioned eyes" over familiar possibilities. And the hero's imperturbability in the face of the violence that erupts (often on his own body) is established by the quiet stoicism with which he endures glowing descriptions *of* that body. It is as if the intensity of the narrator's gaze or the lingering focus of the camera eye had an anesthetizing effect, making violence easier to experience both for hero and reader/viewer (a response discussed more fully in Chapter 6).

The "aimless glance" of the Western ranges far more broadly than across male bodies, however—so much so that the genre sometimes seems to exist to dispense yet another account of horse breeds, or brands of gun, or the customary gear, rituals, and seasonal activities of cowboys and ranch hands. Mostly, however, the Western is devoted to the terrain from which it takes its name, focusing the reader's glance on landscapes apparently as numerous as Westerns themselves. And while the stylistic variations in any landscape define an author's or director's niche, it is the recurrent impulse to evoke a lingering sense of place that allows the Western's explosions into violence to seem less implausible than they otherwise might. The sheer fact that none of these depictions are necessary for the plot—that nothing narratively hangs upon these long descriptive digressions—is nonetheless the basic rationale by which outrageous plots are underwritten.

If Cooper is appropriately recognized as the father of the Western, then, it has rarely been for one of the most appropriate reasons: that he first mastered the technique of aimless gazing. One scornful exception was William Hazlitt, among the shrewdest of Cooper's critics, who anticipated much of Eco's argument in 1829. "Mr Cooper describes things to the life," Hazlitt dismissively wrote of *The Last of the Mohicans,*

but he puts no motion into them. While he is insisting on the minutest details, and explaining all the accompaniments of an incident, the story stands still. The elaborate accumulation of particulars serves not to embody his imagery, but to distract and impede the mind. He is not so much the master of his materials as their drudge: He labors under an epilepsy of the fancy. . . . It is mistaking the province of the artist for that of the historian; and it is this very obligation of painting and statuary to fill up all the details, that renders them incapable of telling a story, or of expressing more than a single moment, group, or figure.[16]

While the terms of analysis are apt, one might do better to reverse their implication (as Eco does with Fleming), pointing out that it is just *because* Cooper's landscapes tend "to distract and impede the mind" while his "story stands still" that improbable activity can have the force it does.

Thus, the recurrent landscape descriptions so admired by Balzac, Saint-Beuve, and Lawrence serve a purpose even they did not explicitly value, lending an illusion of realism to otherwise outrageous plots (soliciting "our credulity" by reducing the implausible to "trifling acts"). As well, those scenes instruct the reader in how to read terrain and surfaces, to maintain postures of silent expectancy in anticipation of the violence that can always suddenly erupt. Natty Bumppo's incredible marksmanship in *The Last of the Mohicans*—whether in defense of the Glenn's Falls retreat, or later when challenged, to corroborate his identity with enemy Hurons—like his first murderous snap shot in *The Deerslayer*, is each presented as a violent moment that intrudes upon the "painting and statuary" of landscape descriptions. Similarly, his suspenseful race of escape in the later novel, like the fatal heroics of Uncas that conclude the former, are prepared for only after the "aimless glance" of the reader has been solicited. What Mark Twain failed to see in dismissing Cooper's implausible plots is that the series compels belief by diverting attention *to* the landscape. This end is achieved through different means in different novels, however, and since *The Last of the Mohicans* and *The Deerslayer* reveal more distinctly than anywhere else Cooper's transformation of the role of fictional landscape, we need to look at each in turn more exactingly.

The Morality of Stillness in a *Nature Morte*

Earlier I noted how fully Cooper animates landscape, imagining settings come alive while one watches. Now it is worth investigating the ideological (as opposed to narratological) implications of this animistic presentiment in *The Last of the Mohicans,* where terrain is acknowledged as something that needs to be opposed, even fought—a "bloody arena" fully as inimical as both the French and Hurons (1:480). Lawrence first noted a "menace in the landscape" of the novel, a tone established in its opening sentences: "It was a feature peculiar to the colonial wars of North America, that the toils and dangers of the wilderness were to be encountered, before the adverse hosts could meet. A wide, and, apparently, an impervious boundary of forests, severed the possessions of the hostile provinces of France and England" (1:479).[17] The following description of Lake George intensifies this premonition of "severing" natural violence as a detachment of soldiers prepares to march through five leagues of threatening forest to help defend Fort Henry from the French.

This depiction inaugurates a series of ever more ominous settings, constraining and even imprisoning characters as they wander through. The first hideout of the escaping party is at Glenn's Falls, which they only achieve by battling the Hudson River's "whirling eddies . . . sweeping them to destruction" (1:524). As Natty explains once they reach safety, moreover,   35 the waterfall defies any observable logic: "look at the perversity of the water! It falls by no rule at all. . . . The whole design of the river seems disconcerted" (I:531). More generally, the landscape appears a nightmare created by the "rebellious stream," so labyrinthine as to confound the narrator's efforts at realistic depiction. "We find ourselves in the midst of huge rocks, and overhanging woods, and tumbling cataracts," so W. H. Gardiner observed in 1826, "with a great mist, and a great noise, and we are utterly unable to settle the relative positions of these objects, so as to form any distinct picture from them in the mind."[18] Fissures, rocks, moonlight abysses, thundering water, a bewildering thicket: all baffle not only the threatened party but the reader as well before the characters successfully withdraw to conceal themselves in a cavern carved out by water.

When the party finally reaches Fort Henry, the scene that greets them is even more horrifying and just as perplexing: a "vast and deserted charnel-house, without omen or whisper," that through the chiaroscuro lighting manifests little but "embodied gloom" (1:691). Later, the Huron encampment consists of a maze of caves so hellish that it can only be compared to "the shades of the infernal regions, across which unhappy ghosts and savage demons were flitting in multitudes" (1:860). For Uncas finally to thwart Magua, he must negotiate the carefully detailed landscape, the "dangerous crags" and gaping precipices that loom above this Dantesque scene. And his destruction at the end seems curiously less the fault of Magua than of the harrowing terrain that has forced him into "leaping frantically, from a fearful height" (1:862). Landscape does part of the informal work usually ceded to evil beings, as if it were itself becoming an agent and thus stealing the capacity for action of human characters, leaving them immobile figures in a *tableau vivant*.

What lends a special eeriness to such scenes is the voices that emerge so unexpectedly as to make nature itself seem somehow vocal: "the woods were filled with another burst of cries" (1:549). In the first hideout at Glenn's Falls, as the fugitive party sings to calm itself, "a cry, that seemed neither human, nor earthly" shocks everyone "to the inmost heart" (1:536). That "same strong, horrid cry" recurs three times, "as if from the bed of the river," further terrifying the party until Duncan identifies it as the shriek of a scared horse (1:539). Soon after, a Huron's "triumphant yell" paralyzes the fugitives; and in preparing to leave, the party overhears similar threatening voices (1:567, 622). Just as appalling are occasions when different registers of sound are juxtaposed, as when the valley reverberates with "merry and cheerful flourishes" of martial music, just prior to the massacre that fills the air with "shrieks, groans, exhortations, and curses" (1:667, 672). Yet even this horrifying contrast does not match extremes of sonic expression embodied so abruptly in Magua, whose "fatal and artful eloquence" on one page becomes a "fatal and appalling whoop" on the next (1:671, 672). The figure whose presence best attests to the sinister associations of voice, however, is David Gamut, the ungainly, incompetent music master. Singing repeatedly "in full, sweet, and melodious tones," Gamut is able to transfix all around him with nothing other than his voice (1:497). During the massacre, "he poured out a strain so powerful as to be heard, even amid the din," winning stunned admiration from the Huron attackers and saving his party from death (1:674).

The reason Gamut's behavior compels attention is because it is so conspicuously aberrant, so different from conventional "gifts" that characterize suitable deportment, red or white. As exemplified by the "last of the Mohicans," Chingachgook and Uncas, masculinity consists in being able mysteriously to merge with the landscape, only to reemerge in moments of crisis. And Gamut's vocal presence helps confirm this conceit, not just in early sonorous outbursts coded as unsuitably feminine but in the startling transformation he undergoes following the massacre, as his own voice gradually disappears from the narrative. His progression toward a more virile manhood is registered as an evolution from arresting vocal pyrotechnics to self-arresting silence. This progression, moreover, engages a gender problem the Western would leave unresolved: of manhood represented as both verbally adroit and mysteriously silent, a cross between Natty and Uncas, unbuttoned garrulousness and mute serenity (discussed more fully in Chapter 4).[19]

Wilderness sometimes comes alive with voices in *The Last of the Mohicans* only to form a contrast with its otherwise mute intensity. Gamut's lively songs, for instance, are met by "the silence and retirement of the forest"— an apparent rebuff that forms less a marked alternative to human behavior than an instructive analogy (1:497). Nature's "breathing silence" is everywhere meant as a model for individual endeavor (1:499). This pattern of silent animation—or more accurately, animated silence—is clearest just before the final attack on the Hurons:

the woods were as still . . . as when they came fresh from the hands of their Almighty Creator. The eye could range, in every direction, through the long and shadowed vistas of the trees; but no where was any object to be seen, that did not properly belong to the peaceful and slumbering scenery. Here and there a bird was heard fluttering among the branches of the beeches, and occasionally a squirrel dropped a nut, drawing the startled looks of the party, for a moment, to the place; but the instant the casual interruption ceased, the passing air was heard murmuring above their heads, along that verdant and undulating surface of forest, which spread itself unbroken, unless by stream or lake, over such a vast region of country. Across the tract of wilderness . . . it seemed as if the foot of man had never trodden, so breathing and deep was the silence in which it lay. (1: 849)

The uneasy balance here between natural setting and preternatural silence, agitated sight and sudden sound, is at once an immediate part of the scene's "treacherous quiet" and a more general characteristic of Cooper's style (1:849). That is, he regularly directs our aimless glance by defining terrain not only in visual images but in terms of sound and silence that seem irrelevant to plot progression. This has been true from the opening moments, which describe how "silence soon pervaded the camp, as deep as that which reigned in the vast forest by which it was environed" (1:483). And when the army departs the next morning, its human noise is absorbed by nature: "until the notes of their fifes growing fainter in distance, the forest at length appeared to swallow up the living mass which had slowly entered its bosom" (1:484).

More compelling than this stress on the gradual muting of landscape is the effect it has on characters who become more intensely quiet and inanimate. The process is only tacitly registered in the opening depiction of the departing army, as the narrative itself coyly imitates its own descriptive processes. Indeed, description seems ever on the verge of co-opting narrative ("swallow[ing] up the living mass"), while characters are conversely admired for an ability to be reduced to sheer physical description (as if inanimate).[20] In addition to its narratological role as guide for the reader's aimless glance, then, landscape serves the additional function of being a paradigm for male behavior, with even the power to enforce that ideal. It both assumes and compels the kind of quiet restraint men are expected to take—restraint effectively dramatized only in contrast with scenes of lack of restraint (impulsive action, unexpected noise). This pattern first is apparent when Natty, Uncas, and Chingachgook undertake to guard the Munro party: "Immovable as that rock, of which each appeared to form a part, they lay, with their eyes roving" (1:543–44). And throughout the novel, this silent arrest becomes a defining stance: "each dusky figure seemed a breathing statue, so motionless was the posture, so intense the attention" (1:759).[21]

Characters are reduced so often to the condition of garden statuary (as Hazlitt derisively remarked) that Cooper seems intentionally to be offering up a series of *tableaux vivants* (or, more strictly speaking, another sort of frozen scene, *natures mortes*). Nor is this simply a reflection of Natty's physical bearing, the reputed "iron-like inflexibility of his frame" (1:528). His stiff demeanor reflects, on the contrary, the method by which Cooper characteristically represents action, by creating a frieze. When Natty takes a shot, it is "as though both man and rifle were carved in stone. During that stationary instant, [his rifle] poured forth its contents, in a bright, glancing, sheet of flame" (1:818). Likewise, when Magua incites his tribe to revenge, he is described as one who "not only maintained his seat, but the very attitude he had originally taken, against the side of the lodge, where he continued as immovable, and apparently, as unconcerned, as if he had no interest" (1:808). Even David Gamut—the bodily antithesis of Magua and most "ungainly man" of the novel—is transformed in the midst of the Fort Henry massacre into a "strange and unmoved figure, rivetted to his post" (1:674).

The central figure of stillness in *The Last of the Mohicans* is the titular Uncas, whose stalwart integrity is manifest directly in his deportment. This is particularly evident after his capture, in the tableau formed by him and his cowardly betrayer as they stand before the Huron tribe—he, with a "calm, elevated, and collected" bearing, while Reed-that-bends cowers "like a cringing statue, expressive of shame and disgrace" (1:749). Uncas persists as an "immovable form" and, despite the taunts of a Huron shrew, "maintained his firm and haughty attitude" (1:751). A full chapter later, he "still remained where he had [been] left" (1:751). Even when an ax is hurled at his head (to be barely deflected by Magua), he continues unblinkingly in a stone-like position, "still looking his enemy in the eye, with features that seemed superior to emotion. Marble could not be colder, calmer, or steadier" (1:761). Self-possession achieves its most extreme manifestation—just as Uncas ironically gains his true stature—in the posture of death, "seated, as in life, with his form and limbs arranged in grave and decent composure" (1:866). The scene is the last of marvelous tableaux that began with the final pursuit of the Hurons through labyrinthine caverns onto overhanging mountain ledges, to the dramatic deaths of Cora, Uncas, and Magua. Now, in the final frieze, sitting before his lost son, Chingachgook embodies his opposite number: "so changeless his attitude, that a stranger might not have told the living from the dead" (1:867).

This moment of physical stillness forms the novel's culmination, as the stunning tableau of father facing dead son is further detailed. The Delaware sage, Tamemund, stands over everyone this final day, while "the multitude maintained its breathing stillness. . . . [N]or had even a limb been moved throughout that long and painful period" (1:867). So "deep and awful" is the "stillness" in which the tribe listens that "even the inanimate Uncas appeared a being of life, compared with the humbled and submissive throng by whom he was surrounded" (1:868). A few characters whisper to Uncas, "as if the empty clay retained the faculties of the animated man," even as Cooper repeatedly highlights Chingachgook's own deathlike   39 stillness—"nor did a muscle move in his rigid countenance . . . every other sense but that of sight seemed frozen" (1:871). Filling out this spectral frieze, General Munro sits in frozen stillness before his own dead child, Cora, until he finally "started, as if the last trumpet had sounded in his ear" (1:872). Moments earlier, the final uncanny sound of the novel has unsettled the scene—beyond comprehension until finally made clear that Chingachgook is singing a faint monody—replicating in that gesture the many other fantastic, eerie sounds that have filtered through the narrative.

The extraordinary detail of this final still life (now, literally *nature morte*) confirms our sense that the novel has been pressing all along toward this spell of descriptive calm. Suspense is drained, narrative is halted, attention converges simply on bodies.[22] Twain's mocking claim is finally apropos: Cooper's readers cannot always "tell the corpses from the others." Beginning with a succession of violently hurried activities, the novel's trajectory has been through a cycle of motionless moments to this near cessation of sequence itself in the ritual hush of death. That concentration on still bodies and silent moments recurs in the Western in various forms, but is best epitomized in the formulaic shoot-out, which forms such a central scene that it survives frequent shifts in medium (novel to film), in syntactic style (prolonged suspense, narrative placement), and in social agenda (revenge, justice, inequity). Cooper's triumph in *The Last of the Mohicans,* however, cannot be measured simply by his capacity to anticipate such motifs and scenes, however ubiquitous they would become. Rather, his astonishing success in altering the possibilities of landscape itself warrants attention. Making description into a narrative act, he deftly revealed the frontier "West" as a mysteriously silent realm in which characters were transformed into mute representatives of masculine ideology.

Absorption

If landscape strikes plot into immobility in *The Last of the Mohicans,* preaching the virtues of human immobility in the form of restraint, then *The Deerslayer* represents something more radical: the absence of plot altogether (in the sense of causational sequence). What is substituted instead is a principal of mere succession evident earlier in the series: initial landscape description; followed by brief, sometimes violent action; followed in turn by the "nattering" reconstruction and interpretation of Leatherstocking. Reiterating this loosely tripartite paradigm, Cooper presents scenes as paintings into which characters belatedly enter, either in conflict themselves or anticipating it with others, before the conflict is resolved and issues arising from it abstractly reviewed. The effect of this modal rhythm is to absorb action, dialogue, character, even time itself, into the landscape, intensifying the experience of stasis established at the end of *The Last of the Mohicans,* defining masculinity as an ahistorical, all but vegetable construct.

The pattern begins with the opening pages, as disembodied voices emerge from dense woodland landscape (like *The Last of the Mohicans*), before Natty Bumppo and Hurry Harry March burst into the meticulously rendered scene, "a vast picture of solemn solitude" (2:496). The narrative builds to March's frustrated choking of an imperturbable Natty—"his countenance remained unmoved; his hand did not shake" (2:507)—after which a discussion of due provocation and "human laws" ensues. The next chapter repeats the pattern once the two men discover a canoe, offering the first description of Lake Glimmerglass. This noontime paean will be repeated in extended descriptions of its "sweet repose" in late afternoon, nighttime, and sunrise—each establishing certain mystical, mythical qualities to the lake (2:513). The two men carefully approach and examine the Hutter "Muskrat Castle" before discussing the subject of racial "gifts." At this point, the tripartite pattern is again recapitulated: a long description of the Susquehanna River and Hutter's floating Ark, preceding an attack by six Huron braves (famously lampooned by Mark Twain), followed by discussion of the morality of scalping: "Revenge is an Injin gift, and forgiveness a white-man's" (2:566). In the next sequence, a lyrical description of dawn on the lake leads to Natty's first killing of a human being, which in turn prompts his soliloquy on Indian treachery and white "gifts" (2:606). That sequence is followed by another description of Lake Glimmerglass before Chingachgook escapes from enemy Hurons to join a discussion with Natty and Judith Hutter about "woman's gifts" (2:635). Later, a singular point of land on the lake is described, as preface to the daring rescue of Wah-ta!-Wah in a maneuver that compels Natty's selfless surrender, heroic footrace escape, and recapture. Closing this sequence is his gruesome account to Hetty Hutter of the physical tortures he presumes he will suffer.

Clearly, a triadic model assists the novel's "aimless glance," validating implausible actions via descriptive jaunts through the countryside. Yet far more than any before, this novel establishes setting as an absolute *condition* of action by resorting to descriptions of landscape whenever action is about to ensue. And what was tacit above in the cursory review of plot can now be made explicit: that *The Deerslayer's* triadic model is as theatrically structured as novelistic practice allows. After the narrative curtain rises, readers are permitted to examine the set, watch players enter before indulging in dramatic exchange, then listen at last to their retrospective accounts. Later, I will argue that the Western is essentially a theatrical genre, cinema *avant la lettre;* but it should already be clear that Cooper anticipates this theatrical 41 register, adopting the idea of setting as stage—in this case a watery one, the "glorious spectacle" of Lake Glimmerglass, which resonates so powerfully as to drown out the significance of any human activity. Once its supernal qualities are described, all narrative action seems plausible. The scenery (like Zane Grey's high Utah plateaus or John Ford's Monument Valley) dissipates through sheer spectacle any reservations one might have about plot.

Yet paradoxically, the very extravagance of *The Deerslayer's* landscape descriptions seems to negate the need for action or narration *at all*. Straightforward exposition of events, even the most exciting, is sandwiched so thinly between preliminary description and subsequent analysis as to be nearly squeezed out *as* action. And much as description overtakes action, it regularly supplants even dialogue. Or rather, the narrator is constantly disposed to turn dialogue into description, by recounting nearly every exchange before going on to decipher its meaning. Instead of characters speaking for themselves, the novel continually intrudes, explaining why it is they say what they do.

So fully do descriptive passages in *The Deerslayer* predominate over narrative sequence that it seems as if individuals themselves are being displaced, thrust into subsidiary roles attendant on the landscape, swallowed up by terrain. Far more than in *The Last of the Mohicans,* where characters are reduced to a silent tableau, here figures seem absorbed by landscape, made to experience quiet self-annihilation. Natty repeatedly loses himself in contemplation of Lake Glimmerglass, feeling "a pleasure at looking on the scene he now beheld, that momentarily caused him to forget the object of his visit" (1:759). "Mingl[ing] with the universe" (as phrased in the Byronic epigraph to the opening chapter), he achieves a state of spiritual transcendence. Late in the novel, he escapes a band of pursuing Hurons by lying face up in a canoe, staring as he floats at "the blue void of space" in a loss of self-consciousness: "a death like stillness pervaded the spot: A quietness as profound as if all lay in the repose of inanimate life" (1:961). His gaze, moreover, suggests an unmediated identification with the firmament that is nonetheless an alert recognition of his own separate status—a curious balance of transcendental union and self-contained independence.[23]

This unusual relation between settings and actors, with landscape encroaching on narrative so persistently as to disrupt our deepest assumptions of personality, reinforces the novel's mythic tone, but only by obscuring a contradiction between the novel's claimed history and its putative timelessness. Cooper's aim was to sketch the youthful origins of an American Adam, providing a historical background to earlier portraits of that figure in middle and old age. As filiation, the series' final novel is set in an earlier era—so precisely, in fact, that the whole is said to have taken place within six "cloudless day[s] in June" in the period "between the years 1740 and 1745" (2:496). Yet more conspicuously than ever before, *The Deerslayer* aspires to a timeless condition in which events are frozen by landscape and narrative absorbed by description.

That aspiration is hardly apparent in Cooper's framing of the narrative, with his opening claim that "events produce the effects of time," and that whatever "seems venerable by an accumulation of changes, is reduced to familiarity when we come seriously to consider it solely in connection with time" (2:495). Nor does Judith's poignant avowal at the conclusion make it clear: "So much, and so much that is important has taken place, within [a week], that the sorrows, and dangers, and escapes of a whole life have been crowded into a few days . . . " (2:1022). Between these two declarations, however, few allusions are made to the fact of time passing, with the narrative further suspending the question in its triadic rhythm of description, event, and dialogue. And if time itself is erased by the recurrent sacrifice of event to description, even its passage between events is for the most part neglected, the hours and days simply ignored, confirming again the novel's commitment to mythical space.

Occasionally, the narrator will make self conscious temporal references: "no time was to be lost," or "In scenes like these, events thicken in less time than they can be related" (2:642, 816). At other points, the reader is alerted to the future by being informed of events still to come, culled from moments in the rest of the series (2:696; also *The Pathfinder,* 2:410–11). It can even be said that *The Deerslayer* is loosely structured by two major commitments to time: Natty's rendezvous with Chingachgook, which has brought him to Lake Glimmerglass; and his "furlough" from captivity, which brings the novel to a close. As Natty repeatedly explains, he is pledged to return to his Iroquois captors "at the appointed moment" of noon on the sixth day, and "to a minute" does exactly that, with tremendous "dramatic effect" (2:946–47). Yet these isolated moments tend to interrupt rather than sustain the narrative, breaking breathlessly into what otherwise seems like a timeless realm.

The novel devoted to providing a historical account of Natty's youth seems oddly bent on avoiding any temporal constraints and finally on escaping time altogether (achieving the silent arrest that Leone so ardently desired). It might, in fact, more generally be said that *The Deerslayer* aspires to a condition of stasis, becoming as inert and self-possessed as the landscape itself. Or as George Dekker remarks: "*The Deerslayer* is a novel in which all things stand trembling on the edge of some other condition," caught in a logic of present fullness, resistant to what the future may bring, hesitating before the onset of history itself.[24] What marks the novel as an evolution in the possibilities for the Western is that this aspiration toward stasis is true even in its nondescriptive parts: whether through the potentially monotonous repetitions of a triadic compositional pattern or through the novel's pervasive resistance to more firmly temporal structures. In contrast to *The Last of the Mohicans*, where the landscape opposes characters, compelling them into model behavior, the later novel establishes a sense of stasis all the more complete. Natty Bumppo's mythical resonance is secured by his becoming as fully a part of the landscape as possible.

Possession and Self-Possession

Differences aside, both *The Deerslayer* and *The Last of the Mohicans* pursue what it means to lose oneself, to become part of the landscape, reduced to a nonhuman world where cultural valuations no longer mattered. The most obvious indication of this is the novels' self-conscious address of racial difference in terms of distinctions at once inherent and conditioned—distinctions characterized by Natty as deriving alternately from "natur'" and "gifts." Little would be served here by adding to extensive commentaries, except to confirm how confused Natty becomes through the series, identifying racial "gifts" as supposedly local, environmental, and presumably corrigible, while a character's true "natur'" is congenital, inherent, and thus ineluctably determined.[25]

What *is* worth investigating in this distinction is its reliance on a notion of "possession," leading characters to wonder which traits they possess as individuals, which as a race, which as a species. Possession, however, encompasses an even more basic logic of persons and objects that is just as regularly addressed by both novels. *The Deerslayer* raises the question directly in asking who should possess Natty's rifle, "Killdeer": the person who can use it best or she (Judith Hutter) who legally owns it? The question had emerged earlier in slightly varied form, in Natty's dispute with the Huron, Lynx, over a pair of free-floating birchbark canoes. And its ramifications are later pursued in a discussion of the contents of Tom Hutter's chest. More broadly, the novel broaches the issue in matrimonial terms: To whom does Wah-ta!-wah belong and to whom will she be given in marriage? It is a question Natty also raises later about himself and Judith, and which was similarly raised about Cora and Alice Munro in *The Last of the Mohicans*.

Indeed, each of the Leatherstocking novels raises the large question of who possesses the American continent itself and how that possession is to be legitimated. Indian rights to the land are explored in *The Prairie* and *The Deerslayer*, both of which predictably side at last with proponents of Judeo-Christian law enforced by European military might. *The Last of the Mohicans* and *The Pathfinder* evolve from a subsequent historical narrative, when France and England have "robbed" the landscape of its Indian names and fought each other "for the possession of a country, that neither was destined to retain" (*Mohicans*, 1:481). *The Pioneers* dramatizes a still later class struggle, establishing the right of a landed aristocracy to control a country the mob would despoil. In a variety of ways, from an array of historical perspectives, Cooper kept pressing the question: Who has the right to hold what? And the signal importance of that question here—particularly in terms of owning land—is that it is constantly restaged in the Western via chronic conflicts between generic groups wresting control of a passing frontier (Indians versus whites, transients versus settlers, ranchers versus farmers, middle versus lower classes).

This obsession with gaining title to land is part of the consideration of possession figured in the Leatherstocking series through many other guises. Even the episodic structure of the novels reinforces this anxiety, with the recurrent narrative rhythm of pursuit, capture, and escape accentuating the effort to "hold on" to property that may not rightfully belong to the possessor. That rhythm, moreover, reflects some of the trouble faced by Cooper himself in possessing his own narrative property, and how consumed he became with the need to control the readership of his novels— dictating conditions in footnotes, haranguing in prefaces and public letters, never readily releasing texts to any but his own authorized interpretations. In sum, the disputes that occur over plots of land within his novels match not only the difficulties that emerge at the plotted level of narrative form but as well the authorial controversies prompted by the novels themselves. None of this posed a liability for Cooper, either in terms of popularity or aesthestic achievement. But does this mean that plotlessness is somehow a necessary ingredient in the construction of Westerns? Those rambling, aleatory narratives of Wister, Grey, and L'Amour; the episodic films of William S. Hart, Budd Boetticher, and Sam Peckinpah: all depend upon an understanding of plot (in both senses) as something always desired but only secured temporarily. What critics have seen as a defect in Cooper's construction of narrative has served on the contrary as inspiration for countless authors and film directors.

One of the reasons plot can operate less forcefully in the Leatherstocking series (as in later Westerns) is the stature of the central character himself, whose presence alone commands attention. Physically unhandsome, Natty Bumppo is nonetheless a figure of unexcelled prowess, with a "lean" build on a six-foot frame and the speed and agility to perform incredible feats (catching a thrown ax in mid-air, for instance, and returning it to kill his antagonist). Above all, he is a marksman whose ability to hit imperceptible targets, quickly, with deadly accuracy, almost suggests a demonic contract. He achieves a state that anticipates the gunslinger hero only in the course of the series, becoming mythically dehumanized in the nearly two-decade transition from *The Pioneers* to *The Deerslayer* as Cooper presents him more closely approximating a condition of landscape.

Landscape is granted a kind of agency, then, in compelling individuals to become like itself: motionless, rooted, fixed, unmoving. The paradox in this position is that the stillness enjoined by Cooper's landscapes results in behavior thoroughly impersonal, even deathlike, yet the embodiment of moral principle. The most important of Natty's characteristics, after all, is his integrity when someone attempts to change his mind, remaining true to himself, firm, unswayed, self-possessed: in short, the opposite of losing oneself. The series' concern with possession, in other words, is thematized in psychological terms as a question of self-possession, of maintaining oneself under strict control. This paradox of deathly stillness revealed somehow as moral integrity is, as we will see in a moment, only possible because the pose of stillness is an empty one.

Self-effacement yet self-possession; invisibility yet stalwart integrity: this conflicted ideal is most woodenly incarnated in the figures of Chingachgook and Uncas. What lends to the novels an interesting tension is the way that Natty negotiates both realms, repeatedly *achieving* command of himself to become what he admires. Indeed, it is his *lapses* in self-restraint—his impulsive displays of marksmanship; his "nattering" on about "natur'," "gifts," and manly honor—that reveal how exacting an effort is required to maintain self-control. Nor is this process apparent at first, as if Cooper only slowly realized the importance of making the gesture of self-possession dramatic. Not until *The Deerslayer*, for instance, does the threat of physical torture give Natty an opportunity to *display* his capacity for unyielding self-control, bearing allegiance to something beyond his immediate pain or comfort. Despite certain death, he never considers breaking his "furlough" agreement to return freely to Huron captivity, or more generally to place his companions in jeopardy—all, simply because he has given his word to an enemy.[26]

Natty's devotion to wilderness, then, is associated with a moral sensibility. Yet it is important to acknowledge how fully Cooper's description of him as a figure absorbed by landscape contributes to our sense of that moral identity as somehow *empty*. By identifying him with native scenes where it is only necessary *not* to do something—to stand fixed, unwavering, immovable—Cooper defines a self-obliteration that is morally equivalent to an unchanging tableau, in which choice is never required. His ethical code, in other words, strikes us on closer inspection not as excessively arbitrary but as inadequately so—less a set of principles for choosing one action over another than a series of habitual practices for how to act when a choice has already been made. Ethics come to seem more a matter of improvised *style* than clear *ideal*. And Natty's code appears little more than a vague sort of masculine Golden Rule, entailing respect for women, keeping one's word, in general treating others fairly. Otherwise, his code offers little more than a formal inducement to act with restraint on behalf of friends—a goal hardly moral at all.[27]

What contributes to the mistaken sense that Natty is truly principled—not simply a creature of mechanical habit but an ethical being—is the quality of his self-control, the studied reserve with which he responds to others. *The Deerslayer* offers a strong version of what is evident throughout the series, accentuating his restraint by providing an account less of dramatic deeds than of potential actions Natty declines to do: refusing to marry Judith Hutter; refusing to kill the treacherous Huron, Lynx (until self-defense requires it); refusing to break a furlough promise; refusing to retaliate against Indian taunts. Considerable as are his skills and aptitudes, the most striking trait is Natty's *not* giving way to the impulse to practice any of them—particularly when provoked to do just that.

Means have begun to replace ends, with personal behavior—the "style" of the hero—itself exhibited as something to admire. And for all that separates Natty from Hurry Harry in terms of explicit moral tenets (the idea of fairness to enemies, say, or keeping one's word, or aiding the weak), those differences are less significant dramatically than the disparity in their degrees of patience and self-control. Westerns adopted this opposition of control and impatience, distinguishing heroes from villains less in terms of principles themselves than in the *fidelity* to which those principles are adhered. All agree "a man's gotta do what a man's gotta do," but as the genre evolves the hero is increasingly distinguished by the perseverance, detachment, and self-possession with which he obeys the tautology.

The fact that a code's imprecision makes it appealing should hardly come as a surprise. Loose standards, after all, allow a broader spectrum of conflicting ideals to be projected onto a heroically restrained persona. Certainly, Natty is pledged to a set of values, declaimed through the series as the cultural "gifts" of a Judeo-Christian heritage. But just as regularly, his character is revealed in moments that occur as eruptions of violence in the text, whether he is coolly resourceful (escaping from enemies, defending himself, rescuing others) or simply self-contained (manifest proof against suasions and threats). More generally, his restraint is emblematic of the role of description in the series. Just as the *The Last of the Mohicans* slowly immobilizes characters, reducing them to statuary or tableaux—and just as depictions of landscape in *The Deerslayer* end by absorbing individuals, action, even narrative itself—so in both novels the consequence of Natty's restraint is to leave him a figure inimical to action. Not only is he (like Lassiter, Shane, Hondo, and countless successors) depicted as part of the landscape—emerging from it at the beginning, returning to it at the end—but in a rudimentary way, he incorporates landscape's resistance to action, description's opposition to narrative. It is this puzzling gestalt of figure and ground, each generating our sense of the other, that is part of the complex legacy Cooper bequeathed to the Western.

Party Politics

But why this static hero, this proto-Virginian, and why at this historical moment? Or put another way, why did forms of morality expressed as stillness and self-possession need so to drench Cooper's novels as to stop time and dismantle activity? Two decades after the fact, Susan Cooper recalled the moment her father conceived *The Deerslayer* as they were returning from a walk on the slopes of Lake Otsego in the summer of 1840:

Mr. Cooper was singing to himself, as he often did on that quiet woodland road,—it was generally some snatch of a song popular in his youth;—upon the afternoon in question it chanced to be an election song of the party with which he did *not* vote. Suddenly we came out of the wood, and a view of the lake opened before us, a familiar view, but more lovely than usual in the soft lights and shadows of that summer evening. There was a pause in the song. The pony indulged himself with a walk. The author's face was turned towards the lake, and the far-seeing look of inventive genius came into the clear gray eye. He was lost in thought for a moment,—figures and scenes foreign to the day and hour seemed to rise before him. Soon the vision passed away. Turning to his daughter with a smile he exclaimed, "I must write one more book, dearie, about our little lake!" Then the song was resumed, the whip cracked, the pony trotted on, and we went our way toward the village.[28]

This account of conception nicely incorporates significant aspects of the novel: the paired figures, the lake emerging magically in a break in the woods, the display of patient restraint, the landscape's transfixing power, even the seemingly moral self-injunction ("I must"). Perhaps the only jarring aspect (and a theme notably absent from Cooper's novels) is the political significance of Cooper singing "to himself" a Whig party song.[29]

Politics seems immediate; landscape mythic, even eternal. Yet this association of the two is hardly atypical in a period when "free soil" was contested more hotly than ever before. What is arresting is Cooper's delight in singing an *opposition* party song as he contemplates his favorite lake, illustrating a genius for holding conflicting ideals in mind simultaneously and suggesting something of the nature of the appeal of his Leatherstocking novels. In a period of intense dislocation when national issues that had seemed settled were newly coming undone—when class, gender, and racial boundaries were transformed in fundamental ways—Cooper achieved a vision precluded in his more straightforward political fables of a national landscape peopled by Americans heroically poised in untoward circumstances. His success, moreover, defied party lines, appealing as fully to Whigs as to Democrats, confirming his genius at resolving ideals that would otherwise have seemed mutually exclusive.

Certainly, his readers in the 1820s experienced a series of major social transformations, both exciting and disturbing. For even as suffrage was finally extended to unpropertied white males, confirming (at last, by some lights) the nation's democratic promise, laborers found economic opportunities diminish along with an erosion of standards of work, loyalty, and independence. Industrialism replaced the artisan-apprentice compact with a competitive system of labor and capital as workers turned for the first time regularly against employers, divided as never before by class. In a period sometimes labeled "the era of egalitarianism," the rich secured ever greater power while politics itself became a markedly less noble calling.[30] At the same time, progressive religion was abandoning belief in man's fallen state only to embrace a less sternly secure but more apprehensive view. Urbanization took place at frightening speed in a demographic explosion that accompanied the first of intense waves of foreign immigration. East Coast cities resembled nothing so much as Third World cities today, with garbage and pigs littering streets that lacked any social services. Access to rural retreats (much less to unspoiled scenes of nature) was increasingly a privilege of wealth and class.[31]

It was the extraordinary success of market capitalism, however, with its encouragement of speculative behavior that made older virtues seem irrelevant yet more essential than ever, leading to a broad range of public expressions marked by an increasing tone of anxiety. The fear of uninhibited self-aggrandizement, of ruthless acquisition, was expressed in sermons, school lessons, political pamphlets, and a variety of other public forms. National crises were interpreted as failures of self-control. Andrew Jackson's famous battles in the 1820s against government corruption and the national debt, like the Bank War controversy of the 1830s, have been read by Michael Paul Rogin as part of Jackson's—and more generally, Jacksonians'—psychosocial fears about bodily control and self-regulation.[32]

Indeed, the touchstone for these fears was ironically Jackson himself, whose Inaugural reception on March 4, 1829 signaled the times. A raucous debacle in which thousands of "scrambling, fighting, romping" citizens tramped mud through the White House, the event caused considerable damage and alarm.³³ Associate justice of the Supreme Court, Joseph Story, sourly noted that "the reign of King MOB seemed triumphant."³⁴ Another observer recalled: "It was like the inundation of the northern barbarians into Rome. . . . They swarmed . . . a sort of Praetorian band, which, having borne in upon their shields their idolized leader, claimed the reward of the hard-fought contest."³⁵ Even those amused by the sight proclaimed it a "regular Saturnalia" and described how "[t]he mob broke in, in thousands—Spirits black yellow and grey, poured in in one uninterrupted stream of mud and filth, among the throngs many fit subjects for the penitentiary."³⁶ At a time when the Apollonian restraints of an older order were still fresh in memory, the new social calculus threatened to make a virtue of the Dionysian. How would traditional Republican principles be cultivated in this new era of unrestrained democratic capitalism?

The answer, of course, was Natty Bumppo, who stood at once as man of the people and in mute defiance of a rabble-rousing "King MOB." The cowboy would wait half a century before riding onto the historical stage, but Cooper clearly anticipated that hero's restrained stance toward civic excess. As much to the point, Natty offered a firm assurance about both public and personal values, a self-confidence about how one ought to behave in even the most disorienting of wildernesses. Only a short generation before, people had lived in more settled circumstances with clearer standards, if no less "tormented with the fear of Sin, and the terror of the Day of Judgment." As Emerson despondently went on to note, however, "These terrors have lost their force, and our torment is unbelief, the uncertainty as to what we ought to do."³⁷ Jackson's accession to power coincided at once with the erosion of ineffectual standards and the release of exuberant social energies, to both of which Natty Bumppo offered an unambiguous response.

Perhaps unsurprisingly, anxiety over erosion of standards appears most baldly in texts devoted to inculcating just such standards: conduct books addressed to young men. In 1827, a handbook advising newly ordained ministers on "mental discipline" encouraged them to maintain their faith with a series of warnings, each phrased as *self-restraining* injunctions: to "repress," "guard against," "limit," "regulate," "discriminate."³⁸ Embracing a host of pitfalls, the reiterated warnings collectively serve the design of ever stricter emotional control. And while times had certainly changed by the 1840s, conduct was to remain more or less the same. As one book cautioned, the loss of "quiet hamlets" and the spread of a perilous credit system had spawned new temptations in an unregulated world. Ever greater self-restraint (or what was more commonly referred to as "decision of character") was required of young men if they were to succeed. Foremost was "the necessity of *steadiness of purpose* and *perseverance* in whatever we first choose in life."[39] Another manual listed the primary virtues as "strict honor, self-possession, forbearance," and concluded: "The greater the liberty we enjoy in any sphere of life, the more binding, necessarily, becomes the obligation of self-restraint."[40]

Conduct books, in short, offer a guide to masculine behavior marked by the tautologies of Cooper's code for Natty Bumppo. Instead of enjoining a specific ethics for relations in school, business, and home, they rely upon a general morality of stillness in which *what* one does is less important than *how*. Not behaving intemperately, not speaking thoughtlessly, not diverging from a course of action, not breaking one's word: the point is that certain performative constraints matter more than the ethics of any given action itself (Who is one's word given *to*? What is the goal of an action?). By contrast, conduct books from the earlier Federalist period tended to prescribe specific acts, to enjoin a fixed set of behaviors: obedience to elders, honesty, frugality, sincerity (among other behavioral standards), and Benjamin Franklin notoriously added to these a list of thirteen primary virtues (including Cleanliness and Order). When these same books counseled reserve, moreover, they stressed the positive, religious, and moral grounds for acting in this way (for example, not to displease or distress others, to gain self-knowledge, or simply to stay healthy).[41] A generation later, restraint was simply to be practiced as an end in itself: the process by which Jacksonian men became men was primarily one of holding themselves back.[42] And when conduct books in the 1830s did venture at being more broadly prescriptive, they risked self-contradiction. One pamphlet urged the "practice of observation" as "the first means of improvement"—"Endeavor therefore to derive some instruction or improvement of the mind from every thing which you see or hear"—only then to return once again to the "Necessity of Having Fixed Principles" based on "decision of character."[43]

That contradictory capacity to be both keenly observant and yet self-contained—at once dependent educationally and yet constitutionally autonomous—forms a rough characterization of Natty Bumppo himself, one worth pursuing in a moment. The larger appeal of the series, however, can be attributed to Cooper's own authorial contradictions as someone clearly opposed to an unregulated rise of "the people," desiring return to older forms, who nonetheless incorporates in his emotional proclivities and social habits a staunch identification with those same newly rebellious forces. In a career-long rebellion against his father's commanding reputation, in adolescent outbursts that resulted in expulsion from Yale, in a later long and self-destructive history of libel battles, in an affinity for conspiratorial theories, and in various other ways: Cooper reveals a dynamic, sometimes impulsive, always strong-willed personality not to be simply identified with the forces of propriety.[44] And while he may in historical novels proclaim political and social biases directly, even allegorically, the Leatherstocking series reveals a self-contradictory tenor in which the very positions Natty upholds are controverted. Racial problems, class and gender issues are presented as controversies over which his woodsman has little control, allowing Cooper to play out voices and positions among a series of contending forces.

It is his central character, however, who embodies the contradictions dividing readers most radically, both dependent educationally and constitutionally autonomous. Natty's woodsman's eye is ever watchful, ever aware, ever attuned to what others are doing, even as he always remains firmly himself, unchanged, self-secure. It is as if he were pitched between mutually exclusive possibilities, at once imperturably self-contained yet ever on the verge of explosive violence—or, as Jacksonians frequently liked to express it, poised on the edge of the "spontaneous."[45] Natty is in fact "a magnificent moral hermaphrodite," and not simply (as Balzac meant) for mediating between the savage and civilized but because he incarnates deep contradictions in Jacksonian ideology itself.[46]

Dislocations in the Jacksonian period led to a predictable investment in putting the lid back on, reinaugurating older values and behavior at a time when market capitalism was inspiring sharply innovative practices. "The movement which helped to clear the path for laissez-faire capitalism and its culture in America," notes Marvin Meyers of the "Jacksonian paradox," "and the public which in its daily life eagerly entered on that path, held nevertheless in their political conscience an ideal of a chaste republican order, resisting the seductions of risk and novelty, greed and extravagance, rapid motion and complex dealings."[47] Even so, those "seductions" appealed to many, who saw signs of national development in a new mentality that, as Michael Paul Rogin has said, "made independence, opportunity, and self-help the cardinal virtues."[48] This divergence between anxious conservatives and eager capitalists helps explain why Natty's "moral code" is expressed *as* performance, as mere show of restraint, the flagrant gesture of holding back from action. He is a man for the times because he clearly knows his social place—or more to the point, knows, from having read the landscape as conduct book, the virtues of emotional accommodation. Unswayed by envy, ambition, or the apprehension that traditional standards of behavior are somehow inadequate, he is (in a word) self-possessed. It could hardly be better phrased than in Andrew Jackson's Farewell Address: "You have no longer any cause to fear danger from abroad. It is from within, among yourselves—from cupidity, from corruption, from disappointed ambition and inordinate thirst for power—that factions will be formed and liberty endangered."[49] The point, once again, is that virtue flows from a certain vegetable stillness and consists in resisting desires that act on the self as if from abroad.

Natty appeals to a forward-looking Jacksonian era because he satisfies a nostalgia about older times that paradoxically often goes hand in hand with hoarse cries for revolution. By allowing his hero to grow more youthful through the series, Cooper creates a character more obviously capable of contradictory beliefs and behavior, at once more morally pure and yet more violent. As important, however, is the way that Cooper depicts the landscape in sensual terms, which embody and even enforce an idealizing masculine stance. Where conduct books proffered avuncular advice in dry tones, the Leatherstocking novels excited interest in the same behavior by presenting its various landscapes as living examples with the force of law. They serve as complicated machines of excess that at once legitimate narrative and paradoxically make it seem inessential, since characters are taught to remain figures of inaction, stilled into postures of quiescent restraint.

Stasis, Landscape, and a Code

As no other writer before, Cooper presented *landscapes* for the reader's "aimless glance," providing an apparently recognizable space where incredible narratives could be not simply credited but given a national flavor. At the same time, he imagined a mythic *character* whose "true sight" never wavered, who seemed to speak on behalf of something more than his own desires, indeed on behalf of higher values. Yet the most striking feature of these dual innovations in landscape description and narrative action is the strange link that connects them—the sense of absolute stasis that becomes apparent as characters achieve heroic stature, approximating the landscape itself, silent and unmoving. Natty, Chingachgook, and Uncas in particular are frozen by terrain, compelled into a mythic quiescence that accords them the power of unspent potential. In the prelapsarian wilderness before the ax falls and history begins, these woodland figures come to seem mythic creatures, displayed in poses that exemplify virtue as a timeless restraint.

Upon closer examination, of course, neither Cooper's luxuriant landscapes nor his character's moral code are more timeless than any other cultural construction. My point has only been that their very confusion is seductive. The very vacuity of Natty's code is compounded by the absorptive power of the landscapes through which he moves—a combination that appealed as it did because unsettled readers could project on the still, silent   53 figure of manly restraint their own mutually exclusive agendas: progressive and reactionary, liberal and conservative, forward-looking and nostalgic. Natty Bumppo prevailed in untoward fictional circumstances much as Jacksonians hoped to do, armed with a code that bound him firmly to principles only vaguely defined, making him at once moral and free. Westerns would borrow assorted features and issues from Cooper, among the most persistent of which was the problem of possessing the land, of imposing "plots" that could be imagined as both narratively and legally binding. Yet Cooper's more critical legacy was his vision of how to constitute America itself as a mythic space where older ideals could be reconfigured and made appropriate for current needs. Before a popular tradition could understand how much Cooper had done, however, a wider array of characters as well as a more spectacular landscape would need to be invented.

3 FALLING SHORT

It's all Bierstadt and Bierstadt and Bierstadt nowadays! What has he done but twist and skew and distort and discolor and belittle and be-pretty this whole doggonned country? Why, his mountains are too high and too slim; they'd blow over in one of our fall winds.

I've herded colts two summers in Yosemite, and honest now, when I stood right up in front of his picture, I didn't know it.

He hasn't what old Ruskin calls for.

"Hank G. Smith, artist" (1870)[1]

I sometimes wonder what kind of work I am doing. I never see anybody whose opinion I value; I never hear any criticism. I grind out the old tunes on the old organ and gather up the coppers, but I never know whether my audience behind the window blinds are wishing me to "move on" or not.

Bret Harte (1879)[2]

Despite the significance of landscape for the Western, despite Cooper's stature as father of the genre, his landscapes are never set in the West nor even resemble actual scenery. Quite the contrary, he creates an anthropomorphized, mildly phantasmagorical world that draws attention to itself as an ethical book to be read, not as a photographically accurate scene. Nor was accuracy expected, since even the most interesting *painted* depictions of far western terrain were rarely direct transcriptions intended as ocular proof. Indeed, one of my themes throughout is that landscapes serve a series of shifting ideological positions through the history of Westerns, and do so through sometimes abrupt metaphorical transformations. The best Westerns treat landscape idiosyncratically, organizing it according to a contemporary emotional logic that often seems lawless from a later perspective.

The person who first seized this insight was, curiously enough, a painter, who showed what was possible in the Far West by notoriously capturing it as just such a realm of optic lawlessness. Albert Bierstadt pulled back from the clear authority of Cooper's landscapes—landscapes intended to compel performances of restraint—to develop in grandiose oils the more purely formal innovations Cooper had introduced, creating a surreal, clearly false natural world capable of naturalizing a broad (and changing) range of behavior as distinctly American. Contemporary with Bierstadt, Bret Harte invented a cast of characters commensurate with the painter's western landscapes—indeed, embodying a series of contradictions that might also be said to be lawless, making them perfect denizens of Bierstadt's phantasmagorical canvases where narrative has yet to begin. Bierstadt first painted not the West but a drop cloth for the Western, as a place waiting to be filled by Harte's eccentric westerners.

Notably, both men burst into fame in the mid–1860s as premier icon-ographers of America's Far West, only to disappear from view in less than a decade. Painter and writer, devoted to similar native subject matter, un-derwent a meteoric rise and fall of reputation in tandem, which prompts the question of what inspired such brief fame. One explanation is simply the obsessiveness with which Americans focused on native identity in a period of Civil War that prompted strong regional loyalties. Hundreds of stories and novels detailed the manners and mores of local scenes: southern plantations, rural New England, frontier farms in the Old Northwest. And demand for such accounts only grew in the postbellum period: John Greenleaf Whittier capitalized on the fad with *Snow-Bound: A Winter Idyl* (1866), for which he received a royalty check for the unprecedented sum of $10,000; the year before, Mark Twain had established a budding national reputation with "Jim Smiley and His Jumping Frog" (1865); three years later, similar plaudits were accorded Harriet Beecher Stowe's *Oldtown Folks* (1869). Countless imitations followed, encouraged by improved means of production and distribution (new printing processes; transcontinental rail-road), and spurred by competition among monthlies like the *Atlantic* and *Harper's,* eager to cater to an interest in provincial landscapes, traditional customs, and regional dialects—all part of what became known as the "Lo-cal Color movement." The initial appeal of Bierstadt and Harte, then, is explained by a fascination with regional difference, even if context alone does little to clarify their sudden loss of favor (especially since the Local Color movement continued to grow). Nor do their declining reputations match the notable influence each would continue to have upon other artists of the Far West.

One answer to this conundrum of lost popularity yet abiding effect may lie in the treatment both artists gave to the West as a "direction of thought" rather than a geographical region. They envisioned a psychologi-cal terrain less local or specific than either the Sierra Nevadas or Rocky Mountains, and in so doing they first mapped a realm that artists could recast symbolically, emotionally, ideologically under the label "Western." The closer one looks at each man's career in terms of the other's, moreover, the easier it is to grasp how overnight fame and nearly instant neglect may have stemmed from an inability to match the other artist's central vision: Bierstadt at his best creating paradoxically lawless landscapes that demand (but do not provide) strong narrative plots; Harte creating paradoxical characters who emerge from overly vague landscapes. Each artist aroused expectations for a West that neither, alone, could satisfy.

Figure 1. Albert Bierstadt, *The Rocky Mountains, Lander's Peak* (1863), oil on canvas, 73¼ × 120¾ inches. The Metropolitan Museum of Art, Rogers Fund, 1907.

Critical Rebukes

In 1853, when Albert Bierstadt returned from America to his birthplace in Germany, it was as a self-confident teenage painter, eager to master techniques at the famous Düsseldorf academy. By the time he sailed the Atlantic again at the age of twenty-seven, he had become a well-respected artist, with career ambitions as grand as his new painting style. Realizing the West would offer "my subject," he accompanied General Frederick W. Lander's 1859 survey to the Rocky Mountains and excitedly began to paint what he found. His landscapes soon won acclaim in New York, but nothing like the international fame he garnered with *The Rocky Mountains, Lander's Peak* (1863), the wall-sized canvas that sold for an unprecedented $25,000 and secured his reputation as the heir to Turner (figure 1). "On this American more than any other," London's *Art Journal* solemnly averred, "does the mantle of our greatest painter appear to have fallen."[3] Yet within the decade, Bierstadt found the mantle slipping, and by 1885 his reputation was such that he was rejected for an international show. Long before his death in 1902, he had grown accustomed to being ignored.

If less convinced at so early an age of his artistic talent, Bret Harte's career nonetheless parallels Bierstadt's. Born in New York, Harte had moved to California at eighteen where he took odd jobs and began in a desultory way to write. Within a decade, his poems and parodies had become familiar to San Francisco readers, but no one anticipated that his first story, "The Luck of Roaring Camp" (1868), would make his name a household word across the nation. Two years later, riding a wave of popular acclaim, he signed a one-year contract to supply the *Atlantic Monthly* with a story per month for $10,000. Traveling east to a hero's welcome, he crossed the continent (in Mark Twain's envious account) "through such a prodigious blaze of national interest and excitement that one might have supposed he was the Viceroy of India on a progress, or Halley's comet come again after seventy-five years of lamented absence."[4] A mere four more years later, another wit transposed the figure, wisecracking that Harte had "reversed the path of the sun. He rose splendidly in the West and set in darkness in the East."[5] His contract unrenewed, his works already neglected, he sailed to Europe in 1878 never to return, countering Bierstadt's example but likewise hoping to attract a public that had swung abruptly away. When he died in London (within months of Bierstadt), he had long been forgotten in America.

In the ninety-odd years since, both artists have gradually been rehabilitated, although Bierstadt's reputation in particular reveals a continuing power to engage and offend. "Bierstadt is an artist toward whom it is impossible to feel indifferent," proclaimed Michael Brenson, the *New York Times* reviewer of the mammoth 1991 one-man exhibition, who then went on to rail against his "showmanship, his gamesmanship, his flattery," and to indict the paintings as "artistically and intellectually dumb," produced by someone who "had no artistic imagination, no introspection, and [who] was incapable of growth."[6] Strong words, to be sure, but hardly stronger than other verbal salvos fired at the painter for well over a century. "Whatever is said about Bierstadt now," his biographer has observed, "much worse was said during his lifetime."[7]

Indeed, the surprise is not that the invective should prove so virulent but that the language associated with Bierstadt has always been as strong, aroused by the "Wagnerian exultations" of his sensational full-length landscapes.[8] Critics have regularly taken offense at his painterly excesses, as if his own intemperateness induced a corresponding intemperateness in the viewer. The aesthetic objection most frequently lodged has been to the influence of the "Düsseldorf school": that Bierstadt's paintings, as Brenson's distant predecessor wrote in an 1867 *New York Times* review, were "superficial, 'beautiful' but 'destitute of sentiment.'"[9] Others have singled out a flouting of perspective, or the dependence on an outmoded panoramic mode, or have more directly scorned a tuft-hunting preference for grandiose canvases and an "effusive temperament."[10]

Bret Harte arouses less antipathy only because he inspires more circumspect praise, with readers continuing to agree to Wallace Stegner's assessment of more than thirty years ago:

> Though the critics have been out in Chinese hordes panning the worked-over gravels of American literature, no critic has made a new strike in him. The consensus on Harte is approximately what it was at the time of his death: that he was a skillful but not profound writer who made a lucky strike in subject matter and for a few heady months enjoyed a fabulous popularity.[11]

While Harte's stories remain in print, they rarely prompt critical study, and when they do faint praise generally evolves into analytical assault, even character assassination. "The tendency to triteness in his dialogues, to flowery writing in his descriptions, to moralizing in his passages dealing with serious questions of personal relationships," one critic has written, "stem from a personality which somehow escaped self-analysis."[12] From the beginning, Harte's reception has been tinged by this propensity to read the art as product of a deformed life. Readers had expected an author as crudely colorful as one of his characters and were disappointed in the "handsome fop" who sported "faultless linen" and a trimmed beard.[13] As well, Harte could be at once the most charming of men and the most insufferable—helping explain why the author's initial reception turned sour so soon. A notoriously patronizing manner and indelicate snubs prompted former supporters, critics, fellow writers, even former collaborators like Twain to retaliate.

Bierstadt's personality even more blatantly antagonized critics, upset at the theatricality of a painter who ingratiated himself with prospective clients, secured entrée to high society through grand balls and formal dinners, and even consented to repaint finished canvases on request. Unlike Harte, he treated his art as a means to social advancement, painstakingly playing a kind of painterly agent to the rich, noble, and famous—a role that ensured him a life of elegant living but invited the disapprobation of those upset that "he deliberately sought fame and fortune."[14] His preference for large canvases was thus construed as little more than a ploy to excite the interest of well-heeled clients with walls to fill.[15] No clearer evidence for such a motive exists than Bierstadt's unashamed willingness to name his western mountains for buyers, a lure that did induce wealthy patrons to pay extravagant prices. From this perspective, Bierstadt appears to have anticipated one of the premises of this book: that viewers (in this case, wealthy owners) saw themselves reflected *in* the canvas, and therefore would have desired more than a merely realistic representation. Strangely unlike any other artist I discuss, Bierstadt needed to appeal in his paintings not only to a popular constituency (who would establish his reputation) but to a moneyed clientele (who could afford his prices), raising questions about the kind of mixed audience to whom they appealed.

Neither Bierstadt nor Harte could afford the style of life to which each aspired, leading to different but equally calamitous choices in their careers. Harte succumbed to a demand for more sustained efforts than was warranted by his mastery of the short story form, turning briefly (unprofitably) to the lecture circuit before publishing his only full novel. The plot of *Gabriel Conroy* (1875), apart from stylistic considerations, is so utterly confused that even Harte had to fiddle with the ending, altering the skin color of the heroine in order to bring the whole to a logical conclusion. It hardly need be added that the novel was scathingly reviewed and sold poorly. At the same time, Bierstadt's grip on a national audience (and therefore on individual clients) loosened, forcing him back on evermore obvious stratagems, reducing him "to public relations tricks that would have been beneath his dignity" only a decade before.[16] Still, a painting like *Sunset in the Yosemite Valley* (1868), which would have garnered accolades in 1862, elicited little more than grunts on its appearance half-a-dozen years later (figure 2). Even Mark Twain found the oil wanting: "Some of Mr. Bierstadt's mountains swim in a lustrous pearly mist, which is so enchantingly beautiful that I am sorry the Creator hadn't made it instead of him so that it would always remain there. . . . We do not want this glorified atmosphere smuggled into a portrait of Yosemite, where it surely does not belong."[17]

Twain rose to fame in the 1870s by distancing himself from standard conventions used to describe the Far West—conventions mastered by Bierstadt and Harte in the 1860s. It is not that Twain was more "realistic" than they were, far from it. Yet the effect of alerting his readers to the conventional status of realistic discourse—of adopting a sardonic drawl and deflationary tactics toward an increasingly tired tradition of Western narrative—made his descriptions *seem* more authentic, reviving interest in the West once again as a genuinely wondrous locale. Before Twain garnered lasting fame through this self-conscious vision of the region's transformative qualities, Bierstadt and Harte would need to perfect the adulatory perspective adopted by so many during the Civil War.[18] It is the formalist story of their rapid rise and fall from such unprecedented popularity that now needs to be told.

Figure 2. Albert Bierstadt, *Sunset in the Yosemite Valley* (1868), oil on canvas, 35¾ × 52 inches. The Haggin Museum, Stockton, California.

Explaining (Un)Popularity

Accounts of Bierstadt's and Harte's careers tend to devolve into either reductive or overdetermined interpretations. Too often, popular enthusiasm for their work is equated with images themselves, as if the complex responses of viewers and readers could be measured in terms of the simple appeal of Western scenes, characters, and icons. The more strictly historical explanations tend to reduce delight in odd stories and extravagant paintings to a diffuse public fascination with the unknown. An alleged national ignorance about details of landscape and life in the Far West had been largely rectified by the 1870s, with the appearance of government reports and the photographs of J. C. Hillers, Timothy O'Sullivan, and William Henry Jackson. According to this explanation, the turn from Bierstadt and Harte is attributable to increasing familiarity with their subject. Western facts, that is, finally caught up with extravagant visions.[19]

More distinctly formalist critics tend to attribute the sudden popularity of Bierstadt and Harte to a momentary lapse in public taste. In both cases, it is easy to itemize flaws in technique that contribute to an overall effect of

63

excess, confusion, or simple incompetence. Bierstadt's obvious problems in maintaining a consistent point of view is reflected in incompatible centers of interest, while the mixed influence of photography on his art, his awkward representation of figures, and his generally poor use of painterly formulas all are adduced to explain why the viewing public finally turned from him.[20] Likewise, Harte's indulgence of the pathetic fallacy, his resort to purple prose, his sentimental plot turns and narratively patronizing tone all wore thin rapidly, and readers simply found his later stories lacking in interest.

Cultural analysts declare that both men fortuitously put their fingers on the pulse of the nation, citing Bierstadt's enthusiasm for the West as consumable empire, a grand spectacle for Americans newly enabled by railroads to visit a region still exotic and dangerous. Such danger is, of course, never presented as either actual or imminent, and in its overaestheticization suggests a theatricalizing of experience, transforming the West into a safe stage set, thereby assuaging the viewer's potential uneasiness about the unknown. Somewhat more economically, a similar end is achieved by Harte through evocations of a mining frontier represented as a region already civilized. Familiar civic virtues emerge from exotic circumstances, and strange wilderness garb only masks a familiar social order. A nation caught in the painful process of Civil War, then Reconstruction, was eager to embrace the pastoral and utopian fantasies purveyed by Bierstadt and Harte. But not for long, as each of these interpretive perspectives helps explain. Before pressing such perspectives further in order to address the altering relationship between artist and public, popular art and reception, we might simply ask what each fantasy seems to be doing. More specifically, beginning with Bierstadt, what aspirations are expressed in his painting and what did he succeed in producing?

A Lawless World

The best place to begin is with the canvas that made Bierstadt famous and continues to be his most celebrated: *The Rocky Mountains, Lander's Peak* (see figure 1). Exhibited in 1864, the over six-by-ten-foot oil painting overwhelmed all but one of six-hundred–odd other entries at New York's Sanitary Fair (a government-sponsored exhibition to raise money for Civil War wounded). And not even Frederick Church's equally grand, equally grandiose *Heart of the Andes* (1859), which hung directly opposite, could vie with the *tableau vivant* arranged by Bierstadt in front of his canvas: nineteen Indians mutely standing among an array of a hundred-odd artifacts. Stripped of this dramatic "frame," the painting still overpowers the viewer through a surreal combination of vast scale and exacting detail—the way it celebrates a panorama of mountain peaks and valley floor even as it details rocks and trees, animals and humans (reminding us of Balzac's observation on Cooper's success "in giving us a sense of both the slightest circumstances and the combined whole"). The painting, in fact, compels attention not despite its contradictory demands but because of them, by deliberately *not* resolving pictorial elements into a balanced whole. The starkness of the lighting itself compounds this effect by cleaving sunlight from shade, while the luminous peaks overhanging the trees are accentuated through their repetition in the mirroring lake below.

Indeed, the contrast of Alpine majesty with the domestic scenes in the valley points to a larger division between the painting's separate modes—of landscape description and genre detail that divide its top from bottom halves. Partially alleviating this disjunction are the mountainous shape of the tepees that appear at the border of these regions. Even so, the perspective is foreshortened so radically that peaks appear to loom on top of the valley rather than in the distance behind. More generally, the painting's topography is broken into discrete *mise-en-scènes,* each with a physical integrity that seems convincing only in terms of itself. Attempts to coordinate these separate moments are stymied, most obviously in the case of the ominous band of shadows broken by light on the waterfall, which are rendered unaccountable by delicately lofting cumulus clouds.

Far from a liability, these contrasts attest to the painting's achievement, with multiple centers of interest competing for attention they never quite command. The group of Bannock Indians arrayed among the shadows of an evening encampment serves in muted tones to lend perspective to the scene, to humanize a landscape that is the site of such disparate efforts. The preparation of the mountain goat to the right; the white dog bounding across the valley floor; the tripod erected to keep food safe, depicted at lower left; the inquisitive prairie dog watching the whole further to the left: among a series of other activities, each of these fosters a separate perspective that threatens but never succeeds in disrupting the overall scene. The artful conjunctions of the painting effect a set of visual tensions, deliberately compelling the eye through a disparate mix of realistic details, narrative enactments, and melodramatic sweep of landscape.

As early as 1864, one of the most prominent critics of the period was provoked by this artful conjunction, and in a review of the Sanitary Fair offered a trenchant observation about Bierstadt's and Church's paintings: "With singular inconsistency of mind," so James Jackson Jarves wrote, "they idealize in composition and materialize in execution, so that, although the details of the scenery are substantially correct, the scene as a whole often is false."[21] Accurate as this seems at first glance (reinforced by a second glance at the landscapes), the question that lingers is what it might mean for "the scene as whole" to be "false"—and false, in particular, when its details are said to be "substantially correct." It is this sense of the false that lies at the heart of so much of the criticism directed at Bierstadt—of someone whose larger vision is allegedly unconvincing although his details are unimpeachable.

This sense of "falseness" depends, of course, on viewers' expectations, which are hard to identify, especially removed from strict painterly contexts. But consider a shrewd insight made only seven years before Jarves wrote about the kind of audience soon to be drawn to Bierstadt's art: "There is another class" of reader, so Herman Melville observed,

> who sit down to a work of amusement tolerantly as they sit at a play, and with much the same expectations and feelings. They look that fancy shall invoke scenes different from those of the same old crowd round the customhouse counter. . . . They look not only for more entertainment, but, at bottom, even for more reality than real life itself can show. Thus, though they want novelty, they want nature, too; but nature unfettered, exhilarated, in effect transformed. . . . It is with fiction as with religion: it should present another world, and yet one to which we feel the tie.[22]

Part of what critics have persistently thought of as the "problem" of Bierstadt derives from this socially transgressive, metaphysically transcendental yearning—the unappeased craving "for more reality than real life itself can show." Like the fiction Melville describes, Bierstadt's paintings represent "another world, and yet one to which we feel the tie."[23]

Bierstadt does this in part through the very profusion of authentic details in his paintings—the surfeit of tiny things that makes the eye pan for so long over so much rendered with such extraordinary care. Like a documentary film, they force the viewer to linger on every crag, tree, and windover in the effort to reveal how much more the painterly perspective (or camera eye) can encompass than any actual eye could register. That comprehensiveness is itself a sign of the surreal in Bierstadt's imagination, of the "more reality than real life itself can show," which prevails throughout his paintings. Yet he succeeded not only by perfecting such stylistic tricks as a crowded visual field but because of a more general enthusiasm in the postbellum period for the "secular sublime." He displayed a series of nonsacred, self-transforming aesthetic tableaux that redefined the West in terms that religion was no longer capable of doing.

This possibility of "nature unfettered, exhilarated, in effect transformed" is exemplified in *A Storm in the Rocky Mountains, Mount Rosalie,* completed in 1866 (figure 3). It is an extravagant painting, complex and

Figure 3. Albert Bierstadt, *A Storm in the Rocky Mountains, Mount Rosalie* (1866), oil on canvas, 83 × 142¼ inches. The Brooklyn Museum.

crowded, with dark, towering mountains on the right sliding us into the foreground pool, then into a series of further pools that lead to the larger lakes in the middle and far distance. Over it all hang Bierstadt's signature clouds that just miss hiding the gleaming peak of the title. Again, half a dozen centers of interest vie for the viewer's attention in a kind of cinematic competition (before the fact) for the plot: from the startled ptarmigans winging into flight, to a dead deer abandoned near the foreground pool, to Indians chasing a frightened horse, to the encampment of tepees near the river that flows through the left middle distance—a river in which mounted Indians ride three horses, on to deer quietly grazing beyond the chasing Indians, and so on, depending on how closely one looks. The point is that there is a surplus of stories, unrelated, unconflicting, randomly disposed, with figures afar as clear as the birds nearby. And while such a foreshortening of perspective is unrealistic, it has the effect of allowing potential narratives to emanate from many points—an effect reinforced by our slight confusion over the source of the picture's light fostered by the rococco shadows, the darkened pines, the distant thunderstorm.

One of the first viewers of the painting, in fact, angrily indicted it for   67 doing just that, flagrantly violating what he assumed was the "truth of nature." "The whole science of geology cries out against him," this critic charged:

> The law of gravitation leagues itself with geological law against the artist. Away up, above the clouds, near the top of the picture, the observer will perceive two pyramidal shapes. By further consultation of the index-sheet, the observer will ascertain that these things are the two "spurs" of Mount Rosalie. Now, let him work out a problem in arithmetic: The hills over which he looks, as we are told, are 3000 feet high; right over the hills tower huge masses of cloud which certainly carry the eye up to 10 or 12,000 feet higher; above these . . . the two "spurs"; what is the height of Mt Rosalie? Answer: approximately, 10,000 miles or so. Impossible.[24]

Clearly, Bierstadt has met his match, even if the attack recalls the Devil's mirror of rationality in Hans Christian Andersen's story, "The Snow Queen": science once again reducing art to a handful of preposterous images.

But in fact, if Melville is right in describing "nature unfettered, exhilarated, in effect transformed," then it was science itself that Bierstadt meant to oppose, as if actually in league against geological law. Repeatedly, even when paintings are named for actual sites, they *seem* fictitious, "wondrous inventions" that depend upon mélanges of topographical features organized far more to theatrical effect than to referential accuracy. He altered actual sites as he wished, working much like a stage designer assembling some fantastic set. And the dramatic excess indulged *in* his paintings extended notoriously to their public display: the Indians posed in front of *The Rocky Mountains, Lander's Peak* clearly testify to this intended effect, leading one viewer to wonder when "the thing was going to move."[25] Likewise, the draped, gas-lit chambers in which *A Storm in the Rocky Mountains* was hung resembled a theatrical backdrop, compelling the viewer to imagine walking into the landscape "through dueling passages of bright sunlight and deep shadow." As Nancy Anderson continues, "even without a darkened room and orchestrated lights, stepping close to the canvas was akin to stepping into the scene."[26]

What is "false," then, is a certain lawless world that evokes too much emotional fervor, too much astonishment at the "sensational," the "lurid," the otherwise extravagant. Paintings like *Valley of the Yosemite* (1864) deliberately exceed faithful geography just as they studiously avoid a reference to recent events or history more generally—this, in the midst of a Civil War, then a Reconstruction era that was transforming all aspects of American life (figure 4). That combination of excess and avoidance, however, is precisely to the point, bleaching out science and history in order more clearly to intensify the experience of his scenes. Their "falseness," in other words, is

Figure 4. Albert Bierstadt, *Valley of the Yosemite* (1864), oil on chipboard, 11⅞ × 19¼). Gift of Mrs. Maxim Karolik for the M. and M. Karolik Collection of American Paintings, 1815–1865. Courtesy, Museum of Fine Arts, Boston.

central to their mass appeal as spectacle, which Michael Rogin suggests requires a certain cultural amnesia:

Spectacle is the cultural form for amnesiac representation, for specular displays are superficial and sensately intensified, short lived and repeatable. Spectacle and amnesia may seem at odds, to be sure . . . but this opposition . . . is what enables spectacle to do its work.

Spectacles, in the Marxist modernist view, shift attention from workers as producers to spectators as consumers of mass culture. Spectacles colonize everyday life, in this view, and thereby turn domestic citizens into imperial subjects. Spectacle goes private by organizing mass consumption and leisure.[27]

Bierstadt's success lay in his ability to make the viewer forget the moment, absorbing the gaze into scenes that allowed one to imagine oneself an "imperial subject."

Bierstadt's most compelling landscapes reflect the crowding together of contextual fragments, the melding of scenic materials whose very excess generates a sense of psychic and moral drama. The viewer is challenged by that excess into a kind of scenic unpacking, an unfolding of the paintings' mixed descriptive moments into relatively consistent temporal successions that resemble nothing so much as the unreeling of film. Scenes that appear simultaneous on canvas are transformed by their unusual perspective and conjunction, as if requiring a narrative explanation that only cinematic sequence can provide. Bierstadt, in short, imagines less a particular place than a singular process—or rather, a place waiting for the process of personal transformation. And thus, his painterly landscapes prefigure the countless, verbally "false" landscapes concocted by the host of Western writers and directors who followed. The Far West memorialized by Bierstadt was a region of psychological transfiguration that itself remains strangely untransformed—a frontier dividing emotional states, a liminal zone invented long before Frederick Jackson Turner described how the American wilderness "masters the colonist." And though countless other painters and illustrators preceded Bierstadt's West, it was his striking vision of landscape that caught the nation's attention. Just as writers were developing materials for the Western, Bierstadt manufactured a "West" in which fictional plots could unfold.

Inventing a West

America's most popular fiction has developed from a concentration on place so intense that landscape descriptions in the Western make it clear how much more than physical place always is. Even in Bierstadt's subdued paintings, landscape reverberates with a special aura. Take *Mount Whitney* (1875), for instance, less idiosyncratic than many Bierstadt completed, where geology does not "cry out" in protest: even so, the landscape signals something other than just itself (figure 5). The viewer's perspective is unusually well-focused, with details contributing to a harmonious whole, verticles and horizontals arranged in a stereotypically classical balance. The paralleled repetition of towering pines, striated cliffs, and thundering waterfalls offsets and contains the lateral sweep of the water's sheening surface, the lengthening shadows beneath the trees. Rising mountains to right and left triangulate the trees, reinscribing the three-sided mass of Mount Whitney in the canvas itself.

Yet the integrating force of these structural effects only highlights a set of thematic oppositions: of waterfalls competing for the viewer's attention at opposite sides of the painting; of soaring falcon and alarmed buck as displacements for the absent human figure in the landscape; of fantastic clouds churning around an indistinct mountain peak; and finally, of light and dark again dramatically dividing up the canvas. The setting itself resonates with a powerful semantic excess (as it does in Cooper), appearing animated once again, made into the character it would become in so many Westerns. And this is what Bierstadt's vast, frequently peopleless landscapes achieve. Indeed, the very absence of human figures in so many of

Figure 5   Albert Bierstadt, *Mount Whitney* (1875), oil on canvas, 68⅞ × 116⅝ inches. Rockwell Museum, Corning, New York.

his canvases has the effect of investing his settings *as* settings with a disproportionate significance. The lack of what Michael Brenson denotes as a "pictorial feeling for people" freed Bierstadt not simply to focus on setting but, paradoxically, to create canvases that seem to beg for characters and plots of the sort that took shape in the paintings of Frederic Remington and Charles Russell, in the stories of Harte and Wister.

This sense that setting is waiting for plot has been described by Ray Allen Billington in terms not of visual arts but of popular literature of the nineteenth century:

Something more than a monotonous landscape was needed by the novelists; they must have oases where adventurers could find haven from desert heat, caves to shelter them from marauding Apaches, towering cliffs where hero and villain could battle with bowie knives, raging rivers where bad men could be swept to their deaths. Hence writers performed feats of geographic legerdemain remarkable to behold as they transformed the Southwest to suit their needs.[28]

Bierstadt helped invent this expectant terrain in a purely visual mode by revealing the ways in which water, rock, trees, clouds, sunlight itself could create a cosmic drama always on the verge of becoming moral and social. It is worth recalling that Cooper's landscapes patrol and suppress action (fostering restraint, counseling stillness and silence), in contrast to Bier-   71 stadt's painterly invitations to excess, his landscapes' plea for a drama yet to begin.

What in particular lends to Bierstadt's paintings such an originary power is their conflicting perspectives, requiring a viewer's moving eye, creating a prototemporal sensation while their surfaces are nervously scanned.[29] In that sense, Bierstadt's landscapes seem to aspire not just to the condition of film but to novelistic description itself, where only one thing can be read at a time and effects are achieved through a gradual accumulation of details. While painting finally should not be confused with either film or fiction (each with its own means of rendering setting and depicting the natural world), Bierstadt does succeed in bringing pictorial representation eerily close to the cinematic and novelistic.[30] More than any other painter before, he revealed the generative narrative possibilities that ensue from seeing the American continent in a particular way. This angle of vision involved a peculiar psychologizing of landscape, confirmed as early as 1869 by Ambrose Bierce when he denounced Bierstadt's influence on countless imitators. "We have had Yosemite in oils," he thundered, "in watercolor, in crayon, in chalk and charcoal until in our very dreams we imagine ourselves falling from the summit of El Capitan or descending in spray from the Bridal Veil cataract."[31] Thus, the unpeopled vistas of Bierstadt's California were magically transformed by viewers themselves—vistas now no longer unpeopled but become the setting for selves in motion, for nefarious plots and hot pursuits, if only "in our dreams."

There is a special aptness to the fact that Bret Harte emerged at this historical moment to fictionalize a Far West being rendered in paint by Bierstadt in a style equally extravagant. And parallels between the two are perhaps nowhere more apparent than in works completed at the same time, *Sunset in the Yosemite Valley* (figure 2) and this description from "The Outcasts of Poker Flat" (1869):

The spot was singularly wild and impressive. A wooded amphitheatre, surrounded on three sides by precipitous cliffs of naked granite, sloped gently toward the crest of another precipice that overlooked the valley. It was, undoubtedly, the most suitable spot for a camp, had camping been advisable. . . . [John Oakhurst] looked at the gloomy walls that rose a thousand feet sheer above the circling pines around him, at the sky ominously clouded, at the valley below, already deepening into shadow; and doing so, suddenly he heard his own name called.[32]

Harte might almost be said to have had Bierstadt's landscape in mind. Yet this owes less to a fortuitous resemblance of topographical features than that both scenes already seem self-conscious fictions, giving an impression of being depictions of other representations more than of actual sites themselves, announcing that re-presentation through "ominous" clouds, "gloomy walls," "precipitous cliffs of naked granite," and a valley spread beneath.[33] The features are tightly fused in two moments that announce themselves as transitional—dramatic, anticipatory, unresolved. The only place the story signally differs from the painting is in Harte's portrayal of what Bierstadt can only suggest: making explicit the solicitation of self from setting through a surprised self-identification, transforming pure description into the literal narrative of one's name emerging "suddenly" from the landscape.

This spectacular scene in Harte anticipates countless moments in the Western where character and landscape are fused together. The problem is that Harte rarely repeated this conjunction, of recognizable Western setting linked almost mystically with representative Western character. His array of newly invented figures would in fact recast possibilities for the genre, but before evaluating those narrative constructions we need to look at "local color" descriptions to understand how the presumed promise of his Far Western landscapes failed (with rare exception) to match what Bierstadt was doing in paint. Harte may first have popularized the Far West as locale for distinctively American endeavors—transferring Cooper's eastern woodland scenes to a California terrain—but he took too much for granted in that mere shift of geography, assuming too readily that redwoods and rock cliffs themselves authenticated a certain transformed consciousness.

Still, part of Harte's appeal lies in his adapting techniques initiated by Cooper, at times so self-consciously that his descriptive prose appears to represent landscape *paintings* rather than actual landscapes themselves. That self-consciousness becomes a significant feature of the Western, as does the collapse of firm distinctions between actor and landscape, narrative and description (discussed in Chapter 2). Even Harte's earliest stories entertain this prospect of fusion, as in this bizarrely ironic passage of murder from "M'Liss: An Idyll of Red Mountain" (1863):

> For some hours after a darkness thick and heavy brooded over the settlement. The somber pines encompassing the village seemed to close threateningly about it as if to reclaim the wilderness that had been wrested from them. A low rustling as of dead leaves, and the damp breath of forest odors filled the lonely street. Emboldened by the darkness other shadows slipped by, leaving strange footprints in the moist ditches for people to point at next day, until the moon, round and full, was lifted above the crest of the opposite hill, and all was magically changed.
>
> The shadows shrank away, leaving the straggling street sleeping in a beauty it never knew by day. All that was unlovely, harsh, and repulsive in its jagged outlines was subdued and softened by that uncertain light. It smoothed the rough furrows and unsightly chasms of the mountain with an ineffable love and tenderness.

73

It fell upon the face of the sleeping M'liss, and left a tear glittering on her black lashes and a smile on her lip, which would have been rare to her at any other time; and fell also on the white upturned face of "Old Smith," with a pistol in his hand and a bullet in his heart, lying dead beside the empty pocket.[34]

The corpse—a father shot by his daughter here at the close of the story's first chapter—is at once the central figure and the most easily dispensable in a strangely articulated memento mori.

What brings the landscape alive in this passage is a conjunction of death and the conditional tense, "as if" her father's passing "magically changed" the very environment in which M'Liss could exist. Or perhaps it is more accurate to say that the brooding, threatening, "emboldened," shrinking, slipping milieu has itself become the transformative agent, now too easily revealed as emotional cause of the human drama in its midst. The narrative inverts the usual placement of active figure and descriptive ground, animating the landscape against the passive forms of M'Liss and her victim, both with "white upturned face[s]." Character is exposed as an animistic force, transcribed from a supposedly intentional subject onto an enchanted western terrain, reminding us of a Romantic tradition exploited by Cooper only two decades earlier.

The reminder, however, also serves to measure the distance between the two authors, marked by Harte's descriptive vagueness and an easy resort to the pathetic fallacy. What Cooper accomplishes through attention to the peculiar animating qualities of landscape and corresponding restraint of character, Harte tries to achieve by simply treating the Sierra foothills as if it *were* a character. This helps explain why silence in Harte is never simply silence alone but a revelation of the landscape's emotional constraint, indeed, of its psychological arrest—as in the "miraculous" birth that inspires the drama of "The Luck of Roaring Camp" (1868): "The pines stopped moaning, the river ceased to rush, and the fire to crackle. It seemed as if Nature had stopped to listen too" (7:4). The same occurs in the converse situation, when the last two exiles of "The Outcasts of Poker Flat" finally succumb to the snowstorm: "The wind lulled as if it feared to waken them. Feathery drifts of snow, shaken from the long pine boughs, flew like white winged birds, and settled about them as they slept. The moon through the rifted clouds looked down upon what had been the camp" (7:35). The hard-won restraint of Cooper's characters in the face of nature they cannot control has been reduced to a simple conceit: the predictable restraint of a landscape on behalf of some vague transcendental affiliation.

When critics disparage Harte's "purple prose," they usually cite the casual ubiquitousness of the pathetic fallacy. Yet simply to identify Harte's anthropomorphizing as a regrettable stylistic tic overlooks the special resonances of the relationship he identifies between individuals and a Western landscape (and, in a sense, the degree to which he imitated and degraded Cooper's more complicated balance). In "The Idyll of Red Gulch" (1869), the evening light "flickered, and faded, and went out" just as Miss Mary's defiant will also expires (7:86). "A momentary shadow" crosses the hero's path in "A Protégée of Jack Hamlin's" (1893) at the very moment a dark thought of murder occurs to him (20:43). "Mrs. Skaggs's Husbands" (1870) opens with "a dissipated-looking hanging-lamp, which was evidently the worse for having been up all night," that lights "a faded reveller of Angel's, who even then sputtered and flickered in *his* socket in an armchair below it" (17:3). Likewise, in countless other passages a symbiosis occurs between the human and the inanimate—a symbiosis Harte would like to suggest forms a distinctively Western process but which he never quite pulls off (as Grey, for instance, would effectively do). Bierstadt's dramatically empty landscapes reveal the West as a transformative region but with no one there to be transformed; Harte's narratives conversely parade dramatic characters through a landscape that usually seems already tamed, essentially no different from themselves.

The immediate appeal of Harte's landscapes, apart from their vaguely Californian flavor, is that he erases the dialectical tension that exists in Cooper's novels between narrative and description, action and landscape— where characters are carefully defined in terms of responsiveness to the natural world. No longer is landscape a test of character, a touchstone for moral agency, distinguishing good from bad, men from women, Indians from whites, and humans from "the lower orders." Erasing invidious moral distinctions, Harte established most of his characters as essentially good, living in a natural world revealed as radically egalitarian. His identification of drunkenness as a kind of sleep, for instance, is less a psychological observation than a metaphysical one, since sleep is also elsewhere identified as a kind of death (and vice versa). Everywhere in Harte's Far West, the customary distinctions of person and place are elided (and not only persons and places, but good and bad persons, good and bad places), with a slightly disorienting effect on the reader unaccustomed to so melodramatic a style.

This readerly disorientation results from a flattening of moral distinctions that, in Cooper at least, were reflected as aspects of landscape—and even so, had already been flattened into terms of sheer restraint. Harte's undistinguished landscapes are more or less equivalent, as are elements within any given view: a moral monochromaticism that paradoxically finds its best analogue in Bierstadt's more vividly melodramatic vistas. Not only does the deft blend of light and shadow in his paintings prevent the viewer from pinpointing sources of light, it compels the eye to flit back and forth indiscriminately across the canvas with an effect akin to Harte's lack of moral discrimination.

In *Sunset in the Yosemite Valley* (1868), light emerges from the center of the canvas, hot enough to be molten lava burning a hole through the cosmos. Yet without the title, the time of day remains indeterminate, anticipating the kind of day-for-night shots produced through filters by cinematographers. The sun, that is, appears too high and bright for actual sunset, or for the valley to be so dark, even with low-lying wisps of clouds. The granite mountains rise out of blinding brightness to tower over the sides of the canvas in Bierstadt's signature mode. The ox-bowing river has been transformed from any realistic association with Thomas Cole in its intensely melodramatic reflection of a western sky. All told, the painting's stunning effect derives from its capacity to at once solicit yet evade our gaze, compelling us thereby into "another world," unreal, excessive, overdone.

An oil completed the same year, *Among the Sierra Nevada Mountains, California* (1868), poses a less dramatic scenario that also succeeds by merging animate and inanimate, and by disorienting the viewer accustomed to mastering a single perspective (figure 6). The minute foreground detail of rocks, vegetation, and rippling water seduces the viewer into stepping toward the canvas (where a fish beneath the water's surface becomes

Figure 6. Albert Bierstadt, *Among the Sierra Nevada Mountains, California* (1868), oil on canvas 72 × 120 inches. National Museum of American Art, Smithsonian Institution, Washington, D.C. Bequest of Helen Huntington Hull, granddaughter of William Brown Dinsmore, who acquired the painting in 1873 for "The Locusts," the family estate in Dutchess County, New York.

finally visible). At the same time, the heroic landscape invites a backward step, to align the canvas's receding spatial perspectives and to follow the gaze of the familiar Bierstadt deer standing in awe of something always beyond—perhaps clouds piled high or mountains scrubbed gleaming white, perhaps the array of waterfalls or something among the shadowed trees across the lake. In any case, our gaze keeps shifting in search of a narrative to explain why the land itself seems struck into contemplative silence.

Harte rarely achieves this odd destabilization, although he adopts analogous strategies to evoke a similarly expectant mood. "Tennessee's Partner" (1869), for instance, presents a scene where human activity is registered obversely as inactivity, through the cloyingly personalized responsiveness of a vigilant natural world:

The way led through Grizzly Canyon,—by this time clothed in funereal drapery and shadows. The redwoods, burying their moccasined feet in the red soil, stood in Indian-file along the track, trailing an uncouth benediction from their bending boughs upon the passing bier. A hare, surprised into helpless inactivity, sat upright and pulsating in the ferns by the roadside as the cortége went by. Squirrels hastened to gain a secure outlook from higher boughs; and the blue jays, spreading their wings, fluttered before them like outriders, until the outskirts of Sandy Bar were reached. (7:67–68)

Like the tints and poses in many of Bierstadt's heroic landscapes, Harte depicts a scene of wonder, of suspense before recognition, of the self at a moment of transformation. Yet here again, nature is too easily animated, too unproblematically personified, with trees simply depicted as human figures (standing "in Indian file") and our putative visual astonishment too indulgently displaced onto an animal world, as hares gaze, squirrels hasten, and jays spread their wings.

Paradoxical Bundles of Character

That Harte's landscapes fail to achieve a desired effect only makes clearer how much the appeal of his stories depends upon singular characters. Bierstadt's melodramatic but empty vistas solicit the reader and demand a plot; Harte fleetingly imagined such landscapes but more successfully created the rogues, heroes, and hangers-on who might inhabit a Bierstadt canvas. And so often do the series of figures he invented recur in the popular Western that they have become leitmotifs extending across time and individual texts. The proverbial whore with heart of gold first appeared in "The Outcast of Poker Flats," then again in "Miggles" (1869) and "The Idyl of Red Gulch" (1869). That latter story, moreover, introduces the prim but passionate eastern schoolmarm who would become (barely) fleshed out as the female lead in Wister's *The Virginian* and in countless later Westerns. In Yuba Bill, profane but colorful, Harte portrayed the first of countless blusteringly drunk, astonishingly competent stage drivers. The twin figures of Jack Hamlin and John Oakhurst epitomize the poised, tight-lipped southern gambler, ready at the drop of a glove to duel over questions of honor. Likewise, the road agents and outlaws, recluses and lonely eccentrics, Chinese immigrants and hard-knuckled miners all emerged from his brief sketches to become stock characters of the genre. Nearly single-handed, as it were, Harte concocted the dramatis personae for the Western.[35]

The clearest instance of Harte's technique for rendering character occurs in his most famous story, in the early passage describing miners gathered at Roaring Camp:

> The assemblage numbered about a hundred men. One or two of these were actual fugitives from justice, some were criminal, and all were reckless. Physically they exhibited no indication of their past lives and character. The greatest scamp had a Raphael face, with a profusion of blond hair; Oakhurst, a gambler, had the melancholy air and intellectual abstraction of a Hamlet; the coolest and most courageous man was scarcely over five feet in height, with a soft voice and an embarrassed, timid manner. The term "roughs" applied to them was a distinction rather than a definition. Perhaps in the minor details of fingers, toes, ears, etc., the camp may have been deficient, but these slight omissions did not detract from their aggregate force. The strongest man had but three fingers on his right hand; the best shot had but one eye. (7:3)

The group is as strangely constituted as the separate personalities themselves, bound together by little other than individual recklessness and contradictory traits. As Wallace Stegner has observed, Harte's "characters seem made because they *were* made, according to a formula learned from Dickens: the trick of bundling together apparently incompatible qualities to produce a striking paradox."[36] Those paradoxes, moreover, suggest one reason for the durability of Harte's characters: they can bear the weight of countless repetitions and reinterpretations. Characters formed as crude "bundles" of contradictory qualities appeal to different readers for different reasons, in the process bearing out the premise that undergirds so much popular fiction: appearing to lend equal support to readings directly contradictory.

Apart from the obvious visual disparities generated by Harte's contradictory construction of character—of one-eyed sharpshooters, gentle giants, adolescent vixens, and aggressively timid heroes—the most striking paradox involves the use of time-honored references to identify frontier personalities (a "Raphael face," the "intellectual abstraction of a Hamlet"), as if to suggest that the highest civilization was already imminent in California's mining communities. Harte hews to this pattern throughout, rarely

78

invoking classical names with even the hint of parodic intent, as in the enumeration of Mrs. Morpher's children in "M'Liss: An Idyll of Red Mountain": Lycurgus, Aristides, Octavia, Cassandra, and Clytemnestra. Bacchus and Malvolio are elsewhere cited comparatively, as is "Una and her lion"—with classical allusions in the West springing up so frequently that Jack Hamlin's "Greek face and Homeric gravity" are somewhat incoherently confirmed by an "Indian stoicism."

This conflation of races and classes—or rather, of classical Greek and "noble savage" behavior—borrows from a venerable literary tradition that celebrates the appearance of patrician breeding amid egalitarian circumstances, usually with disguised aristocrats mastering lower-class skills and only revealing themselves at the plot's conclusion. Whereas that conceit actually confirms class distinctions, however—joining nobles and commoners only to sequester them properly at the end—Harte invokes it on the contrary as a means of erasing fears of social stages. Beneath the wild and woolly veneer of frontier life in the Sierra foothills, he suggests, civilized values are firmly in place, and plots are simply there to reveal beneficent beings for what they already are. Character is not transformed but revealed, with the arduous process of civilizing the West represented as nothing more than regeneration. More precisely, civilization only affirms virtues already in place, already possessed by those supposedly about to be "civilized." The appeal of Harte's stories lay in the paradox of ne'er-do-wells capable of ultimate self-sacrifice, of ruffians and whores responsive to the most conventional moral imperatives. At a time of increasing uncertainty about European and Asian immigration, about working-class assimilation, even westward expansion, there was a strong appeal to the sentiment that American social organization and middle-class values actually might be innate.

The unruly residents of Roaring Camp, for instance, automatically feel a "first spasm of propriety" with the birth of a child:

And so the work of regeneration began in Roaring Camp. Almost imperceptibly a change came over the settlement. The cabin assigned to "Tommy Luck"—or "The Luck," as he was more frequently called—first showed signs of improvement. It was kept scrupulously clean and whitewashed. Then it was boarded, clothed, and papered. (7:12)

In a similar fit of "regeneration," Poker Flat decides to expel four "outcasts"—the town having been moved by "a spasm of virtuous reaction, quite as lawless and ungovernable as any of the acts that had provoked it" (7:19–20). The "outcasts" themselves undergo a similar transformation after their encounter with the maiden, Piney Woods, and "the Innocent," 79

Tom Simson, who help create a self-sacrificing family of "happy laughter" (7:29). In "M'Liss: An Idyll of Red Mountain," the titular waif magically exhibits "some natural instinct" for Victorian dress (174), while in "How Santa Claus Came to Simpson's Bar," Dick Bullen just as inexplicably alters into a kindly, hard-riding St. Nick. Nearly everywhere, Harte's stories exhibit his sentimental dictum that "much good feeling may be found in the breasts of wicked men."[37]

Gambling with Gender

The one flagrant if rare exception to the assumption that virtue is already ensconced in the West occurs in another of Harte's paradoxical constructions of character: women with pious demeanors revealed as cheats or hypocrites. Much as social and class distinctions seem elided in the stories, conventional assumptions about gender are confirmed, with even the women Harte celebrates condemned to marginal roles or behavior: whores may be blessed with golden hearts, but they remain whores nonetheless, while their socially elevated sisters are either deceitful or priggish. If the narrator occasionally speaks in patronizing tones of the "large-hearted and discriminating sex," that sex is also implicitly compared to beasts of burden. Yet serving at the same time to undermine this condescension is the delight the stories take in aggressive female sexual behavior, and particularly in the frequency with which women commit adultery. The central narrative tension in "A Passage in the Life of Mr. John Oakhurst" (1874) concerns the wayward affections of Mrs. Elsie Decker, whose affairs with the close friends, Oakhurst and Dick Hamilton, lead to their deadly duel and her scene of defiant courage. That scenario partially repeats the plots of "Brown of Calaveras" (1870) and "A Protégée of Jack Hamlin's," in both of which Jack Hamlin is subject to the forceful attentions of strong-willed wives.

From a narrowly moral perspective, such portrayals may seem a narrative means of reducing women to the same base status of untrustworthy, lascivious behavior: *cosi fan tutte*. Wives run off in "Tennessee's Partner," "Mrs. Skagg's Husbands," and "How Santa Claus Came to Simpson's Bar" (1872), all blithely forsaking marital obligations. As Yuba Bill bellows, "Where is Jack Adams' wife? Where is MY wife? Where is the she-devil that drove one man mad, that sent another to hell by his own hand, that eternally broke and ruined me? Where!" (17:54). And yet, Harte's resistance to drawing moral distinctions suggests the possibility of another interpretation—one that turns the tables on misogyny expressed more explicitly in these stories. Adultery, from this perspective, offers forceful women an enviable freedom from the dolts they have married, releasing them (if only temporarily) from the consequences of decisions binding them against their wills.

Plots of sexual transgression help to restore to women control of their bodies (as much, at least, as men are allowed), in the process granting them greater autonomy in a world where social and financial constraints have led to incompatible unions in the first place. Moreover, women now resemble men in satisfying sexual drives, even if doing so requires breaking moral precepts and social laws that patriarchy has established to rein them in. Where the Victorian wife had stereotypically been caricatured as a simple, virtuous dependent in marriage—unexciting, unexcitable—Harte portrays western women as fiercely independent, endowed with the pluck to escape matrimonial slavery and gain their emancipation in a West clichéd as the region of individual freedom.

Significantly, the men toward whom these strong-willed women find themselves belatedly drawn are professional gamblers, which raises an important question about Harte's cast of characters. Why does he choose the gambler as the most attractive of his figures, and what are the gestures and assumptions Harte lends him that make him the predecessor of the gunfighter hero? Even more simply, what is the narrative rationale for poker as the gambler's game, other than the historical fact that it was the game of choice in the Far West? One reason certainly is that unlike bridge, say, or gin rummy or canasta, poker depends less on intellectual skill than personal character, less on what one happens to know than on how one comports oneself. Not only is poker a highly individualistic game (involving neither teams nor partners), but the deal of five cards obviates any need for special expertise (such as facility at card counting). The bets one places depend as much on reading others' psychology as on odds defined by the cards, with self-presentation finally more important than the hand one holds. "Success is determined as much by character as by skill," Philip French has claimed, "and personalities are determined by their attitude to the game and the way they play it."[38]

The requirements of the game itself, then, dictate the importance of the gambler's character, which clearly resembles the model of self-restraint that Cooper had popularized in the figure of Natty Bumppo. By now, however, skill has come to matter less than self-possession. The player's inscrutable response to cards that happen to be dealt becomes the sign of how well emotions can be controlled in the face of any chance event: as Oakhurst says of bad luck generally, "If you can hold your cards right along you're all right" (7:31). And while Harte never depicts an actual game of poker, he consistently plots his stories in terms of its vocabulary—of figures who rely in dire circumstances on the strength of inner conviction and not, as Oakhurst reminds his fellow "outcasts," "'throwing up their hand before the game was played out'" (7:23). Both Oakhurst and Hamlin have a laudable gift for remaining "calm," with demeanors repeatedly admired as "inscrutable," "impassive," and "silent," reflective of an ability to let the turn of a card decide their fate.

Harte's gambler forms the predecessor to the gunfighter hero because of his smooth self-composure in confronting the dictates of fate alone. Able to ignore their immediate welfare, both gambler and gunman stand figuratively outside themselves in poses of modest self-regard, contributing in turn to their keen aptitude for reading the motives of others. Cultivating that aptitude, however, involves a familiar pattern of life, of long dull stretches of time punctuated by sudden moments of intense emotional excitement. The narrative logic in this pattern is that self-control can only be revealed in moments when presumably it is least easily maintained. Or as Harte discloses in his portrait of Oakhurst: "he could not help feeling the want of that excitement which, singularly enough, was most conducive to that calm equanimity for which he was notorious" (7:23).

This conception of the gambler as one who breaks from the monotony of quotidian existence is an image of the nonlaborer, the rival to time-card employment, the individualist who turns his back on urban-industrial life. In a postbellum period defined increasingly by assembly-line employment, by mechanical models of labor and scientific studies of work efficiency, Harte's gambler chooses to confront fate alone. And because his background is so often mysterious, his presence suggests that considerations of race, class, and region can be simply transcended. The gambling table is the great social leveler where men meet one another as equals, distinguished only by luck and the ability to keep a poker face.

The importance of gender to Harte is signaled by an unlikely alliance of setting and plot, in the frequency with which he conjoins the masculine site of the saloon with plots that involve women—as if his stories were deliberately engaged in maintaining a kind of ideological tension. Women stereotypically embody an aversion to the saloon, whether to the sale of drink (with its power to loosen inhibitions) or the staging of poker (with its demands for tighter self-repression). In either case, the question of male control remains at issue, and the middle way defined by feminine Victorian codes—of strict bodily restraint aligned nonetheless with expressive ease—is depicted by Harte as a continuing (and mysterious) threat to masculine self-construction. In short, men fail to grasp what it is women want, even while they cannot escape the lure of trying to understand.

One way to conceive the issue is that women become equivalent to the
82   game of poker itself: inscrutable, unpredictable, needing to be patiently

read and dealt with carefully, invariably introducing the prospect that one may lose one's shirt in the encounter. When Jack Hamlin observes an attractive woman, he breaks into a "smile of cynical philosophy. Not that he depreciated the sex, but that he recognized therein a deceitful element, the pursuit of which sometimes drew mankind away from the equally uncertain blandishments of poker" (7:89). Likewise, John Oakhurst's only loss of control occurs when he falls in love with a married woman, thereby reducing him to self-mortification in betraying the loyalty of his closest friend. Yet more important than the adulterous deceits and betrayals that persistently spice Harte's plots is the compulsion with which he reimagines the sexual attraction between gambler and housewife: between the fiercely individualist nonlaborer and the stalwart defender of middle-class propriety. Harte is unable to press his insight very far—that footloose, irresponsible men and solidly domesticated women represent an engaging opposition of powerful cultural imperatives. But he does imagine the basic premise of illicit romance set in a supposedly "Wild West," and thereby inaugurates a striking transaction across both class and gender lines that will be renegotiated through the course of the Western.

The Spectacle of Melodrama

Reading Harte against Bierstadt helps clarify the modal structure they share, compounded of emotional sensationalism, sententious phrasing, narrative exorbitance, phantasmagorical settings, paradoxical medleys of contradictory materials: in short, melodrama. The mode, customarily disparaged by critics, is considered something of a formal embarrassment because it "implicitly insists that the world can be equal to our most feverish expectations about it," as Peter Brooks has claimed; "that reality properly represented will never fail to live up to our phantasmatic demands upon it." Or as he later adds, "Nothing is *understood*, all is *overstated*."[39] While melodrama normally seems a verbal or narrative mode, a glance at *Storm in the Mountains* (ca. 1866) suggests how fully Bierstadt engaged its hyperbolic logic (figure 7).

The painting, highly praised at the time, depicts an apparently western terrain that resembles his other heroic landscapes (though, ironically, it may have been based upon a German scene). The magnitude of the panorama is again offset by a series of carefully arranged details, eliciting from the viewer the familiar impulse to move both backward and forward. Tiny red farm buildings sit amid an overwhelming confluence of natural forces, as swirling clouds highlight the mountain peak above the valley. The eye is drawn from mountain to fields and back, shifted among the bands of white

Figure 7. Albert Bierstadt, *Storm in the Mountains* (ca. 1866), oil on canvas, 38 × 60 inches. Gift of Mrs. Maxim Karolik for the M. and M. Karolik Collection of American Paintings, 1815–1865. Courtesy, Museum of Fine Arts, Boston.

and yellow that parallel each other in painterly tension, producing a dramatically "overstated" effect that defies either plausible meteorology or familiar topography. Once again, the entire confluence of elements seems "false" by insisting so entirely, so inconceivably on providing a view "equal to our most feverish expectations."

Harte indulges as freely in melodramatic excess, not only in feverish plots but in diction and style that epitomize the concept of "purple prose" (which itself derives from a visual analogy with the idea of regal excess, costumed brilliance, ornateness, a gorgeous, lurid show). Constantly straining to dress up clichés, he drains them of any life they still may have. Cherokee Sal is only the first victim of overstated prose in "The Luck of Roaring Camp": "Dissolute, abandoned, and irreclaimable, she was yet suffering a martyrdom hard enough to bear even when veiled by sympathizing womanhood, but now terrible in her loneliness. The primal curse had come to her in that original isolation which must have made the punishment of the first transgression so dreadful" (7:1–2). Tightening (or rather, loosening) descriptive adjectives to a dramatic pitch, the narrator succeeds at last in getting all Nature to succumb:

> Above the swaying and moaning of the pines, the swift rush of the river, and the crackling of the fire rose a sharp, querulous cry—a cry unlike anything heard before in the camp. The pines stopped moaning, the river ceased to rush, and the fire to crackle. It seemed as if Nature had stopped to listen too. (7:4)

Like Bierstadt, Harte welds sharp particulars to grandiose claims, alternating perspectives in a series of stark oppositions. That irrepressible impulse to overstate—to find the most extreme expression of local, subjective knowledge—results in a scene of unsurpassed bathos.

Elsewhere, the process is inverted, with vaguely sentimental expectations punctured by an explosion of immediate action. The title itself of "How Santa Claus Came to Simpson's Bar" belies the possibility of a realistic plot, and the story's opening scenes increase the emotional pressure for a soapy conclusion to a boy's Christmas hopes. Yet Harte then strikes through grandly inflated abstractions with a moment of visual extravagance.

> There was a leap, a scrambling struggle, a bound, a wild retreat of the crowd, a circle of flying hoofs, two springless leaps that jarred the earth, a rapid play and jingle of spurs, a plunge, and then the voice of Dick somewhere in the darkness, "All right"! (17:71)

And so, Santa Claus appears in a melodramatic swirl, representing before our eyes the play of expectant emotion.

One of the advantages of the melodramatic mode for painter and writer alike is that it consists of a kind of sign language by which values can be arrayed outside of social contexts. In Bierstadt, this is achieved through a nervously floating eye that never establishes priority of perspectives; in Harte, through diction and plots that undermine moral distinctions by distributing equivalent virtues everywhere, like colored glass strewn on a floor. "In a universe of such pure signs," Brooks has said, "we are freed of a concern with their reference . . . and enabled to attend to their interrelationship and hierarchy."[40] While the subject here sounds like music, with its interplay of pure structure, the individual "signs" agglomerated in Harte's stories or Bierstadt's canvases are also pure—their semantic purity guaranteed by their very extravagance, their flagrancy, their dramatic élan, their "falseness." Whether a verbal realm of events staged sententiously or a visual sphere of depictions inflated exorbitantly, the effect of melodrama is always the same: to press against realistic conventions in order to evoke that other fancifully charged "world . . . to which we feel the tie."

Figure 8. Albert Bierstadt, *Night at Valley View* (1884), oil on canvas, 34 × 27⅛ inches. The Yosemite Museum, National Park Service.

This melodramatic logic in Bierstadt achieves a special clarity in *Night at Valley View* (1884), with cliffs abruptly interrupting each other, breaking through their respective picture planes, and the moonlit surfaces of water and mountains competing with the campfire's bright reflection (figure 8). Obviously indebted to the pictorial Gothic, the scene focuses on blasted trees, shaggy cliffs, distant mountains enveloped in glowing mist, even a rushing cataract—all in the apparent effort to isolate them as pure painterly "signs." Bierstadt confirms this isolation through a self-conscious representation of space, in sharply perpendicular cliffs and powerful vertical shifts of paint. Normal topographical expectations are once again subverted, as a middle distance evaporates in the overall flattening of perspective. And light itself is obscured, emerging mysteriously from lake, sky, campfire, even from the mountains themselves.

The result of this semiotic self-consciousness—of painterly flourishes and embellishments whose very excessiveness draws attention to their inadequacy as signifiers—is rarely allowed to remain in Bierstadt merely at the level of conventional painterly reference. Rather, the viewer comes to recognize something beyond the everyday as "the ordinary and humble and quotidian [reveals] itself full of excitement, suspense, and peripety, conferred by the play of cosmic moral relations and forces."[41] This effect is achieved in Harte through the use of narrative voice, which consistently transgresses against the convention of muted third-person consciousness. "And here I must pause," the narrator claims, or interrupts himself with "I stay my hand with difficulty," or hurries on with "I shall not stop to inquire." Interjecting anxiety, he adds, "I regret to say," or "grieve to say," or "fear": all part of the obsessively recurrent self-consciousness of narratives willing to draw attention to their fictive power. Indeed, Harte's stories (like Bierstadt's paintings) eagerly embrace the very qualities that so alarm critics, who scorn both artists as victims of excess.

Harte's stories and Bierstadt's landscapes exposed as nothing but melodrama: the observation is a commonplace in the mouths of angry critics, though the term need hardly be denigratory. For their most successful art appeals not as transparent depictions of actual scenes but as self-conscious occasions for the exhibition of people and landscapes—of gamblers, prostitutes, and stagecoach drivers, or clouds, mountains, pools, and trees—regardless in either case of actual, historical referents. Critics predictably treat this as an aesthetic liability, rejecting Harte's claims of realistically portraying the Sierra Nevadas or observing that "Bierstadt's problem with detail lay not in its overabundance but in its visual isolation. Individual forms stand out and interrupt movement between larger units; their edges are too taut and their colors and tones too distinct from surrounding forms."[42]

If we instead treat both Harte's narrative patronizations and Bierstadt's painterly details as "pure signs," their supposed liabilities can emerge as assets. The energy with which each artist mixes "signs," compelling oppositions that seem exaggerated and confused, attests to possibilities in which melodramatic surfaces are asked to bear an excess of meaning. In the case of Bierstadt, we are put in the presence of stark abysses, brilliant ascents, gigantic trees, blazing reflections, impassable (and impossible) terrains that

Figure 9. Albert Bierstadt, *The Domes of the Yosemite* (1867), oil on canvas, 116 × 180 inches. St. Johnsbury Athenaeum, St. Johnsbury, Vermont.

remind us (as they did Bierce) of nothing so much as our dreams—if always dreams with us as the dreamers removed, and therefore with narratives yet to be plotted. In the case of Harte, we are put in the presence of kind-hearted prostitutes, noble gamblers, ruthless housewives, and amiably drunken stagedrivers who supply our dreams with figures larger than life, waiting for plotted landscapes to be drawn. In both artists, the "plot" that is called for can only be supplied by the reader/viewer.

The Domes of the Yosemite (1867) confirms this impression of Bierstadt's supplicating narrative power (figure 9). The second largest of his customarily large paintings, it represents a view of mountains again climbing the side of the frame, with a gigantic waterfall feeding a river that divides the landscape in two. Without detailing again the way in which our eyes are moved around the canvas, we can still note how trees are depicted in various states of health and disease—in the absence of other animate life, standing in for human figures. Characteristically, intense theatrical swirls dominate the canvas, lending a self-conscious effect to features that draw attention to themselves *as* features: the nearby rock fissured in patterns that announce its texture as rock; the waterfall whose mist of billowing white declares its thundering presence; the distant cloud-covered mountains, heavily hugging the landscape; the meandering stream in the midst of the scene, proclaiming its slow pace; and so on. The landscape, like so many others, seems at odds with itself, composed of features that assert their reality at the expense of any overall realistic belief. Never quite cohering, they finally lend a refractory tension to the scene that confirms our sense of dislocation.

Michael Brenson claims that Bierstadt repeatedly fails to focus our interest, to subordinate parts into a visually organized whole: "There is no artistic identification with any part of the landscape," he complains, and he goes on to censure Bierstadt's "interest in spectacle, not song"—as if an ear for the "notes of nature" would have been preferable in a painter.[43] It is Bierstadt's uncanny ability to decenter our point of view, however, that allows him to invest an imagined landscape with the spectacle of melodrama. More than any contemporary other than Harte, he imagined the West as a dramatic (and therefore moral) terrain rather than a geographical one. That ability to reveal the West as a place of pure and mixable signs— signs that seem at times all but self-referential—enables the viewer to delight in a landscape that thereby becomes distinctly American. The West is "American," in other words, not for supposedly natural reasons (whatever that might mean), or even for simply political ones (which is to say, as an accident of history), but because the West, as Bierstadt visualized it, could excite the dreams and plots that would themselves become characteristically American. He gave the viewer an almost physical sense of westward transfiguration. Or as one reviewer advised in 1863, all those seeking "an interval of unalloyed happiness" need only "go up a staircase or two, through a passage or two, round a corner or two, into a darkness, into a light—and—you are no longer in the studio-building on Tremont street, you have crossed rivers, lakes, woods and valleys. You have left behind you railroads, and batteries, and Boston and civilization. You have stridden out to the border-lands. . . . You have struck the trail of the Savage."[44]

It is ironic, therefore, that the person who would become our most American figure should have been the one to offer a detailed examination of *The Domes of the Yosemite* when it first appeared in 1867. Mark Twain could authenticate from a Californian perspective the correctness of each detail, only to conclude that the atmosphere was "altogether too gorgeous": "It is more the atmosphere of Kingdom-Come," he scoffed, "than of California." As Nancy K. Anderson wryly notes at Twain's expense, however, "California as Kingdom-Come, California as the Promised Land, was exactly Bierstadt's subject."[45] Likewise, it was Twain who most effectively spoofed Harte in *Roughing It* (1872), exposing an extravagant emotional drama he found unrealistic.[46] But again, Twain missed the point that realism was hardly Harte's subject, nor the basis of his phenomenal appeal.

Expectations Aroused

Nothing like the extraordinary careers of Bierstadt and Harte had been imagined before the Civil War. Both men achieved fame early and easily; both mastered similar styles; both were entranced with glittering prizes and lives of high social standing. The widespread esteem they enjoyed from the mid–1860s through the early 1870s and the unprecedented sums they received attest to the enthusiasm with which their striking visions of the Far West were welcomed. By the same token, their sudden fall from the limelight into frustrating years of neglect—of diminished fees, mounting critical attacks, and letters of flat rejection—attests to an abrupt transition in popular opinion. Nor was the fault entirely theirs, as even a brief review of their art confirms; they altered little in subject matter or technique, from early years of acclaim to long, productive years of neglect. The epigraph to this chapter suggests the forlorn confusion Bret Harte felt, in confessing to his wife only a decade after his greatest acclaim: "I grind out the old tunes on the old organ and gather up the coppers, but I never know whether my audience behind the window blinds are wishing me to 'move on' or not." In fact, both artists' audiences simply melted away, unwilling in the '70s to countenance what, a bare decade before, could hardly satisfy popular demand.[47]

One explanation for this shift in popular appeal has been adumbrated all along, and lies in the expectations both men aroused—expectations for their own art and for each other's. Each was perceived upon his debut as something of a genius, the best practitioner of his chosen medium and someone promising greater things to come. Bierstadt was touted as the successor to Turner, Harte as a possible rival of Dickens and Cooper. That very overinflation of reputations led in turn (by a predictable process of self-correction) to their collapse.[48] Neither was able to live up to admirers' expectations, and the fact that Harte's stories and Bierstadt's paintings remained essentially the same only proved that neither was the great American artist so many had anticipated. It is almost as if their postbellum audience craved the fantastic images they offered, and—soon embarrassed by that craving—repressed its expression as soon as it could. That should not be too surprising, since repression is usually the fate of melodrama, a mode that arouses critical resistance in its very refusal to be moderate, restrained, commonsensical.

90   Ironically as well, both artists raised expectations that contributed to

dissatisfaction with the other. Bierstadt's landscapes and Harte's characters represent two halves of a more powerful enterprise, which itself was first suggested by their independent success. Bierstadt's canvases, in other words, were waiting for Harte's characters to people them, while Harte's narratives needed a more distinctively western setting. The expectation left unfulfilled in the paintings is the assurance of dramatic renewal, of personal transformation, of transcendence beyond the physical facts of topography itself—a promise that cannot be redeemed until the Western is invented. Exciting a melodramatic imagination he cannot fulfill, Bierstadt succeeds nonetheless more spectacularly than, say, Thomas Moran's realistic oils of Yosemite and in a more identifiably national style than Frederick Edwin Church's equally spectacular monuments to the Andes.

Harte bears out the promise of Bierstadt's paintings through his characters' regeneration, which gives the impression of personal transformation but actually requires no labor of change. Miners, whores, and gamblers are already what they supposedly have yet to become: morally abiding citizens disguised by exotic customs and rough-hewn behavior, upright Americans hidden under wild and wooly costumes. Where Harte fails, however, is to imagine a distinctive western landscape adequate to this process of regeneration. His California frontier is largely indistinguishable from parts of New England, the Midwest, the South, even England's Lake Country: in short, a conventional woodland landscape. His characters caught the public's fancy only long enough to make readers aware that their fantasies needed landscapes more elaborate, more detailed, more distinctly Far Western.

While both artists fell short, it is still worth acknowledging what they achieved in view of their own aspirations—something Michael Brenson ignores in his 1991 review of Bierstadt, which closes on a disdainful note that also applies to Harte: "With just a little imagination and culture, Bierstadt might have constructed images of a real West that could still be believed." The problem, however, is rooted in Brenson's belief in "a real West" and in his corresponding failure to envision what Bierstadt's first viewers saw (or Harte's first readers imagined). Neither artist aspired to photographically faithful images of landscape or elaborate studies of character, nor are those the reasons they warrant our attention. Rather, Bierstadt maps a Far West terrain and Harte molds a set of Western characters that together inspire a host of subsequent melodramas—whether on Wister's Wyoming cattle ranch, Zane Grey's high plateaus of purple sage, John Ford's Monument Valley, or in countless other mythic places.

Some inkling of what happens when Bierstadt's and Harte's separate insufficiencies are erased and their two modes combined can be gained from briefly considering a cinematic Western often taken as the triumph of

Figure 10. Stage crossing Monument Valley in John Ford's *Stagecoach* (1939).

the genre: John Ford's *Stagecoach* (1939).[49] The film opens in Tonto, Arizona, with the preparation of a stagecoach ride to Lordsville, New Mexico, and the introduction of the passengers: the kind-hearted whore, Dallas (Claire Trevor); the southern gambler, Hatfield (John Carradine); the philosophic but alcoholic "Doc" Boone (Thomas Mitchell); the platitude-spouting, larcenous banker, Gatewood (Berton Churchill); the priggish army wife, Lucy Mallory (Louise Platt); and the meek whiskey salesman, Samuel Peacock (Donald Meek). The appearance of the hearty stage driver, Buck (Andy Devine), only confirms the film's full debt to Harte. Through the course of the narrative, a further influence becomes apparent in the revelation of each character's redeemable trait (with the notable exception of the banker in this late-Depression film). The whore reveals her maternal self-sacrifice; the whiskey salesman, his stalwart mettle; the drunken physician, his capacity for sober medical aid; the prim wife, her sympathy; even the disreputable gambler offers his veneration of female honor. Morally commendable traits are achieved through a narrative that suggests nonetheless that those traits were already in place, if unapparent at first.

This process, however, only commences with the stage's departure from Tonto, passing a rail fence that establishes the transition from town to desert. Accompanied nondiegetically by trumpet fanfare and triumphal music, the coach is framed against a commanding view of Monument Valley that stretches out phantasmatically (figure 10). The towering buttes (including the Mittens), immense mesas, jutting rock outcroppings, all posed against a broad expanse of desert: the verticle and horizontal planes of landscape seem to defy each other in a vertiginous setting that Ford would repeat in ten other film Westerns, that would regularly be copied by others, and that has since become the dominant stereotype of the Far West. Into the midst of this optically lawless Bierstadtian landscape comes the cowboy outlaw in the person of Ringo Kid (John Wayne), twirling his Winchester, challenging the stage to stop (even as the camera keeps zooming in on him in close frame). With Ringo's addition to the passengers as a mediating figure, the democratizing process of regeneration can begin. Throughout the film, moreover, that Americanizing process is defined by identification with a landscape that is itself lent a heroically national cast—in part, through sheer immensity; in part, through the Apaches who peer down in domination from the heights. Ford's self-conscious incorporation of Bierstadt and Harte in a single enterprise, moreover, serves as a representative instance of the Western's more general reliance on conventions first invented by those two artists.[50]

The scenes Bierstadt fixed in paint established how convincingly the Far West could be seen as a magical land that was also America writ small—a place where troubling issues of justice, manhood, and social control might be for the moment resolved. Harte then imagined characters and encounters that would focus that narrative resolution and produce, over and over in various guises, an assent of recognition. By mapping out regional plots wherein narrative plot can unfold, Bierstadt figuratively cleared the ground for Harte's distinctive set of characters, enabling their reinvention by hundreds of writers and directors over the following century. No longer would protests on behalf of geology or sociology stand warrant against the challenges both men had mounted, reshaping the landscape as well as history into a logic conducive to Americans' dreams.

4 SEXUAL EQUALITY

Now for your judgment of The Virginian. *You say 1) It's piecemeal. 2) Last chapter superfluous. 3) Heroine is the failure. 4) That it's of doubtful morality, as to the justification of lynching, and as to the hero's conduct.*

Owen Wister to his mother, July 5, 1902[1]

[T]he mahogany landscape, the florid-faced, blue-eyed roughriders, the prim pretty schoolteacher arriving in Roaring Gulch, the rearing horse, the spectacular stampede, the pistol thrust through the shivered windowpane, the stupendous fist fight, the crashing mountain of dusty old-fashioned furniture, the table used as a weapon, the timely somersault, the pinned hand still groping for the dropped bowie knife, the grunt, the sweet crash of fist against chin, the kick in the belly, the flying tackle; and immediately after a plethora of pain that would have hospitalized a Hercules (I should know by now), nothing to show but the rather becoming bruise on the bronzed cheek of the warmed-up hero embracing his gorgeous frontier bride.

Humbert Humbert (1955)[2]

Choose any history of the Western, and Owen Wister's *The Virginian* (1902) will invariably be cited as *the* transitional text—responsible all by itself for making the restrained, soft-spoken, sure-shooting cowboy into a figure worthy of sustained popular interest. Thousands of subsequent novels by authors like Zane Grey, Luke Short, Max Brand, and Louis L'Amour, along with hundreds of cinema and television Westerns, have simply embellished the image of quiet violence introduced in Wister's runaway best-seller. Even the first full-screen version of *The Virginian* (1929) celebrated the hero as a man of few words, typecasting Gary Cooper in his talkie debut as the "yup and nope" actor. The film followed a formula already established in dramatizing the Virginian's antipathy to Trampas, tightening the silent tension between them into the prototypical walk-down and shoot-out.

Like most other versions, however, that film only barely resembles Wister's novel, a disparity that should give us pause in reading *The Virginian* according to the genre it inspired. The supposedly classic functions of the Western are either absent or vaguely implied: the hero is not a mysterious loner nor is the villain a menacing figure, and neither one poses a significant threat to the social order. The novel, in fact, so disappoints expectations based on later films and novels as to seem at last scarcely a Western at all. Far from being a stranger, the trusted Virginian guides the narrator around Sunk Creek Ranch, and like everyone else he has little more than contempt for the pusillanimous Trampas. Ignoring gunplay all but completely, the plot focuses on the Virginian's rescue of a schoolmarm from danger, his transport of Judge Henry's cattle to Chicago, and his safe return of the crew to Wyoming. Not even the pattern of violence familiar in the conventional Western occurs as we have been led to expect: after being wounded in an Indian ambush and nursed back to health, the Virginian helps lynch a pair of rustlers and is finally coerced into a shoot-out.   95

More to the point, this summary itself misrepresents a curiously un-eventful narrative—one in which actions that do occur are marked at best only obliquely. Scenes soon to become the Western's most distinctive stock features are never actually shown: the Indian attack, roundup, and lynching each forms instead a narrative lacuna, alluded to proleptically and after the fact but never represented directly. Conversely, the rescue of the schoolmarm and shoot-out with Trampas are dramatized too directly—the result of an abrupt shift in narrative voice to the bewildered perspective of the principals themselves. Yet strangely enough, this skewed presentation leads to a certain misgiving about events akin to the effect that results when scenes are excluded from the narrative altogether. And herein lies one cause for the novel's initial success and later history, since readers resist uncer-tainty by automatically bridging textual gaps. Possibilities left by the author in a state of unresolved tension are foreclosed as readers make sense of texts (and, in particular, of popular texts) through assumptions that appear natural at the time. If those assumptions are generally less than obvious to later generations (as previous chapters have shown), it is only because the conditions that produced those assumptions have altered so fully.

The circumstance that makes *The Virginian* a very special case is its nearly immediate translation into a popular stage adaptation that avoids ambivalence and simplifies plot, in the process highlighting the very con-ventions for which Wister's novel would be considered prototypical. The novel, in other words, raised expectations for a genre it did not actually quite define, prompting readers to exceed the text in their own reconstruc-tions. Like countless other translations, imitations, and reviews, the first theatrical script testifies to only one of several possible readings of Wister's novel, which itself helps explain how he could so compellingly have cap-tured his contemporaries' imaginations.[3] Hardly what it seems, *The Virgin-ian's* importance thus lies in what readers first assumed it to be, which can only be measured against a reading that registers how such effects were in fact produced.

Before turning to the novel itself, it is worth recalling the general inter-est during the 1890s in the West and the cowboy, epitomized in the enthu-siasm of Wister's close friend, Theodore Roosevelt (discussed in Chapter 1). Joined by another Easterner, Frederic Remington, they had responded to the broad cultural mandate for histories, sketches, sculptures, stories, and novels of western horsemen and landscapes.[4] Buffalo Bill Cody had already mounted a "Wild West" show that would prove over thirty-odd years (1883–1916) to be one of the nation's most popular commercial en-tertainments, commanding an audience only gradually lured away by a new film industry. Already before the end of the century, the proliferation of cheap periodicals with huge circulations had spawned a "magazine revolution," spelling at once the decline of the dime novel (with its exclusively juvenile readership) and the heyday of the historical romance. From this perspective, Wister could hardly have devised a more appealing plot, of spirited schoolmarm courted by handsome cowboy in an exotic high plains locale.[5]

Moreover, Frederick Jackson Turner's announcement in 1893 that the frontier was closed corresponded to a larger public sense that unique western experiences were passing and needed to be chronicled before it was too late.[6] Urban and industrial transformations had begun to feed a nostalgia for supposedly simpler ways of life, contributing to the celebration of an unindustrial West—a celebration that was also, of course, a barely disguised effort at restoring cultural hegemony. In a period of unprecedented economic depression, labor violence, and political dissension (sparked by fears of Populism, unionism, and free silver agitation), it is not hard to see why so many looked for renewed social control or felt so ambivalent about the tenets of democracy.[7]

Wister's inclinations resembled those of many of his contemporaries, but what distinguished his efforts as novelist was an uncanny realization that the popular figure of the cowboy needed to be imagined against a sublime setting, conjoining character and landscape, melding Harte at last with Bierstadt.[8] Wister played to a nostalgic sensibility by dramatizing the prospect of psychic renewal in a context that left one nonetheless looking and feeling the same. Aware that that context needed to be a distinctly national one, he hit on the idea of uniting East, West, and South in the form of a historical romance. Even his loose-jointed plot itself served a notable function by giving this paradoxical vision something of a less self-contradictory air—as if the novel's narrative slackness helped foster an otherwise mythic conjunction. Wister had been slow to realize the possibilities of an entire novel about the Virginian, having essayed a number of stories in the 1890s with his hero as subsidiary and central figure. But again, his very lack of success in integrating stories and points of view only contributed to the novel's appeal (as becomes clearer below). In short, Wister's confused response to the West resulted in a novel engaging his readers' own confusion in a way that encouraged repetition—or rather, encouraged a series of imitations that strained to clarify Wister's materials but ended reinforcing generic tendencies that allowed mutually contradictory possibilities to co-exist.

To reiterate: much of the appeal of *The Virginian* lies in not being quite what readers first took it to be, which becomes apparent when we consider the effect of textual omissions. For more important than what the novel says is what it seemed to say, leaving only the most cautious reader to realize how less transparent and more evocative Wister is than many assumed. Such a perspective, foreign as it may be to the late nineteenth century, requires us to acknowledge how fully the novel celebrates language at the expense of actions it describes. Only then can we see that quick wit is prized over quick draws and that the Virginian's dramatic stature depends less on brief confrontations with Trampas than on elaborate conversations with Molly Stark Wood. Through the course of the novel, he astutely begins to match her verbal sophistication and her early condescension to him as an untutored cowhand gives way before his rhetorical skill. In contrast to the genre's requirement that gentility tame a lawless West, *The Virginian* presents a hero who triumphs not only through bullets but through words that convincingly riddle her eastern ideals. Molly's affirmation of political equality is quietly refuted by his claim for innate difference, which culminates in his eloquent argument for a natural aristocracy. Once the novel is seen in terms of rhetorical as well as physical duels, moreover, a series of otherwise disconnected scenes come to seem narratively justified.

Instead of reducing the novel to a single strong reading (thereby sustaining the formulaic imperative initiated by the novel), this perspective releases *The Virginian* to a series of mutually opposed interpretations—or more generally, as the first Western and yet something like an anti-Western. On the one hand, the fabled world of the cowboy that Wister claimed "will never come again" represented the past as Americans longed to conceive it: a time of supposedly staunch individualism and a place where problems were physically resolved.[9] On the other hand, the setting of the novel drew attention less to the past than the future and to an uncertain future at that. Wyoming's pioneering on behalf of women's suffrage had led to the nickname of "Equality State," and the turn from text to context reveals another source of the novel's appeal. The thesis of sexual inequality that weaves through *The Virginian* seems at odds with the implications of its locale—a contrast of which neither Wister nor his readers could have been unaware. In a region becoming rapidly eastern-like, at a time when the suffrage movement was regaining strength, Wister offered an elegy for the old West that was also a defense of male hegemony. Indeed, more important than any action performed in the novel is the Virginian's careful rationale for women's subordination. The melancholy vision of his retirement from the saddle and from the life of action it denotes is offset at the end by a celebration of woman's narrow "place" in the home. The novel's extraordinary appeal lay in its ability to do two things at once—to recall and yet anticipate history in ways that calmed middle-class uncertainties.

98

Wordsmiths and Gunslingers

Common sense resists the claim that events in the first Western are mere occasions for words, perhaps especially since dialogue has rarely seemed memorable in the genre. Whether verbal play is unusual or has simply been repressed, the curiously ambivalent status of language in *The Virginian* has certainly contributed to its prototypical status. Indeed, the remarkable power of the novel's dialogue to direct attention away from itself—to be at once source of high entertainment and yet apparently beside the point—is perhaps the most extraordinary aspect of Wister's narrative accomplishment, helping to ensure his cowboy hero is a compellingly enigmatic figure. And this forms a paradox well worth investigating: that a novel enjoyable for rhetorical legerdemain should have been read for scenes of action, and then inspired a genre notable for its exhibition of tight-lipped violence (given quintessential expression by Humbert Humbert in this chapter's epigraph). Before attempting an explanation, however, we need to establish the prominence of scenes devoted less to pistol spins than verbal flourishes.

In a West repeatedly described as "silent," the eastern narrator first finds his interest piqued by the teasing of Uncle Hughey. "Who is the lucky lady this trip?" the Virginian begins, and then, anticipating the novel's major theme, he unfolds Hughey's checkered history of courtship and missed marriage (4). Following this opening sequence, western talk is again the issue when the Virginian imaginatively convinces an eastern drummer to relinquish his bed for the night. And soon afterward, the narrator overhears his own tenderfootedness deftly ridiculed, which contributes to his rueful admiration for the man who seems otherwise "grave of bearing and of speech" (96). Inappropriate as the well-hewn standard of historical accuracy may seem in this particular instance, Wister seriously championed the Virginian's rhetorical mastery as a characteristic western skill. Elsewhere, he even claimed that the cowboy was a master of the "craft of wordmaking."[10]

The finest illustration of the Virginian's discursive skill, in the best tradition of tall-tale humor, is his invention of a California frog farm. He had earlier been puzzled by a menu listing "Frogs' Legs à la Delmonico," and had asked the narrator: "Are they true anywheres?" (150). Assured that they are, he later uses the information to regain the confidence of his crew. The restless men have been persuaded by Trampas to desert and seek their fortunes at the next rail juncture, but while their car is stalled near a bog, the Virginian conceives the idea of cooking frogs' legs. As he serves his hungry men, he concocts an incredible story of capitalist expansion, corporate battles, and a wildly fluctuating market for frogs:

" . . . there was millions. You'd have said all the frawgs in the world had taken charge at Tulare. And the money rolled in! Gentlemen, hush! 'twas a gold mine for the owners. Forty per cent they netted some years. And they paid generous wages. For they could sell to all them French restaurants in San Francisco, yu' see. . . . "

"Forty per cent, was it?" said Trampas.

"Oh, I must call my wife!" said the traveller behind me. "This is what I came West for." And he hurried away.

"Not forty per cent the bad years," replied the Virginian. "The frawgs had enemies, same as cattle. I remember when a pelican got in the spring pasture, and the herd broke through the fence—" (194–95)

A mangy Tower-of-Babel audience of cowboys, Indians, and wide-eyed tourists remains as alert to the Virginian's verbal craftsmanship as to the preposterousness of a narrative with "frawg trains tearing across Arizona— big glass tanks with wire over 'em—through to New York, and the frawgs starin' out" (196). In vivid contrast, his flat-footed crew are easily seduced by the Virginian's "diabolical art" (194) and credulously begin to envision themselves part of a forty-niner frog-rush. Their hopes fluctuate with the narrative economy until at last a collapse in the market signals their own deflated expectations: "Frawgs are dead, Trampas, and so are you" (200).

The Virginian's conquest illustrates an unusual form of social control, narratively inducing belief in his account despite its thorough implausibility—or, as the narrator comments on another such triumph: "It had been so well conducted from the imperceptible beginning. Fact and falsehood blended with such perfect art" (180). That skill makes him adept at exposing others' self-aggrandizing rhetoric, and his next major triumph occurs on returning the crew to Sunk Creek Ranch, when he learns of the hellfire-and-brimstone sermons with which the Reverend Mr. McBride plans to reform the West. On the minister's first (and only) night, he excoriates his cowboy congregation before retiring to the new foreman's cabin for what turns out to be an interrupted night's sleep. The freshly "converted" Virginian, now wary of possibilities for backsliding, pleads repeatedly through the night for pastoral support, and is wholly convincing by "using some of the missionary's own language" (244). Not until morning does the exhausted preacher waken to his victimization, when he angrily rides off into the sunrise toward a more accommodating East.

The point is that words shape consequences in the novel as powerfully as action does, so fully that even physical encounters are absorbed into contexts that seem self-consciously discursive. Dramatically, the culminating gunfight is brought on by Trampas's drunken "talk"—careless slurs excessive enough for the hero's friends to intercede. Just as the Virginian's "tall" talk bespeaks a pattern of habitual self-control, so Trampas's "loose" words expose him as merely a casualty of language. And since the Virginian declines to "say the word" to his friends, Trampas is left in his final hours to contemplate the irrevocability of verbal excess: "now his own rash proclamation had trapped him. His words were like doors shutting him in to perform his threat to the letter. . . . [H]e dared not leave town in the world's sight after all the world had heard him" (478). By contrast, the Virginian's self-imposed silence paradoxically confirms his rhetorical powers. Never victimized by words, his own or others, he knows what Trampas does not: that silence also speaks, and that like language it must be carefully exercised.

This cautious stance toward the possibilities of language is at once an extension and transformation of Cooper's thematization of restraint and is similarly meant to represent a moral capacity. Unlike Natty Bumppo, however, who rarely submits to silence in the face of opportunities to hear himself talk, the Virginian's self-restraint is manifested in a severely laconic style—the emotional sangfroid that registers his ability to maintain himself apart from others, their judgments and desires, repeated in countless subsequent taciturn cowboy heroes. It is not that the Virginian cannot be eloquent when so inclined but rather that he refuses to do so when not, resisting easy familiarity with first the narrator, then the drummers—"the being too soon with everybody, the celluloid good fellowship that passes for ivory" (22). Others must watch what they say before him, evidenced most dramatically in his abrupt challenge to Trampas to retract slurs made against Molly Stark Wood.

A number of elements contribute to the strange oscillation in our view of the Virginian as at once decidedly verbal and yet somehow inarticulate, including most pointedly the overinvested narrative perspective. The narrator's delight in the Virginian's verbal shenanigans and resentment at his restrained silence are both the result of a distantly third-person perspective, of standing self-consciously apart from the figure he is also so clearly drawn to know.[11] Compounding this paradoxical effect is the structural incoherence of the novel, which alternates between first- and third-person perspectives as a result of Wister's incomplete consolidation of eight earlier stories.[12] Midway through the novel, an omniscient view of the Virginian is established that gives a more intimate insight into his sensibility and makes it clear how much his silence is a matter of intentional self-restraint.[13] Moreover, it is worth pointing out that language and action always exist in a fragile balance, requiring that words be backed by actions just as much as silence is. If it is not enough for the Virginian simply to be faster or stronger or more brutal than Trampas, it also does not suffice for him simply to be better at tall tales and restrained silence. His notoriously "cool art of self-preservation" (30) depends upon knowing the difference between the two contingent realms, when words need to be backed by actions and when not.[14]

This central equilibrium between action and silence, words and restraint, is defined most suggestively in the final shoot-out between Trampas and the Virginian, which occurs in a stunning paragraph of only three brief sentences:

"It is quite awhile after sunset," he heard himself say.

A wind seemed to blow his sleeve off his arm, *and* he replied to it, *and* saw Trampas pitch forward. He saw Trampas raise his arm from the ground *and* fall again, *and* lie there this time, still. A little smoke was rising from the pistol on the ground, *and* he looked at his own, *and* saw the smoke flowing upward out of it. "I expect that's all," he said aloud. (480; emphases added)

The showdown that has since become formulaic—indeed, by some accounts, the sina qua non of the Western—appears from a bizarrely self-distancing perspective that seems all but to defy formulaic reconstruction. The sentences are curiously detached from one another, the gunshots themselves are unseen and unheard, and the narrator's ordering point of view has been relinquished for the sake of emotional immediacy.

More important, it is as if the very possibility of objective description were being denied; the accumulated conjunctions and repetitive syntax draw attention to the process of the prose itself, a prose no longer transparent or comfortably outside the experience it purports to describe. In a sense, action *becomes* language through a transition so radical that the fatal gunshot is identified in conversational terms: "he replied." And it seems clear that the Virginian's triumph in the duel owes as much to his precision with words as with bullets. Despite being reduced to a narrowly focused inner perspective, uncertain as he is of the dangers around him, he retains a grip on language in the face of his greatest physical crisis. The very brevity of the scene's description confirms the difficulty of this process, as linguistic command is equated with the challenge of maintaining physical self-control.

Appropriate as this parallel is for *The Virginian,* a certain irony attaches to the fact that the scene's brevity has, more than anything else, dictated its prototypical status. The very concision and indirectness with which Wister represents the shoot-out has encouraged countless re-presentations of what has become the classic Western scene. Paradoxically, the suggestiveness of the passage directs attention not toward but away from its language, permitting a tantalizingly brief, straightforward sequence to be reproduced in innumerable permutations that play out the problematics of violence. Notably as well, this scene is one of the very few moments of actual violence in the novel, though Wister's successors quickly realized the appeal of such scenes and turned to them more regularly and with an intensive imaginative vitality. The prospect of a moral confrontation that could be adjudicated simply through gunslinging skills—played out in front of our eyes as the triumph of restraint over excess, honor over unscrupulousness, self-possession over preening self-regard—was all encapsulated in the three brief sentences of Wister's novel. Nothing else about the Virginian (including his handsome appeal, his commanding stature, even his studied silence) would seem so inexorably central to his construction, despite the fact that he is never described as having such refined martial skills and that their depiction is so fleeting.

Home in the Ranges of Western Talk

Invariably, the setting for such confrontations is a landscape endowed with the power to transform casual violence into something at once more venerable and evocative (or as the tourist says of the Virginian's deadly tall tale, "this is what I came West for"). Wister's own enthusiasm for western landscape approached a nearly Wagnerian intensity, leading him repeatedly to feel that words were inadequate to the feelings aroused (as he wrote of his first trip to Wyoming, "I can't possibly say how extraordinary and beautiful the valleys we've been going through are").[15] Yet as no one since Bierstadt, he converted that initial response into graphically plausible if incredible forms. Consider this 1896 letter from the Wind River Mountains of Wyoming, "extraordinary country that no one has described":

Red mounds . . . are turned to rich rose by the green of the cottonwood trees which green is by the rose reciprocally glistened to transparent emerald; and all between the folds of level & slant go from green through buff and saffron to brown and grey, the whole thing graded and mingled so subtly & softly as to seem made of some rare wonderful plush. Crude is the very last word for it. When you take sage-brush, which of itself is between lavender and the olive leaf, and find it looks white, green, blue, purple, & violet, according to the angle of slant and the value of background against which it happens to be thrown, you are moving among intricacies for which painting would have to devise some wholly new conventions and methods to be able to state them all. And while written down, these mixtures sound so violent, their blend in the landscape is inexpressibly delicate and evasive.[16]

The transformative magic of natural setting is compounded by shimmering oscillations of light and leaf, which suggest an enchanted realm well beyond realistic expectations. Moreover, Wister captures here a sense of violence in landscape coloration itself, borrowing from Cooper that conflation of animate and inanimate, human and inorganic, that lends its allure to the Leatherstocking series, and in the process anticipating the vividly tinted, highly sexualized landscapes of Zane Grey.

Like Grey, Wister conceived of the West as a region suffused with rejuvenative powers, where dry air and pristine scenes would revive one's spirits   103 and restore one's health. Landscape is not only a model but a medicine. S. Weir Mitchell had prescribed the West in 1885 for a nervously exhausted Wister, whose first trip led within weeks to a miraculous sense of renewed self-possession, physical and mental. Unlike Remington and Roosevelt, who slighted the wonders of western terrain in favor of picturesque local types and regional activities, Wister placed his auchtocthonous figures squarely in the West from which they seemed to spring.[17] In his first novel, *Lin McLean* (1897), and in *The Virginian* even more powerfully, he presents the high mountain terrain of the Wind and Snake Rivers countries as something attentively to be observed, whether the narrator and the Virginian are climbing over the Tetons, aware of Trampas and Shorty ahead, or simply watching a train slowly disappear across the unending plains.[18]

And yet, for all his skill at detailing the characteristic wonders of terrain, the special ambience that Wister associated with the West had less to do with topography than with literal atmosphere. From the beginning, even amid the unutterable squalor of Medicine Bow, the narrator observes a certain "immaculate and wonderful" atmosphere: "serene above their foulness swam a pure and quiet light, such as the East never sees" (12). And thereafter, such scenes punctuate an often dreamlike account, whether simply waiting for lost luggage ("like swimming slowly at random in an ocean that was smooth" [47], or riding from town across "the clean plains," where "the great, still air bathed us, pure as water and strong as wine" [49]). This motif is best exemplified in Scipio LeMoyne's response on the railroad trip to crossing the border from Midwest to West: "'That's Montana!' said Scipio snuffing. 'I am glad to have it inside my lungs again'" (170).

The purity of western air is confirmed by an atmosphere so unadulterated that its stillness itself becomes worthy of note, with Wister's narrator repeatedly expressing amazement at the landscape's noiseless calm. The silence captured so well by Bierstadt in grandiose panoramas is given narrative form in descriptions of "this voiceless land, this desert, this vacuum" (58)— where sound is dislocated from sight by vistas so immense that things are seen long before they are heard, as the narrator marvels in watching a distant train (50). So fully does he "luxuriat[e] in the Rocky Mountain silence," in fact, that the landscape itself becomes gradually associated with the sheer absence of sound (53; also 374). Owls may hoot, spurs clang, voices chatter to be overheard, but all are simply milder versions of the mechanical noisemaker that awakens Medicine Bow with a "staggering, blinding bellow" (40): they only accent the preternatural silence that otherwise pervades the West. And through the course of the novel, the narrator's admiration grows until Medicine Bow finally appears in a suggestive hypostatization: "Over all this map hung silence like a harmony, tremendous yet serene" (445).

The characteristic silence of the West has the contrary effect of encouraging a verbal commotion, vividly different from a sedate East where "they were talking about the same old things." That is why the Virginian left home at fourteen: "I put on my hat one mawnin' and told 'em maybe when I was fifty I'd look in on 'em again to see if they'd got any new subjects. But they'll never" (262). Eastern conversation is as exhausted as its soil and through mindless repetition likewise drained of significance. By contrast, the linguistically unsettled West encourages a contest of verbal wits, a regeneration fostered in part by a landscape still unacquainted with noise. The absence of the chatter and hum that resonate through an urban East only seems to extend the dynamic range of western vocabulary. And as if prompted by the quiet landscape itself, the narrator begins to take as much pleasure in the Virginian's reticence as in his teasing. Eastern drummers may rattle away, devaluing linguistic currency by a kind of Gresham's law, but the Virginian's alternating quiet spells enhance his verbal grace. Indeed, his successful tale of frogs seems to require the "nine days' silence" that follows (203). Like a West where silence is punctuated by rumor, quiet space by explosive outbursts, he swings between moods of rhetorical play and uninterrupted quiet—times when "the talking part of him deeply and unbrokenly slept" (203).

The novel, in fact, can be read as a progression in the narrator's willingness to follow suit, as he learns sometimes awkwardly the lesson that it is often better to hold one's tongue. When he first overhears the Virginian ridicule his affable immoderation he pouts, and "this unusual silence of mine seemed to elicit unusual speech from him" (71). Unlike Cooper, whose landscapes define *all* talk as excessive, Wister develops a more resonant vision of landscape where only certain speech is marked as *de trop*. Among a sullen crew, for instance, the narrator attempts to say "a number of things designed to be agreeable, but they met my small talk with the smallest talk you can have" (171). Thereafter, Scipio must explain to him how fully he has aided Trampas's cause through his articulate amiability: "'I do believe you'd oughtn't to be let travel alone the way you do'" (206). Such experiences transform the narrator, until finally he loses his greenhorn status on an occasion significantly marked in the narrative: "after twelve hours of pushing on and on through silence, still to have silence, still to eat and go to sleep in it, perfectly fitted the mood of both my flesh and spirit. . . . I wanted no speech with any one" (374). Without teaching him anything about pistols, the Virginian has given the narrator a western standing by awakening him to the value of silence.

Unsurprisingly, the tranquility of a landscape that induces respect for the unsaid compels an awareness of how unnatural are the words evoked

on its behalf. The emphasis on silence alerts us by contrast to the importance of linguistic conventions, whose arbitrariness is exposed more directly in the narrative possibilities for naming and reference. The Virginian
remains unnamed throughout, which of course lends him a mythic dimen-
sion.[19] But in addition, his anonymity (like that of the narrator) draws attention to social pressures for naming, as he acknowledges at one point in
recalling a friend's understandable mistake: "'Steve used to call me Jeff,' he
said, 'because I was Southern, I reckon. Nobody else ever did'" (421).
While nicknames typify the self better than given names, the Virginian's
reference to a mistaken nickname in a narrative that omits his proper name
only draws attention to how any name helps establish social identity.

The point is memorably dramatized in the scene at the Swinton's ranch
barbecue when Lin McLean helps the Virginian switch infants in what is
described as a "crime against society" (124). Their practical joke inadvertently jeopardizes powerful twin assumptions—that identity is a matter of
natural differences and that names are therefore somehow intrinsic—the
strength of which can be measured by the impassioned consternation of
the ranchers and their wives once they discover the trick. Yet the stripping
of babies to naked equivalence forms less a threat to social stability than a
comic exposure of the arbitrary logic by which it is sustained. For the only
marker that clearly distinguishes the infants (other than biological sex, at
least) are the parents' nervous claims that Alfred or Charlie or another is
their own. Implicit here is a recognition that infants may well be inter-
changable, and the scene whimsically intimates that clothes and names,
not natural capacities, enable social definition.[20]

Parents may not appreciate how fully personhood is a social construct,
but the novel extends this thematic issue in Scipio LeMoyne's appearance as
Colonel Cyrus Jones, the flamboyant restaurateur. The restaurant's original
owner had actually died long before, but LeMoyne explains that "his palace
was doin' big business, and he had been a kind of attraction, and so they
always keep . . . some poor fello', fixed up like the Colonel used to
be, inside" (167). When he later introduces himself in his own person,
LeMoyne likewise explains his name in terms of strict family conventions:
"the eldest of us always gets called Scipio" (158). Instead of referring to
natural entities, proper names identify points of social accord, which is
precisely why the Virginian acquires a certain mythic stature: his anonymity has the effect of suspending conventions and thus of broadening consensus.

Yet conventions can no more be suspended at will than meaning can
be identified solely through names, especially given the importance of con-

text in defining any discourse. The Virginian understands this relation, as expressed in his most famous utterance: "When you call me that, *smile!*" (29). Earlier, Steve's affectionate reference to his friend as a kindly "son-of-a– ————" had startled the eastern narrator, who knew the phrase only as "a term of heaviest insult" (15). Again, the untamed West offers greater opportunities for verbal play, as is clear when the Virginian's smile turns to anger at Trampas's use of the very same words. The term conveys either affection or insult depending on how and with whom it is used—available to either possibility as a particular context happens to dictate. Not even the narrator realizes, however, that context encodes the term triply, not doubly; synonymous with either affection or insult, it also forms a breach of written decorum (this, even though he notes how a joyous Steve applied "to the Virginian one unprintable name after another" [38]). Indeed, the literal gap in the text created by the editor's customary dash confirms more than any scene the way social expectation dictates verbal usage. Proscribed by publishers, the oath foregrounds the sheer conventionality of language through a triple layer of possibilities in which only the referent remains the same. And if profanity best reveals limits to convention (because scandalous by definition), there is a certain aptness in the superior ability of the verbally adept to transgress. When a frustrated Virginian exclaims "Oh, damnation," the narrator observes of Molly: "Had she heard him swear, she would not have minded. . . . He possessed that quality in his profanity of not offending by it. It is quite wonderful how much worse the same word will sound in one man's lips than in another's" (365).

A source of delight as much as a tool, western talk emerges from a region whose vast expanses of silence encourage the colorfully extrareferential possibilities of discourse. The Virginian, for instance, imagines a Delmonico angered by the soaring price of frogs: "Lorenzo raised his language to a high temperature, they say" (200). And his own tall tale confirms the impression that the West can raise words to a heated pitch. Scipio LeMoyne's rhetorical deftness is second only to the Virginian's, and it is significant that the narrator is first attracted by his disembodied voice in the streets of Omaha: "the language of Colonel Cyrus Jones came out to me. . . . It was spring and summer since I had heard anything like the colonel . . . and his vocabulary met me like the breeze of the plains. So I went in to be fanned by it" (148–49). Later, in a verbal tour de force, Scipio erupts at a barely missed train:

"Think you've got me left, do yu'? Just because yu' ride through this country on a rail, do yu' claim yu' can find your way around? I could take yu' out ten yards in the brush and lose yu' in ten seconds, you spangle-roofed hobo! Leave *me* behind? you recent blanket-mortgage yearlin'! You plush-lined, nickel-plated, whistlin' wash room, d' yu' figure I can't go east just as soon as west? Or I'll stay right here if it suits me, yu' dude-inhabited hot-box! Why, yu' coon-bossed face-towel—" (160)

Against the silence of baffled intention, the tall talk of Wister's West re-shapes the landscape and declares in the process that language forms a vehicle of play, not regret. Words ride experience, not the other way around.

Verbal Quality and Sexual Equality

This reading of *The Virginian* suggests more than enough differences with the typical horse opera. In it, the laconic hero keeps faith with a code that demands quick draws and vigilante justice before the influence of love in-duces him to accept a feminized civilization. Not only does the Virginian's rhetorical aplomb contrast with this image of thin-lipped silence but his verbal triumphs over Molly are developed more elaborately than his show-downs with Trampas. The narrative logic becomes clear when one realizes that however less skilled Trampas is as a wordsmith, he shares the Virgin-ian's conviction in the shaping power of words. It is Molly who disputes this view right up to the moment she finally capitulates, posing a radical alternative to the Virginian's legitimation of male hegemony. He stalwartly resists Molly's egalitarian logic, holding to a premise of social inequality, confirming in the process that rhetorical control looms larger in the novel than physical conflict.

The major division between the Virginian and Molly is presented in chapter 12 as the novel's single sustained debate. Entitled "Quality and Equality," it begins when she responds to his avowal of love with the clichéd lover's rejection:

> "I am not the sort of wife you want."
> "All men are born equal," he now remarked slowly.
> "Yes," she quickly answered, with a combative flash. "Well?"
> "Maybe that don't include women?" he suggested.
> "I think it does."
> "Do yu' tell the kids so?"
> "Of course I teach them what I believe!" (143)

This seems an odd exchange to have been prompted by Molly's rebuff, mov-ing as it does so abruptly from a lover's rejection to discussion of political equality. Yet the Virginian realizes she has rejected him out of simple social snobbery (which her democratic principles prevent her from admitting), and that to win her heart he must get her first to clarify those principles. Paradoxically, as he points out, a system of true political equality would have the opposite of a leveling effect by giving free rein to any natural *ine*-qualities of mind and of talent: "No, seh! call your failure luck, or call it laziness, wander around the words, prospect all yu' mind to, and yu'll come out the same old trail of inequality" (144). Of course, having convinced her of this premise, he can demonstrate his own inherent superiority and prove that, despite his immediate station, he is worthy of her affection.

The narrator has long shared this creed and succinctly states it in social Darwinist terms: "true democracy and true aristocracy are one and the same" (147). Democracy, that is, erases artificial class distinctions that allow the inadequate to be valued above their merit, thereby ensuring that "natural" aristocrats will achieve a deserved social cachet. This constitutes little more than a thinly veiled defense of ideals held by Roosevelt, Remington, and other privileged eastern readers concerning the "true nobility" of the western cowboy, by which they meant exclusively Anglo-Saxon sons of the soil (33). And like them, Wister's political assumptions were radically confused, the result of a desire to preserve democratic principles while promoting traditional civic virtues in a period of high immigration, working-class unrest, and economic distress. Self-rule meant knowing one's place and having good manners (for Wister, much the same thing), and the hatefulness of the new egalitarianism could be measured in the sordidness of communities newly developing in the West (viewed in miniature in Medicine Bow). Or as the narrator pronounces, "All America is divided into two classes,—the quality and the equality" (147).[21]

The implications of "quality" are clarified at the novel's beginning, when the Virginian is identified as a natural "gentleman" (12) whose honorable bearing is apparent in his gestures on behalf of the engineer's sick wife: halting the loud party in Medicine Bow, making a gift of flowers the next morning. Likewise, when Trampas resignedly greets him in his role as newly appointed foreman, he reveals his true character by refusing to use his power to fire the rogue. Much as Wister yearned to associate such "aristocratic" virtues with democratic processes, however, he could not quite accept his own premise that Trampas and the Virginian were politically equal, nor quell an abiding fear that fewer Virginians than Trampases resided in the republic. More transparently than anywhere else in the novel, therefore, the Virginian's debate with Molly (chapters 12–16) reflects his own anxieties. And the power that Wister invests in language can be measured by his willingness to identify a political distinction in terms of verbal dexterity—or, as the narrator sums up the tall tale triumph of "frawgs" over Trampas, "the Virginian had been equal to the occasion: that is the only kind of equality which I recognize" (202). Ben Merchant Vorpahl has wryly observed that this is "the most beautiful—the most American . . . of all" moments, because the crew can "make the right choice between gentlemen like [Wister's] hero and shrewd schemers like Trampas."[22]

Merely pointing to Wister's confusion, however, does little to clarify the remarkable extent to which he stakes his vision of society on the capacity for verbal discrimination and linguistic play. More generally, by 1902 Wister had come to believe that society depended on inherent differences much like the structural oppositions that Ferdinand de Saussure was even then asserting as foundational to language itself. There is therefore a certain ironic appropriateness to the fact that the Virginian champions social inequality in ways that correspond to his rhetorical competence. The reason the novel nonetheless appears to offer conflicting claims for the self is that the logics of language and behavior are finally not equivalent. Trusting to the rightness of innate differences, the Virginian (speaking for Wister) assumes that society will benefit by leaving individuals unconstrained, even as he seems to recognize the self as fully a product of cultural forces. Or, to state the issue conversely: the individual can never exist outside society though personal capacities prior to any socializing process dictate chances for success.

This striking paradox is clarified in Molly's plea to the Virginian before his shoot-out with Trampas:

"But if you know that you are brave, and if I know that you are brave, oh, my dear, my dear! what difference does the world make? How much higher courage to go your own course—"

"I am goin' my own course. . . . If any man happened to say I was a thief and I heard about it, would I let him go on spreadin' such a thing of me? Don't I owe my own honesty something better than that? Would I sit down in a corner rubbin' my honesty and whisperin' to it, 'There! there! I know you ain't a thief'? No, seh; not a little bit! What men say about my nature is not just merely an outside thing. For the fact that I let 'em keep on sayin' it is a proof that I don't value my nature enough to shield it from their slander and give them their punishment. And that's being a poor sort of jay." (474–75)

Molly invokes a transcendent morality out of a characteristically American trust in the dictates of conscience. And one might have expected the Virginian to agree, given pride in his own exceptional nature. At the same time, however, he appreciates the social context of moral definition and recognizes that self-worth must always be sanctioned by mutual regard. In this sense, the Virginian resembles Molly less than he does Trampas, who cannot escape from a shoot-out he knows he will lose: "he dared not leave town in the world's sight after all the world had heard him" (478).

Long before Wister, Cooper had loosened the hold of belief in a transcendent morality by defining his hero's moral code in terms of still landscapes. The mere performance of restraint replaced an ethics based on right and wrong, augmenting a changed understanding of moral behavior. Although Natty Bumppo's behavior hardly seems lawless, Cooper implies that those who act with restraint may be permitted greater latitude in what they do. That turn from fixed ideals toward a contingent ethos was extended by Bierstadt and Harte in melodramatic conceptions that rely on "pure signs" freed from any social context. The optical lawlessness of Bierstadt's landscapes, like the semiotic excess of Harte's stories, contributed to a purely performative strain that would come to characterize the Western. The pleasure that Wister's hero takes in the possibilities of verbal legerdemain, in other words, is intimately related to his (and his author's) willingness to flout the common law. In this vein, it might even be said that his keen delight in Shakespeare's Mercutio itself is a sign of his disposition to take the law into his own hands (lynching, shoot-outs).

This conflict between moral absolutism and a performative ethos is staged more elaborately through the Reverend Mr. McBride, who cavalierly dismisses the tall tale of frogs in terms that ironically contrast with the Virginian's: "No matter how leniently you may try to put it, in the end we have the spectacle of a struggle between men where lying decides the survival of the fittest. Better, far better, if it was to come, that they had shot honest bullets. There are worse evils than war" (228). Preacher and cowboy both speak for action but argue from opposite points of view: one from a perspective of self-righteous absolutism, the other acknowledging how fully culture encodes behavior. The minister espouses the claims of a self that precedes social considerations—a position that, despite initial disagreement, Molly clearly comes to share. She also will separate action from circumstance and look to the claims of conscience, not context, before the Virginian impresses on her the need for accountability.

So fully is Wister committed to this vision that the novel even argues against the rule of law when circumstances dictate a need for extralegal remedies. The Virginian's lynching of Steve for cattle rustling addresses this issue directly: "He knew well enough the only thing that would have let him off would have been a regular jury. For the thieves have got hold of the juries in Johnson County" (411). Relying on the same historical context chosen by Jack Schaefer for *Shane* (1949)—the 1890 Johnson County cattle "war" in Wyoming—Wister places his hero firmly on the side of ranchers against the small farmer, on the side of privilege in opposition to democratic processes. Judge Henry's sophism that citizens "made the courts" and can therefore make their own justice—like the narrator's protest that the Virginian was ultimately right in doing "evil"—are not enough to alter Molly's opposition, based on the just conviction that such circumstances represent nothing more than "ordinary citizens tak[ing] the law in their own hands" (432–34).[23] And later, prior to the final shoot-out, the narrator reiterates a resistance to Molly's faith in claiming that "it is only the great mediocrity that goes to law in these personal matters" (463).

If Wister seems confused in his respect for law and order—committed to both as ideals yet willing to skirt the former when the latter demands—his larger point is that meaningful action cannot exist outside terms settled by public discourse. And it is in this respect that *The Virginian* achieves a remarkable effect, developing its hero's conventional claims by presenting behavior as always mediated by language. Indeed, the novel in some ways compels attention as a "battle of the books," presenting a sequence of seemingly Chinese-box enclosures of "texts" within one another. Just as Molly's presumptuous claims are progressively revised by an unnamed Virginian, his story is in turn incorporated into the text of a narrator who remains unnamed. Molly first appears as a "sheet of note paper" in a chapter entitled "Enter the Woman," and it is that playfully self-descriptive letter which first attracts the Virginian: "a girl had talked as the women he had known did not talk. . . . [H]ere was a free language, altogether new to him" (63). Later, at the Swintons' celebratory barbecue, she demands he be formally "introduced," despite his recent rescue of her from a stagecoach accident. This self-conscious ploy, moreover, reveals to her a name never given to the reader, in a scene that further compounds the novel's intense concern with naming and reference.

From their second meeting, however, the Virginian establishes rhetorical control and in a calmly effective way proves he is more than an adequate adversary. Their verbal parrying attests to his psychological acuteness and self-possession, and he soon reduces a mocking young woman to frustrated incoherence:

> "I did not see you. I knew it must—Of course I did not tell any one. When I said I said so from the first, I meant—you can understand perfectly what I meant."
> "Yes, ma'am." (131)

His direct logic and forceful expression fluster Molly's efforts to maintain a tranquil teacherly manner, and her only alternative is finally to silence him, stopping him completely from expressing his love.

As the relationship grows, the Virginian demonstrates a surprising verbal sensitivity in scenes intended to begin his "education." Molly has from the outset assumed an air of eastern cultivation and lends him a selection of "uplifting" books that inadvertently comment on the novel's major issues. George Eliot's *Mill on the Floss* (1860) impresses him less than Turgenev's *Fathers and Sons* (1862), but both novels present societies in which men and women fail each other and where traditional roles come unmoored to leave desire unconstrained.[24] Predictably, Dickens and Scott appeal to the Virginian more than the "frillery" of Jane Austen, although all three again explore the interdependence of rhetorical, sexual, and social control. That Shakespeare most fully excites him, however, seems surprising only until we discover the figures to whom he is drawn. Mercutio appeals more than Romeo for his ability entertainingly to "talk of nothing," while Othello even more obviously anticipates aspects of the Virginian's own situation: "Rude am I in my speech," claims the Moor, yet his rhetorical magic wins Desdemona. Conversely, what impresses the Virginian in *Henry V* is the speech in which the Archbishop analogizes "the state of man" to a hive of bees, deftly expressing his own belief in solid class distinctions.

Not only do the ideological tensions of these texts reflect issues central to *The Virginian* but they lend a significance to the gradual reversal in the relationship between student and teacher. When Molly at last introduces him to Robert Browning, "her idol, her imagined affinity" (346), the Virginian dismisses the first poem she reads in a judgment that irritates, then impresses her. Still not attentive to his response, she turns next to Browning's "Night and Morning," misreading the elusive lines as a lovers' quarrel. The Virginian instead interprets the poem as the sad parting of two lovers, caused by the narrator's bending to the "need of the world of men." The larger thematic implications are clear, both in Molly's misreading and the poem's anticipation of the novel's later crisis. More generally, not only does each textual instance work in a sort of literary progression but this "education" takes up more narrative time than any other activity—confirming from another perspective the importance of discursive control in the West. Physical events no more than implied by the novel are prominent in the formula reading, but the detailed drama of rhetorical triumphs suggests an alternative interpretation.

The "Equality State"

The Virginian only vaguely satisfies expectations aroused by the Westerns it inspired, which raises the question of what at first could so strongly have appealed to readers. Why should a novel of Wyoming cowboys have become *the* best-seller of 1902, fifth on the list in 1903, and continue as a perennial favorite for many years thereafter? Certainly, enthusiasm for the West and the cowboy, fostered by Roosevelt, Cody, and Remington, meant that Wister's audience was already predisposed to his materials. And he benefited further from a novel that lent itself readily to expectations—beginning with its first playwright adapter, then countless scriptwriters and

113

novelists, right up to television writers who made Trampas rather likable in a feckless sort of way. Still, there is something improbably circular to the claim that variations inspired by the novel help account for that novel's initial popularity, and we need now to consider more fully the implications of having turned from genre to idiosyncratic text, from scenes of action back to language itself, and in particular from the theme of physical violence to that of gender conflict. Those implications add up to a striking conclusion—which does not so much contradict as contribute to other explanations for the novel's success—that *The Virginian* offered a muted resolution to the crisis over woman's suffrage developing at the turn of the century.

Near the novel's conclusion, Molly threatens to break off their engagement should the Virginian hew to his code of honor. Nonetheless, following the gunfight with Trampas, she rushes into the street to embrace her lover, confirming under pressure his mastery of her and acknowledging the clear reversal of roles she had assumed would define their relationship. Molly's capitulation forms more than simply a personal defeat, however, as suggested by the rhetorically inflated description of her change of heart: "At the last white-hot edge of ordeal, it was she who renounced, and he who had his way. Nevertheless she found much more than enough, in spite of the sigh that now and again breathed through her happiness when she would watch him with eyes fuller of love than of understanding" (496–97). This maudlin passage helps explain the ready concession the author made to his acerbic mother when she complained (in a judgment more or less shared ever since) that "the heroine is a failure."[25]

Yet Molly's flat characterization can be seen as essential to the novel's thematic deployment, which requires less of her as developing character than merely as resident of Wyoming. For in the new territory, she possessed a right denied to nearly all her countrywomen: access to the ballot box. The territorial legislature had been the first, in 1869, to extend suffrage to women, and when it sought statehood in 1890, it likewise proposed the first constitution with an equal-suffrage clause. Indeed, despite a meager population Wyoming was admitted to the Union *because* of the widespread attention its experiment had attracted. By 1902 most readers were aware of a political situation a third of a century in the making and might well have found instructive the absence of any allusion to suffrage—perhaps especially since Wister so proudly proclaimed the novel's historical verisimilitude.[26] Molly's lack of definition thus serves a distinctive narrative end by emphasizing her simple representativeness as a woman in the "Equality State." And if one can measure by sales and reviews, contemporary readers approved of the way the role of a newly enfranchised American woman was being defined: by an independent schoolteacher who at last accepts her social and intellectual dependency in a man's world.[27]

As Susan B. Anthony wearily noted at the time the novel appeared, relatively few Americans supported the cause of equal suffrage, which only began to win broad support more than a decade later (resulting at last in the passage of the Nineteenth Amendment in 1920). Part of the problem lay in the self-contradictory logic invoked by moderate suffragists to defend a woman's right to the ballot. "They claimed equal suffrage because women were morally superior to men," Peter Gabriel Filene explains:

> They asked for public power because of their experience as housekeepers and mothers. These tactics successfully co-opted the arguments that traditionalists had been using to keep women in their sphere. But the co-optation also backfired upon its authors. By exploiting the Victorian premises, the suffragists never fully abandoned them. . . . In the end they made her the better half, a woman on a public pedestal, and to that extent still a Victorian creature.[28]

And if even those inclined to extend the franchise fell back on the traditional assumption of woman's proper role, one can understand how resistant most others were to any such political change.

Americans were hardly prepared to abandon the idea of innate sexual differences and corresponding social roles, which explains the strong conservative backlash that developed against the suffrage movement.[29] This is the same period that recent historians have described as increasingly concerned with issues of masculine identity, apparent in the proliferation of fraternal organizations, the rise of mass sports, physical fitness, and martial ideals, and (perhaps surprisingly) a vital change in the paternal role to a newly nurturing model.[30] The evidence, in fact, suggests that Americans were caught at the turn of the century between traditional gender ideals and new imperatives, leaving them far from self-assured about their sexual identities. Wister's own marriage forms an exemplary instance: he proposed in 1898 to his cousin, Molly Wister, who had already earned a reputation as an outspoken feminist; although he was firmly opposed to her speaking in public, he still recognized his own ideas as "feudal" and did not stand in her way.[31] America's future may have pointed toward women's fuller equality, but the advantage of fiction for Wister lay in its power to transform conditions imaginatively to something like a *status quo ante*.

Granted, then, that though Wyoming's electoral experiment was broadly seen as progressive, readers of *The Virginian* did not need to fear that even so great a political change would alter domestic relations. The irony nonetheless is that the actual history behind Wyoming's extension of the vote would have alarmed few opponents of women's rights and have reassured even fewer of those striving for social equality. No suffrage society existed in the territory nor was a petition ever submitted, and when the original legislation was passed Wyoming's declining population barely exceeded 8,000 (with only one woman for every six men). The considerations that induced twenty-one territorial congressmen to vote a suffrage bill were neither idealistic nor feminist but simply a matter of prudential economics. They construed the legislation as public relations with the aim of attracting women to their rough-and-tumble realm of railroad camps and mining towns. And once there, women were expected to exert political influence in support of a traditional social order. As it happened, the new dispensation in practice seemed little different from the old exclusion, confirming women in a "separate sphere" as repositories of education, culture, and religion.[32]

Patriarchy Renewed

Still, most readers were unfamiliar with the ins and outs of Wyoming's history and would have regarded its political experiment as an affirmation of full social equality—especially since suffrage simply construed denied any special nature to women. From an eastern perspective, it was not at all clear that theory and practice stood at odds in the West or that suffrage could be, as in Wyoming it was, effectively antifeminist. Against this misunderstood history, Wister's fictional confrontation of the Virginian with the schoolmarm acquires symbolic importance by engaging only to dismiss the twin possibilities of female enfranchisement. Radical suffragists had argued, on the one hand, for women's equal humanity, and they denied any intellectual or emotional, indeed all but physical differences between the sexes. Molly cogently expresses this position in arguments and actions, and yet we have seen that the Virginian's rhetorical edge persuades her of his superior logic. Not only are individuals innately different but the sexes are so as well, and (according to him) those differences should be reflected in political rights and social roles. On the other hand, the more common counterposition (already described above) had been adopted by the legislators who passed the territorial bill. They deemed women morally superior to men in terms of innate sensibility and openly hoped a feminine influence would help civilize the still unsettled territory. Again, the Virginian refutes this logic by educating the schoolteacher in books and civil behavior, demonstrating his superior moral sensibility.[33]

At times, the novel reinforces this imperative of gender roles simply by pointing out what happens when they are transgressed. Early on, the Virginian wryly compliments Molly as a man for having been honorable enough to admit that she was wrong—"You're a gentleman!" (133)—and when later wounded, he tersely informs her, "You have got to be the man all through this mess" (331).[34] More pervasively, the narrator's homoerotic perspective on the Virginian itself implies a certain feminized dependency in its mixture of incompetence and marginality, as if only the hero's stereotypically masculine behavior could warrant his attention. The most striking instance occurs with the episode of the "manly-lookin" bantam hen, Em'ly, who "came near being a rooster" (73). Unaware of her proper female function, even of her species, she frantically sits on potatoes, onions, and balls of soap, all in the effort to reproduce. The perfect embodiment of female energy driven by mistaken notions of behavior and duty, this "egregious fowl" even sits on a brood of puppies before the Virginian places an egg beneath her. Surprised by the unexpected hatching of a chick, Em'ly dies from the sheer "terror" of the event, a victim of basic gender confusion and terminal hysteria (82). If the bathos of this narrative set-piece barely disguises its sardonic puncturing of feminist pretensions, its importance for the novel as a whole can nonetheless be measured by the fact that it marks the first true affinity between the narrator and the Virginian, whose relationship of stiff formality immediately becomes one of "thorough friends" (83).

Like the Virginian, the narrator shares the assumption that women are neither equal to men nor even superior in traditional ethical terms but rather (like children) dependent upon their partners in matters of social and political control. Near the novel's conclusion, the implications of this attitude are made explicit:

Having read his sweetheart's mind very plainly, the lover now broke his dearest custom. It was his code never to speak ill of any man to any woman. Men's quarrels were not for women's ears. In his scheme, good women were to know only a fragment of men's lives. (452)

This reactionary thesis of inequality between the sexes ends the novel, only to be further adumbrated, embellished, and otherwise strenuously rationalized in countless Westerns that follow. Masculine principles, talents, and constitutions all combine to justify the patriarchal structure of American society as it has always been, and as *The Virginian* promises it will be once again.

Yet the narrator complicates this paternalistic and familial perspective in the very attention he pays to the Virginian's footloose, twenty-something existence in Wyoming. Pointed simultaneously forward and backward as successfully as any subsequent Western, Wister's novel encourages both adolescent nostalgia and parental expectation: celebrating a fancy-free realm of adolescent male rivalry even as it envisions masculine privileges in family life under the counterlogic of patriarchy. As the narrative concludes, Molly has become the traditional wife and mother cloistered at home ("She shall teach school no more when she is mine" [372]); the Virginian is socially dominant in a more established civic context, with coal reserves on his land ensuring a future fortune; and their eldest son sits astride his father's horse, Monte. Henry James may have preferred that the Virginian achieve mythic greatness through violent death, but his own suggested "better ending" is only among the first to transform the novel into a less ambiguous, more formulaic construction, thereby helping to unstring the flexible ideological web that Wister had devised.[35]

The achievement of *The Virginian* resides instead in its capacity to satisfy contradictory expectations: the desire for nostalgic escapism into an exclusively masculine West and yet the need for a resolution to the more immediately vexing national issue of gender relations. If in 1902, the prospect of life in an "Equality State" seemed unsettling to readers, their uncertainty would have been eased by the drama of the Virginian's courtship of Molly. That few were consciously aware of the novel's contradictory possibilities did not diminish their enjoyment. On the contrary, *The Virginian* would never have won so large a readership had its terms been presented unambiguously, and the very ability to have things both ways contributed to its success. Evading issues it seems to confront, it even celebrates principal cultural terms only to redefine them. Centrally, the concepts of "equality" and "democracy" are invoked to divide, not unite—whether men from women, superior from inferior, shrewd from simple, or the hero from the rest. At a time when republican ideals seemed inadequate to the pattern of a new urban industrialism, the novel reshuffles definitions in ways that middle-class readers would have found comforting.

Of course, such a consoling interpretation was hardly Wister's primary intention; though gratified with the novel's sales, he continued to feel he had failed to convey his message of a threat to republican institutions in the breakdown of older class constraints. Nearly a decade later, in the preface to the 1911 edition, he described his memory of the book's appearance, "when political darkness still lay dense upon every State in the Union," and reiterated his deep antipathy to thinly disguised Populist forces. "Our Democracy has many enemies, both in Wall Street and in the Labor Unions," and only the example of the Virginian's "sincerity" and virtuous self-restraint holds promise that such threats to self-government can be successfully withstood.[36]

In fact, despite repeated obeisances to the principle of equality, an aging Wister became ever more firmly aligned with the prerogatives of the "quality," and took exception to his inability to control the readings of his own text. As Ben Merchant Vorpahl has sardonically noted, "Wister found the number of readers with whom he wished to identify shrinking, while the size of his reading public grew."[37] His own initial conception of the West as a setting for youthful competition and fluid class boundaries became less fully attractive as he himself became less youthful. Like Remington and Roosevelt in their mid-forties, family men and worldly successes, he began to feel threatened, even displaced by the very forces that they had all identified with the free and open West.

But if Wister grew more single-minded as the years went by, secure in his Philadelphia study and uneager to venture West again, the legacy of his novel was profoundly other, and through its richly ambivalent strains stimulated an abundant array of responses. The Wyoming landscape that is at once vivid and silent, colored so violently as to seem a physical assault yet so pure as to seem otherworldly, would be altered by later practitioners of the genre into countless topographical settings—but always with the power to restore one to oneself. As in Bierstadt's panoramas, Wister captured a certain self-contradictory quality he identified with the West, lending his characteristic narrative a characteristic setting that would come to seem nationally distinctive as well.

Even were it possible to extract the central figure of Wister's narrative from the landscape, the Virginian would still be part of the process of contradictory interpretation that it initiates. His valuing of silence, for instance, places him ahead of a long line of laconic Western heroes—even though he is also the novel's master of talk. And because the narrator is a tenderfoot, the Virginian appears a bit distant, despite being as convivial and committed to marriage as anyone else in the novel. That external perspective lends him the aura of a man of action rather than one of deliberation. Clearly the contradictions of the novel extend well beyond its redefinitions and narrative perspective, but they exemplify why it fulfilled expectations for a genre it nonetheless resists. Individualism versus social consensus, physical dexterity versus rhetorical control, masculine independence versus patriarchal commitment: in each of these pairs of opposed concepts, the Western has tended to celebrate the former. That its prototype also aligns with the latter reveals how fully a casual logic of literary history applies, with context genuinely creating the text that readers recognize. Moreover, that capacity to elicit such a variety of responses suggests why *The Virginian* would continue to be so influential for later writers and directors, each of whom tried to define more exactly for expectant contemporaries what Wister had been willing to leave unresolved.

119

5 WHITE SLAVES IN PURPLE SAGE

The most frightful thing, and the most alarming about the White Slave Traffic is that it has become a system, one powerfully organized of groups operating it may be independently, but relying upon and aiding each other brazenly. A girl in the clutches of any one of them has practically no chance of escape, since the agents of all of them are on the lookout. Their eyes are everywhere and upon every girl, including those already fallen as they do the innocent. No Black Hand, no secret organization of any kind is more silent or insidious, or, in the end, more ruthless.

Robert J. Moorehead (1911)[1]

Oldring's Masked Rider sat before him, a girl dressed as a man. She had been made to ride at the head of infamous forays and drives. She had been imprisoned for many months of her life in an obscure cabin. At times the most vicious of men had been her companions; and the vilest of women, if they had not been permitted to approach her, had, at least, cast their shadows over her. But—but in spite of all this— there thundered at Venters some truth that lifted its voice higher than the clamoring facts of dishonor, some truth that was the very life of her beautiful eyes; and it was innocence.

Zane Grey (1912)[2]

Arthur Conan Doyle's most famous character made his debut in 1887 with the publication of *A Study in Scarlet*. As lovers of Sherlock Holmes know well, the novel tells of Dr. Watson's service in the Afghan Wars, his meeting with Holmes, their renting of rooms at 221B Baker Street, and the discovery of Holmes's devotion to "analytic thinking," that characteristic process of working from mystifying effects to hidden causes, from possible discourses to a single story. Or, to put it in Holmes's self-preening terms, "the whole thing is a chain of logical sequences without a break or flaw."[3] Yet if the novel sets the terms of detective stories inimitably English, it does so via an immense detour into a narrative coded as wholly American.

The framing Watsonian chronicle depicts the mystery of two violent deaths in closed rooms and ends with Holmes's luring of the murderer, Jefferson Hope, to public arrest in his own smoky chambers. The embedded narrative, told by Hope, begins half a century before, "in the central portion of the Great North American continent" (71). This "Western" account traces the history of two survivors of starvation, a man and a girl saved by Mormons. Years go by, during which the girl falls in love with the Gentile, Hope, even as Mormon elders secretly decide she is meant for one of their own. Given a deadline, she makes "a flight for life" (91) past the guard encircling her house, but is taken back against her will to be coerced into a Mormon marriage, after which she pines away and dies. The novel ends with Hope's account of tracking down the responsible Mormons and his justification of their brutal murder through an appeal to manliness: "I determined that I should be judge, jury, and executioner all rolled into one. You'd have done the same, if you have any manhood in you, if you had been in my place" (116).

This stark resort to the logic of manliness, with its echoes of the Western, is only one reason for invoking a novel that develops its central narrative tension through the abduction of a woman. Doyle foregrounds the dark side of what we refer to as plot—as conspiracy, as secret and determining shape. And plots are concocted by all involved: by Mormons most insidiously, later by Hope, and then by Holmes and Watson. More importantly, death itself is dragged dramatically into the foreground, enacted through the novel's numerous bodies lodged in postures of pain, jammed into narrow rooms that contrast vividly with the wide-open wilderness at the heart of the novel. Indeed, Watson's famous search for London digs—a quest for a cozy, protective space—ironically initiates a novel whose other chambers are grim and soaked in blood. Closed rooms and endless space create a dialectic of constraints upon the body that is imaged not only in the Mormon's threatening encirclement of Lucy's ranch, but in Holmes's gradual withdrawal to his own narrow room when he has solved the mystery and is able to lure the murderer to him.

Exactly a quarter-century later, Zane Grey published what would always be his most popular novel, *Riders of the Purple Sage* (1912), a book that firmly established the modern Western by offering a convincing sequel to Wister.[4] It opens with the scene of a man about to be whipped by Mormons in order to pressure Jane Withersteen into marrying against her will. Suddenly, the hero Lassiter appears, a gunman in black leather, who routs the threatening men and gradually recounts a history of endlessly searching for a woman abducted long before by Mormons. Once again, a Mormon conspiracy collides with the secrets each character guards. A woman is threatened, deprived of her wealth and peace of mind, and finally forced to dramatic escape in a narrative that focuses on contested notions of masculinity. And again, the novel juxtaposes interior spaces with the same Utah wilderness, though Grey imagines his characters in transit to ever more open spaces, unlike Doyle, who shuts us up with his detective at the end.

At issue here is not the birth of separate genres. Doyle cannot be credited with the invention of detective fiction any more than Grey can be charged with having thrust the Western upon us. (It is enough that both authors adapted elements from their predecessors to fix the separate genres into shapes by which we know them best today.) Nor is it a matter of more tempting questions: why, for example, the misanthrope Holmes has emerged as a distinctively British Victorian figure while America's misanthropic man took shape as a gun-toting, leather-clad cowboy. Or, why the mystery novel should have been pedigreed by its engagement of intellectuals while the Western has always remained non-U. What is compelling at the moment is the fact that two such dissimilar texts generating divergent literary histories should require so singular a set of bizarre motifs for their plots: Mormons, the great western desert, conspiracy, closed and blood-soaked rooms. Two different writers on separate continents near the turn of the century—and more importantly, their countless readers—found tremendous pleasure in that unsettling litany.

Pointedly for our purposes, Grey's novel forms a remarkable turn in the evolution of the Western, selling well over a million copies and solidly establishing the career of the author most closely identified with the genre—indeed, whose novels were instrumental in actually defining the Western *as* a genre.[5] Grey created a professional career just as the "culture industry" consolidated its hold on the public, best-seller lists first governed publishers' attention, and film emerged as a captivating form of entertainment. The extraordinary success of *Riders of the Purple Sage* not only signaled the kind of treatment that would fascinate a national audience but announced to that audience itself (defined at the time by female readers) the certification of a new narrative form with its own characteristic turns and codes. Thus encouraged, Grey went on to write over fifty Westerns by the time of his death in 1939, most still in print, nine having dominated the best-seller list for their year, and dozens converted by Hollywood into feature-length films.[6]

The significance of *Riders of the Purple Sage*, then, is at once generic and historical, due as much to its influence in consolidating formal aspects of the Western as to its immediate impact in allaying contemporary anxieties. While these effects are interconnected, they are best treated sequentially: first, the novel's revision of features that others had contributed to the Western; and second, the novel's engagement of more immediate eastern dilemmas. Grey transforms Harte's and Wister's investigation of gender, for instance, into an obsession with secrets, plots, conspiracies—all devised to draw attention toward the ways in which gender is not only biologically complex but culturally *constructed*. In the process, landscape description is complicated beyond what earlier writers had imagined, making Grey's wilderness settings a living maze that induces helpless capitulation. Incorporating a captivity narrative structure more fully as plot than even Cooper had attempted, Grey reveals the process of transformation now as simply a confirmation of what one is.

So successful were the innovations Grey introduced in novels over the next four decades that he all but single-handedly confirmed the shape of a powerful new narrative form. Yet none of these technical alterations, nor their combination, would have struck readers so forcefully without a peculiar state of panic that happened to exist in 1912. Grey's triumph lay in his responsiveness to anxieties about standards of female behavior—indeed, his ability to arouse yet assuage fears of a global conspiracy to abduct white females through an intricate plot of Western riders and purple sage. At   123 once reinforcing and undercutting an emergent discourse on women's independence, the novel celebrates the possibility of the New Woman even as it cautions against her. In that oscillation, moreover, Grey follows in a strong line of precursors extending back to Cooper.

Worthless Secrets

One of the standard ploys invoked by many of Grey's novels is to have Mexicans, outlaws, Mormons, or other supposedly unsavory groups succeed in enslaving white women. Drawing on the long tradition of the captivity narrative, he offers elaborate plots, dark secrets, and powerful conspiracies that invariably threaten his independent-minded heroines. And it is the risk of being captured (with the ever-present injunction to "save the last bullet for yourself") that lends a perversely erotic charge to this basic narrative line—one borrowed from Cooper and the dime novel (with their unerring cycle of pursuit, capture, and escape).[7] *Riders of the Purple Sage,* in fact, brings two captivity plots together. The first involves Lassiter's eighteen-year search for his sister, Milly Erne, who has been seduced by a mysterious Mormon, abducted and "chained in a cave" (172), had her own child "captured" in turn from her, and dies in sheer despair two years before Lassiter comes to the rescue. He now decides to help the rich rancher Jane Withersteen resist similar attempts to force her to marry a Mormon against her will—attempts that include the abduction of her own adopted daughter Fay. The novel ends with Jane brutally dispossessed of her ranch, having barely escaped with her life, her virtue, and her newly constituted family (Lassiter, Fay) into a mountain stronghold.

The second captivity plot involves the rustler Oldring, who has raised Milly's daughter Bess as his own and forced her to become a masked bandit. Wounded (in self-defense) by a gentle gunman named Bern Venters, she is carried by him to a secluded valley where once again she thinks she is a captive. Their Edenic experience develops in tandem with the relationship between Jane and Lassiter, and at the novel's conclusion this second couple likewise eludes the Mormons by racing "back to my old home in Illinois" (252). Tellingly, however, and despite these separate escapes to freedom, the Mormon conspiracy remains in place, undeterred by the plot's happy end. Indeed, the conspiracy itself escapes the novel's conclusion to re-emerge in a sequel a generation later, when the Mormon cabal looms larger than ever to torment Fay Larkin, now a grown woman herself.

In short, the novel organizes materials according to a conventional captivity plot, with Mormons and outlaws replacing the traditional villainous Indians as the alien Other.[8] Insistently driving the narrative is what Richard

Hofstadter once described as "the central preoccupation of the paranoid style—the existence of a vast, insidious, preternaturally effective international conspiratorial network designed to perpetrate acts of the most fiendish character."[9] This strongly marked sexual threat succeeds in cutting Jane Withersteen off from friends, suddenly "calling in" her riders, and finally setting her own servants to spy on her. When her foreman defiantly returns to service after his hostaged mother has died, he is ruthlessly murdered. Even Oldring's outlaw band agrees to conspire with the church of Jesus Christ of Latter-Day Saints in stealing Jane's herd. More important than this ubiquitous power of the Mormon conspiracy is the representation of the church as always "binders" of women, enslaving them in efforts to exact submission to a creed—whether the woman is Jane's ward Fay, or Milly Erne, or Bess Oldring, or Jane herself. Physical enslavement offers an analogy to the alleged condition of women in Mormon society, revealed in one of the few explanations they ever offer: "You haven't," the leader Tull sternly explains to Jane, "yet come to see the place of Mormon women" (6).

The fact that Latter-Day Saint ideology is never elaborated—and that additionally it seems to entail nothing more complex or taxing than enforced wifely obedience—lends a powerful irony to Jane's metamorphosis through the novel into an unquestioning partner to Lassiter. Ironically, it is her staunch resistance to being transformed by the Mormon leadership ("they would find her unchangeable" [60]) that initiates her ultimate transformation, making her into the "changed woman" (60) who contentedly, even eagerly, bows to a forceful male perspective. The novel, that is, eventually seems to sanction pressures on women to conform to a standard even though it has firmly coded those pressures as evil, as belonging to the alien race.

Self-transformation in itself is hardly a process to be disparaged—certainly according to Grey, whose innumerable novels self-consciously celebrate the transfiguring potential of western life. Removed from the oppressive climate and artificial constraints of the East, his characters typically discover renewed health, resurgent happiness, and appropriate social roles. *Riders of the Purple Sage* forms no exception to this social Darwinist pattern in depicting the arduous metamorphosis of each of four main characters, each achieving full manhood or womanhood through sustained resistance to the closed room of Mormonism. And that resistance is explicitly allegorized as an escape into unlimited landscape, a turn from claustral confines into the prospect of psychological openness and sexual health.

In apparent opposition to its own plot exertions, however, the novel oddly relies on occult narratives and clandestine spaces, sharpening suspense through the promise of secrets revealed about characters' pasts—

secrets that seem to hold the key to former identities and that should explain the nature of various characters' relation to Mormonism. Everyone is driven by secrets, wanting first to know who the mysterious Lassiter is and about his relationship to Milly. He, likewise, has pursued the mystery of his sister's abductor for eighteen years and must continue to wait through most of the novel to have that mystery resolved. Venters as well is initially mystified by the motives of those who steal Jane's cattle and later wants to be fully informed of Bess's life as the Masked Rider. She playfully withholds from Venters her discovery of gold, just as Oldring refuses to speak of his relationship with Bess.

Throughout, the novel operates by a process of painfully delayed recollections, of information grudgingly divulged and secrets never willingly laid bare. The central captivity narrative of Milly Erne is constructed piecemeal, in patchwork parts, through partial revelations elicited from various figures at sundry times—Venters first, then Lassiter, and later the rustler Oldring. Not until all but the end is the name of the mysterious man who eighteen years earlier masterminded Milly Erne's abduction finally divulged, when Jane reluctantly admits that her own Mormon father was the legendary figure with "blue-ice eye and the beard of gold" and that Milly Erne was part of his imperial plan (227). As if in collusion with this obsessively secretive pattern, the novel functions as characters do, transforming actions into enigmas by absenting the narrator at crucial moments. The violent, off-stage encounter between Venters and Tull is only recounted to Jane by Lassiter after she has wheedled the story from him. Later, after suddenly fainting (as the narrator again absents himself), she must entice Judkin into revealing the cardinal fact that Lassiter killed Bishop Dyer.

While secrets (plots, enigmas, conspiracies) can be said to be the novel's obsession, then, curiously little depends on them, as if they no longer matter once the truth is disclosed. "There is something strange about these stories, secrets, and revelations," Christine Bold has observed; "by the time they are told, they are inconsequential not only to the reader . . . but to the other characters."[10] The darkest secret of Bess's past, guarded with singular caution, is that Oldring is her father—a secret only revealed with Mormons in hot pursuit and almost immediately supplanted by Lassiter's long-delayed revelation that she is actually his niece, the daughter of Frank and Milly Erne. In either case, Bess's parentage is a matter of small consequence to Venters (the man from whom the secret was kept), if only because in the interim he has been transformed by love for her. And Jane's similarly delayed parental revelation leaves Lassiter equally unaffected. "I've outgrowed revenge," the gunman simply declares (221). As elsewhere, the desperate pursuit of secrets that has driven so much of the novel is here merely abandoned, with the need for plot itself evaporating once secrets are finally known. Individuals attain true selfhood by imparting shameful revelations to those they love, who are no longer troubled by the revelations once they have been made.

In contrast to this mutual process of personal transformation, which results in a gradual devaluing of secrets, stand the Mormons, a people who resolutely refuse to divulge anything of themselves. Venters marvels at "how Mormons hide the truth" (20) and comes to realize that what most distinguishes them is this "strange secretiveness," a habit that seems to him an "expressionless expression of mystery and hidden power" (201). Mormons, in other words, incarnate untold enigmas, unnarrated plots, negative energy, and their resistance to giving up secrets is phrased ("expressionless expression") as an oxymoron that suggests their staunch resistance to the process of narrative itself. They resolutely pose themselves against all accounts, obstructing any reports, in the process serving as a black hole for narrative energy. Milly simply disappears, with nothing ever told about her, except for fragmentary evidence beaten out of church witnesses and skeletal explanations garnered from her few letters (themselves abruptly foreshortened by her conversion to Mormonism). The "locked lips" of the Mormons offer mute testament to antinarrative elements within the novel that serve as a force of entropy, eroding the stories that the good characters are finally willing to tell. And thus, the Mormons make their own master claim to narrative power by locking narrative itself away.

Of course, the effect of the Mormons' behavior is the very opposite of what they intend—not to suppress narratives but to get people talking in the effort to fathom their esoteric doctrine and conspiratorial ploys, their abductions, whippings, seductions, confinements, thefts, enforced marriages, and murders. Through their own obsession with silence, they paradoxically induce a narrative proclivity in others, generating an interest in the possibility of alternative plots. The complete lack of information about their supposed "black plot" against Jane, for instance, has the effect of sparking the melodramatic expectations they had hoped to silence.

Even more notably, that Mormon plot is imaged by Jane and others with the bizarre visual metaphor of an "invisible hand": a conspiratorial intelligence figured forth metonymically as a sexual gesture, a seductive caress so powerful that it forestalls anything other than blind submission. Depriving Jane of choice itself, the "unseen hand" (35) erases indeterminacy through the effects of its physical strokes. This ambivalent process becomes most explicit in the novel's central chapter, entitled appropriately "Invisible Hand," when Jane ponders her now frighteningly circumscribed situation:

127

If that secret, intangible power closed its toils round her again, if that great invisible hand moved here and there and everywhere, slowly paralyzing her with its mystery and its inconceivable sway over her affairs, then she would know beyond doubt that it was not chance, nor jealousy, nor intimidation, nor ministerial wrath at her revolt, but a cold and calculating policy thought out long before she was born, a dark, immutable will of whose empire she and all that was hers was but an atom.

Then might come her ruin. Then might come her fall into black storm. Yet she would rise again, and to the light. God would be merciful to a driven woman who had lost her way. (130)

The linking here of plot, causality, conspiratorial power, and sexual innuendo is far from fortuitous, with the Mormons imaged as something like an ultimate seductive threat, forcing narrative itself into passive quiescence.

Given that premise, it is odd that the narrative once again seems to support these gestures—that the novel itself should oppose the proliferation of women's stories and, like the Mormons, celebrate their repression. We have already seen how secrets are both forsaken and devalued, self-consciously revealed at last only to be treated as inconsequential by those who have learned to love. Yet love in itself does not explain how the novel's most crucial secrets—secrets finally answering questions that have troubled everyone from the beginning—can now be deemed irrelevant. Jane's and Bess's painful revelations about their fathers are simply disregarded, ignored not only by lovers but by everyone else as well. The scenes are striking in their sudden deflation of the very female narrative energies that have been so carefully erected, suggesting that one of the major premises of *Riders of the Purple Sage* is expressly to extract secrets from women that are only denigrated once revealed. This in itself forms a Mormonesque turn, resembling their own explicit denial of the process of narration.

More generally, the novel reinforces the Mormon threat in its shift from the dramatic implications of narrative into unalloyed description of landscape itself. From this point of view, it is hardly irrelevant that the two intertwined plots come to an end not through formal resolution but through a simple retreat into the desert, with Venters and Bess riding away from it all to "home in Illinois," and Lassiter, Jane, and little Fay walling themselves into the isolated security of Surprise Valley. Once again, that is, the novel invests in the Mormon point of view, shifting repeatedly from the melodramatic entanglements of plot to offer instead lush descriptions of landscape. Cooper had already anticipated this retreat from narrative as an "aimless glance," helping to validate explosive scenes of violence through a luxuriating attention to flora and fauna, topography, even climatic conditions. If formal reasons for the strategy remain the same, however, Grey's descriptive turn also reinforces part of the novel's thematic agenda, suggesting a covert and pleasurable endorsement of the silencing preached by the "alien" Mormons within a novel that otherwise seems to despise their "black hands."

What the Landscape Says

Grey deliberately invokes a specific historical time and space, the landscape of southern Utah where small Mormon towns were already well-established in the summer of 1871. Yet although Lassiter has been on the trail of his sister since her abduction in 1853, the novel is all but silent about any recent developments. Never, even indirectly, are the ravages of the Civil War apparent, or the completion of a transcontinental railroad, or the astonishing emergence of the cattle industry in the years immediately following. Like Bierstadt's landscapes, Grey's are so unhistoricized that the setting could be almost anywhere in the West during the half century prior to the novel's appearance.[11] The question then arises: What effect is achieved by this indeterminacy, this de-historicizing of space in a descriptive style laden with baroque cadences and a landscape embellished with verbal sounds?

The glorious sunlight filled the valley with purple fire. Before him, to left, to right, waving, rolling, sinking, rising, like low swells of a purple sea, stretched the sage. Out of the grove of cottonwoods, a green patch on the purple, gleamed the dull red of Jane Withersteen's old stone house. And from these extended the wide green of the village gardens and orchards marked by the graceful poplars; and farther down shone the deep, dark richness of the alfalfa fields. Numberless red and black and white dots speckled the sage, and these were cattle and horses. (25–26)

Elementary syntax and simple diction, transformed through a lavish proliferation of gerunds and adjectives, "paint" the landscape in what might be called a gaudy version of Stephen Crane (the last sentence, in particular, replicating the split-second cognitive delay so typical of Crane's literary impressionism). Nor is this passage unique in the novel; on the contrary, it is matched by countless others offering an eyesighted Far West in prose that more than once tumbles through the color purple.

Perhaps, with the advent of black-and-white cinema, this text served as a verbal surrogate for visual luxuries yet unattainable, as if Grey had devised a Ted Turner colorizing process for fictional narrative still unavailable to film. Unintentionally, Grey successfully vied with the new cinematic medium—a medium defined in its early years as much by the Western as by any other genre—even as his novels soon provided material for frequent film translation.[12] Part of the lure of his descriptions lies in their endowing the land with an Edenic quality at a time when the banalities of a new tourist literature were generating considerable interest in the West, reinvesting it with dramatic fascination just when it had been made safe in reality.[13] Grey's depiction of Jane's ranch at Amber Springs, the town of Cottonwoods, the highlands of purple sage, and most especially Deception Pass and Surprise Valley map out a high-calorie vista for the eye, paralleling in words the accomplishment half a century before of Bierstadt and Church.

Yet the *mise-en-scène* is less academy painting than stage set—dark wings, draped backdrops, the fanciful and improbable platform for melodrama, a visual scene that suddenly takes on a performative life of its own in the very process of being written. After Venters carries a wounded Bess to Surprise Valley, she thinks she has awakened in heaven, and the prelapsarian scenario that ensues does more to confirm than deny the supposition. The first "purple" thunderstorm is nothing less than an *opera seria:*

> The tips of the cottonwoods and the oaks waved to the east, and the rings of aspens along the terraces twinkled their myriad of bright faces in fleet and glancing gleam. A low roar rose from the leaves of the forest, and the spruces swished in the rising wind. It came in gusts, with light breezes between. As it increased in strength the lulls shortened in length till there was a strong and steady blow all the time, and violent puffs at intervals, and sudden whirling currents. The clouds spread over the valley, rolling swiftly and low, and twilight faded into a sweeping darkness. Then the singing of the wind in the caves drowned the swift roar of rustling leaves; then the song swelled to a mourning, moaning wail; then with the gathering power of the wind the wail changed to a shriek. Steadily the wind strengthened and constantly the strange sound changed. (150)

The landscape is invested with an unusual animistic energy, as the narrator strains to describe (through a series of "strange," self-exampling "changes") a storm that will continue to rage for another five pages.

Or perhaps it is more accurate to say that the landscape itself appears to resist conventional forms of representation, thus compelling the narrator to devise exceptional means of scenic depiction. By invoking the immediately heard (instead of merely the distantly understood)—through alliteration, assonance, anaphora, parachresis, word repetition, and so on—the narrator invests the earth itself with a sonically expressed temperament usually reserved for characters. This is a pattern with solid analogs to the animated landscapes of earlier authors, if more extreme than Cooper and more convincing than Harte. The point is that scenery constantly seems to evade the narrator's attempts at control, throbbing with a defiantly passionate life ascribed to it in a metamorphosis that recurs through the novel—of springs that "leaped down joyously" (29), of sunsets creeping across cañons "to mount the opposite slope and chase and darken and bury the last golden flare of sunlight" (36), of "singing of the wind in the cliffs" (97), or of "silent" stone bridges and balancing rocks that "guard" the landscape like giants (84, 86). Animation, even personification, is never quite so vague or bathetic as the process so regularly instanced by Harte's use of the pathetic fallacy.

Even so, such exorbitance is disturbing as much because of nature's contorting transformations as the narrator's contorted efforts to describe them—as much because of the strangely phantasmagorical status of the landscape itself as to the somewhat "purple" terms of its description. The problem (minor as it seems at first) lies in distinguishing how truly exorbitant the narrator is, how much he supplements what is otherwise clearly a site of excess. Insoluble as that problem may be, the landscape does undeniably live, with characters normally depicted escaping to an outer world "peopled" by natural phenomenon, whose sky or terrain expresses their own particular emotional states. Human bodies appear almost magically incarnated in the natural world. At first, Venters thinks "the details of his wild environment seemed the only substance of a strange dream"; later, he is startled to find the mountain storm truly does embody his own tumultuous feelings. In the opening pages, Lassiter literally rides out of the landscape simply in response to Jane's "strained gaze." And the novel's obligatory final sunset takes an inordinately long time (continuing for a full twenty-five pages), conveying an impression that the landscape itself is expiring along with the narrative motion.

The larger sense of an animate environment resisting the narrator's efforts to tame and depict it contributes to the peculiar intensity of his descriptions. Repeatedly, the narrator's landscapes defy our sense of normal topography, much as M. C. Escher's engravings play with perspectival assumptions by making water fall uphill and people run downstairs to the floor above.[14] Characters themselves are "deceived" by a geography that should in fact be straightforward, venturing at once a "climb and descent into Surprise Valley" (90), or discovering the opening to Deception Pass forms "five hundred feet of sheer depth" (37). Venters, it is true, may masterfully wend his way through the elaborate mountainscape even though he is occasionally bewildered by "this stone-walled maze of mystery" (52). The reader, however, is constantly frustrated in the imaginative attempt to map his trail, not because too little but too much is accessible to the eye (in an optical lawlessness reminiscent of Bierstadt's landscapes now forced to an even greater extreme).

The setting vibrates in an almost literal "frenzy of the visible," an effect ascribed by Jean Louis Comolli to the late nineteenth-century in which "the whole world becomes visible at the same time that it becomes appropriable."[15] A newly enabled, newly imperializing eye discovers how little it can control, as the narrator likewise finds when the land repeatedly escapes his attempts to describe it, resorting to depictions that resemble a confusing maze, a dream or drug-induced vision capable of luring the unwary reader along. This deracinating conception of landscape is part of the genre's conventions, extending all the way back to *The Last of the Mohicans,* as W. H. Gardner noted at the time in the passage quoted more fully in Chapter 2: "we are utterly unable to settle the relative positions of these objects, so as to form any distinct picture from them in the mind." Moreover, this phantasmagoria offers one possible trace of the landscape's persistent, secret double identity as a human body.

Through the course of the novel, the body of earth becomes human, simultaneously female and male, via the sensually evocative terms invoked by the narrator to describe it. He seems eager to control a landscape that otherwise ever escapes his will and produces a gendered setting into which direct sexual activity is often displaced. Immediately after Venters discovers the Masked Rider is Bess, not a boy—having opened her shirt to nurse the wound he made and discovering her breasts—he carries her to safety:

His concern was to avoid jarring the girl and to hide his trail. Gaining the narrow canon, he turned and held close to the wall till he reached his hiding-place. When he entered the dense thicket of oaks he was hard put to it to force a way through. But he held his burden almost upright, and by slipping sidewise and bending the saplings he got in. Through sage and grass he hurried to the grove of silver spruces. (46)

Shortly thereafter, thinking of Bess, he "penetrate[s] the thicket" (53), and every subsequent time he must check her wound, the landscape is suddenly feminized (91–92). Citing such instances becomes a bit like critical leering, but the larger point is that the narrative itself indulges in such sexual innuendo, whether here directly or less straightforwardly in the sensuous descriptions of purple sage.[16]

Venters's discovery of his affection for Bess is directly identified with the exploration of his high country retreat: "She fitted harmoniously into that wonderful setting; she was like Surprise Valley—wild and beautiful" (142). Likewise, Jane "resembles" the "wild, austere" land of purple sage (19). At the end of the novel, a wounded Lassiter and an exhausted Jane will struggle up to Surprise Valley, implicitly recognizing the physical correlative to their entrance into a marital relationship. And the imagery is once more suggestive:

A glistening, wonderful bare slope, with little holes, swelled up and up to lose itself in a frowning yellow cliff. Jane closely watched her steps and climbed behind Lassiter. He moved slowly. Perhaps he was only husbanding his strength. But she saw drops of blood on the stone and then she knew. They climbed and climbed without looking back. Her breast labored; she began to feel as if little points of fiery steel were penetrating her side into her lungs. She heard the panting of Lassiter and the quicker panting of the dogs. (263)

Perhaps the passage requires no comment, except to note how thoroughly humans and their inanimate understudies have been intertwined. Significantly, however, the landscape is once again imbued with a latent eroticism that is not identified as specifically female. In turn, both sexes are depicted responding physically and emotionally to its sensual allure, with women as well as men vainly endeavoring to curb their responses. The open space of wilderness evokes not agoraphobic fear but erotic release, eliciting from the body that libidinous energy associated by Freud not with unbounded space but its opposite: the closed room.

Clearly, Grey's sage-covered landscape differs radically from that of his predecessors (Wister's realm of Rocky Mountain silence, say, or Cooper's Adirondeck conduct book), even though all share the assumption that the West is a setting for self-transformation in which characters reflecting *on* the landscape find themselves gradually reflected *in* it. That mutual identity of character and landscape is not always apparent at first, or must be achieved, as David Gamut shows in *The Last of the Mohicans* and the narrator of *The Virginian* realizes. This may explain why some of Grey's characters vainly spend time taming the wilderness into forms of domestic space. Venters struggles for scores of pages to build a rustic "home" in the wild for Bess just as Jane is concerned in more luxurious circumstances to make "a real home" for Fay (115). Yet *Riders of the Purple Sage* unsettles the possibility that space might actually *be* domesticated, delighting instead in vertiginous dislocations and maze-like misdirections more confusing than anything even Cooper had imagined in the nightmarish vision of *The Last of the Mohicans*. At this point, it is worth asking what can possibly be gained by such a bewildering strategy, of eroticized fictional landscape posed as displaced home yet baffling ordeal.

One thing is certain: the reader is led along as much by the syntax of Grey's unfolding landscape as by its Escheresque allure—as much by the riddles of the narrator's purple prose as by the topographical improbabilities of purple sage. And a conspicuous reason the terrain succeeds in mystifying as it does is that we are swept along by the language through a suasive mix of dependent clauses, repetitive prepositional phrases, and "colored" modifiers. At times, the narrator persistently reiterates a single adjective as a way of apparently offering the reader a stylistic still point to orientate perceptions:

Perceptions flashed upon him, the faint, cold touch of the breeze, a cold, silvery tinkle of flowing water, a cold sun shining out of a cold sky, song of birds and laugh of chil-   133 dren, coldly distant. Cold and intangible were all things in earth and heaven. Colder and tighter stretched the skin over his face; colder and harder grew the polished butts of his guns; colder and steadier became his hands. . . . (205)

On other occasions, the narrator shifts to active verbs and gerunds that persistently suspend the subject, floating it (or him, in this case) ever onward to the next clause:

Bounding swiftly away, Venters fled around the corner, across the street, and, leaping a hedge, he ran through the yard, orchard, and garden to the sage. Here, under cover of the tall brush, he turned west and ran on to the place where he had hidden his rifle. Securing that, he again set out into a run, and, circling through the sage, came up behind Jane Withersteen's stable and corrals. With laboring, dripping chest, and pain as of a knife thrust in his side, he stopped to regain his breath, and while resting his eyes roved around in search of a horse. (241)

In the continuous eros of spectation, the reader is nearly as breathless as Venters and must also pause to collect him- or herself. Everywhere, the novel works to instill the sensation of helpless capitulation—a feeling of being stroked or seduced—that contributes to the unsettling aspects of a mysterious plot, as if language were conspiring with narrative somehow against the reader. That pattern is only a more forceful version of a strand that will frequently characterize the Western, but to understand it more fully we need to turn back to a literary history Grey at once copied and recast.

Captivity and Self-Transformation

Surprising as it may seem, Westerns differ little in basic structure from other popular genres. Mysteries, spy movies, detective novels, thrillers, science fiction, even romance adventures also tend to work from the resumption of an originating crime, a "plot" in need of detection, requiring one to follow trails, extract secrets, interpret signs. As Roland Barthes has pointed out, all fiction operates through a hermeneutic code that constitutes "the various (formal) terms by which an enigma can be distinguished, suggested, formulated, held in suspense, and finally disclosed."[17] One of the features that does distinguish the Western from other genres, however, is its characteristic positioning of the necessary "enigma" somewhere else, on the outside, beyond the immediate locale. Instead of the threat of plot emerging within one's midst (the murdering butler, the Russian mole), Western characters post themselves against forces from without, represented by aliens bent on incorporating all to themselves.

Usually, those aliens have been represented as Native Americans, which explains the force of Leslie Fiedler's contention that "the heart of the Western is not the confrontation with the alien landscape . . . but the encounter with the Indian, the utter stranger for whom our New World is an Old Home."[18] To remain itself, that is, the Western cannot afford to abandon a benighted attitude toward "the Indian," since the less alien they become, the less reason remains for a genre committed to a reactionary view of cultural process. Whether or not Fiedler's claim is true, Westerns frequently arouse the fear of confronting an Other so deeply threatening to entrenched values as to imperil one's cultural moorings themselves. Like the engulfing aliens of science fiction, the Other in the Western forms a cultural threat not simply because she is an exotic menace but because part of so ubiquitous, so enveloping a group: Indian tribes, Mexican bandits, Mormon riders, outlaw gangs.

Anxiety about this threat to culture, so central a feature in many Westerns, seems more or less an American preoccupation, explained in part by the recognition that American cultural identity originates as a matter of choice. "Being an American is not something to be inherited so much as something to be achieved," Perry Miller once proclaimed, which may sound like a strange premise to Italians, Chinese, Moroccans, and others for whom culture is less a question of choice than a predetermined convergence of race and birth.[19] Americans have been inordinately anxious about their culture *as* a culture—as foreign visitors for centuries have observed—if only because forms of that culture appear to have emerged more from common agreement than historical necessity. A freedom of self-determination involves a corresponding fear of mistaken choice.

One symptom of this anxiety has been the broad appeal of the captivity narrative, by far the most popular fictional genre in America through the eighteenth century and in various other forms a continuing fictional structure up to today. Based upon a residual belief that other cultures represent forms of psychic entrapment, the captivity narrative could not help but become self-conscious about the idea of culture itself, with the prevalence of a "captivity plot" in recent Hollywood films suggesting this narrative legacy remains a persistent anxiety.[20] In general, popular texts suggest that part of what being American has long meant is fear of cultural loss—a fear only to be allayed by recasting the traumatic scene of external threat, to confirm one's culture as not simply a matter of choice but of choice well-made.

The captivity narrative established initial conventions for depicting threats of violation that have continued ever since, stressing the transfigurative effect of alien setting as much as of alien beings. The emphasis Cooper and Grey set upon landscape description, then, corresponds to the exorbitant demands that the frontier has always been imagined as making, both psychological and physical. And the Western would further engage the prospect of personal transformation by adapting the captivity narrative's scenario of altering individuals against their will by a combination of savage abuse and oppressive environmental conditions. The earliest such account, Cabéza de Vaca's *Relàçion* (1542), depicts eight years of wandering westward, enslaved by a succession of native tribes, as a long series of encounters resulting in his own metamorphosis.[21] That pattern was reinforced in Mary White Rowlandson's extraordinarily popular *The Sovereignty and Goodness of God* (1682), which likewise relies on the premise of physical "removes" as a means of marking her transformation: "now it is otherwise with me."[22] Cooper revitalized this fictional paradigm at a time when the captivity narrative had fallen from favor by stressing the stalwart self-possession of Natty Bumppo, the "man without a cross," who stands between cultures without ever being in doubt about which one is his. As important, Cooper established physical torture as a test of self-control, to dramatize as vividly as possible the scene of threat and corresponding resistance.

If the persistence of the "captivity plot" suggests that Americans have from the beginning felt insecure in their cultural identity, *Riders of the Purple Sage* marks nonetheless a special moment in the history of that narrative form, appearing at a moment of particularly acute anxiety about American culture that the novel itself helped to form. That paradox—of Grey inscribing his own conception of American culture in a novel that claims to be only describing the way things have always been—needs to be unpacked in the following pages. But first we need to acknowledge how fully the Western in general—and, more particularly, Grey's novels—represented a popular response not simply to vague, generation-old misgivings but to an explicit set of emerging anxieties about the nation in an industrializing, imperializing age of new global power. The achievement of *Riders of the Purple Sage* lay in its convincing ability to explain his vision of America— of a place where individuals would be transformed in certain important contemporary ways and yet still remain recognizably the same—even as he convinces the reader that that vision is what American identity has always represented.

Becoming What One Already Is

Perhaps the captivity narrative's most important legacy to the Western is a lingering ambivalence about the risk of personal transformation, as if not only appalled by the prospect but also vaguely attracted to it. Frequently, the threat of being taken against one's will had been represented as a diptych, with the second if notably smaller panel illustrating the final assurance of newfound identity. This familiar pattern of narrative tension was left unaltered by the dime novelists who emulated Cooper, and (despite Harte's achievement) not until Wister's *The Virginian* would the diptypch's second panel be enlarged in the unnamed narrator's effusions at his gradual westernization. Grey adapted Wister's example and pressed even further, churning out dozens of novels in which the benefits of personal transformation were unequivocally acclaimed. Repeatedly, characters are more or less coerced into reconstructing their lives in the West, acquiring there the means to become at last physically and emotionally whole.

A powerful irony is nonetheless concealed in this stock metamorphosis, which represents less an attenuation of earlier strains of ambivalence than their confirmation. Like Harte before him, Grey exalts the individual's transformation without ever genuinely crediting the process, since unable to conceive what might be meant by truly altering social relations—and more particularly, by renegotiating gender roles. While Grey's characters learn to value behavior appropriate to their biological sex, then, as well as newly savoring the sexual nature of desire, their recognition differs only nominally from what they have ostensibly known all along. Transformation occurs (again, as in Harte) as a regeneration, an affirmation of what one already is, even if Grey invests far more energy in dramatizing the process as a redemptive one by celebrating the supposed mystery of true men and women. The force of that mysterious process is itself sustained by the attention devoted to masking desire, to keeping secrets secret from a narrative that continually demands to know. Even though desires throughout the novel remain more or less the same (and more or less hidden), the increasing pressure to reveal oneself—and the willingness to resist—makes it seem as if one were being transformed.

Riders of the Purple Sage forms a sustained investigation into sexual secrets, with the plot melodramatically teasing the reader much as the landscape does, persistently raising questions about what it means to be a sexual being. Jane Withersteen is the most prominent example, openly exploiting her "womanly allurement," her "grace and beauty and wiles," to win Lassiter from his vow of vengeance against the church (62). So unwavering is her faith that she contemplates sexual solicitation ("Lassiter, I almost gave—all myself to soften you to Mormons" [163]) and later pleads with him to "take me" in exchange for a promise of nonviolence (226). Strangely "repelled yet fascinated" by his "great black guns" (119) she persistently endeavors to strip them from him, only to be surprised when, worn down, he at last agrees. Yet seeing how he then becomes a notably "smaller man," she quickly commands him to don them again (215). For

137

all Jane's efforts to justify her behavior as simple altruism, her desire for Lassiter is revealed as a response to the same compellingly masculine "power over women" that allows the mysterious Mormon elder to seduce Milly Erne (217). Jane's inadmissible secret is that her deepest passion is sparked by the sight of guns and the threat of violence they introduce.

The novel sustains a paradoxical relationship between sex and gunplay, manifested with a certain sadomasochistic tinge in the "vague joy" Jane feels "in her very fear of him" (232). Notably, she falls into a faint both times Lassiter is forced to shoot—a charged response that not only releases sexual tension but occurs as a narrative ellipsis forcing the reader to share her perspective. Like erotic arousal, violent encounters invariably seem to occur somewhere else and must therefore repeatedly be represented indirectly, either through displaced descriptions of landscape, analeptically as flashbacks, or in the dramatically skewed terms that structure the one scene of direct violence in the novel: Venters's surreal, first-person shoot-out with Oldring. Violence is invoked by the narrative, in other words, much as is sexual activity, only to be repressed.

The counterplot of Venters and Beth presents a complementary experience, with the man's transformative gaze now focused on the woman, awakening her to true womanhood through both an emotional and physical conversion. Like Jane with Lassiter, Venters hopes to redeem himself through Bess: "if I can win back your strength . . . help you somehow to a happier life—just think how good that'll be for me!" (101). And during their interlude in Surprise Valley, she does shed her "stripling" (100) stature to become a suitably physical woman: "she no longer resembled a boy. No eye could have failed to mark the rounded contours of a woman" (142). At the same time, Venters himself is transformed: having "gone away a boy— he had returned a man" (164). Or as he vaunts to Bess, "I'm a man—a man you've made" (185).

The assumption behind this narrative deployment was hardly unfamiliar at the time: that men and women will discover in the West their true (and separate) sociobiological purposes. Anticipated in Frederick Jackson Turner's frontier thesis, Teddy Roosevelt's political speeches, and Wister's fiction, the premise of this assumption was that cultural meaning emerges through binary oppositions patterned on the central distinction of simple sexual difference. And if women are necessary to the definition of manhood, that necessity rests on a notion of gender as a biological given, not a cultural construction. Society (especially effete, eastern society) perverts supposedly natural rhythms, and true sexual identity can be recovered only in an unsettled, unrestricted West. The effect of Grey's (as well as many other turn-of-the-century authors') conception is to foreground biological imperative over social choice or individual character.

Grey reinforces the point through a decided accent on blood relations, and the scene that dramatically marks this theme occurs when Bess discovers she is Frank Erne's child, not Oldring's. Even though reminded that Oldring "learned to love you as a daughter" (242), she expresses (and seems to feel) no regret for Venters's murder of him. Her grotesque response confirms that lifelong parental affection means nothing apart from biological affiliation, as bonds of culture simply fade before certain natural truths. This one-sided weighting of the issue is silently reinforced through religious belief itself, since Mormon doctrine requires a recovered genealogy in order to "save" dead family members through the legitimation of formal baptism. As Lassiter succinctly puts it, "blood tells" (284). The choice of Mormons as villains is not simply because they ruthlessly "bind women" or steadfastly refuse to divulge secrets but because their attribution of a sacred value to biological affiliation corresponds with one aspect of a dilemma explored throughout Grey's novel.

The cultural crisis at the time most powerfully evoking this conflict of natural and acculturated traits was that of gender roles, of determining behavior appropriate for each sex. Controversy had raged over the topic for well over a decade before Grey's novel appeared, which also happened to be the initial period of scholarly interest in the teenage years. In 1906, G. Stanley Hall invented the term "adolescence" for a mammoth study of this developmental stage, openly addressing a dispute between essentialist and constructivist views of sexual behavior that was of considerable public moment, involving contentious debates about manhood, womanhood, the conduct suitable to each, and the best ways of ensuring a culture adequate to the two roles.

Contrary to what might be inferred from above, *Riders of the Purple Sage* stands in the midst of this cultural dilemma, collapsing together useful distinctions between nature and nurture. In part, it does this by emphasizing how fully Jane and Bess are *naturally* women even though they still need strenuously to become what they already are. The paradox is played out most obviously at the rudimentary level of clothes, with both women frequently dressed in male garb as if to challenge categories prescribed by the narrative. Indeed, Grey teases the reader at times by having the women cross-dress, introducing genuine uncertainty about their sexual identity. Lassiter is surprised when Jane changes her costume: "'If I didn't take you for a boy,' he exclaimed. 'It's powerful queer what difference clothes make'" (62). Likewise, Jane can still repeat at the end a question that has lingered

139

about Bess all along (despite her celebrated transformation into "full" womanhood): "Is this a girl—a woman?" The very revelations that the plot has struggled to produce must be reproduced, again and again (238).[23]

Uncertainty over gender identity fosters a more general uncertainty discussed above about libidinous desires and sexual activity. Jane assumes her seductive behavior with Lassiter is impelled by religious disagreement, not physical desire, lending weight to the impression that conflict with others can only be negotiated through bodily wiles—but the wiles of a body that finally cannot claim its yearnings for itself. Analogously, Venters assures Lassiter on first meeting Bess, "And the *hell* of it is that in spite of her innocence and charm, she's—she's not what she seems!" (209), by which he means not that she is better than appearances suggest, but worse—the Masked Rider, an outlaw, possibly a killer whose gentle demeanor reveals nothing of her history except to raise suspicions about her sexual activity. The process by which women become women in the novel is reinforced, incongruously enough, by granting them active desires they are then not allowed to claim as their own. Finally, it is as if women were being imprisoned less by Mormon conspiracies than by the narrative itself, which condemns them to bodies over which they have no control.

White Slaves

Only a decade separates *Riders of the Purple Sage* from Wister's *The Virginian*, yet conspicuous differences between the two novels suggest something of the dramatic changes that had occurred in public life. Wister's romance offers a largely Victorian conception of class and gender, as an upwardly mobile hero is paired with a traditionally dependent woman in a plot that intimates little doubt about the established social order. The novel's unexpected success combined with the immense popularity of the stage version spawned an enthusiasm for sequels that Wister was unable to fulfill. Film compounded that public interest: Western one-reelers had titillated audiences ever since the huge success of Edwin S. Porter's *The Great Train Robbery* (1903), and Bronco Billy Anderson had already become the first cowboy star. By the time Grey's novel appeared, then, the ground was ripe for the Western to be reestablished in a version appropriate to an era when patriarchal assumptions were promulgated less confidently than they had been by Wister, and when Americans felt far greater anxieties about recent changes in social (and particularly gendered) relations.

Any brief description of the century's opening decade risks claiming too much or too little: either overstating changes that had begun well before and continued long after the decade; or slighting the cumulative effect of such changes on a population more and more anxious about the continuing acceleration of industrial development, urbanization, consumerism, and class strife. Mark Thomas Connelly has described this transition as one from "a predominantly rural-minded, decentralized, principally Anglo-Saxon, production-oriented, and morally absolutist society to a predominantly urban, centralized, multi-ethnic, consumption-oriented, secular, and relativist society."[24] Among other developments, the general acceptance of shorter working hours contributed to greater demand for a new entertainment industry and prompted changes in urban living arrangements that gradually released young women from parental surveillance. Those changes understandably provoked a clash between traditional standards of family life and a new ethos that would come to be considered distinctly American.

The invention of the "working girl" and the "career women" led in this decade to what was thought of as the problem of the New Woman, a figure at the center of debates about birth control, new divorce and property laws, prostitution, and suffragism. Moreover, the middle-class impulse to control "excessive" sexuality led to increasing surveillance of the lower classes and a generalized scare about prostitution.[25] In fact, "the oldest profession" had become a matter of such grave concern that a social action movement known as the "Purity Crusade" was organized by a loose federation of women's groups, former abolitionists, temperance associations, and ministers, all anxious to revive traditional sexual morality through public means. The movement fastened on the problem of tens of thousands of independent, urban young women, often of immigrant parents, who came to dominate the workforce during this period—a period of increasing sexual freedom and decreasing privacy.[26] It seemed obvious to many that sexual immorality was linked to a new contagion of venereal diseases, and a surprising rash of pronouncements appeared in the form of federal investigations and state inquiries, urban vice commission reports, Supreme Court decisions and presidential fiats, even best-selling tracts and novels, all opening up the discussion of contemporary sexual mores.

The Progressive era represented a newfound faith in the power of social science to cure age-old civic ills, and this outburst of official surveys was prompted by the need for statistics to justify broad corrective measures. The Social Purity movement, then, embodied a serious effort to restore to women control over their own sexuality by redefining sexual activity as a cultural construction, not a biological imperative, and thus behavior subject to women's restraint. Moreover, "men were to be held to a female standard even though, as many in the 19th century believed, women's sexual desires were less insistent." As Carl Degler has further observed, "No more

141

persuasive measure of Social Purity's fundamental concern for women could be imagined."[27]

Yet Social Purity activists were caught by largely conflicting demands, hoping to grant all women more autonomy in sexual matters and to abolish prostitution as a privileged outlet for men, even as they struggled to control young working women whose sexual behavior they described as "clandestine prostitution." The reason these demands represented dual agendas is that it was so hard to define what prostitution actually was. "Clandestine" prostitution, after all, covered a broad range of activities—from professional solicitation to simple adolescent experimentation, from outright adultery to affairs between unmarried people, and even activity well within the bonds of legitimate marriage. One popular magazine described it in 1912 as any "attempt to isolate the sensuous element in love from the social affections and family responsibilities it was meant to support." The next year, a New York physician peremptorily claimed that a prostitute was simply a "woman who will cohabit with any man for the pleasure it gives her."[28]

Obviously, women did not always agree. But conventional belief coincided with the view that sexually active women could only have been compelled for dire economic reasons. Or as the Illinois Senate Vice Committee report announced in 1913: "low wages are to blame for most of the immorality among our young girls."[29] Repeatedly, federal studies concurred that Progressive legislation should raise minimum wages in order to alter the conditions that drove so many lower-class women into "clandestine prostitution"—which is to say, into active sexual lives. More generally, this fear expressed a sense of growing anxiety among the middle class that traditional ideals of female behavior were being seriously challenged. And the evidence seemed to be everywhere: in the advent of new means of birth control, the growing resistance among middle-class daughters to conventional family strictures, the notable display of more aggressive manners, supposedly smart language, and daring fashions. In short, a strong connection appeared to link the large-scale anxiety that lower-class daughters were being led against their will into "clandestine prostitution" with the more obvious fact that middle-class daughters were being swayed from traditional standards. Powerful forces over which individuals seemed to have little control led to the development of a conspiracy theory that seemed so reasonable at the time, explaining why women needed protection, that it took the nation by storm.

Over the course of a number of decades, a swelling number of reports had confirmed (with little actual evidence) the existence of a vast international traffic in young women moved from country to country for the sole purpose of prostitution.[30] And the international agitation that began in the

1880s had led in 1904 to a treaty signed by thirteen nations (including the United States) pledging to suppress what had become known as the White Slave Trade. An alarmist mentality easily linked rising levels of prostitution, venereal disease, and immigration, drawing its language from the social Darwinist rhetoric of racial purity. The urban vice commission report served as a kind of twentieth-century jeremiad, proclaiming a new class of sinners, divulging the clear and present danger they offered to public welfare. Americans became so panic-stricken that, in 1910, Congress passed the White Slave Traffic Act (more commonly known as the Mann Act, after its sponsor, James Mann of Illinois), which allowed for the surveillance of immigrant women and the arrest of any man who kept more than one woman in a house.[31]

Only a year before, a highly popular genre that became known as the white slavery tract had made its appearance. Such tracts were a fictional species of salacious vice-commission reports that detailed how innocent girls became prostitutes not because of low wages but because of a powerful, all-encompassing conspiracy controlled by foreigners. Again, the genre clearly drew on the Indian captivity narrative, with rural women abducted to urban wildernesses and held sexually against their wills. Books like Reginald Kauffman's best-selling *The House of Bondage* (1910) or Clifford Roe's *The Girl Who Disappeared* (1914) were transformed into popular movies that emphasized a strident conspiratorial mentality. Groups of slavers worked together, "aiding each other brazenly" (in the words of the tract cited in the epigraph), leaving "a girl in the clutches of any one of them [with] practically no chance of escape, since the agents of all of them are on the lookout." Sleepless, ever-watchful captors rivet their attention on young women—"their eyes are everywhere"—in a pattern curiously similar to that of the readers of tracts themselves. Indeed, the tracts (and films made from them) play out a paradox common to this form of inquiry, in requiring a combination of sexual dread and sexual curiosity by imagining women forced into compromising positions. Perhaps the most significant consequence of this contemporary fervor was the appearance of a film that not only used sex openly as a major ingredient but was "blatantly exploitive": *Traffic in Souls* (1913). According to Garth Jowett, "the incredible success of this film has been credited by many film historians with ensuring that sexual themes became an industry staple."[32]

Just as curious a feature of the genre as its sexually explicit nature is the level of conspiratorial intention represented in white slavers who are ceaselessly vigilant, ever prepared to abduct young women whose own vigilance lapses.[33] With a minimum gesture to evidence, the tracts claimed anywhere from 40 to 100 percent of all prostitutes were held as white slaves, kept forcibly against their will in houses of ill fame. The pervasiveness of this conviction, especially given the paucity of convincing proof, suggests parallels with other sustained moments of cultural psychosis in American history, beginning with the Salem witchcraft trials of the 1690s and extending through the Illuminati alarm of the 1790s, the Masonic conspiracy menace of the 1820s, the anti-Mormon legislation of the 1880s, and the McCarthy hearings in the 1950s.[34] Yet these parallels do not help clarify the particular frenzy with which Americans in the Progressive era felt that standards of sexual behavior were being threatened, nor the extent to which such fears were apparently resolved through forms of popular culture—even forms conspicuously removed from the subject of white slavery tracts.

Westerns and Tracts

Riders of the Purple Sage appeared in the midst of this cultural ferment, this paranoid fear of a worldwide plot to erode American sexual mores. Grey, in fact, rewrites the white slavery tracts, giving us three separate plots of women abducted, enslaved, or under threat: first, Lassiter's sister taken by Bishop Dyer ("the man who dragged Milly Erne to hell" [61]), who then in turn abducts her daughter; second, Jane Withersteen pursued by these conspiratorial powers while her adopted daughter, Fay, is likewise snatched away; and third, Bess Erne (Milly's grown daughter) seized by Venters from her foster parent, the outlaw Oldring ("who had held a girl in bondage, who had used her to his infamous ends" [94]). Each of these women might have come to the realization given to Jane: "She asked only the divine right of all women—freedom; to love and to live as her heart willed. And yet prayer and her hope were vain" (25). In short, Grey replaces the panderers of the white slavery tracts with equally ruthless Mormons whose practice of polygamy is likened to enforced female slavery.[35]

Even more striking analogies emerge when one compares the fate of women captured by Grey's Mormons with that of young country maidens ensnared by white slavers. In both cases, the female body is reduced to a supine position, serving as little more than pliant receptacle for male lust. Female desire in each species of narrative is signaled only to be denied. As Mary Brandt pleads with Jane: "Marry Tull and be one of us. . . . You'll feel no rapture as his wife—but think of Heaven! Mormon women don't marry for what they expect on earth" (72). Likewise, the working-class women whose mores were being so closely investigated—in either official reports or the more salacious fictional tracts—were granted no self-determining sexual pleasure. And in both tracts and novel, environmental descriptions serve at least in part as displacement, standing in metonymically for the sexual allure that both men and women might otherwise feel—either the lush decor of rooms in which white slavers supposedly worked their wiles or the sensual Utah landscape in which Grey's characters are immersed.

Grey's signal achievement, however (akin to Cooper's and Wister's), is that despite narrative and structural similarities, it is hard to tell whether *Riders of the Purple Sage* supports or subverts the popular tracts—whether it seeks to confirm or deny their reactionary vision of female sexuality. True, the novel functions much of the time like the tracts, as a voyeuristic account: most obviously in recounting Venters's wounding of Bess, opening her shirt and seeing "the graceful, beautiful swell of a woman's breast!" (45)—a sight rehearsed repeatedly in the days to come (48, 92–93). Moreover, this shooting ironically enacts–if now benignly–the white-slave description of young country girls, drugged and taken to a guarded house. Her words to him upon awakening likewise echo a refrain from the tracts: "Do what—you want—with me" (79; see also 160). And his refusal to take advantage of her traces a common plot, of rescuing the compromised maiden from men who have compelled her to work as the Masked Rider. As if to mark this borrowed strain and keep our suspicions aroused, Venters expresses constant doubts about her actual innocence.

Against the standard plot of white slavery tracts, the novel encourages a set of ambivalent readings, silently raising the question, for instance, of whether Venters has genuinely saved Bess or in shooting her has only succeeded in isolating her from her "family." A starker, more important ambivalence occurs in the novel's view of women as captured, compelled, bound against their wills, and finally enslaved in forms of behavior they do not have to admit to relishing. Bess is the exemplary embodiment of this narrative oscillation, and (tellingly, once again) her situation is best depicted in Venters's reflections about her:

Oldring's Masked Rider sat before him, a girl dressed as a man. She had been made to ride at the head of infamous forays and drives. She had been imprisoned for many months of her life in an obscure cabin. At times the most vicious of men had been her companions; and the vilest of women, if they had not been permitted to approach her, had, at least, cast their shadows over her. But—but in spite of all this—there thundered at Venters some truth that lifted its voice higher than the clamoring facts of dishonor, some truth that was the very life of her beautiful eyes; and it was innocence. (109)

Innocence and dishonor collapse here as a viable distinction, with Venters acknowledging that Bess has been transformed against her will ("you couldn't help yourself?" [101]) into what she most enjoys: a rider dressed in male garb.

Bess can, in fact, be best conceived as having been captured into manhood, and the premise of the novel is then to have her regain a female biology (a "figure," "curves"), while retaining her considerable skills as a male horseman—skills amply evident in the final race to safety, when Venters finally concedes she is a better rider than he.[36] His satisfaction in Bess (and, though one is forced to imagine, hers in herself) is due to the fact that she *had* been enslaved, which is to say rescued from the confining possibilities that usually exist for women, and transformed by supposedly transgressive forms of behavior into a more interesting figure.

Jane likewise personifies this oscillation in views of female sexuality, as both a woman threatened by bondage in a forced Mormon marriage and as a Mormon herself using all her "womanly allurement" to compel Lassiter against his will: "through her an evil man might be reclaimed" (62). She wants to "bind his hands" (126), much as Bishop Dyer tries with her, and succeeds by the end in transforming the leather-clad gunman into a domesticated "Uncle Jim" who "follers her like a dog" (241, 203). At once victim and victimizer, she suffers an inner turmoil about her Mormon beliefs that resembles the distress of the New Woman, caught between older patterns of sexual behavior and new ideals. Even so, to effect her aims she ends by invoking the same seductive ploys that the Mormons themselves have used against her.

Interestingly, the scene of abduction that generates both of the novel's plots is itself recounted ambivalently. Lassiter claims his sister had been seduced and abducted by a man with enormous sexual "power over women," a "quick an' passionate" preacher who "went after people, women specially" (217). Although Milly's letter finally confirms that she was abducted, the narrative recurrently flirts with the possibility that she ran off voluntarily and must warn her brother to desist because she is "with the man she had come to love" (219). Conflicting possibilities are kept tantalizingly in play, with Milly placed as the object of competing male claims (lover's, husband's, brother's) even as she is granted an abstract autonomy.

There is a sense, then, in which the novel celebrates the New Women by stressing independence of character—whether Jane runs the ranch at Amber Springs, or Bess performs as the finest "rider of the purple sage," or both women independently embrace the prospect of sexual love outside the bonds of marriage. At the same time, the narrative emphasizes the compelling force of the Mormon conspiracy—driving women against their wills into alien, degrading bonds.[37] It might even be said that the novel itself enslaves women, transforming them into helpless figures unable to control their own lives. Bess is left prone and defenseless through most of the narrative as she recovers from a well-examined wound, while Jane is repeatedly described as "blind" by the narrator as well as by Lassiter. Both women think of themselves in crucial scenes as literally "nothing" without their men—as Bess exclaims, "I am nothing—I am lost—I am nameless!" (157)—and both are willing to give "all myself" in order to save their "masters" (163, 226). In short, *Riders of the Purple Sage* looks longingly backward and forward, lauding the New Woman even as it warns of the perils she entails, as if to frighten a female readership so clearly drawn to its plot. The novel encourages a new era of open sexuality, of experimentation with gender roles, at the same time that it confirms the traditional stance of women standing by their men. The very secrets the novel so desperately wants to unveil, moreover—all secrets involving women and their pasts—are part of a narrative that does not require them and that continues quite nicely once they are revealed.

Duplicitousness

Grey's triumph was to create a Western so radically ambivalent that it resists its own structures of exploitation, at once spurring and reining in attention to the sexual politics that are its recurrent theme. By eroticizing the landscape, for instance, the narrator invests the terrain with a strongly sexual identity that seduces the reader as successfully as it does any character. Yet the narrative itself never transgresses established bounds of sexual decorum, and characters never willingly act upon their transgressive desires. Likewise, the novel seems to offer women entirely new fictional freedoms, portraying Jane as an independent rancher and successful manager of men, and Bess as the most skillful rider on the range. This utopian social vision is achieved, however, only as more traditional constraints on female behavior are reinscribed that emphasize women's fixed (and unequal) sexual identity.

The significant question left at the end is whether Jane and Bess are less bound by the men they have than by those they elude. Having escaped the "invisible hand" of the ominous Mormon conspiracy hardly means that other "hands" do not remain. As Lassiter attests: "There's that unseen hand of power, an' Tull's black hand, an' my red one, an' your indifferent one, an' the girl's little brown, helpless one. An', Venters, there's another one that's all-wise an' all-wonderful. *That's* the hand guidin' Jane Withersteen's game of life!" (181). And even this last hand, though meant by Lassiter as divine, is in fact simply authorial, encoding sexual difference according to the contradictory standards of the day. How that hand might make a difference is never explained, anymore than is the ambiguity of the text's own eroticism, which figures forth objects of desire in the bodies of men like Lassiter and

Venters, lingering over their surfaces and elaborating those features that rivet a heterosexual woman's attention.[38] Yet these objects of the New Women's desire are celebrated in terms that characterize the Mormon conspiracy, and their compelling erotic force works surprisingly like those conspiratorial coercions. The landscape, that is, serves warning that sexual desire is always at least bewildering and often a dangerous activity well worth avoiding. Moreover, the very exoticism of Venters and Lassiter as sympathetic men who nonetheless master the women they love represents a portrait only marginally different from the Mormon men in the novel.

So all-embracing are the social problems posed by *Riders of the Purple Sage* that the single response authorized at last is to retreat from the world altogether, apparently out of narrative itself. Venters and Bess ride off at the end into an East that remains undetailed (except for proleptic fears of that "big outside world with its problems of existence" [155]). At the beginning of the novel, Jane had feared the very "prospect of untoward change" that Venters and Bess find themselves forced to embrace, and instead "wished only to go on doing good and being happy" (4). By the end, so committed is she to living this banal dream of static social relations that she commands Lassiter to roll the Balancing Rock over the entrance to Surprise Valley, "forever."

The last word of the novel, "forever" closes a scene that itself spectacularly forecloses the possibilities of any other social or political engagement. One could read that closing back into the novel as part of an incipient national mood of isolationism, evinced in Woodrow Wilson's 1916 election promise to keep the United States free of foreign entanglements.[39] Or *Riders of the Purple Sage* might well be construed as an allegory of labor relations, starting with the claim that Jane was trained by her father "in the management of a hundred employees" (56), and then noting the problems she experiences with striking workers, labor consolidation and union concessions, a closed shop against Gentiles and the accompanying management violence involved in scaring her riders or stampeding her herd; in short, all the myriad issues involved in any rivalry with an "empire builder" (141). The novel, like other popular texts, engages a medley of pressing concerns more inclusive than simply the fear of White Slavery and "sexual anarchy," as a more exhaustive reading might show.

Here, however, it is enough to agree that Grey transformed materials Wister had only barely incorporated into generic form, reaching back to the phantasmagorical landscapes of Bierstadt in order to establish the Western we know today. Grey at once refines certain stereotypes (silent gunman, explosive violence, villainous aliens) and complicates the issue of gender neatly resolved at the end of *The Virginian*. Indeed, so radioactive has that issue become a decade later that the only solution Grey can provide is a falling rock to close off discussion—a solution that registers just how charged the question of gender had become and would continue to be for the Western. Grey delivered the Western over to more explicit treatments of sex and violence that continue to be its legacy (and that of popular culture more generally). But he also showed how a literary (and cinematic) mode created through a combination of familiar characters, resonant landscapes, and still confrontations could become the theater in which expectations for manhood and womanhood play themselves out. The fact that those gendered expectations are so often at bottom unconvincingly tautological hardly detracts from their interest; quite the contrary, the Western's ability to disguise that tautology and make the issue seem either natural or necessary forms its greatest gift from Grey, especially since he seems himself attracted so fully to other possibilities. Given the importance of his reconfiguration of possibilities for considering gender, however, it now seems appropriate to turn from individual texts to a larger exploration of the Western as it has persistently defined a masculine ethos throughout its variegated history.

6 A MAN BEING BEATEN

They that have power to hurt and will do none,
That do not do the thing they most do show,
Who, moving others, are themselves as stone,
Unmoved, cold, and to temptation slow;
They rightly do inherit heaven's graces,
And husband nature's riches from expense;
They are the lords and owners of their faces,
Others but stewards of their excellence.

William Shakespeare, Sonnet #94

Posture, gesture, movement, bone structure, ranges of individual ex-
pression—these inevitably suggest underlying social ideas and emo-
tions and motives in terms of typical form.

Constance Rourke (1942)[1]

I don't just do something. I stand there.

Clint Eastwood (1992)[2]

No other genre has men bathe as often as Westerns, where they repeatedly strip down to nothing more than an occasional hat, cigar, and bubbles in order to soak the dust away. But is that really the reason? After all, so much hot water, so much soap does not simply register the passage from barbarism to civility (cleanliness being next to godliness in the period when Westerns are set). There seems to be a deeper logic at work in such scenes, requiring the man to disrobe, put his body recliningly on display, then slowly soak back into a rejuvenated, upright condition (figure 11). And the pendant to the bathing motif is the customary visit to the barbershop, where viewers are asked to gaze at stubble shaved, hair trimmed, mustaches waxed, as faces emerge from suds to be slowly reconstituted before our eyes (figures 12 and 13).

These scenes actually serve as miniature convalescence sequences in which the hero is reduced to a prone position so that the camera can display him recovering himself. We watch, that is, men becoming men in the principal way the Western allows, by being restored to their male bodies. Interestingly, this restoration is different from the process by which women become women (at least as Zane Grey imagined it), since so little emphasis there is placed on bodily transformation. Granted, Bess develops "curves" in recovering her female identity, but more important to that recovery (and stressed far more) is the developing love for Venters that schools her in patience, deference, self-control. Grey's women learn how to become women through appropriate behavior, not appropriate bodies, which explains why his Westerns are as much conduct books for women as for men. Even more so, in fact, since the problem for men is already a matter not simply of learning how to act but of proving one's male body (or rather, proving the body male)—a proof that, ever since Grey, has required a series of ever more elaborate confirmations.

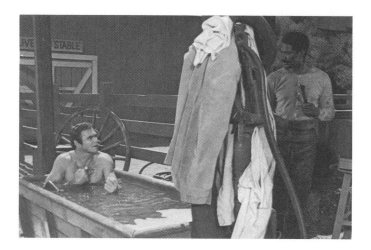

Figure 11. Sam Whiskey (Burt Reynolds) taking a bath in Arnold
Laven's *Sam Whiskey* (1969).

Grey's ambivalence about the New Woman was the shadowed side of
a larger question central to Westerns from the beginning: What does it
mean to be a man? The stakes involved in that preoccupation with gender
have altered with nearly every decade (as the Wister-Grey juxtaposition
shows), but a certain ornamental style associated with the question persists.
The sense of an ongoing problem in becoming, then remaining a man has
provoked a series of recurrent gestures so thoroughly inflecting the genre
(baths, barber shops) that they now invite clarification on their own, independent of more specific functions in a given text. The risk in such a proce-
dure is that strict historical specificity is lost; the gain comes from grasping
why a familiar narrative grammar of stylistic tics and plot turns should have
served the Western so well in meeting a history of contemporary crises.

Before turning to larger patterns, however, we should recall that the
emergence of the Western coincides with the advent of America's second
feminist movement, and that the genre's recurrent rise and fall coincides
more generally with interest aroused by feminist issues, moments when
men have invariably had difficulty knowing how manhood should be
achieved. Initially, "feminism aroused such furious debate," Peter Gabriel
Filene has observed of Wister's contemporaries, "less because of what men
thought about women than because of what men were thinking about
themselves. They dreaded a change in sex roles because at the turn of the
century they were finding it acutely difficult to 'be a man.'" As he adds, "To

Figure 12. Will Kane (Gary Cooper) getting a shave in Fred
Zinnemann's *High Noon* (1952).

'be a man' was an exquisitely difficult and ambiguous ideal," largely because
"purity and wild oats formed a contradictory masculine mythology."[3]

Half a century later, much as the conventional polarities of manhood
had altered, the difficulties of achieving an ideal of masculinity were just as
exquisite, the ambiguities just as tantalizing. At a time (following World
War II) when women had gained more independence outside the home,
men were increasingly anxious about the prospect of being "domesticated"
in the workplace even as they tried to become better helpmates in the sub-
urbs. And almost every study of sexual roles in the forty years thereafter
has been preoccupied with the question, "What makes men less masculine
than they should be, and what can we do about it?"[4] All sorts of otherwise
equally consequential issues through the century, involving class rivalries,
racial conflicts, and regional disputes, have repeatedly been deflected by
this concentration on the problem of gender roles.

Granted other issues engaged by Westerns in fiction and film, then, the
one question linking them is how to be a man.[5] That question cannot be
addressed by parables about the containment of women, since men do not
come into existence simply when women behave in a certain way. In this
respect, Westerns prove more intelligent than many a conservative cultural   153

Figure 13. Wyatt Earp (Henry Fonda) getting a haircut in John Ford's
My Darling Clementine (1946).

critic. They know, as it were, that keeping women in the kitchen does not itself transform men into Men. The alchemy for "making the man" is more complex, dependent on an intricate mixture of bodily and behavioral traits that results in a double logic of the male body visibly making itself, even as it needs to disappear *as* a body to ensure the achievement of masculinity. This latter component of the process may seem less obvious than baths and shaves, though it has been adumbrated all along in the posture of restraint first dramatized in Cooper's Natty Bumppo. Achieving that restrained state is never an easy matter, any more than it is to make such an achievement itself seem dramatic, converting a sequence of nonactions into a convincing display of masculinity.

The point is that masculinity is not evident *prima facie* in the Western—not simply a blunt biological fact (a matter of correct anatomical parts, as it were)—but is as well a cultural fiction that must be created, then re-created. Carol J. Clover has intriguingly observed of gendered roles in the horror film: "Sex, in this universe, proceeds from gender, not the other way around. A figure does not cry and cower because she is a woman; she is a woman because she cries and cowers. And a figure is not a psychokiller because he is a man; he is a man because he is a psychokiller."[6] If Westerns seem less forthright, it is because they oscillate between sex and gender, between an essentialism that requires the display of a male body and a constructivism that grants manhood to men not by virtue of their bodies but of their behavior.

In the following, I survey a broad range of examples to explore the arresting process by which men become men in Westerns, both fictional and cinematic. Beginning with the hero's body, the question arises why so much attention is paid to physical features, costumed appearance, and upright stance. The frequency with which the body is celebrated, then physically punished, only to convalesce, suggests something of the paradox involved in making true men out of biological men, taking their male bodies and distorting them beyond any apparent power of self-control, so that in the course of recuperating, an achieved masculinity that is at once physical and based on performance can be revealed. In short, the Western is invariably pitched toward an exhibition of manly restraint, thereby requiring the proof of generic excess in the form of repeated violence. The first step in this process, and the basis on which everything else rests, is the body of the Western hero situated always at center frame.

If Looks Could Kill

Among other seminal features of Wister's *The Virginian* is its narration by an outsider, a tourist on his first trip West who finds everything in Wyoming an object of delight. The novel opens with the unnamed narrator newly arrived in Medicine Bow, caught in a gaze of wonder at another man, overwhelmed by the sight of the stranger's "drop-dead" good looks:

Lounging there at ease against the wall was a slim young giant, more beautiful than pictures. His broad, soft hat was pushed back; a loose-knotted, dull-scarlet handkerchief sagged from his throat; and one casual thumb was hooked in the cartridge-belt that slanted across his hips. He had plainly come many miles from somewhere across the vast horizon, as the dust upon him showed. His boots were white with it. His overalls were gray with it. The weather-beaten bloom of his face shone through it duskily, as the ripe peaches look upon their trees in a dry season. But no dinginess of travel or shabbiness of attire could tarnish the splendor that radiated from his youth and strength.[7]

Then, referring to Uncle Hughey's marital prospects, the narrator avows: "Had I been the bride, I should have taken the giant, dust and all." As it happens, the narrator himself will be "taken" by the "slim young giant" on the long trip to Judge Henry's ranch. Before they set out, however, he finds himself staring at the Virginian: "But in his eye, in his face, in his step, in the whole man, there dominated a something potent to be felt, I should think, by man or woman" (9). The narrator tries to avoid making too frequent, too furtive glances: "But the eye came back to him—drawn by that inexpressible something . . . " (33). Indeed, the very syntax in which the narrator describes his scopophilic delight is enough to give him away, marked by the recurrent conjunction "but" ("But in his eye," "But the eye"), as if it were futile to resist the gazing slide into homoerotic desire. Later, his slack-jawed wonder at the Virginian's ability to win a bed for the night— by accepting an invitation to share the bed with another man—confirms what we have suspected all along.

Among numerous possibilities Wister initiated for the Western, perhaps the most important (and least discussed) is the male body itself, which is repeatedly presented as a desirable object, worthy of sexual interest. Even more to the point, especially for good-looking stars who appear in so many other roles, Western films focus not simply on attractive men but on their pleasing features in ways considered essential to the delineation of masculinity. One might compose a catalogue aria not simply to these male delights, then, but to those moments when the camera frames certain attributes in a fashion that seems generically distinct. Start with eyes: the inarticulate gaze of Gary Cooper, highlighted in over thirty years of cowboy roles (from George B. Seitz's *The Vanishing American* [1925] to Anthony Mann's *Man of the West* [1958]), but brought to a peak of intensity in Fred Zinnemann's *High Noon* (1952), as the cinematographer Floyd Crosby focuses on the diffident, anxious, scrupulous regard with which Cooper confronts a series of mutually exclusive choices.[8] Or the unblinking, steel-blue eyes of Henry Fonda, reinforcing on the one hand the stiff, emotionally vacant integrity of Wyatt Earp in John Ford's *My Darling Clementine* (1946), and on the other the eery heartlessness of the cold-blooded killer in Sergio Leone's *Once upon a Time in the West* (1969), not to mention a full dozen Westerns in between.

Turn to the lower half of the face: strong jaws in Randolph Scott and Joel McCrea, expressive of rugged sensibilities played off against debonair styles, combining manifest integrity with a certain airy aplomb. Long careers in Westerns meant both men defined the genre's cinematic aging, as they matured jointly into roles requiring chins be held high despite pain and hardship, until Sam Peckinpah cast them in his requiem-like *Ride the*

Figure 14. Lewt McCanles (Gregory Peck) admired by Pearl Chavez
(Jennifer Jones) in David Selznick's *A Duel in the Sun* (1946).

High Country (1962), where all they had left was the stalwart pose: mouths
stoically set. Or glancing lower yet, consider bodies themselves: Jack Beutel
as Billy the Kid, in Howard Hughes *The Outlaw* (1943/1950): according to
André Bazin, "one of the most erotic films ever made" as much because of
Beutel's muscles as because of Jane Russell's cleavage.[9] Whether he is
soaked in water and revealed in a tight shirt or saved by Russell when she
cuts the shirt off, the film self-consciously celebrates Billy's lithe body in a
manner that reinforces the supposedly Western emphasis on physical tautness and self-control.

This bodily performance is matched nowhere as fully in 1940s Westerns as in David Selznick's *Duel in the Sun* (1946), where Gregory Peck
flaunts a virile assurance in matching his body against that of Jennifer
Jones, whether stretched out on hitching rails or positioned on rocks, in
athletic poses more common in fitness studios than on the range (figure
14). With bodies as developed but with reputations still to be built, Rock
Hudson and Jeff Chandler appeared frequently in Westerns as bare-chested
braves, allowing the camera to focus on hairless torsos and muscular arms.
One could continue with other handsome faces and virile bodies: Burt Lan-
caster and Alan Ladd (in over a dozen Westerns apiece), whose cool reso-
luteness is revealed through muscular stances; or Paul Newman's and Robert Redford's azure gazes, both in half-a-dozen horse operas, confirming

the wry self-confidence and sprightly intelligence that made them a matched pair in George Roy Hills's *Butch Cassidy and the Sundance Kid* (1969).

From the beginning, Western stars have been celebrated for their physical attractiveness—for clear eyes, strong chins, handsome faces, and virile bodies over which the camera can linger to disclose what it is that supposedly contributes to self-restraint. This self-conscious revelation of character through the body is parodied wittily in Mel Brooks's *Blazing Saddles* (1974), when the camera introduces the newly appointed Sheriff Bart (Cleavon Little) by focusing in closeup first on his embroidered Gucci saddle, then (to the accompaniment of nondiegetic big band music) sliding up slowly from his pearl-handled holster past his open suede shirt to his brightly smiling, handsome face. Riding away from the camera, he passes Count Basie sitting at a white grand piano directing his orchestra; bending from the saddle to shake Basie's hand, he then continues riding off over the distant high plains.

The one possible exception to the Western's erotic deployment of male features is no less a figure than John Wayne, perhaps America's most important postwar symbol of masculinity (as Hollywood's number one box-office star from 1950 to 1965). Certainly, his trademark dark-flannel shirt with its placket front forms an icon of male power—its buttoned panel creating the illusion of a fortified chest. Yet even in earlier, youthful roles, the camera lingers on Wayne less out of sheer aesthetic delight (as it does upon Cooper, Fonda, or Eastwood) than as an investigation of the paradoxical gentleness of a figure who, at 6 feet 4 inches, 220 pounds, regularly dwarfs everyone around him. The mask-like cragginess of his features (hooded, slanting eyes; blunt, large nose; furrowed brow; thin lips) and the massive inflexibility of his frame (broad shoulders, thick neck, undefined waist) are repeatedly undercut by his surprisingly expressive eyes and highly inflected voice.

Whether as army officer, sheriff, or hardened cowboy in nearly ninety Westerns from 1930 through 1976, Wayne offered a smile, a forthright manner, and assurance—all establishing masculinity as at once proudly self-contained yet stumblingly responsive, both stiff and faltering. In the process, he offered a curiously modern version of Cooper's Leatherstocking (middle-aged, somewhat homely, rather garrulous, unromantic). Occasionally, in the role of romantic lead (in John Ford's *Stagecoach* [1939], say, or John Farrow's *Hondo* [1953]), the camera plays over his body in a way familiar to other Western stars (and interesting, of all Wayne's films, *Hondo* elaborates the treatment described in this chapter as customary for male heroes, by torturing Wayne's body with hot coals, then watching it recover

Figure 15. Thomas Dunson (John Wayne) and Matthew Garth (Montgomery Clift) in Howard Hawks's *Red River* (1946).

under a woman's gaze). More generally, in films for John Ford and Howard Hawks following World War II, Wayne takes a paternal role with figures younger and less experienced (figure 15). His very aging in the process of his career as Western star helps explain why he is so rarely subject to the kind of treatment this chapter describes as customary—an enigma that nonetheless warrants fuller reflection in any further treatment of Wayne.[10]

Otherwise, not only is the Western a genre that allows us to gaze at men, this gaze forms such an essential aspect of the genre that it seems covertly about just that: looking at men. To state the issue so starkly already suggests how problematic that process has always been, and it is no surprise that the hesitations, distortions, and evasions that accompany this male-centered "look" are customarily interpreted as a deep-seated nervousness over homoeroticism.[11] But if so, that is only part of the story. I'd like to argue instead that this concentration on male physiques also feeds a broader cultural longing for renewal, one that occurs in a special landscape (the American West) because that landscape is associated with personal transformation. Becoming a man (which is conventionally expressed as doing "what a man's gotta do") has been such a tired cliché of the Western that it hardly warrants comment. Yet this banal tag line of gender identity is tied up in the Western's focus of our gaze on the male body—a body that must, as I shall argue, be beaten, distorted, and pressed out of shape so that it can paradoxically become what it already is. The American West is thus associated with crucial transformations to an untransformed body— as if the West and only the West were a place in which manhood might emerge yet remain what it was. Given the nervous contortions aroused by the male body in any genre, however, how can we first understand the way our gaze is solicited by the Western—directed so often, so pointedly at bodies that critics assume are not worth comment (unlike the narrator of Wister's *Virginian*)? In short, why is the Western so invested in this bizarre "look-but-don't-look" experience?

Let's Get Physical; or, *Just* Looking?

One way to begin to answer this question is (as usual) by asking another: Why do film theorists so persistently ignore this particular "look"? Most in fact agree that classic Hollywood cinema operates patriarchally, ever putting the female body on display for the male spectator. Laura Mulvey opened the discussion with her influential essay, "Visual Pleasure and Narrative Cinema" (1975), in which she described the pleasure of film as one of a persistent sexual imbalance between "woman as image, man as bearer of the look."[12] That distinction applies not only to male and female characters but to the audience as well, where women have learned to look as men do. By contrast, films refuse to linger over men because their bodies, as Mulvey explains, "cannot bear the burden of sexual objectification. Man is reluctant to gaze at his exhibitionist like."[13] In short, both men and women viewers identify with the male hero in attending exclusively to the heroine's image—or so Mulvey asserts, and for two decades her position has shaped a heated discussion.

Feminist film critics claim that even when women are physically present on screen they nonetheless are cinematically excluded, since they only appear as spectacle or fetishes for the process of male narcissism—a process that never takes place directly, and therefore must be negotiated through the diversion of the female body.[14] Raymond Bellour translates that insight into a reading of film Westerns, which he argues are organized according to a classic Oedipal scenario "in which the woman occupies a central place only to the extent that it's a place assigned to her by the logic of masculine desire."[15] More generally, theorists like Mary Ann Doane, E. Ann Kaplan, Teresa de Lauretis, Tania Modleski, and D. N. Rodowick have prominently adapted Mulvey's insights to define the identification that takes place between viewer and star, usually concluding that any such iden-tification is more complicated for women than men.[16] Even those ready to challenge Mulvey directly, who agree with Carol J. Clover that "gender is less a wall than a permeable membrane," often find themselves, in Linda Williams's phrase, "caught up . . . in the either/or oppositions that Mulvey herself posed."[17] Instead of "proliferating sexualities," critics keep falling back on the notion of unified or bipolar sexuality, in the process flattening out the complicated responses involved in any cinematic experience.[18]

Given such consensus about the male gaze and the female body, it may seem odd that the Western so obviously celebrates the male body, as if that tall, handsome, bright-eyed, broad-shouldered figure who rides through our national dream represented some radical inversion of the stereotype.[19] But here we should recall the obvious: that film Westerns are descendents of literary Westerns, whose equally "shocking" celebration of the male body descends straight from Wister. The vision of the handsome man returns as if an obsession. Zane Grey (having read *The Virginian*) opens *Riders of the Purple Sage* (1912) with a description of Venters "tall and straight, his wide shoulders flung back, with the muscles of his bound arms rippling and a blue flame of defiance in [his] gaze" (5). Two pages later, the heroine's own "strained gaze" literally conjures up the novel's second hero out of the land-scape—a leather-clad Lassiter, who dismounts from his horse with a "lithe forward-slipping action" (8) that matches the Virginian's first movements a decade before, "climb[ing] down with the undulations of a tiger, smooth and easy, as if his muscles flowed beneath his skin." Later, Lassiter is de-scribed as "looking like a man in a dream" (16)—a motif sustained by Grey in most of his other Western novels, where he depicts with a lingering gaze men who are "good to look at."[20]

Literary Westerns thus invented a dream man, a tiger in high-heeled boots and chaps, and then placed him prominently as the target of all eyes. In no other genre is such an emphasis laid upon youthful male good looks, confirmed by contrast with the "comic old man," the old-timer whose aged lines, limping walk, toothless garrulousness, and ill-tempered petulance represent an alternative to the cowboy's twenty-something vibrancy (only in the Western did a troop of character actors specialize in this one role). The fetishizing mental gaze on youthful beauty that authors induce in read-ers, moreover, has the effect of deferring the onward motion of narrative in erotic moments of contemplation. Repeatedly, the presentation of the West-ern hero is accompanied by a sense of sheer spectacle, helping explain the often static or cyclical quality of Western plots. The fetishizing gaze tends to lose interest in narrative complications because sated with what it already sees, as John Ellis has noted in pursuing a distinction first tendered by Laura Mulvey:

> The voyeuristic look is curious, inquiring, demanding to know. The fetishistic gaze is captivated by what it sees, does not wish to inquire further, to see more, to find out. Hence those films which incline towards a fetishistic attitude, like those of Josef von Sternberg, tend to have cyclic plot structures, which repeat variants on the same scenes of desire and rejection. The fetishistic look has much to do with display and the spectacular. It is present in our enjoyment of displays of landscape, of technology.[21]

The entire history of the Western as well as of its individual avatars can be thought of as a "cyclic plot structure," replaying the already known in the effort to allow us simply to gaze.

Such concentration of descriptive delight in the male physique duplicates the Western's affectionate lingering over landscape—that heavily detailed, fantastic place we know as "the Far West." Or, to put it conversely as Homer Bannon (Melvyn Douglas) does in Arthur Penn's *Hud* (1962), "Little by little the look of the country changes because of the men we admire." If Cooper first worked to stop plot in moments of spectacle, the later Western more exactingly defines its landscape *as* "Western" by the absence of those familiar signs encoded as somehow female—the pastures, fields, farms, and more obviously schoolyards, church steeples, and store-window displays that signal the domestication of space. Likewise, Western heroes are described within fixed gendered proscriptions, precluding any sign that might encourage the male to be regarded as simply pretty, hence female. This pattern as well was initiated by Cooper, for whom male beauty was morally suspect, at least in white men. Despite Natty's progressive rejuvenation over the course of the Leatherstocking series and despite some narrative pressure to combine both youth and beauty in a single figure, Cooper refused to make his hero an object of aesthetic pleasure. That position could only be taken by noble Indians like Hard-Heart and Uncas, or conversely someone like "Hurry" Harry Marsh, whose Apollonian features are merely the sign of a narcissistic temperament. Ever since Cooper, putting the male body in an object position has required evasive narrative stratagems, as if in overcompensation for making that body not appear female.

All of this raises large questions about our range of cultural heroes and more particularly about the cowboy as an object of desire. Several reasons for that overdetermined choice are worth recapitulating: the cowboy's job, consisting of moments of excitement embedded in hours of waiting and riding, reflected larger cultural assumptions about masculinity, in terms of constrained violence; during an era of increasing anxiety over constructions of family life, he was conspicuously without family; in openly displaying guns, he appeared radically individual; in appearing to coalesce *out* of the landscape, he is identified with it. If these suggested a national hero, his repackaging in Wister's stories and Roosevelt's histories, in Charles M. Russell's paintings and Frederic Remington's sculptures, completed a heroicization that would come to depend less on what the hero was or did than with the way he looked.

Tall (and Silent) in the Saddle

From the beginning, observers have delighted in the cowboy's picturesqueness—a term that here gains a literal force in his capacity to encourage others to make him into an icon. Richard Harding Davis (himself notorious as a flamboyant, self-regarding journalist) exclaimed somewhat enviously in the early 1890s:

The cowboy cannot be overestimated as a picturesque figure; all that has been written about him and all the illustrations that have been made of him fail to familiarize him, and to spoil the picture he makes when one sees him for the first time racing across a range outlined against the sky, with his handkerchief flying out behind, his sombrero bent back by the wind, and his gauntlets and broad leather leggings showing above and at the side of his galloping pony. And his deep seat in the saddle, with his legs hanging straight to the long stirrups, the movement of his body as it sways and bends, and his utter unconsciousness of the animal beneath him would make a German riding-master, and English jockey, or the best cross-country rider of the Long Island hunting club shake his head in envy and despair.[22]

This iconic force was hardly a spontaneous by-product of signing on with a ranch crew (an unearned increment, as it were, of riding the range). Which makes it perfectly understandable that the most famous painter of cowboys should have been aware of how fully self-conscious the effect in fact was (figure 16). As Charles M. Russell observed:

Cowpunchers were mighty particular about their rig, an' in all the camps you'd find a fashion leader. From a cowpuncher's idea, these fellers was sure good to look at, an' I tell you right now, there ain't no prettier sight for my eyes than one of those good-lookin', long-backed cowpunchers, sittin' up on a high-forked, full-stamped California saddle with a live hoss between his legs.
Of course a good many of these fancy men were more ornamental than useful.[23]

If there is an odd reciprocity here between scopic delight and "fashion leader" self-consciousness, the intriguing element lies in the cowboy's preening self-regard—how much interest he has found in himself as an object "good to look at."

Such vanity seems remarkably out of place in the open spaces of the Far West, and only in part because fashion is presumed to be an urban,

Figure 16. Charles Russell's engraving of "A Center-Fire Fashion Leader," in *Trails Plowed Under* (1927).

courtly affair rather than a pastoral one. Yet it may well be that one of the reasons the cowboy attracts so much notice is precisely because of this sensitivity to the power of the gaze, of looking itself. He draws our attention, that is, by positioning himself as an object worth gazing upon. And he does it, as both Russell and Davis attest, through a close attention to costume in the belief that clothing properly worn conveys a personal, highly gendered meaning. Once again Wister has been there first, portraying the Virginian as a man capable of being "a trifle more than satisfied with his appearance." Later, in a long passage between the Virginian and Molly before they go East to meet her family, she draws attention to his good looks:

> "If you could," she said, laughing. If only you could ride home like this."
> "With Monte and my six-shooter?" he asked. "To your mother?"
> "I don't think mother could resist the way you look on a horse."
> But he said, "It is this way she's fearing I will come."
> "I have made one discovery," she said. "You are fonder of good clothes than I am."
> He grinned. "I certainly like 'em. But don't tell my friends."[24]

It has often been observed that the working cowboy depends more on a specialized garb than almost any other modern worker—so much so that his dress has become a kind of language, signaling in fiction the kind of moral, emotional being he is (the excess of two guns versus the restraint of one, for example, or the contrasting claims made by fringe, silk, leather, and silver). As well, however, the cowboy's elaborate, sign-laden costume permits the eye to roam across the male body without seeming to focus on that body as flesh. In Western novels as much as in film, the eye is trapped and held up by fetish items associated with parts of the body, as our gaze is directed from eyes, chins, chests, legs, and various muscle groups to articles instead that either cover or exaggerate them. Hats of assorted shapes and tilts (few of the proverbial ten-gallon variety); handkerchiefs knotted round the neck; ornate buckles, gun belts worn low, and of course, an array of holsters and six-shooters; pearl-buttoned shirts, fringed jackets; leather gloves carefully fitted and as carefully stripped off; leggings, chaps (with the groin area duly uncovered and framed), and tight-fitting Levis or leather pants (in the only genre that allows men to wear them); long, stylized white linen dusters; pointed, high-heeled boots and spurs: all the way up and down, the cowboy's costume invites and deflects our gaze, doing so in a characteristic moment of oscillation, of nervous distortion that seems ever attached to the scandal of aimlessly gazing at men.[25]

Reinforcing this wavering response is the cowboy hero's self-presentation. For despite a calculated attention to costume and otherwise flamboyant self-presentation, the most notable aspect of his performance is the effort to maintain an inexpressive persona. Self-preening vies with self-effacement, exhibitionism with restraint, as the visual "busyness" of his demeanor is balanced by a vocal inactivity, a sonic stillness that regularly offers a nearly physical pause in the narrative line (think of the narrative clefts registered by the stony faces of Gary Cooper, Alan Ladd, or Clint Eastwood).[26] So entirely self-contained is the later Western hero that he seems to exist beyond everyday commonplaces of talk and explanation, of persuasion, argument, indeed beyond conversation altogether. Valuing action over words, marking silence as the most vivid of actions, the cowboy hero throws us back onto the male physique, shifting attention from ear to eye in the drama of masculinity. Such an extreme laconic tic forms something of an ambivalent trait—a matter of knowing when to be silent but also an inability to make oneself known. In this regard, it is hardly surprising to learn that silence is a constitutive feature of narcissism or that resistance to language characterizes the reversion to a pre-Symbolic state in which the self looks to find its needs echoed back unaltered from the world.[27]

The restraint that the Western hero wears as part of his sign-laden cos-   165 tume sharply distinguishes him from other men—indeed, it requires the distinction of others whose lack of restraint provides a foil to the true man's achieved coherence. Talking too much or laughing too easily or expressing fear too readily are more than mere signs of bad form; they reveal a general inability to maintain composure under the pressure of vivid sensation. And in the recurrent enactment of such scenes of emotional excess, the Western offers a silhouette that helps construct its shadow image. The exemplary instance of such inadequate men occurs in George Marshall's *Destry Rides Again* (1939), with Mischa Auer's performance as Boris "Callahan" Stavrogin, the man who is garrulously unable to decide "what to do, what to do," who loses his pants to Frenchy (Marlene Dietrich). Up to the end he even fails to be called by his own name, referred to instead (despite eye-rolling objections) by the name of his wife's first husband, Callahan. A similar role was played that same year by Donald Meek in *Stagecoach* (1939), as the whiskey drummer Samuel Peacock, whose name and profession no one remembers despite patient, repeated reminders. His obvious fear of being scalped, played off against his gleaming bald pate, recurs as a broad comic gag. This role of marginalized man defined by hypersensitivity, social affectations, and verbal exorbitance was represented by Walter Brennan in countless roles later in his career—as the sometimes limping, invariably toothless, always interfering friend who talks or drinks too much, for instance, in Howard Hawks's *Red River* (1948) and Anthony Mann's *The Far Country* (1954). He enacts not so much the failed man (a role more properly defined by the villain) as an unworkable combination of masculinity and feminine excess.

Further tracing this silhouette of masculinity is the frequency with which the town drunk stumbles through the Western, and the stakes seem significantly higher when the drunkard is, as so often, a figure of education or expertise—a doctor, say, or newspaper editor, or even a former sheriff. It is as if the rationale behind such figures of complex talents and skills were that, unlike the hero, they fail to control their desires. Again, these professional derelicts appear most notably in *Stagecoach* and *Destry Rides Again*: Thomas Mitchell's Doc Boone and Charles Winninger's Sheriff "Wash" Dimsdale. Driven downward by oral compulsions into ever more drunkenly reclining postures, these figures of excess are posed against the upright hero who, in a scene multiplied countlessly in saloons across the fictional West, declines a whiskey, or orders a soda pop, or accepts a glass of milk. By withstanding the censure of a saloon full of drinkers, the hero confirms a claim on our attentions as a figure of restraint set against the chaos of non-men.

Not only do such barroom scenes display human foils that foreground the true man, they dramatize the cowboy hero's sense of being watched, of creating himself *as* a man in a self-consciously social process. That self-construction requires him continually to observe himself, controlling behavior in a world where desire so easily leads to social disorder. And in turn, that self-constraint helps explain the gunfighter hero's descent from the western gambler, especially as Harte imagined the figure. The irony is that restraint can only be demonstrated through narratives of excess, since restraint takes shape as a given capacity only by contrast with surrounding conditions. Without plots in which such control can be marched out and displayed—without scenes in which this supposedly masculine virtue can be needled into action, revealed in its strength, strained to the breaking point—the blankness of the hero's countenance expresses only blankness, not the deliberateness of prudent intention or the saving power of self-control.

The vacillation between restraint and flamboyance informs not only the Western's descriptive polarities, then, but its narrative terms as well. And if "narrative expectations are thus worked out through costuming," as Jane Gaines remarks, other expectations are also satisfied in a genre that ever denies it is doing what it does: gazing at the male body.[28] Even the Western's classical moment of unleashed violence is descriptively coded as a moment of displaced sexuality, when the prose perspective or camera angle turns to focus on a hand hovering over a gun. This splitting of the body into parts with typical "gear" offers more than a fetishizing displacement of inadmissibly homoerotic desires, which is my central point: the "oscillation" (of aimlessly gazing/not gazing) upon which costuming is based marks a potential for disrupting the body into costumed parts and anticipates the ways that manhood will be emblematically stretched, distorted, and slowly rehabilitated.

Just as the failed man offers a foil against which the true man's restraint can be measured, the ground against which this figure of bodily disruption emerges is the unfractured, undistorted, fully coherent male body, which the Western celebrates in the phallic image of a man on horseback, sitting high above the ground, upright and superior, gazing down at a world whose gaze he in turn solicits. The power of this image lies in the contradictory gesture of sitting yet moving, remaining motionless on display even while traversing the landscape, registering supreme self-control in the nonetheless energetic process of crossing (and recrossing) our field of vision, fixed at the center of the frame. Of course, it is also true that "horse opera" depends on a special relation of man and horse that vibrates with mythic sexual power. The fact that horses can be tamed and ridden, and in the riding seem actually to extend the body, is important to other displacements in the Western, where woman are also meant to be tamed to male domination.

That Centaur-like union of human and horse is sexualized asymmetrically in masculine terms, as Parker Tyler has observed: "The horse is not only a power-symbol as a fleshly engine but as an extension of the man's personal power and, more specifically, of his sexual power."[29] And the very fact of sitting astride a horse is taken in Westerns to be a necessary (if hardly sufficient) condition for manhood. As if to confirm that image's meaning is its counterimage, considered the most severe of "western" humiliations: a man pulled down from the heights to be dragged in the dust by a horse clearly out of control. Coincidentally, the scene itself involves one of the most dangerous stunts in the cinema (made famous by Yakima Canutt in numerous films): the phenomenology of the performance, that is, confirms the very anxieties the Western itself means to introduce.

Indeed, the Western can be reduced to oppositions between those who stand and those who fall down—between upright men on horseback and those whose supposedly "natural" position is prone. The prone are always revealed in the end to be non-men (a category that generously embraces Indians, preachers, Mexicans, small children, Easterners, and women). And the central plot conflict therefore involves those who try to act like men, with villains distinguished from heroes by being compelled to stretch out on the ground. Thus against the strong narrative pressure for men to remain erect, astride their horses, the Western imagines them brought low, tripped by their own inadequate masculine skills into lying down, either for the moment or for good. Even the predictable barroom brawl works to this scenic end, as a means of knocking men down so that they can rise again. Carried to ridiculous ends in B-Westerns, that process of rising before or after the final punch is given a scenic space in which we can observe once again the male body in ascent. When Shane (Alan Ladd), for example, recovers his feet in the barnyard brawl with Joe Starrett (Van Heflin), there is a mythic sense that nothing human will ever be capable of crippling him. Or again, in *Red River,* the colossal Oedipal brawl between Tom Dunson (John Wayne) and Matthew Garth (Montgomery Clift) suggests how difficult it is for men to stand erect by the relative ease with which they continue knocking one another down. Space is organized in similar terms through the inevitable final shoot-out, with the stakes involved in standing or lying down by this point having risen dramatically. It is as if the narrative energy of a genre primarily about men on horseback was invested in showing how easily they could be reduced to prone inactivity.

Getting Knocked Down

Scenes of violence are highlighted in other genres fully as much as in Westerns, but not primarily to provide the hero with conditions for self-definition. In the Western, that is, violence poses less a social or moral dilemma than an emotional one. Even Robert Warshow, who first broached the question of the genre's ethical status, found himself drawn (as if despite himself) to this strange conclusion. In a powerful declaration, he claimed that the Western "offers a serious orientation to the problem of violence such as can be found almost nowhere else in our culture," and that in "acknowledg[ing] the value of violence," the Western helps us understand moral terms by which violence might ever be exercised.

Yet then, in an apparent about-face, he went on to argue that

it is not violence at all which is the "point" of the Western movie, but a certain image of man, a style, which expresses itself most clearly in violence. Watch a child with his toy guns and you will see: what most interests him is not (as we so much fear) the fantasy of hurting others, but to work out how a man might look when he shoots or is shot. A hero is one who looks like a hero.[30]

Violence in the Western, in other words, is less a means than an end in itself—less a matter of violating another than of constituting one's physical self as a male.[31] The purpose is less defeat or destruction than (once again) display. And if this celebration of violence confirms it as a masculine emotional prerogative (that is, as an activity released and controlled by men), it does so by putting the male body distinctively on show. The shoot-outs, brawls, and scenes of horse taming, the shots of "riding herd" as well as assorted Indian chases: each compels a man to exhibit broad shoulders and narrow waist, allowing us again to gaze at masculinity in action.

Given the genre's celebration of the male physique, why does violence so often destroy that body, especially since it is one of the Western's chief reasons for being? What, in other words, can be made of the almost obsessive recurrence of scenes of men being beaten—or knifed and whipped, propped up, knocked down, kicked in the side, punched in the face, or otherwise lacerated, clubbed, battered, and tortured into unconsciousness? Consider this representative passage from Zane Grey:

But was that Cal? She saw an unrecognizable face or what had been a face, but now scarcely human, beaten and swollen out of shape, purple in spots, raw like beef in others. Nose and mouth were bleeding. His hair was matted with blood, and his shirt, that appeared torn to shreds, was black with stains.

Through seven pages of Grey's *Code of the West* (1923), we read how the hero's hands were "bruised, swollen, skinned raw in places," how "he was breathing heavily, almost gasping, and a bloody froth showed on his swollen lips" before he "turned his disfigured face to the wall." Later, he "lifted his bleeding, bruised face, and it touched Georgiana's hands, burning her with its heat."[32]

This powerful image of a face so damaged that it becomes itself a "burning" actant, an agent in the world, looks forward to many similar moments in film Westerns. But it also looks backward, rewriting a central moment in Wister's *The Virginian* two decades before, when Molly discovers the Virginian's "motionless figure" lying next to a spring, left for dead by Indians: "One of his arms hung up to its elbow in the pool, the other was crooked beside his head, but the face was sunk downward . . . and the man's whole strong body lay slack and pitifully helpless" (325–26). Unable to move his dead weight, she finally rouses him, only to hear the "clear impersonality sounding in his slowly uttered words" (328). Soon "she began to feel a greater awe in this living presence than when it had been his body with an ice-cold hand." And when at last home, "she undressed him. He was cold, and she covered him to the face" (333–34)—then to spend the next thirty pages nursing him back to health.

The repetition of this scene over the next ninety years in countless novels and films attests to the central importance of beating scenarios in the Western's construction of masculinity. And to borrow again from Carol J. Clover, if one is physically punished simply because one is a man, one also becomes a man by being punished. Even so, it is far from apparent why the genre takes such pleasure in punishment, offering up a vast panorama of sadomasochistic scenes that lead invariably to even more protracted displays of the hero's convalescence and recovery. Consider only three: Billy the Kid (Jack Beutel) in *The Outlaw,* critically wounded and unconscious, attended by Rio (Jane Russell) in the notorious sequence when she cuts off his shirt. To raise his body heat, she jumps into bed with him, though that only induces a fever that contributes to his delirium over the next few days.

More vivid is the Roja gang's prolonged beating of The Man With No Name (Clint Eastwood) in Sergio Leone's *A Fistful of Dollars* (1964)—as blood trickles down his cheek, his right eye swells shut, his ribs are repeatedly kicked, his bruised hand is cruelly stepped on, and he falls unconscious. The film later tracks his painful escape as he crawls under a long boardwalk, climbs into an unfinished coffin, and is then carried out of town. Slowly, in an abandoned mine, his wounds heal, he rebuilds his strength and recovers his shooting skills. Or more vividly still, the beautiful Angel (Jaime Sanchez) in Sam Peckinpah's *The Wild Bunch* (1969) is towed in the dust by General Mapachi's car (in a "modern" variant of the humiliation of being dragged by a horse). His face badly beaten and bruised, his torso and arms dreadfully lacerated, finally in a mortal stroke his throat is cut, full face to the camera.

Western films of the past thirty years have reinforced the violence practiced on the male body through cinematic style (though this, of course, is hardly unique to the Western). Increasingly, the "face" of the film has been distorted, as the standard cinematic image is broken up through a complicated series of telephoto closeups, zoom shots, flash cuts, deep-focus long shots, and a host of other fragmenting techniques. *The Wild Bunch* offers the most intense such assault on the viewer, with an extraordinary number of cinematic "edits" splintering the narrative sequence. With a radically different design in mind and making the close-up his signature style, Leone turned his "spaghetti Westerns" into a catalogue of body parts, tightly focusing the camera on sections of face or eyes alone, or on hands, guns, legs, and torsos. As if intentionally complementing this cinematic technique, Clint Eastwood (and later, Lee Van Cleef) performed in an impassive, inexpressive style, giving the impression of being deadened before the movie had begun. As Gilles Deleuze has argued, the cinematic close-up tends not to intensify personality or focus a sense of character but to void any sense of individuation at all.[33] Curiously, then, the spatial discontinuities of Leone's metonymic close-up have an effect akin to the temporal ruptures of Peckinpah's editing—in both cases, serving to nullify conventional assumptions about unified character.

Necrology

In this late phase of the film Western (with the advent of Leone and Peckinpah), masculine restraint has been heightened beyond what Cooper had in mind when he invested Natty Bumppo with a self-constraining temperament. Now that temperament occurs as little more than a sign of absence. In a world with no larger vision of progress or of a coherent past, rules no longer apply, and all that distinguishes the hero from anyone else is mere emotional detachment—a style that seems like nothing so much as death itself, with the hero's body become a corpse, as motionless and stark as desert landscape. In particular, Leone's "reign of violence" strips character down in scenes of walking-dead, where individuals only seem to come alive once they have been shot (and either cry out, or are seen to twitch). The particular success of spaghetti Westerns as parodies lies in revealing how the genre has always relied on some version of the living dead (even if characters have not always been so corpse-like). The theme is nowhere better expressed than in *A Fistful of Dollars,* when No Name explains his ruse to Silvanito (Pepe Calvo) in propping up dead soldiers (a scene quoted from Cooper's *The Pathfinder,* as discussed in chapter 3, fn. 22):

The dead can be very useful sometimes. They've helped me out of tough spots more than once. First they don't talk. Second, they can be made to look alive if I manage it right. And third, well third, if you shot 'em there's no worry because they're dead already. Understand?

In fact, Silvanito does not understand and is openly shocked by the notion.

Oddly enough, however, the Western itself operates roughly this way, tirelessly resuscitating caricatures into characters, reachieving a hold on our imaginations by revitalizing dead clichés, taking figures who "don't talk" and making them "look alive if you manage it right." Silvanito's response to this pronouncement reveals his own insufficient understanding of the way the genre has always worked:

It doesn't make a bit of sense to me, and I'm getting out. I'm alive, and I want to remain with the living, understand? And when I'm dead, I want to remain with the dead and I would be unhappy if somebody living forces me to remain with the living.

The Western, on the contrary, has always celebrated a certain necrological impulse, verging ever on the edges of death, invoking violence only to show how the restrained, fetish-laden body is not to be deprived of life but made to stand as a desirable emblem of masculinity, as a self-contained, animated (if finally inanimate) object. The process of beating the hero can thus be thought of as a kind of artificial respiration, raising his temperature and bringing a bloom to his cheek—even if that "bloom" is blood on the surface rather than just beneath. And what occurs as convalescence in earlier Westerns now appears more ambiguously, as the hero "convalesces" back into the white-cheeked, frozen-faced image of death.[34]

This late phase of the Western recasts familiar materials in a way that not only exposes the genre's dynamics but also has a powerful popular appeal. Slavoj Zizek has recently observed that "if there is a phenomenon that fully deserves to be called the 'fundamental fantasy of contemporary mass culture,' it is this fantasy of the return of the living dead: the fantasy of a person who does not want to stay dead but returns again and again to pose a threat to the living." According to him, the reason the dead keep returning is because they have not been properly buried, requiring a symbolic debt that still must be paid and then repaid: "the funeral rite exemplifies symbolization at its purest: through it, the dead are inscribed in the text of symbolic tradition, they are assured that, in spite of their death, they will 'continue to live' in the memory of the community."[35] While the process of literally rising from the dead never occurs in the Western (at least, in other than "vampire B-Westerns"), the gesture of emerging from the landscape is there from the outset, mutating slowly into a more uncanny form as characters and landscape are both drained of life. What had started in Cooper as an autochthonous motif of "natural man" in "nature's nation" has become a strangely emptied-out notion of men whose link with landscape is only negative, defined through a mutual inanimacy. And what we see in these late films is that the dead "'continue to live' in the memory of the community," a community formed by those whose refusal to let the Western die has become a progressively more ghoulish activity.

The reason this joining of body and landscape persists as a central dynamic of the Western is in large part because it helps define an ideal of masculinity. Various as the terrain may be—whether Wister's high Wyoming mountain reaches, Grey's Utah plateaus, Ford's Monument Valley, or Leone's Spanish wasteland—landscape description always defines the essential attributes of manhood. L'Amour's Hondo emerges from the Arizona desert as tough, ungiving, quick changing as the land through which he travels. Wister's hero is defined by the silence that is everywhere associated with Wyoming. Leone's No Name is chiseled from barren desert attributes, while both Grey's Lassiter and Jack Schaefer's Shane emerge directly from high mountain landscape, to which they both return at the end. Even Liberty Valance first appears melodramatically in what is patently a stage set—testament to Ford's late recognition of the Western's debt to the power of culture.

The persistent motif (extending back to Cooper) is that the hero is identified with whatever natural setting he inhabits, at home in the wilderness, familiar with its laws, capable of thriving in conditions that others find oppressive. Mastering the space around him fully as much as he does his horse, he nonetheless realizes how little mastery he actually exerts over either animal or setting, living in an intimate relationship that often defies any distinction of one from the other. To be a man, as the genre has it, is to be at one with terrain yet able to rise above it. The interconnections between landscape description and character portrayal are so closely aligned, in fact, that gender becomes a matter of defining the body vis-à-vis the earth. Narrative must ever work out the limits of masculinity by defining those who align themselves with the landscape (emerging from it, respecting its powers) against those others who simply submit to it (lying down, being put in the ground).

This link between landscape and death, inaugurated in the tableaus that close *The Last of the Mohicans,* recurs most compellingly in the Western as a process of bodies being returned to their source, forced back into the landscape from which they emerged. This motif helps explain the ubiquity of cemeteries in the fictional West, as settings for the numerous funerals and burials that punctuate its narratives. Each town has its own Boot Hill not simply because violent times require it, when men who die with their boots on must be buried. Other genres, after all, are just as violent without evincing a similar regard for the recently deceased (spy movies, say, in which bodies disappear; or detective novels, in which the bodies stay inexorably put; or war movies, in which bodies merely pile up). Even in a genre like the gangster film, where lavish funerals occur, the rituals of death confer no dignity upon the "dearly departed." By contrast, the measuring for a rude coffin, the digging of a grave, the lowering of a body into the ground, the solemn reading of a few last words, the depiction of mourners standing speechless or singing a hymn off-key, the slow turning away at last: all are part of a ceremony as central to the Western as the shoot-out or the lynching.[36]

The more specific, gendered reason for this obsession with acknowledging death is that it serves as a liminal marker in the construction of masculine identity. After all, the hero always convalesces from his body's disfiguration, and even Leone's living dead man ultimately rises from the ground. But the process of putting bodies *into* the ground reminds us of what it is he risks, and in the process reveals a key distinction between his sometimes deathlike mask and the actual fact of death itself. This distinction illuminates the frequency of cemeteries in Westerns, since they counterpoint the fetishized physique of the cowboy, identifying that signal instance when the body's supreme moment of cold self-restraint has become nothing more than rigor mortis.

From this perspective, it is clear that Western heroes are knocked down, made supine, then variously tortured simply so that they can recover in order to rise again. Or rather, the process of beating occurs so that we can *see* men recover, regaining their strength and resources in the process of once again making themselves into men. The paradox lies in the fact that we watch them become what they already are, as we exult in the culturally encoded confirmation of a man again becoming a biological man.[37] On the one hand, the genre advertises itself as committed to an essentialist ideology, showing how men are always already there, biologically fixed by the accident of genitals. Gender is repeatedly extolled in the Western as somehow natural and unchanging, often via an exchange between characters who defend the notion of heredity roles for men and women. From this perspective, men (like women) are historically found, not culturally made, and even if they happen not to live up to inner potential, that potential is never in doubt.[38] On the other hand, Westerns depend upon means that everywhere expose this ideology, relying on plots that demand instead the creation of manhood, then its re-creation. That ongoing process draws into question the assumption everywhere else reinforced—that a "man's man" always exists before the effect of cultural processes are seen. The double logic of this process, moreover, is echoed in our own oscillating response to the image of the male body violated—although before that response can be clarified, the question of who this "our" may mean needs to be specified.

Whipped into Shape

Film critics have, as if in choir, interpreted the Western's concentration on the male body as a disguised, displaced, inadmissible homosexual pleasure, and that the beatings so often sustained by the hero are to be understood in these terms as punishment of the audience for what it cannot allow itself openly to enjoy. As Steve Neale asserts of Anthony Mann's Westerns, "The mutilation and sadism so often involved in Mann's films are marks both of the repression involved and of a means by which the male body may be disqualified, so to speak, as an object of erotic contemplation and desire."[39] In other words, the erotic potential of the male physique can only be embellished when suppressed—a suppression regularly achieved through the open administration of pain. The director is therefore in effect said to be beating the viewer for what critics presume must have been socially naughty behavior.

In fact, however, it seems to be less the director than film critics who are in a punishing mood, warning viewers away from the screen by pointing out how its pleasures can only be taken as pain. This kind of argument, for all its evident political correctness (liberal, feminist, antihomophobic), quickly comes to seem indistinguishable from the position it condemns: the viewer is once more reminded of reasons for not enjoying the film, with scenes of violence serving as didactic instruments in the hands of critics turned schoolmarms, slapping the wrists of the viewer. Indeed, so hard is the labor to convince us that there is "punishment for transgression," that despite disapproving of the ends to which violent scenes are supposedly elaborated (the suppression of homoeroticism), such interpretations seem to sanction the suppression, affirming that those who "don't look now" will escape being reproved by pain.

The problematic essentialism of this view aside, it ignores the history of this cultural fantasy, especially as elaborated in the popular captivity narrative.[40] That narrative's central image was the prospect of danger as often to women as to men, with the implication that violation of the female body placed colonial culture metonymically under attack. John Vanderlyn painted the most famous of these scenes in *The Death of Jane McCrea* (ca. 1804), depicting a hysterical woman about to be brutally slain by a pair of

Figure 17. John Vanderlyn, *The Death of Jane McCrea* (ca. 1804). Wadsworth Atheneum, Hartford. Purchased by the Wadsworth Atheneum.

fierce, virile Indians (figure 17). Yet an ambiguity in bodily representation is nicely caught in Vanderlyn's composition, which lingers as fully over male physiques as over the female one: on the prominent, darkly muscled chest and back of the Indians who bracket McCrea, as if in self-consciously stylized frontal and rear poses of the male body. Their gaze directs our own to the bright gleam of her exposed breast, but the very posture of the figure on the right makes his own gaze ambiguous, directed as much at the other man as at the woman who holds his wrist. Moreover, the fourth figure in the painting, the diminutive, helpless husband—so nearly invisible in the

176

upper left corner that he seems to fade altogether from the painting—
stands as evidence of the insufficiency of male desire, in a position replicated throughout the Western, of masculinity yet untested, untransformed
into itself.[41]

Violence against the body has been a persistent theme of the popular
arts, elaborated with so much imaginative vitality that fascination rather
than fear seems to have been the inspiration. A catalogue of only a few of
the physical torments concocted by nineteenth-century novelists suggests
the baroque appeal such embellishments must have held for readers:

> Captives were nailed to trees to be consumed by animals, skinned alive, roasted over
> slow fires, buried in the arms of an already dead comrade, their flesh sliced off and
> eaten as they watched, sulfur matches lighted between their fingers, wooden splinters
> thrust under their nails, their faces coated with honey to lure bees that would sting
> them to death, molten gold poured into their mouths (a favorite means of disposing of
> miners), thongs slipped through gashed skin and used to suspend the sufferer, eyes
> plucked from their heads and the sockets filled with live coals.[42]

If we reject the argument that male bodies are tortured to punish us for
desiring them (whether we are men or women), the question then worth
asking is why in the Western it is men—not women, children, or other
"non-men"—who are made the visible victims of violence? And while the
answer to that question has been shadowing us from the beginning, to understand it we need to see what happens *after* the beating, when the body
convalesces.

The fiction of the most influential Western author, Zane Grey, can be
described as a series of "convalescence narratives," with plots that concen-
trate on scenes of rehabilitation in which true manhood or womanhood
is at last discovered. Dozens of Grey's books imitated his initial success,
The Heritage of the Desert (1910), in which the invalid John Hare travels to
Arizona to recover from the dehabilitating life he has led in the East. It is
the West's "isolation from the world" that ensures the region can serve as
the scene of self-repossession, and in a series of body-building, mind-
expanding, consciousness-raising scenes, John Hare is transformed.[43] Subsequent novels compound the "wound" of modern life by more predictable,
Western-style shootings, but always a process of slow recovery leads to renewed strength.

In his thematic obsessions, at least, Zane Grey might be thought of as
the Thomas Mann of American literature, persistently offering scenes of
sickness and recuperation, compulsively depicting the process by which
the body recovers not only firmer muscle tone but a firmer emotional tone
as well. *The Lone Star Ranger* (1915) depicts Buck Duane's near-death at the
hands of a woman whose affections he does not requite, his two-month

recovery nursed by another woman, then a prolonged scene of wounding and pursuit that keeps him in mental torture for days—plagued by heat, mosquitos, a festering wound, and deprived of food—until he escapes, and once again "in a couple of weeks he was himself again." Finally, losing a shoot-out, consciousness begins to fade:

Light shone before Duane's eyes—thick, strange light that came and went. For a long time dull and booming sounds rushed by, filling all. It was a dream in which there was nothing, a drifting under a burden; darkness, light, sound, movement; and vague, obscure sense of time—time that was very long. There was fire—creeping, consuming fire. A dark cloud of flame enveloped him, rolled him away.[44]

Later, recovering consciousness, he feels "all his bound body racked in slow, dull-beating agony"—an agony unabated by the novel's conclusion. Here as elsewhere, Grey is probing the borders of pain, narratively testing the limits of sentience as a means of investigating male sensibility reduced to a minimum.

The presence of Duane's lover, Ray Longstreth, by his side throughout his recovery constitutes another signally important leitmotif for the Western. As in similar scenes alluded to above—Molly caring for the wounded Virginian, Georgiana ministering to Cal in *Code of the West,* Rio tending Billy the Kid in Hughes's *The Outlaw*—the woman does more than simply nurse the man back to health. From a narrative perspective, of course, she represents the exemplary reader/viewer in attending so closely to the hero's recovery (often foregoing sleep for days in her heroic efforts). Yet the regularity with which convention demands that a woman be present in such requisite scenes suggests that narrative highlighting is a less significant aspect of her role.

In part, her importance lies as reminder of the psychological roots of male violence, if only because aggressive behavior is seen by psychiatrists as resistance to the threat of reversion to an infantile stage of development characterized by maternal care and woman's control.[45] She stands, in other words, as a vivid token of what violence is all about—the primary reason the male body lies beaten, waiting to recover. Just as significantly, however, she serves as catalyst for that recovery, a midwife between two states of consciousness, who ensures through a feminine presence (anxious gaze, compassionate gestures, verbal expressions of concern) that masculine restraint will be restored, unimpaired, to full strength. Instead of "signalling incompleteness and inability," then, these scenes register femininity as a gendered self-sufficiency the man must analogously reattain.[46] Paradoxically, the woman's gaze is both reminder and promise, evoking the developmental moment when manhood's violence first emerged even as it ensures

the hero's reaccession to full masculinity. Without her presence, his convalescence fails—or as Anthony Mann declares, "without women a western
wouldn't work."[47]

Originating with Wister, this pattern is obsessively repeated by his fictional successors, from Grey through Max Brand, Ernest Haycox, and Luke
Short. In Louis L'Amour's novel, *Hondo* (1953), for instance (as in the movie
with John Wayne), Apaches torture the hero with hot coals ("he felt the
pain shoot through him, smelled the burning of his own flesh"), and Silva
leaves a knife buried in his shoulder when his spent body is delivered to
Angie Lowe to be nursed back to health.[48] Putting him to bed, "she looked
down at the blistered and swollen hand, the lacerated wrists, the bloody
shirt," before beginning to clean and bandage his body and nurse him back
to health (129). The restorative female "gaze" at the male body, written into
the Western text itself, forms a necessary catalyst to the re-creation of that
body. By contrast, the death of the villain in *Hondo* is represented from a
startlingly dramatic, first-person perspective, almost as if the very absence
of a female gaze condemned the man to die: "Phalinger looked up at the
sky and saw the cloud fade and knew he was gone and he tried to speak
past the blood and there were no words, there was nothing any more"
(111).

It is in film preeminently, however, that the convalescent narrative is
visually displayed, clarifying its implications. The simplest forms of convalescence are most often predicated by a fistfight or brawl, usually in settings
where the primary energy of male violence can be dramatically inflated. By
stepping up the volume, adding strong (often excessive) nondiegetic music
to the sound track, and relying upon self-consciously elaborate camera
angles, films convert even fistfights into apocalyptic events, as though the
process of assaulting bodies were being transposed, recast into realms (of
sound, vision, music) having nothing to do with them. In Fred Zinnemann's *High Noon* (1952), for instance, Will Kane (Gary Cooper) is as-
saulted in the town's stable by his deputy, Harvey Pell (Lloyd Bridges). According to Carl Foreman's screenplay (in which Kane was originally
named Doane):

They punish each other mercilessly, nothing barred. The horses, becoming nervous,
rear and whinny in their stalls. . . . Once, Doane is knocked down under a horse, and
narrowly escapes being trampled. As the fight reaches a climax, the horses go completely wild. . . . Doane stands over him, panting and dazed . . . his breath whistling
through his bruised lips.

What Foreman's screenplay cannot suggest is how disproportionately loud
the horses' whinnying becomes or how aggressively the sequence of camera   179

angles shifts from beneath horses to high corner angles and back again. Nor can it capture the bruised, anguished countenance of Gary Cooper on which the camera lingers as he trudges off to the emotionally overwrought, mildly feminized barber to be washed and brushed. His haggard expression (prompted, as we otherwise know, by chronic back problems, a recent hernia operation, and a painful ulcer) is at once cause and effect of his beaten state—part of the Oedipal reason why Harvey Pell feels the need to assault him (thereby destroying the father figure) and yet as well the direct physical consequences of that assault. The filming of such beating and recovery scenes, moreover, makes us strangely aware of the makeup artist—breaking us out of film consciousness at the very moment Cooper reclines in the barber chair, prompting us to think, "Ah, now, he's sitting in the makeup chair, waiting to be reconstructed." Self-consciously alerted to how well the wounds have been created, how easily their erasure can be effected, we realize once again how fully manhood is always already there, just beneath the plaster and paint.

In *Shane* (1953), George Stevens presents Alan Ladd in a pair of exaggerated brawls: the first provoked by Chris Calloway (Ben Johnson) in Grafton's saloon; the second by Joe Starrett (Van Heflin) in his own stable yard. The cinematography of both scenes again relies on camera placement under animals, over swinging doors, through windows, and behind stairs, while the soundtrack is so singularly heightened that it seems like the world is coming unglued. That is the point of these hyperbolic fights, to shatter the seamless surface of masculinity by destroying the expressionless eyes and vacant glance that confirm Alan Ladd's mysteriousness. The film itself draws attention to that narrative pattern in the convalescence scene in which Marian bandages his head, when for the sake of Joey he breaks out in a (self-consciously faked, entirely uncharacteristic) expression of pain.

Other examples are rife: *Red River* presents Matthew Garth brawling fiercely with his foster father, Tom Dunson—a scene so dramatically powerful and at the same time so derivative that Howard Hughes successfully sued United Artists for having "copied" it from the final shoot-out of *The Outlaw*. Anthony Mann's *The Far Country* (1954) dramatizes the wound received by Jeff (James Stewart), his nursing back to health by Renée (Corinne Calvet), and his rewounding once again with the camera obsessively focused on his bandaged hand as he dramatically unwraps it, clenches and unclenches it, then at the end repeats the process with the image fading before the final credits. Mann's *The Man from Laramie* (1955) suggests in turn a convalescent cinematic sequence, showing Jimmy Stewart once again with wounded hand, now able to make a miraculous recovery. An even more elaborate example is Tom Gries's *Will Penny* (1967), with the

Figure 18. Ringo Kid (Marlon Brando) being whipped in Brando's
One-Eyed Jacks (1960).

titular hero (Charlton Heston) beaten, knifed, burned, and left for dead.
Having crawled back across the winter landscape in long underwear, he
finally returns to his cabin where Catherine Allen (Joan Hackett) nurses
him in a series of prolonged scenes over many days, stitching him up, bathing him, making him soup.

Perhaps the most spectacular cinematic instance of abuse to the male
body occurs in Marlon Brando's *One-Eyed Jacks* (1960), a strangely psychological Western that traces once again an Oedipal conflict between the
Ringo Kid (Brando) and his former partner, "Dad" Longworth (Karl Mal-
den). The paternalistic sheriff Longworth punishes Ringo in the film's
central scene by lashing him to the town's hitching post, then brutally
bullwhipping him before smashing a rifle down on his gunhand. Throughout, Brando remains expressionless, and even as he slips to his knees his
body retains its dignity while the camera lingers on the smooth face and
emotionless eyes that stay characteristically untransformed (figure 18). The
rest of the film traces his slow recovery on the Monterey coast, as his lacerated back is nursed by the quiet, loyal, feminized Mexican friend, Chico
Morelles (Timothy Gilman). Finally able to fit a leather thong to his gunhand, he practices shooting for long, aimless hours in preparation for revenge. The film, however, swerves from the generic demands played out in   181

Rio's brooding thoughts of revenge, as he finds his Oedipal love for Longworth's stepdaughter gradually transforming him. What betrays this newly pacific intention is his rejuvenated body itself, as if he could not prevent himself from carrying out the revenge against Longworth his body has so long demanded, despite a change in emotions that has finally committed him to a peaceful life.

The film that, as in so many other respects, forms the clearest example of dynamics at work in the Western is Ford's *The Man Who Shot Liberty Valance* (1962), at once epitomizing and undercutting nearly all the claims made in this chapter. The very opening of the flashback sequence presents Jimmy Stewart (this time as Ransom Stoddard) violently flogged by Valance (Lee Marvin), reduced to the same corpse-like state that Tom Doniphon (John Wayne) maintains in the frame narrative. As in *One-Eyed Jacks,* the film highlights his convalescence (at the hands of Hallie [Vera Miles]), but only to attain the status of aproned dishwasher and again to be tripped by Valance, revealed as ever a victim of gravity, bent over, crouching, prone to fall, in a posture of feminized vulnerability (starkly contrasted with the erect bearing of Tom and Hallie).[49] From this perspective, the film becomes a meditation on the Western's devotion to violation and recovery and prepares Stoddard for the genre's most clichéd scene of manly self-possession. His final, limp-wristed confrontation with Valance ends in what seems an improbable triumph enforced by nothing more than sheer generic demands (the sequence of beating and recovery itself requiring a scene of physical mastery). Ford's ironic double perspective attests to both the impossibility and yet the necessity of a sequence central to the Western.

Who Was That Masked Man?

Is a man's face and body little more than a gendered mask, in need of being destroyed and reshaped to confirm that manhood exists beneath? The Western, at least, seems to think so, requiring that masculine identity be pressed out of shape, initially deformed so as to make "man" all but unrecognizable. Or more accurately (given the way in which masculinity itself has been constituted *through* the body), Westerns treat the hero as a rubber doll, something to be wrenched and contorted so that we can then watch him magically recover his shape. His convalescence reassures us in the reachievement of a form we had presumed to be static, somehow inorganic—like Humbert Humbert's deflated image of "the rather becoming bruise on the bronzed cheek of the warmed-up hero" after "the shivered windowpane, the stupendous fist fight, the crashing mountain of dusty old-fashioned furniture, the table used as a weapon, the timely somersault, the pinned hand still groping for the dropped bowie knife, the grunt, belly, the flying tackle." The whole dramatic process reveals how the cherished image of masculinity we had dismissed as simply *learned* behavior is in fact a resilient, vital, biological process. Stretching of the body proves the body's *natural* essence, and all the leather, spurs, chaps, pistols, handkerchiefs, and hats may now be excused as dead talismans. In this, they are a kind of fetish to the highest power since they "hide" a male body that has proved itself coherent. The compensatory satisfaction they offer is no longer really necessary since the physique they disguise has revealed itself as unmistakably male.

Yet the contradiction of the Western is that masculinity is always more than physical, and that in favoring an ideal of restraint well beyond bodily considerations it reveals how manhood is as much learned as found. Restraint, of course, is essential to our most fundamental ideals of selfhood even as it poses a concept difficult to represent. Therefore, the Western signals restraint always *through* the body, in its vacillations and hesitations under the threat of danger—in eyes alerted to peril, or shoulders stiffened in response to a verbal slight, or the gesture of a hand hovering over a gunbelt. Before restraint can be said to exist dramatically, in other words, it needs to be needled, stretched, otherwise exacerbated by the continuing threat of violence.

The point of violence directed at a physical body is to arouse a tension that allows an emotional self to exhibit its capacity for restraint. In that mutual pressure of threat and restraint, the terrain is mapped in which masculinity in the Western is ever contested. Because no particular form of behavior happens to be prescribed by the genre, however, the disparity between hero and villain is less a matter of defined characteristics than of maintaining different capacities in a certain fragile balance. As Martin Pumphrey has observed (in the passage quoted near the end of Chapter 1 above), heroes succeed in incorporating both stereotypically feminine and masculine traits, bridging "the anxiously guarded (ambiguously experienced) frontier between the two worlds usually coded as masculine and feminine." In short, the terms of masculinity are always essayed if never quite resolved in the Western, a lack of resolution that itself contributes to the genre's appeal.

Despite lingering over tableaux, despite an emphasis on costumed bodies outlined against empty horizons, the Western's most intense investigations of the problematic of manhood take place out-of-sight and within, at select moments over given choices, as a performance of self-restraint against the imminent threat of the body's dissolution. Again, Owen Wister anticipated the pattern in *The Virginian*, through his contrast not of hero and villain but of two villains themselves, Steve and Trampas: the former, dignified by silent self-possession in his last moments before being lynched; the latter, demeaned by slipshod talk, flaccid emotions, and drunken recklessness in the hours before his final shoot-out. That contrast persists throughout the genre's long history.

Difficult as it is to remain a man according to the contradictory demands of the Western, there are very few moments when the hero ever actually considers abandoning the effort—and those ocasions are instructive. The Ringo Kid in *One-Eyed Jacks* foregoes avenging himself out of love, only at last to be forced by Dad Longworth into retaliating. Likewise in *Riders of the Purple Sage,* Lassiter finally vows to put aside his guns out of love for Jane ("I've come to see an' feel differently. . . . I've outgrown revenge" [260]), only moments later to be compelled into putting them back on for her sake, to kill Bishop Dyer and rescue a newly abducted Fay. In *Stagecoach,* Ringo similarly accedes to Dallas's plea to forget the Plummer brothers, who murdered his father and brother. His classic self-justification ("Well, there's some things a man just can't run away from") elicits her angry retort: "How can you talk about your life and my life when you're throwing 'em away? Yeah—mine, too! That's what you're throwing away if you go to Lordsburg!" Ringo agrees and is only prevented from abandoning his quest by an Indian attack. *High Noon* offers an analogous scene of Will Kane encouraged by friends to leave Hadleyville ("Think of Amy"). He and his new wife drive out of town, nearly out of the Western itself, before he turns his trap around and back into the genre. "They're making me run," he persists in explaining, "and I've never run before."

In each of these four unusual cases, the text actually proposes that the effort of continuing to be a man be abandoned. And it does so not because of bodily threats or violent beatings but out of a too powerful feminine force in the hero's life. The narrative demand for a shoot-out, which helps make these identifiably Westerns, is disrupted by the hero's slide too far toward virtues associated unequivocally with one side of that gendered "frontier" noted by Martin Pumphrey. In his possible abdication of duty, the hero accentuates once again how difficult it is to remain a man, how confusing the demands of gender can be, and more particularly how much is required in balancing masculine and feminine traits in the self one constructs as a true man.

Given how accustomed we have become to speaking of the self as a construct of language, it is clear that any threat of the self's dissolution is already a threat to its powers of self-expression. Intense physical pain seems incommensurable with language, then, for as Elaine Scarry observes, "whatever pain achieves, it achieves in part through its unsharability [*sic*], and it ensures this unsharability [sic] through its resistance to language."[50] A nice symmetry thus emerges in the scenes adduced above, of otherwise laconic, taciturn men repeatedly beaten, battered, and whipped, reduced by pain into only further confirmation of their apparently constitutional silence. Yet part of the meaning of the beating scenario, which helps explain its centrality to the Western, lies in the startling recognition it offers to those being tortured—of "what atrocities one's own body, muscle, and bone structure can inflict on oneself" (48). Scarry goes on to describe this uncanny experience of dissociation as a feeling of body split off from oneself (the self, as constituted in and through language), in which strict borders between public and private, inner and outer experience are elided (53). At their deepest, most secure levels, our self-identities are, as she points out, identities with and through the body, learned as a curious physical grammar (otherwise known as "body language") that is thereafter only forgotten with extreme difficulty. Given "the refusal of the body to disown its own early circumstances, its mute and often beautiful insistence on absorbing into its rhythms and postures the signs that it inhabits a particular space at a particular time," one can even speak, as Scarry does, of "the political identity of the body" (109).

More single-mindedly than any other American drama, Westerns focus our attention on the way in which bodies have absorbed "the rhythms and postures" of a particular region. And the curious aspect of that wide-open landscape is how fully it is depicted as a male terrain, identified as the "Far" West by its distance from a middle region of domesticated farms and settled communities. What the Western plays out is how masculinity emerges as a bodily phenomenon that is nonetheless cultural, and it does so by identifying manhood in characteristic ways with the terrain: as hard but gentle, generous yet unforgiving, inexpressive if nonetheless capable of being read, and so on. Yet to be absorbed into that landscape (through burial, or simply lying prone) is to fail as a man, since what the landscape also teaches is the need to resist it on its terms.

What comes as a surprise is not this "political identity of the body" in the Western—an identity that characteristically alters with each generation—but rather the fact that the Western hero is so obviously schizophrenic, split by conflicting cultural demands in the construction of masculinity over the past century. Ironically, that split in the tortured Western hero corresponds to the split we feel in the threat posed to his masculinity. For our fascination with the Western is over those supposedly masculine forms we want to recognize as biologically fixed—forms the Western nonetheless presents through scenes that can only be read on the contrary as bringing the biological into question. The paradox is always expressed once

185

Figure 19. Clint Eastwood as "The Man with No Name" in Sergio Leone's *For a Few Dollars More* (1967).

again in the amount of effort it takes to *remain* a man, whether Shane or Hondo or even a Man with No Name—the amount of work invested in reshaping the body, relearning the skills, honing the image, mastering once again the terms of restraint. That is the reason for the recurrent narrative pattern of imperiling the body to watch it convalesce, since that pattern reinforces our ambivalent sense that masculinity has as much in common with physical therapy, say, or bodybuilding as it does with breathing or giving birth—is as much, that is, a distinct cultural *effect* as it is a natural *cause* or biological imperative.

More specifically, we come to realize how fully silence is a sovereign condition not simply and passively assumed but arduously achieved—or likewise, how restraint is a chosen mode of behavior rather than simply an automatic response, a mere psychological tic or symptom of warped, antisocial tendencies. From this perspective, the Western hero's notorious inexpressiveness can be seen as conduct intended to focus our attention on his physical body, compelling us to heed that body as a fully constructed form uninflected by evidence of any ongoing process of fabrication. But his silence also has the opposite effect, of reinforcing our sense of the amount of continuing effort expended to maintain this state of masculinity, to ensure it as a condition not otherwise given or prescribed. Clint Eastwood's appearance as No Name, an impassive, zombie-like creature, serves as only the most extreme, ironic form of this condition (figure 19).

Whenever a man is being beaten in the Western, it is less to punish us for our delight in the male body than to prepare us for the process by which he becomes what he already is. We find ourselves, male and female, identifying with that subject of suffering and in that moment also identifying with the masculinizing process itself as one of American culture's most powerful (and powerfully confused) imaginative constructions. For it is the Western hero—unlike the leading men in any other genre—who is placed before us precisely to be looked at. And in that long, oscillating look, we watch men still at work in the unfinished process of making themselves, even as we are encouraged to believe that manhood doesn't need to be made.

7 SENTIMENTAL EDUCATIONS

Whatever else may have to be set aside in the Western, there is always time for a little instruction. . . . For every Showdown at Wichita there's a little Teach-In in Dodge City.

Philip French (1969)[1]

Trust yourself. *You know more than you think you do. . . . Don't take too seriously all that the neighbors say. Don't be overawed by what the experts say. Don't be afraid to trust your own common sense. Bringing up your child won't be a complicated job if you take it easy, trust your own instincts, and follow the directions that your doctor gives you.*

Dr. Benjamin Spock (1946)[2]

That's just what I need—to get advice from a guy who never saw Shane.

Arthur "The Fonz" Fonzerelli (1970s)[3]

In the opening moments of *The Deerslayer*, in the earliest view we have of Natty Bumppo, the youthful hero is already doling out sententious advice, lecturing "Hurry" Harry Marsh on his benighted view of Indians: "'That matter is not rightly understood—has never been rightly explained,' said Deerslayer earnestly."[4] Over the next half-century of adventures chronicled in the Leatherstocking Series, Natty continues in this hectoring role, garrulously tutoring the ignorant and enlightening the misinformed, backed by an author similarly prone to lecture the reader, adducing facts, invoking maps, footnoting supportive texts, and otherwise aggressively trying to instruct.

A violent historical juxtaposition: almost exactly a century later, the most popular book ever sold adopted a similar tack, complaining how little the "correct" view of infants was properly understood.[5] Take, for instance, the common practice of urging babies to eat too much—against which Dr. Benjamin Spock contended in hearty tones:

In the long run, urging does more than destroy appetite and make a thin child. It robs him of some of his positive feeling for life. A baby is meant to spend his first year getting hungry, demanding food, enjoying it, reaching satisfaction—a lusty success story, repeated at least three times a day, week after week. It builds into him self-confidence, outgoingness, trust in his mother. But if mealtime becomes a struggle, if feeding becomes something that is done *to* him, he goes on the defensive and builds up a balky, suspicious attitude. (81)

Strange as it seems, the developmental stakes in the child's evening feeding have acquired grand, Manichean dimensions (a point of pediatric psychology to which we will return).

For the moment, substantive issues matter less than presentational mode: that a New England pediatrician successfully addresses anxieties in American culture by adopting the bearing and tone of a prototypical West-   189 ern hero. Obviously, that bearing and tone do not match the hero in the preceding chapter, who suffered his beatings in silence resistant to possible self-transformation—indeed, was beaten to allow us to watch him become what he already was. Still, there is another facet to the Western (apparent in the discussion of Cooper) in which landscape plays a paternal role, serving as conduct book, offering advice on how boys might become men. And it is this tension (elaborated in the chapter on Wister) between calm silence and tall talk, between mythic stasis and comic transformation—between, that is, the elegaic, uncanny status of a hero being beaten and the more prosaic, pedagogical role he is so often asked to play—that needs now to be assessed. For in both versions of this narrative dynamic, the problem of "making the man" is the same even though they lead to radically different solutions (physical distortion; commonsense advice).

Spock hardly saw himself in the role of gunslinger savior, but in adopting an avuncular manner to edify parents on raising children, he confirms how much the authority figure of the Western retains a cultural charm that resonates with rare intensity at certain historical moments. The Western's recurrent dependence on the conduct book of nature, with landscape providing a moral guide to be interpreted by experts, offers a powerful paradigm that has continued from Cooper down to the present. And if Natty's hectoring and Spock's lecturing form a linked pair of performances, it may be less than fortuitous that *The Pocket Book of Baby and Child Care* became a runaway best-seller just as the "classic Western" achieved its greatest popularity.

Cooper's emphasis on a pedagogic (not to say pedantic) strain convinces even those unconvinced by his fiction. Mark Twain notably demolished the Leatherstocking novels only by unconsciously emulating them, adopting Cooper's expert stance to expose the "literary offenses" that registered how little Cooper "rightly understood."[6] Just as vigorously, the shadow of Natty Bumppo lives on in genre writers and film directors who invoke the tactic of historical accuracy to authenticate their own fictional forms. So regularly does the tactic recur that it often appears as a self-conscious plot motif, with the education of characters presented as one of the Western's chief reasons for being, in the process edifying readers and viewers about tools, terrains, and local techniques.[7]

Persistent as this pedagogical impulse has been throughout the history of the genre, never was it so urgently pressed as in the early 1950s, the "golden age" of the Western, when fictional, film, and television exemplars concentrated on teaching boys to become men. Driven by plots of sons seeking fathers, of fathers looking for reliable sons, of both locked in the highly contested structure of the nuclear family, the genre exaggerated as never before the process of "growing up." Consider three of the most popu-lar and influential Westerns of the era: Louis L'Amour's *Hondo* (1953) pres-ents a boy's instruction by a hero encyclopedically versed in dogs, horses, axes, swimming, Apache medicine, and military strategy; George Stevens's *Shane* (1952) depicts a boy's more modest tutoring in how to comport him-self with a gun; and Fred Zinnemann's *High Noon* (1952), where juvenile instruction never occurs, is haunted by the lack of paternal authority in a world gone awry.

This exaggerated attention to education, even in its absence, suggests a larger cultural anxiety about parenting emergent in the early 1950s—about instilling character and civic ideals, about defining proper gender roles, about the larger project of raising children into capable men and women. The Western's singular capacity to address such pedagogical issues, moreover, contributed to its unprecedented popularity during this period. Again, as in earlier chapters, the appeal of *High Noon, Shane,* and *Hondo* lay not in resolving issues they address (issues so complex as to be irresolvable in any event) but in offering varied contexts in which the "problem" of adolescence might seem to disappear. Soliciting readers and viewers di-vided on the most basic premises of gender and upbringing, these West-erns spur interest in the problem only narratively and cinematically to elide it, appearing to resolve deep cultural anxieties without in fact actually do-ing so. Before exploring more fully the general anxiety that led to an interest in fathers and sons, however, we need to turn to each text in turn to identify the singular structural effects that mask their common strategy.

Complacency at *High Noon*

Not only was Hollywood losing viewers after World War II, it was under attack from a Congress alarmed that the entertainment business had been infiltrated by Communists. As conservatives saw it, the American public (and younger viewers in particular) needed to be protected from subversive cinematic messages. By 1952, the extraordinary powers wielded by the House Un-American Activities Committee had aroused such fears in the film industry that Carl Foreman was induced to write the screenplay of *High Noon* as an anti-McCarthyite tract. The stalwart marshall Will Kane (Gary Cooper) is portrayed in the mold of men like Dalton Trumbo and Alvah Bessie, who not only defied HUAC orders to inform on others but refused to appear before Congress at all.[8]

As many have noted, however, the political allegory can just as easily be read conversely, with the strong individualist who refuses to compro-mise akin to Senator McCarthy himself, continuing to fight against foreign

191

aggression when others fall back on a complacent, do-nothing policy.[9] It is even possible to argue *High Noon* as an *à clef* depiction of the Korean War, equating Will Kane with America, Frank Miller with international communism, Amy Kane with isolationists, and the town of Hadleyville with nations content to let the United States go it alone in Korea. Yet less important than pedigreeing any single reading of plot is the need to recognize how closely Foreman's liberal polemic resembles the arguments of those he attacked. McCarthy viewed liberals as responsible for selling out the nation; opponents instead viewed him as the threat to fundamental freedoms. But pro- and anti-McCarthyites shared a conviction as deep as anything dividing them: that the true enemy was civic complacency. And this capacity to provoke a common assessment of America's current malaise explains much of the film's appeal. No matter one's political stripe, all agree that the citizens of Hadleyville have regressed to a state of infantile dependency, requiring a paternal figure to protect them. And the very elaboration of Will Kane's self-restraint, moral authority, and masculine skills suggests by contrast what calm maturity might actually entail.

This indictment of civic complacency as akin to juvenile self-indulgence is reinforced by *High Noon*'s notorious obsession with time—an obsession that eerily emulates the adolescent parent's stereotypical injunctions, constantly reminding the child to be conscious of the clock, to organize time more effectively, to be aware of how fast or slowly it is passing. The film reflects real time on-screen minute for minute, almost tyrannically, beginning with a temporal self-consciousness in the hurried glance Jack Colby (Lee Van Cleef) gives to his watch as he waits for his partners. The action then extends for eighty-five minutes through Sunday morning, concluding in a classical Western shoot-out. Other Aristotelian unities are observed not only with the setting in small-town Hadleyville but by limiting the cast of characters to Kane, his wife, ex-lover, deputy, and the threatening Miller gang, with townspeople presented as interpolating chorus. What make these formal constraints apparent *as* constraints is the brief contemplation of other possibilities (as when Kane flees town with his new wife only to stop and turn back), gradually leaving the viewer with a regressive sense that time, place, even character itself are all beyond one's control, dictated by others, contrary to any more ordinary sense of mature self-possession.

Compounding the effect of this temporal tautness are the film's compilation of facial close-ups, enabling us to stare hard at characters' strengths and flaws. Will Kane's battle of wills occurs at the level of tightly focused grimaces, again approximating a psychological pattern common to adolescence (of overly intense responses to unintentional tics and misperceived mannerisms). For the moment, we need only note that this intense cinematic style mirrors a technique associated with television's small screen, as if Fred Zinnemann (and his strong-willed producer, Stanley Kramer) were imitating the limited methods available to television directors. In doing so, they revealed unsuspected possibilities in those methods through frequent cross-cutting that posed a silent counteroffensive to television's predominately static images.

A more obvious allusion to television lay in the grainy, flattened quality of *High Noon*'s filmic image, especially surprising in the context of major studio productions in the early 1950s. Defying the newly glamorous promise of Technicolor production, Kramer adopted a black-and-white, newsreel tone that seemed to reflect the influence of Rossellini, De Sica, and the Italian neorealist school. Nonetheless, Kramer's rationale, like nearly every other practitioner of the genre, was a desire for historical authenticity—in his case, to match the grimly documentary atmosphere of Matthew Brady's Civil War photographs. Shooting without filters, he created in the dull, washed-out sky of Hadleyville an effect radically different from other Westerns of the period—from either the nostalgia of *Shane* or the highly staged pageantry of Delmer Daves's *Broken Arrow* (1950).

Pressing an earlier analogy perilously further, that effect corresponds to a strained tone of adolescent self-consciousness, as the emotional detachment of individual characters and the collective anomie of the community is confirmed through a repeated series of empty scenes—of vacant railroad station and tracks, of abandoned streets and silent town, of Will Kane regularly striding across an unobstructed sky while "proper" citizens are seated at church. Reinforcing that sense of personal isolation are the dull strokes of ticking clocks and a corresponding musical ostinato—both sounds that converge at noon as each character is brought into separate focus just before the blast of the train whistle shatters the stroke of twelve. More evidence must be adduced to confirm how such moments reveal a preoccupation with growing up, but we need to turn first to an equally popular film to see how similar considerations might be enacted quite differently.

"Galahad on the Range"[10]

Instead of an allegory of civic complacency, *Shane* offers a distillation of the Western itself, glorifying the larger social processes of American history in a glowingly nostalgic mode. Like Stanley Kramer confronted by the genre's demands, George Stevens strove for historical accuracy in transferring Jack Schaefer's 1949 novel to the screen. Archival research led him to create a cinematically unconventional town, lining buildings on only one side of the   193 street in standard western style and introducing other notes of authenticity (filming on location near Jackson Hole, watering down the set to resemble nineteenth-century photographs of sodden Wyoming towns in spring). Yet such historicizing efforts do little to alter what Robert Warshow first identified as the film's "aestheticizing tendency" or what Slavoj Zizek has defined as its nostalgic "purity."[11] The combination of Tetons and Technicolor automatically transmutes landscape into Bierstadtian spectacle, with Loyal Griggs's cinematography lending a radiant tone to even moon-lit scenes.

Where *High Noon* deliberately avoids mythic innuendo, *Shane* as deliberately embraces it, impelled by the mental perspective of the boy whose gaze dominates the film. In the long opening shot, Joey Starrett (Brandon De Wilde) watches the buckskin-clad hero (Alan Ladd) ride down from the mountains, framed by antlers of a grazing buck. Shane's first words to the boy then simply confirm the specular identification of viewer with Joey (and with Marian Starrett, who shares Joey's gaze): "You were watching me down there quite a spell, weren't ya? . . . I like a man who watches things going around." And because Joey's prepubescent angle of vision dominates the film, characters are metonymically equated with the spaces through which they move. Scenery imparts a mythic power that is accepted by Joey as natural, explaining why Shane is the only figure filmed alone against mountains, the villainous Rikers never appear this way, and the farmers only with Shane.[12] So closely is this standard observed that when Shane and Joe Starrett (Van Heflin) ride into town, the road they take faces the mountains, while the Riker gang rides down that same road filmed from the opposite direction. Other characters are likewise bound to identifying locales—the saloon, the store, or simply (in the case of homesteading wives) buckboard wagons.

Part of this aestheticizing tone derives from the film's unusual attention to bodily violence. Joey's flinching gaze at any unexpected gesture or sudden sound points from the beginning to a cinematic sensitivity to physical transgression. And when Shane finally provokes a brawl with Chris Calloway (Ben Johnson), the scene in Grafton's saloon is corroborated by the boy's wide-eyed stare, the exchange of bodily blows punctuated by his chomping on a candy cane. Confirming an emotional intensity to this childish view is a heightened sound track that underscores the impact of punches and the sound of tired gasps. That aestheticization continues even in a more violent scene unobserved by Joey: the one-sided gunfight between the hired gun Jack Wilson (Jack Palance) and the Southern farmer "Stonewall" Torrey (Elisha Cook, Jr.). After years of stylized shoot-outs with gunmen simply collapsing in pain, this scene revealed the shock that flesh is heir to in Torrey's body abruptly knocked over by Wilson's bullet. Again, the moment is dramatically heightened through the coincidence of a thunderclap, lending Torrey's death the significance of a natural event.[13]

While the film's aestheticization of violence lends a newly realistic tone to such scenes, it also creates an apparently contradictory impression of mythologizing them. Both effects result from the film's investment in Joey's gaze, which helps explain why violence seems required and yet is so often deferred. From the beginning, the aimless gaze at Shane's body arouses a longing for action—"Bet you can shoot. Can't you?"—followed by impetuous queries and exclamations that prompt the viewer's longing as well: "Aren't you goin' to wear your six-shooter, Mr. Shane?"; "Can you shoot as good as Shane, pa?"; "Could you whip Shane?"; "I bet you two could lick anyone"; "Let me see you shoot, Shane." The repeated deferral of Joey's desire prompts a regressive response in the viewer, whose own generic expectations are stymied yet sharpened by curbs on the boy's consciousness—as if we were being co-opted into wanting the exhibition of violence that the genre always promises.[14] When violence finally does erupt, its presentation only confirms a child's mixed perspective, appearing at once realistically brutal and yet magically inconsequential. The long, climactic brawl between Shane and Starrett, for which Joey has secretly waited, pictures the fierce violation of both men without leading to any obvious physical damage (much like the fight in Grafton's saloon).

Indeed, both men are mythically elevated above their precise historical context: the summer of 1889 before the onset of the Johnson County range war. Contributing to the film's "meta-western" status is its transformation of that actual moment into a conventional contrast of past and future, tradition and progress, East and West. Even here, however, where history and myth coalesce, a contradiction exists in the southerner Shane collaborating with forces of innovation. Westerns ever since Wister have typically identified the hero as a man of tradition posed against the easy expediencies of northern technocracy (notably, the film takes care to characterize Wilson as "a low-down rotten Yankee"). Instead, Shane allies himself with a progressive group of homesteaders who battle the independent, unreconstructed rancher, Rufus Riker (Emile Meyer).

As if further to compound the film's confusion of roles, Riker's nighttime speech in defense of his rights (delivered on the Fourth of July, no less) is oddly persuasive, based on values otherwise clearly associated with Shane:

We *made* this country, found it and we made it, with blood and empty bellies. Cattle we brought in were hazed off by Indians and rustlers. Don't bother you much anymore because *we* handled them, and made a safe range out of this. Some of us died doing it, but we made it. And then people move in who've never heard the rawhider through the old days. They fenced off my range, and fenced me off from water. Some of 'em like you plow ditches and take out irrigation water, and so the crick runs dry sometimes. I've got to move my stock because of it. And you say we have no right to the range!

While Riker is soon reduced to stock villainy in defense of his "rights," this honorable self-description serves not only to express Shane's independence (and therefore his necessary departure from the valley) but to prefigure the obligatory displacement of Starrett himself. The power of this elaborate moon-lit scene lies in its multiple representations of manhood, with Wilson and Shane alternately drinking from a water cup in a balletic exchange of stares while Riker and Starrett plead their separate causes.

That staged, self-conscious lingering over masculine possibilities is due once again to the powerful condensations effected through Joey's juvenile perspective. Contrary to the fast-paced, suspense-laden, politically charged atmosphere of *High Noon, Shane* indulges a nostalgic mood of childhood revisited. Boyish impatience for action is coupled with an equally intense urge to understand, both signaled through Brandon De Wilde's wide-eyed gaze. This sense of preadolescent consciousness is reinforced through unusual camera angles, dramatic lighting and sound track, an etherealizing use of frequent dissolves instead of sharp cuts (fade-ins and fade-outs rather than framed edits), even the film's rich Technicolor hues. It is hard to imagine a vision less like Stanley Kramer's than this, that nonetheless as Western engages similar substantive concerns.

Giving One's Word

Of the three films infused with anxiety about "growing up," John Farrow's *Hondo* most obviously seizes cinematic possibilities by offering a 3-D Western, allowing the viewer to feel temporarily as if *in* the landscape. Once more, the opening shot is of a boy watching a man approach, this time riding directly at the viewer, while the woman who will finally pair with the man is again given the boy's perspective. The difference from *Shane,* however, lies only in part in the 3-D perspective, in larger part in the intensity with which filial bonds are emphasized—a thematic consideration stressed even more in L'Amour's novelization. The same logic invoked by Vittoro to explain the Apache retaliation ("my sons are dead—in a white man's prison") explains his urging Angie Lowe to secure a father for her own son.[15] And if Lieutenant Davis's success with his troops is attributed to little more than his fatherly presence, Angie likewise responds to Hondo largely because he resembles her own father. This paternal theme is so strong that the novel's only biological father, Ed Lowe, is saved from a mortal bullet by his son's tintype in his breast pocket. "What man does not want a son?" Hondo wonders, in a strain repeated half-a-dozen times; "What man wishes to die and leave no man to carry on?" (122).

Just as strongly, boys need fathers, and L'Amour again exceeds the film in the variety of pedagogical scenes he offers between Hondo and Johnny Lowe. "Watching with excited attention" (20), the six-year-old eagerly absorbs a set of lengthy lessons in wilderness lore and Apache ideals (themselves uncannily similar to middle-class American values). Moreover, *Hondo* strenuously reiterates—in a pattern reflective of '50s anxieties about sex-role identification—that it must be men who train men-to-be.[16] Women are simply too solicitous, too bent on sheltering children from dangerous truths; or as Hondo growls, it "spoils a boy to be protected" (138). The narrative suggests instead that an open, matter-of-fact, supposedly masculine approach produces self-trust in Johnny that makes him feel "almost as if he were a man himself" (20).

This stress on clarity, directness, and mutual trust between generations is reinforced through Hondo's opening exchanges with Angie, which reveal his mildly adolescent indignation at the impulse to prevaricate. His anger first emerges over her lies at her husband's absence ("Mrs. Lowe? You're a liar. . . . An almighty poor liar" [21]); later, it is because Apaches have been deceived by duplicitous whites ("There's no word in the Apache language for 'lie,' and they've been lied to" [24]); much later, he simply declines Vittoro's request to betray the army he serves ("Figure he was testing me. Indians hate a lie. I got to feel the same way" [154]). Callously honest (in the film, at least) about Angie's "homely" appearance ("I got a bad habit of telling the truth"), Hondo later wants to reveal to Johnny the painful fact of his father's death ("If I don't, somebody else will. And I got a belly-full of lies"). Only at this penultimate moment does Angie firmly stand her ground, pronouncing his attempt at truth to be (in her own candid outburst) simply an expression of "fine vanity." The final embrace that then ensues registers Hondo's transition from an adolescent ideal of fixed integrity to a more flexible conception of behavior, bound by mutual relationships.

Given the thematic centrality of integrity and veracity, there is a peculiar irony to the history of the text's metamorphosis from story idea to screen, then in turn to full-length narrative. For unlike *Shane*, which was scripted from an original novel to which the film is faithful, *Hondo* was written out by L'Amour as a novel only *after* the film's appearance—a novel that then went on to become his most popular book. And since L'Amour is the single most prolific Western author, whose 101 books are still in print (with almost 225 million copies in circulation), this unusual inception of his career has implications for the ways in which popular culture defines ideas. Or rather, the surprising success of the film helped define the demands of a contemporary audience—demands that could then be transformed into generic conventions that would shape a novelistic career.[17]

The film was developed from L'Amour's short story, "The Gift of Cochise" (1952), and recast by James Edward Grant as a screenplay with a significantly different plot and newly named hero. At the time the film was released, L'Amour had failed to interest paperback publishers in his short story and, according to John Tuska, had "novelize[d] James Edward Grant's screenplay and published it under his own name, as if it were *his* story." Tuska offers an acerbic description of L'Amour's "novelization," which follows "Grant's screenplay very closely, using much of Grant's dialogue," before he goes on to substantiate how fully Grant's social Darwinism became L'Amour's own, not only in *Hondo* but in subsequent novels.[18] Never acknowledging his debt to Grant, L'Amour carved out a remarkable career based on innovations introduced in "his" first success (that the novel highlights the imperative of honesty only sharpens the irony of L'Amour's plagiarism). It is as if he were establishing his own authority in starkly Oedipal fashion by figuratively clearing the field of his predecessors. And appropriately, that impulse is literally confirmed in the *mise-en-scène* of *Hondo,* which recurrently invokes an empty landscape by erasing all signs through which the terrain might be known. Repeatedly, the word "nothing" appears in the text as a description of locale, giving little sense of the Arizona desert setting (sky and cloud formations are better described than the land itself).

One effect of this descriptive void is to highlight Hondo's mythic status as master of empty, unidentifiable desert, virtually of space itself, and therefore a figure more imposing even than Shane, whose mythic association is with a heroic but nonetheless actual setting, the Grand Tetons. By contrast, Angie's ranch seems full of objects and rich with signs, and thus a precisely historical, clearly domestic and social alternative. Yet more significant than any such immediate thematic purpose is that this narrative pattern clears out the landscape, making way for an author resolved to find a niche in the market for his own often formulaic fiction. By creating a vista that is more or less indeterminate, L'Amour secured a place for his novels in the overcrowded realm of the Western.[19]

Even though the West-as-nowhere is a peculiarly L'Amourian device, repeated endlessly by an author never quite willing to claim his own terrain, he too (like Kramer and Stevens) was unable to resist the genre's injunctions to authenticity. His appeal to the reader's fluid imagination vis-à-vis landscape, then, belies the pedantic precision exacted everywhere else in his narratives (a precision that, once again, never registered the sources of his own first success). As fully as anyone since Cooper, L'Amour stressed self-conscious attention to historical accuracy, making his trademark the close regard to cowboy's gear, breeds of horses, local biographies, even the geographical idiosyncrasies of the Old West.

The Pain of Adolescence

So different are *High Noon, Shane,* and *Hondo,* so varied in plot, pacing, and cinematography, that their common obsession with male adolescence is little apparent at first. Distinctively as each one manifests that obsession, however, all converge on the importance of gender roles rightly understood, which itself suggests anxiety about the process of boys becoming men. Most forthrightly of the three, *Hondo* simply stresses the naturalness of conventional gendered behavior, with males becoming men by avoiding behavior coded as feminine. Hondo's and Angie's "true" selves emerge in response to the other's difference—"like a woman," "like a man"—as if biological pairings were essential to cultural self-construction: "This was as it should be . . . a man and a woman working toward something, for something. Not apart, but a team" (151).⁴⁰ L'Amour's descriptions of soldiers, otherwise spare in psychological detail, depict their frequent thoughts of their wives, as if they were only partial men without them. So universal are conventional roles assumed to be that even the Apaches charge Angie with taking a husband merely for the sake of her son. And her absent husband's villainy is revealed by that very absence, having selfishly forsaken his parental responsibilities. In L'Amour's conservative vision, a larger society only interferes with the natural relationships that bind the nuclear family together, and nothing less than escape to a dreamlike California at the end (like the final flights from history concocted by Zane Grey) can ensure the recovery of family solidarity.

Shane likewise stresses the importance of conventional family norms, but does so by conversely dramatizing the insidious emotional forces that regularly imperil them. Or as Marian counsels Joey (speaking for herself), "Don't get to liking Shane too much." Her warning already betrays the desire they both express through body language: Marian staring through the cabin window at a slowly approaching Shane; he drawing her out through the door to watch his gunplay; she physically obscuring her husband while serving Shane the first piece of pie. Donning her wedding dress to celebrate a tenth anniversary, she immediately looks for the gunman, only to discover him paternally teaching Joey to shoot. The bathos of their relationship, which never comes closer than a handshake and a smile, underscores the fact that all is being seen from her son's adult perspective reconstructing

199

the events of "that summer of '89." A narrator of events he could not fully have comprehended at the time, Joey nonetheless reveals how both he and his parents fostered the threat posed by Shane, each through transgressive desires. The plot can therefore only be resolved through Shane's renunciation, in voluntarily departing from the valley so that the family can continue: "Joey, take care of her, both of them."[21]

High Noon presents yet another conception of appropriate gender roles, with men and women mired in mutual conflict and misunderstanding. Foreman adapted his screenplay from Wister's conflict of hero and schoolteacher, but the stakes had risen considerably in the intervening half-century, as men and women everywhere chafe at each others' sense of appropriate behavior. The marriage itself of aging lawman and virginal Quaker forms an odd conjunction, a union of opposites replicated in other strained relationships: between Kane's deputy Harvey Pell (Lloyd Bridges) and his lover Helen Ramirez (Katy Jurado), or Kane's erstwhile friend William Fuller (Harry Morgan) and his wife. No couple seems capable of living at peace with their differences, and the film's resolution seems inadequate to the divisions it dramatizes.

Nor are filial relationships less disappointing, beginning with Kane's disillusionment at Judge Mettrick's (Otto Kruger) cynicism as he hurriedly leaves town. Kane's later admission to ex-sheriff Howe—"Ever since I was a kid I—I wanted to be like you Mart. You've been a lawman all your life"—only evokes another cynical outburst of regret that he had ever influenced Kane. The most important such alliance is the rivalry of Kane with his ambitious deputy, who harbors growing resentment at Kane's refusal to be a mentor. Harvey first interprets this stance as a paternal judgment that he is "too young," but Kane's intransigence turns the conflict into an Oedipal struggle, as Harvey now suspects that his affair with Kane's ex-lover lies at the heart of the matter: "You've been against me from the start, sore about me taking over Helen from you." Moreover, once defeated by the older man, Pell simply drops from sight.

The two films reinforce a father-son dynamic through inspired casting, most obviously with *Shane*'s sexual triangle. Van Heflin's broad forehead, earnest gaze, and wide smile underwrite Starrett's wholesome integrity—in short, an earthy realism meant to contrast with Alan Ladd's "ethereal detachment." As Philip French goes on to observe, Shane is "like an angel in an otherwise realistic medieval painting," with flat, expressionless eyes and a blank face that reinforce his narrative mysteriousness.[22] Jean Arthur's Marian Starrett mediates between the two men as the older, unfulfilled pioneer mother, in "singularly dowdy costuming and makeup," alternately coaxing Joey and imploring them in bronchial tones to restraint.[23] And finally, Brandon De Wilde's Joey articulates what his mother cannot be allowed to express, with a piercing voice and yearning eyes that explode melodramatically whenever his mother's feelings are conflicted. Shrewd casting everywhere augments the plot's essentially lateral pressures on a conventional family structure.

By contrast, conflicts in *High Noon* are more obviously vertical than horizontal, imaged in the Oedipal strains between young men and old. Gary Cooper's very demeanor—an aging face that Godard once claimed belonged "to the mineral kingdom"[24]—already confirms the film's premise: Will Kane is retiring and is clearly old enough to do so. The dark shadows under his eyes; the lack of makeup; the black-and-white film that literally drains color from his cheek: all lend to Cooper's haggard expression a sense of grim determination in the Oedipal struggle that aligns them all. The foil to this casting is Grace Kelly, whose blonde, blue-blooded, translucently white-skinned Amy Kane offers a stunning physical alternative to the patriarchal logic Kane affirms. Even this contrast (confirmed in Kelly being half Cooper's age) only intensifies a generational tension that is unresolved at the end by the wayward child wife's reacceptance of a repressive patriarchal structure.

Unlike the two films, L'Amour's *Hondo* stresses a developing trust between both sexes and generations, as if to agree with Angie's maudlin belief not only that "the right two people are going to meet by an arrangement of destiny" (15) but more generally that "everyone needs someone" (12). The awkward domestic arrangements of *Shane* and the marital conflicts of *High Noon* are cited as potential problems only to be quickly eliminated through Ed Lowe's abandonment of his family, then craven death. L'Amour further sentimentalizes the romance by making Angie "a beautiful woman" (15) and Hondo a "lean, hard-boned" figure with "no softness in him" (1)—this, in contrast to John Wayne's burly physique and Geraldine Page's self-consciously plain appearance ("I am fully aware that I am a homely woman, Mr. Lane"). The casting for Farrow's film, that is, underscores better than L'Amour that personal integrity matters more than "pretty people"; as Hondo responds to Angie: "some others, something comes out of the inside of them, and you know you can trust 'em.'" Both versions of *Hondo* nonetheless reiterate the importance of mutual trust and the ease with which personal relations can be established—as if resentment, envy, anger, and other darker emotions were simply bleached out of the family romance. Or as the film economically condenses such exchanges into a single response: "Gosh, Uncle Hondo, I want your opinion."

Fatherhood, the '50s, and the "Classic Western"

The emphasis on fatherhood, initiation, and the nuclear family—either through external threat (*Shane*), ideological conflict (*High Noon*), or thematic insistence (*Hondo*)—reveals a clear self-consciousness in the early '50s about domestic responsibility. Traditional definitions of family roles had shifted in the postwar "baby boom," with an unprecedented surge in marriages and births (a million more each year than in the 1930s) coupled with a recently strengthened economy that encouraged Americans to purchase automobiles and suburban homes. The new regime of working father and isolated mother meant that "'filiarchy' had replaced traditional patriarchy," as Steven Mintz and Susan Kellogg observe; "suburban children 'tended to be pampered as never before.'"[25]

New parents accustomed to first the Depression years, then wartime conditions, discovered their own expectations (as partners, parents, and children themselves) no longer at all like those of their own parents. Margaret Mead opened her 1949 "study of the sexes in a changing world" with just such a consideration:

How are men and women to think about their maleness and their femaleness in this twentieth century, in which so many of our old ideas must be made new? Have we over-domesticated men, denied their natural adventurousness, tied them down to machines that are after all only glorified spindles and looms, mortars and pestles and digging sticks, all of which were once women's work? Have we cut women off from their natural closeness to their children, taught them to look for a job instead of the touch of a child's hand, for status in a competitive world rather than a unique place by a glowing hearth? In educating women like men, have we done something disastrous to both men and women alike?[26]

Familiar behavioral models came to seem less appropriate than before, leading in turn to a spate of sociological studies that grappled with what was newly seen to be the problem of youth, and especially of adolescence.[27]

Only around the turn of the century had adolescence been deemed a transitional phase as emotional development first came to be considered the primary sign of maturity.[28] In the nineteenth century, teenagers had not even been considered a separate group, since bodily size mattered more than age and self-sufficient youths were treated as adults. Carl Foreman nicely captures this presumption in Will Kane's exchange with a would-be volunteer:

KANE: "You're a kid, you're a baby."
YOUTH: "I'm 16, and I can handle a gun."
KANE: "You're 13. What d'ye want to lie for?"
YOUTH: "Well, I'm big for my age."

Little more than a generation later, the prevailing view of teenagers was less as troublesome figures heedless of adult authority than as vulnerable adolescents, passive and awkward, caught in years of prolonged indecision.[29] And by 1950, an entire industry had mushroomed to meet their needs, of teachers, athletic coaches, guidance counselors, adolescent psychologists, tutoring specialists, market research analysts, clothiers, disc jockeys, and record producers.

So fervent an attention to youth reflects an underlying uneasiness about adolescents left on their own, and suggests by extension the discomfort that adolescents themselves felt in a society unprepared to accept them as adults.[30] Part of this anxiety surfaced in family melodrama of the 1950s and such mainstream films as Marlon Brando's *The Wild One* (1953), Elia Kazan's *On the Waterfront* (1954), and Nicholas Ray's *Rebel without a Cause* (1955), all of which dramatize adolescent aspirations as a panic about growing up.[31] Yet the genre most successfully engaging the problem of youth was the Western, which achieved its greatest popularity during this period. Defying a radical decline in general movie attendance (to half of what it had been a half-dozen years before), Westerns constituted fully a third of feature films produced in the early '50s (and well over a quarter through the decade).[32]

Interesting as well, they proved among the top-grossing genres: King Vidor's *Duel in the Sun* was the second highest moneymaker in 1947, Howard Hawks's *Red River* was third the following year, Delmer Daves's *Broken Arrow* came in ninth in 1950, *High Noon* was eighth in 1952, and *Shane* won third place in 1953.[33] Technical breakthroughs in color cinematography and the advent of widescreen cinema surely aided this popularity, enhancing a genre based as much on evocation of landscape as on revelation of character. But television Westerns likewise dominated the "electronic hearth" in this period, with dozens of weekly, half-hour series competing on a small screen where lavish visual suasions could not be a factor.[34] Perhaps part of the attraction of films in particular is the recurrent Oedipal plot that keeps redefining larger configurations of father-son relationships.

Certainly, as in no other genre, the '50s film Western highlighted the conflict between aging stars and their successors. In 1950, John Wayne was already forty-three, Alan Ladd thirty-seven, Gregory Peck a mere stripling at thirty-four, James Stewart forty-two, Randolph Scott forty-seven, and Gary Cooper verging on fifty. With so many of the film Western's faces growing lined, it is no surprise that growing old should have become a persistent theme, accompanied by ever more frequent plots of nostalgia, regret, and introspection. The decade began with the most noted of these, Henry King's *The Gunfighter* (1950), exploring the impossibility of heroes   203 growing gracefully old and the odds against other men growing into roles to which their elders no longer seemed adequate (the irony of Gregory Peck having won the coveted role of the aging hero was hardly lost on older stars). Issues of succession came to dominate the genre, both in cinematic plots and behind the scenes (in casting and studio contracts), until the 1960s launched violent "sunset Westerns" representing even more heightened Oedipal struggle between actor-fathers and young male stars before whom they refused to give way.

In short, the Western was ideally equipped to engage and deflect fears about adolescence, and what is now required is a better grasp of the way those materials worked in particular texts. Before turning back to *High Noon, Shane,* and *Hondo,* however, we need to understand what adolescence meant in the '50s, a view nicely summarized in the *Book of Baby and Child Care.* Yet what emerges from Spock's book is less a straightforward solution to the problematics of adolescence than their reproduction, creating the very condition parents hoped to avoid. While Spock cannot therefore explain the preoccupation of '50s Westerns with adolescence, his own self-contradictory resolution of problems offers a parallel popular text that reveals more directly the cultural pressures surrounding the "problem" of adolescence.

Dr. Spock's Common Sense

Dr. Benjamin Spock's *Book of Baby and Child Care* first appeared in 1946 and in subsequent paperback versions has become the most popular book ever sold in America.[35] No other pediatrician has so powerfully influenced the view an entire culture has cast on its children—enjoining a "common sense" that has seemed obvious to millions of parents. Spock's predecessors in the field of pediatric advice had been far more patronizing and firmly authoritarian. His mother's standby, Dr. Luther Emmett Holt's *The Care and Feeding of Children* (1895; 14th ed. 1929), demanded that babies be bowel-trained at two months, not played with before they were six months old (play would agitate delicate nervous systems), and weaned at the age of two, even if that meant starving them for a number of days. Other, more recent texts perpetuated similar advice in more anxious tones, for as Dr. John B. Watson lamented, *"No one today knows enough to raise a child."*[36]

Spock's claim to distinction lay in his Emersonian call to self-reliance, encouraging mothers' and fathers' faith in their "natural" impulses. His Rousseauistic theory of human development led him to think of details of child care as matters of mere technical tuning: the mechanism runs adequately if left in a steady state (all else being equal, of course). And the message of his book is therefore:

Trust yourself. You know more than you think you do. . . . Don't take too seriously all that the neighbors say. Don't be overawed by what the experts say. Don't be afraid to trust your own common sense. Bringing up your child won't be a complicated job if you take it easy, trust your own instincts, and follow the directions that your doctor gives you. (3)

Appearing after a long history of pediatric patronizing, this opening is a refreshing change, with Spock eagerly handing control of the infant back to parents.

Yet much like the rest of the book, this passage shifts responsibility from parent once again back to doctor, slipping from the easy counsel of "trust your own instincts" to an injunction to "follow the directions that your doctor gives you." And the parent's relationship with the child accords with a similar pattern: seeming to trust the infant's behavior yet actually imposing a regulatory scheme.[37] The problem for Spock (as it was for Emerson) is in knowing what self to trust, especially since parents' impulses are frequently more constraining than he would like. Thus he responds in much the same way about all decisions concerning an infant: patting parents on the back for their innate "common sense," then offering expert alternatives. "The Doctor" becomes a sometimes invisible, otherwise looming authority, quietly warning parents in ways that arouse an adolescent uncertainty at the very moment they are themselves admonished in the raising of a future adolescent. Seemingly neutral opinions about breast-feeding, circumcision, even constipation are slyly weighted to encourage parental self-distrust: "If your child becomes constipated, take it up with the doctor—don't try to treat it yourself, because you aren't sure what it is due to. It's very important, whatever treatment you use, that you shouldn't get the child concerned about his bowel function . . . otherwise you may turn him into a hypochondriac" (122).

This paradoxically benign yet aggressive view of parental intervention derives from Spock's contradictory premise of infancy as a self-regulating state that requires constant surveillance.[38] On the one hand, thumb-sucking, left-handedness, perverse eating habits, and toilet training should be of little concern because "the baby will mostly 'train' himself."[39] On the other, battles with children occur, creating hostile adolescents and adults, and therefore should be avoided by simply avoiding needless options: "You are keeping away from choices, arguments, cross looks, scoldings—which won't do any good but will only get his back up" (212). In short, "it is better not to give him a choice" (265). Even when dysfunctional behavior is troubling—stuttering or nail-biting at two, bed-wetting at four, excessive masturbation after six—Spock's advice is always upbeat and therapeutic. As he reiterates, "find out what some of the pressures on the child are and try to relieve them" (288, 303, 403). A "casual, friendly" manner and affectionate "attentiveness" will, in a properly run household, lead to easy parent-child relations (198).[40]

Just as the child is allowed what he wants as long as those wants are perpetually regulated, so the parent is told to trust to "common sense" as long as it doesn't conflict with medical counsel. At the very moment Spock winsomely appointed parents as experts themselves, he reduced them to the status of adolescents in need of parental advice. He replaced an older system of harsh but clear-cut requirements with a far more ambivalent model that at once incited and disabled self-trust. Nearly everywhere else in the culture as well, this oddly relaxed yet nervous stance toward youth was apparent, in the combination of freedoms newly accorded and public anxieties about where those freedoms might lead. Juvenile delinquency continued to be such a prominent issue that by 1957 even Spock revised his book to emphasize parental failure for children's alienation.

This context clarifies the prevalence in '50s Westerns of plots of "growing up," a phrase that itself keeps recurring from film to film. And while Spock cannot explain the phenomenon, his popularity nonetheless parallels theirs, with readers and viewers responding to similar paradigms and dilemmas. The striking feature of these Westerns, moreover, is that a genre given to celebrating the loner should now turn to the nuclear family. The cowboy's choice as popular hero was due in no small part to his freedom from family ties, his abandonment of domestic obligations at a time of their renegotiation (as discussed in Chapter 1 above). What forced the Western to turn at mid-century back to the family and its dynamics was the persistence, the saliance, the sheer importance of Oedipal conflicts that Spock had so assiduously attempted to train out of middle-class life—that by rights (and appropriate management) should have disappeared in the child's early years. The popular success of '50s Westerns lay in their capacity to engage those conflicts, not by offering more self-consistent resolutions than Spock but by reproducing them in parables that were equally self-divided.

Growing Up

Each of the three popular Westerns that appeared in 1952–53 appealed to an obsession with "growing up": *High Noon* by invoking adolescent resentment of adult authority, *Shane* through a juvenile condensation of impulses

Figure 20. Joey Starrett (Brandon de Wilde) peering out from between swinging doors at fight in saloon in George Stevens's *Shane* (1952).

toward both the real and the mythic, *Hondo* via a straightforward assertion of the signal importance of father-son bonds. Yet much as Spock freed parents from pediatric authority only to create a new set of anxieties, these films address a common filial theme as a way of resolving Oedipal issues they at the same time compound or evade. And in each, the difficulty of maturing into a desirable sort of man is emphasized not only at a thematic but a more powerfully formal level associated with threshold situations. Cinematically, that developmental transition is evidenced in the ubiquitousness of borders and liminal scenes; narratively, through abrupt scenic transitions and suspended temporal sequences. Granted that doors, windows, fences, and other frames have been essential to cinematic composition from the beginning; granted even that experiments with narrative sequence and temporal suspension have been essayed more inventively than in most Westerns: still, the frequency with which liminal structures and moments appear in '50s Westerns suggests a strong ideological purpose at work.

Shane is filmed with nearly every camera frame arranged this way, particularly those of the domestic interiors at Grafton's store and Starrett's farm. Transitional moments are stressed in swinging doors that separate saloon from store (figures 20 and 21a and b), or the kitchen door that opens on a farmyard, or the window that connects Joey's bedroom to Shane standing in the rain-filled night. Each of these threshold points is stressed cinematically by people lingering at the edges, peering over at scenes to which they

Figures 21a and 21b. Joey and Marian Starrett (Jean Arthur) watching fight from under swinging doors in *Shane*, in successive frames.

are not admitted, conversing across borders that are not traversed. And when spaces *are* breached, the moment is self-consciously signaled, as in the constant reminders to shut the gate: Starrett ordering his son, then Shane; Shane prompting Joey; Morgan Riker later being cautioned in ominously threatening tones. The only scene that escapes clear architecturally liminal forms is the central episode of "Stonewall" Torrey's funeral on the high Wyoming plateau (accompanied by a harmonica riff and sounds of a whimpering dog) (figure 22). And even here, the transitional quality of open space is stressed in contrast shots of town and reverse shots of Rikers's gang watching from the saloon.

Within these strictly bordered scenes, *Shane* moves by allowing people's gaze to break the frame, introducing fleetingly transgressive moments in which the plot of filial and sexual identification can be developed.

Figure 22. Funeral of Frank "Stonewall" Torrey (Elisha Cook, Jr.) in *Shane*.

Joey's look of stark admiration intersects over and over with Marian's gaze of growing affection—both directed toward the unreal figure who becomes at once father, older brother, adulterous lover, and pampered child. The gaze in this film is aligned recurrently with wife and child, not the man, as the camera insistently reveals Alan Ladd's handsome features and lithe body to be more compelling than aging Jean Arthur's.[41] Ladd's inexpressive face itself defines a kind of mask guarding emotion from expression, as if certain facial bounds were not to be traversed by feeling no matter how strongly felt. The film makes a self-conscious gesture to this "border" when Shane unexpectedly expresses mock pain at Marian attending to his minor abrasions, duly surprising Joey with the theatrical outburst. Here, Shane acts out a certain contempt for the cliché of convalescence, with the effect of rendering him more mythic than otherwise, a hero undeterred and undamaged by the violence that would destroy a lesser being.

The sound track itself presents a threshold situation, defined most clearly by excesses that at dramatic moments punctuate the film's sonic world. Artificial amplification sets off and borders such moments, lending them a rhetorical intonation—whether a clap of thunder accompanies Wilson's gunning of "Stonewall" Torrey, or Shane's and Wilson's spurs jangle

209

too loudly as they walk across a room, or a calf explosively knocks over a milk can, or a canteen drops abruptly, or Johnny shouts "Bang!" unexpectedly, then later clicks his unloaded gun. It is as if a sonic contract with the viewer were shattered in order to corroborate the mythic importance of the film's *mise-en-scène*. The nighttime brawl between Starrett and Shane abruptly augments the volume of horses neighing, cattle screeching, punches landed, and grunts and groans expelled, leading one to believe that the entire natural order itself were somehow being imperiled.

Shane revels in threats to the nuclear family to test the constraints that keep it in place, much as the Western more generally defines its informing issues through threatening pressures—beginning with Cooper's testing of manly restraint through excess, and extending through the misshaping of the male body itself to watch it recover its shape. The energy with which George Stevens engages conventional cinematic borders indicates how much he wants to confirm a vision of manhood as at once realistic and mythic. The film's highly stylized quality—whether of outsized acting and eruptive music or extreme color saturation and strained camera angles— lends to the whole a visionary quality, the nostalgic tones of a boy's fond dream. And Joey's final yelling of "Shane" into the mist, echoing off the mountains, reflects us back to the haunted moment of a man recollecting how he became a man. At every juncture, the film declares its elaborately liminal tendency, as if to reinforce an obsession with the problem of what kind of man to become.

The cinematography of *Hondo* produces a radically different effect, and not simply because John Farrow exploits 3-D possibilities in predictable ways: in the torture of Hondo Lane, staked to the ground with coals thrust into his (and the viewer's) hand; in the fight between Hondo and Silva (Rodolfo Acosta), when both slash angrily at the camera; in the escape of wagons from an Apache attack by driving straight at the audience. The film more inventively adapts this brief cinematic fad to Hondo's gradual passage from fierce desert terrain into a series of comfortably appointed interiors. That transition into domesticity corresponds to a gradual acceptance of responsibility, with an impact in 3-D that offers a psychological inducement for the otherwise straightforward sequence of plot: the evolution of an embittered Indian fighter into a man redeemed by love of a widow and son, able to move from empty space into closed rooms, from independence so intense that he denies even owning his dog ("He doesn't need anybody") to acceptance of necessarily constraining choices and mature commitments ("end of a way of life—too bad").

By contrast, L'Amour's subsequent novel transforms this cinematic
210 evocation of consciousness into a series of still moments, beginning with

the vivid temporal arrest that results from a recurrence of the word "nothing" to evoke Hondo's thoughts and actions. His very stillness is equated with the static landscape—"He did not move. . . . Nothing moved. . . . He thought none of this" (2)—as if to match the kind of descriptive arrest achieved in the Leatherstocking series. When Ed Lowe first unknowingly confronts Hondo, time stops once again: "A fly buzzed in the room. Outside somewhere a horse stampeded and there was a clang of iron on iron. Ed Lowe stood very still" (72). Later, "a frozen instant" is accompanied by instant paralysis: "Hondo lay still, listening, scarcely able to breathe. A bee buzzed near, landed on a bush. Hondo could see the texture of the wings, the flexing of the tiny muscles of the body. . . . Not a sound disturbed the clear, bell-like beauty of the morning. There was nothing. And then there was" (109). Two pages later, "and there was nothing" once more reappears, only to reappear later again. In contrast to *High Noon,* where the clock always ticks, or *Shane,* where protracted glances and calculated gestures seem somehow to slow the clock, *Hondo* arrests time altogether, holding action for the moment in complete abeyance.

Even syntactically, time is suspended through a frequent resort to ellipses—an effect paradoxically reinforced by the simple sequential syntax of "Then" followed by "and then," as scenes with little in common but stark images (swirling "dust," "nothing") suddenly displace one another. Narrative advance is checked by the sheer arbitrariness of scenic progression, as more or less motionless moments appear, chapter by chapter—the subject of equally sudden shifts of point of view within each chapter (aligning the reader first with Hondo, then Angie, a horse, Ed Lowe, various army personnel, and so on, in quicksilver fashion). No special logic governs the shifts in perspective from Angie's ranch to army massacre to Hondo's "reading" of that slaughter to Ed Lowe's treachery, back to Angie awaiting Hondo.

The effect of this narrative confusion is to turn the reader back to characters themselves for a model of what reading should be. Angie reacts through a series of mental questions studiously represented in each of her sections, while Johnny (by contrast with Joey Starrett) seems to have little response at all, his admiration reduced to simple reflection. It is rather through Hondo's instantaneous assessments of any context he finds himself in that a rationale for the narrative's temporal arrest and arbitrary shifts becomes clear. His ability at once to understand others by their own account (whether Angie, Johnny, or even his horse), like his ability to anticipate a surprise attack or reconstruct a three-day-old assault, is meant to confirm how easily, effortlessly, he can interpret the world around him. Acting naturally through well-hewn experience, on the basis of inherent capacity yet hard-learned skills, Hondo offers Johnny a conventional paternal model that exemplifies a somewhat magical combination—indeed, that clarifies how easy yet impossible are conventional expectations for parental knowledge.

L'Amour's achievement in *Hondo* lay in conjoining public with private, history with dream, collaborative effort with an ethos of individualism. Moreover, this conjunction corresponds to that hybrid period of adolescence so nicely captured in Hondo's celebrated position as scout—essential to army maneuvers yet independent and out of uniform, obligated by official duties yet free of normal constraints (or as Major Sherry facetiously remarks, "We've orders to stop anyone—anyone at all. . . . Lane, be careful" [82–83]). Hondo is released from the conventional expectation to take orders and work by the clock—released so fully as to inhabit a narrative world where time is as indeterminate as space, awash in the moment. And invariably that moment occurs as a child-centered one, with Johnny's presence iterated either as imagined or real, joining Hondo and Angie together, proof against any possible misunderstandings or disagreements.

By contrast with this narrative erosion of boundaries, *High Noon* reinforces even more fully than *Shane* the leitmotif of the threshold, making it easier to adduce a catalogue of liminal images. The obsessiveness of such images, however, does little to suggest how highly charged the conflicts are in *High Noon* between fathers and sons—sons who desperately want adult prerogatives yet disdain expectations for adult behavior. As Helen Ramirez repeats to her irritated lover Harvey Pell, in a voice inflected (according to the screenplay) with an "almost maternal pity in her laughter and manner": "When are you going to grow up?" The answer, as the film reveals, is: Never. That theme of maturation is ruthlessly pursued in terms akin to *Shane,* with a parallel concentration on borders imaged explicitly in windows— of people moving toward or away from them, catching themselves gazing through them. Staring through the saloon's plate glass, Harvey resentfully watches a Kane he can neither emulate nor defeat (figures 23 and 24); later, Amy indignantly scrutinizes a Kane who gains in integrity through a window's stark outline. The film's most famous shot (which became a distribution poster) pictures an anxious Kane peering through a fragmented window frame just before his wife is wrenched through a door across the street (figures 25 and 26).

A brief catalogue can sum up the film's even more obsessive invocation of framing doorways: Amy walking out of her marriage by walking through Judge Mettrick's door, reversed in her later decisive return to her husband's office when she hears the sound of shots (figure 27); Harvey proudly making his "final" exit from Helen, the Judge leaving town with his office door wide open. Later, Harvey adolescently tries to stop Kane from entering his office, while Amy strides through the hotel's wide doors into Helen's room

Figures 23 and 24. Harvey Pell (Lloyd Bridges) watching Will Kane (Gary Cooper) from inside saloon window in *High Noon*.

and into face-to-face confrontation with a different set of feminine values. Countless other occasions are marked by dramatically closed doors: of Sam walking into church, followed by Kane asking for help; of Kane blocked at the Fuller's front door by Mildred, his friend's wife, then forced to exit through a picket gate; of Kane repeatedly entering and leaving his marshall's office (figure 28), or of his elaborate release of the town drunk, Charley (Jack Elam), from a jail cell, then from the office (figure 29); of Kane climbing stairs to Helen's room, reentering her life, only to turn away; and of walking to the livery stable where Harvey Pell attacks him, then heading to the barber shop to recover; of his constant retreat through other doors in the vain search for aid. Throughout, Zinnemann maintains an unusually low camera angle, forcing the viewer to look up to Kane through windows or doors, much in the way that *Shane* adopts Joey's perspective.   213

Figures 25 and
26. Will Kane peering
through broken glass at
end of *High Noon*.

The fact that *High Noon* is thematically pitched toward a later stage of
development than *Shane* helps explain its more frequent sequence of
frames, windows, doors, and lines. Such liminal scenes reinforce a sense
of phases involved in the rite of passage to manhood, and contribute more
generally to the charged emotional atmosphere so often associated with
adolescence. Instead of simply gazing transgressively across given boundaries, however, characters in *High Noon* enact their uncertain self-
possession through the kind of face-to-face confrontations adduced above.
The most dramatic instance of these occur as startling encounters at street
corners: when Kane nearly collides with Ben Miller leaving the saloon; or
when boys playing sheriff-and-outlaw collide with him, yelling "Bang,
bang, Kane, you're dead"; or in the series of shocked confrontations that
ensue in the final gunfight. The sharp cross-cutting and frequent close-ups

Figure 27. Amy Kane walking through Judge Mettrick's door in *High Noon*.

that ensue with each confrontation prompts the viewer as well to feel a certain confrontational resistance. These powerful meetings lend a special significance to the fact that the only figures who never cross doors are Pierce and Colby, the outlaws who remain until noon at the railroad station. It is as if they were meant to represent a state of arrested development, wanting to return things vengefully toward the past, unable to enter the spatial dynamics that represent emotional growth. Other characters are always, by contrast, on the verge of another space—beginning with the image of Kane attracted to the idea of leaving town with his bride, and ending with him and Amy ready at last to depart.

The paralyzing impact of threshold moments in *High Noon* is offset by a clock-driven rhythm, which repeatedly jump-starts a plot that becomes momentarily halted (unlike the more complete suspensions that recur in *Hondo*). Indeed, the balance between these two impulses generates much of the film's appeal, with brief moments of narrative arrest punctuating an otherwise taut plot sequence. That combination was only an afterthought in the film's genesis, following the failure of a prerelease version that prompted Stanley Kramer to add remedial effects: additional close-ups of Gary Cooper's pain-ridden face; multiple shots of watches and clocks building to the toll of noon; in particular, the opening ballad sung by Tex Ritter, "Do Not Forsake Me, Oh My Darlin'," which became a popular hit.

The fine appropriateness of Dmitri Tiomkin's ballad, which recurs   215

Figure 28. Will Kane entering marshall's office in *High Noon*.

throughout as off-screen (nondiegetic) music, consists in expressing in musical form the film's tension between motion and stasis, onward progression and liminal scenes. While the ballad form is conventionally circular, with a single musical refrain repeated for different text verses, Tiomkin's words themselves accentuate the temporal arrest of sheer "waiting" made explicit in the final line of the refrain: "Wait along, wait along, wait along." And that textual refrain (intoned repeatedly through the film) is uncannily mirrored in the musical motif of the opening line—of scale degrees 1-1-2-3-1, 4-3-2-1 (or C-C-D-E-C, F-E-D-C)—a circle returning invariably, monotonously, to its initial pitch in C-major. The music itself both carries us on and folds us back, that is, returning us to the same place, much as the film does cinematically in its own repeated delays of plot—a claim given further credence by the fact that the song was interjected at lulls in the storyline.[42]

Much as Kane longs to "go home," however, *High Noon* makes it clear that the time for such longing is simply too late, as temporal limits tighten inexorably. And the ability to live within the constraints of a clock's minute hand defines Kane's hard-won maturity by contrast with Harvey Pell's impatient strivings. Someone who more dramatically personifies an adolescent eagerness to defy time is the outlaw, Ben Miller, who opens and nearly closes the film with the explicit desire simply to push things along. Pierce's opening question, "You in a hurry?" elicits the response, "I sure am," while Frank Miller's final admonishment, "Can't you wait?" (after Ben impulsively breaks a store window to steal a lady's hat) likewise evokes a quick, "Just want to be ready." The film itself similarly pressures the viewer, building

Figure 29. Release of town drunk from jail in *Shane.*

suspense through music, cross-cutting, close-ups, and physical confrontations, almost as if to evoke a stereotypical adolescent consciousness that time is out of one's control.[43]

Part of what it means to be an adult in *High Noon,* more emphatically than in *Shane* or *Hondo,* is to accept the fact that temporal limits are firmly fixed, neither easily elided nor transgressed—something Harvey Pell never quite understands. Lloyd Bridges (in his mid-twenties) played the role as an impulsive adolescent annoyed at Kane's paternal response, eager to prove his manhood with Helen, who finally reminds him, "You're a good-looking boy. You have big broad shoulders. But he is a man. It takes more than big broad shoulders to make a man, Harvey, and you have a long way to go." This admonition forms an important lesson, despite the previous chapter's claims for the body as constitutive of masculine identity, since simply *having* a body is never quite enough in itself. Of course, the male body must be challenged, painfully taken apart to see if it can survive, but it must also submit to education, painstakingly learning to read the contemporary landscape as conduct book. Beating scenes may sometimes serve as short circuits of that pedagogical strain, displacing the process of "growing up" into manhood with scenes of simple violence. But they never dispel the need for education, which helps explain why the Western is split between stasis and didacticism, between the necrophilia of violated men and the sentimental promise of future achievement for a new generation able to master the lessons.

Manhood consists once again of assorted intangible qualities, as much   217 culturally created as biologically given, because it involves a learned capacity to remain in position, able to resist being swayed by personal inclination or social exigency. Harvey Pell bows to both sorts of pressure in order to gain respect, yet the very lack of self-restraint at transitional moments confirms his adolescent stature in a film where he is often imaged either following others through doors or looked at through windows. He refuses to believe in himself simply because he lacks external authorization, unlike Kane, who asserts to Amy while pointing at his marshall's badge, "I'm the same man, with or without this."

Gender

All three 1950s Westerns engage not simply this general issue of manhood but more particularly the question of how a boy is to become a man. Partly, this is done through vivid displays of the male body itself, as if to remind both characters and viewers of the biological issues at stake. But the process of growing into manhood only really exists in contrast with the idea of what it means to be a woman, represented in these three Westerns most compellingly as a breaching of borders, an erasure of limits, a bridging of otherwise incompatible possibilities. Marian Starrett, Amy Kane, and Angie Lowe each express similar bewilderment at the structure of masculine behavior and attempt to alter it most radically by modifying the hero's resolve.

Thus, the problem of adolescence for the male child is to learn how to maintain that resolve, standing stalwart in a world of suasions and humiliations coded as feminine. *Shane,* most forthrightly, addresses this conflict between manhood's conventional behavorial signs (drinking, rough language, aggressive address) and its essential principle (self-restraint) through a series of scenes that augment a tension over forms in which manly behavior can be displayed. Rikers openly taunts Starrett about wielding a boy's rifle in their opening encounter: "Expectin' trouble?" Later, in a much more elaborate (justifiably classic) scene in Grafton's saloon, Chris Calloway ridicules Shane's purchase of soda pop as "womanish."

Restraining himself in the face of repeated challenges to his manhood, Shane succeeds in defining manhood itself as a process of controlled self-presentation. Unlike an emotionally self-indulgent Calloway or even an overly eager Starrett, Shane warily resists encroaching on thresholds, either criminal or domestic. He carefully stands to one side in the contest of ideals between ranchers and farmers, resisting Starrett's earnest efforts to identify him with either party. More important, he resists Marian's fear that skills will transform a man into something he is not or that she should have misgivings over Johnny's education in the tools of manhood ("A gun is as good or as bad as the man using it"). Earlier, he and Starrett resist her suggestion to "hitch up a team" to clear out a stump, in order to do the job the old way. The biological aspects of manhood are manifest in Shane's shirtless display, but as significant is the equation of manhood with the nonphysical principle of maintaining one's resolve, working toward a fixed ideal in matters even so inconsequential.

Becoming a man is presented at once more straightforwardly and problematically in *Hondo* through the plot's attention to the transition into domesticity. The novel, even more than the film, celebrates Hondo's ability to get along without domestic pleasures, so much so that he seems a different species from Angie rather than simply a different gender. The contrast is first underscored by the abrupt transition from Apache-infested desert to her oasis of a ranch, "green, lovely, and peaceful" (7–8), and thereafter develops as a series of culturally acquired differences presented as if innate, beginning with a conventional stress on Hondo's alleged "hardness" ("There was no softness in him. His toughness was ingrained and deep" [1]). Angie understands this quality in him no better than in his dog, Sam, who "doesn't take to petting" (9), or in his unnamed horse whose very savagery is an asset. Such fierce independence appears a biological given, part of a quickly adaptive, inarticulate, unemotional nature so unlike her own that the narrative defies expectations in having her respond to Hondo. Like Marian Starrett and Amy Kane, who also express their feelings freely, her attraction to him is presented once again as an inexplicable biological drive.

Contrary to this understanding of gender as something innate, however, both novel and film reveal it as a learned distinction, capable of being confused and therefore requiring constant attention. Different spheres of influence are natural for men and women, but Hondo appreciates Angie's supposedly masculine skill in sharpening axes, and after claiming, "A woman should be a good cook," adds impetuously, "I'm a good cook myself" (13). Repeatedly, characters behave in ways that deny the assumptions they make about gender—assumptions that L'Amour's novel invokes more explicitly than does the film. Men supposedly feel an innate need to wander, while women settle: "A man might drift, but a woman must belong somewhere" (96–97). Women are constitutionally drawn to serve men while "a man must live as he must" (87). The biological truth of such claims, however, is belied by the novel's emphasis on Johnny's need to learn certain masculine skills in order not to "be spoiled." The protracted scenes of education in what it is a man must do all tend to confirm how unnatural such behavior is. And Angie's reservations about Hondo's "cruel," "unbelievably brutal" tactics (140–41) are simply part of what Johnny will need to learn about women.

219

High Noon does even more to problematize the innateness of such distinctions by identifying Amy as a feminist and Will Kane as a man who "can't be managed."[44] The attractiveness of male independence, both to the traditionalist Helen Ramirez and to Amy, the New Woman, reinforces classical oppositions represented by their bodily types: the passionate brunette with a past and the conventionally respectable blonde. Contrasting outfits—all white, all black—only reinforce this allegorical distinction. Yet almost as soon as it seems in place, the distinction is unsettled when Helen asks questions that already bother the viewer: "What kind of woman are you? How can you leave him like this?" The Western's commitment to standard kinds of women (and correspondingly, standard kinds of men) is undermined by Amy's unexpected answer, in which she expresses a principled antipathy to violence based on her family's own destruction: "I don't care who's right and who's wrong. There's got to be some better way for people to live." Her Quaker commitment to pacifism is a choice, then, not a biological need, resembling the Western hero's own practiced self-restraint, his ability to resist being compelled or coerced by inner emotions or public pressure. While she herself claims not to understand Kane's need to defend the town, her behavior seems strangely similar. And by the film's conclusion, the viewer is left undecided about who has prevailed and what might more generally be meant as a triumph of supposedly masculine or feminine ideals.

All three texts present men and woman as biological givens, only then to reveal gender as a process of cultural construction. *Hondo* in particular belabors the process of male creation through the narrative of Johnny's education—whether warned about dogs or informed of horses, axes, and Apache lore. Less important than sheer information, however, is the larger ideological frame where, as Hondo intones, "people learn by gettin' bit" (17). Hondo teaches Johnny to swim by simply throwing him into deep water, and his advice about mortal danger is that any man "must at all costs die well." The lesson of both novel and film, as of many '50s Westerns, is that men want sons to teach, if only to reveal what it is to be a man. So strongly is this urge presented that it comes to seem innate, with the impulse toward cultural transmission itself identified as biological—and usually as a gesture opposed to whatever women are proposing. The lessons men offer in Westerns are invariably ways of taking boys from their mothers, much as Dr. Spock appears to have done under the cover of pediatric advice. And that helps explain why the genre has become such a highly didactic instrument, suggested by the epigraph from Philip French.

Given how often the '50s Western devoted itself to educating boys, it
is striking how few films actually show the adolescent passage into man-

hood itself. Instead, most focus on one or the other end of the spectrum of development, either casting inexperienced boys in roles where they might be educated or casting experienced but youthful men in roles of adult frustration. Part of the explanation may be that the intermediate stage of adolescence so important to the early '50s was simply assumed to be an extension of a boyhood trajectory. Yet this absence of adolescent possibilities lends itself to a darker interpretation. "In film after film in the 1950s," Don Graham asserts, "there is no young person worthy of assuming the responsibilities of adulthood. Thus Westerns in this period express a view quite different from what the youth-oriented movies were telling us. *Rebel without a Cause* and *The Blackboard Jungle,* for example, took the side of youth." As Graham goes on to observe, *High Noon* "impugns both generations, fathers and sons," and gives the impression that no one will be capable of assuming true civic authority.[45]

The prospect that boys will fail through education to negotiate their way into manhood offers another explanation for an increasing pattern of violence in the Western ever since the 1950s. After all, when slow maturity is no longer granted a cultural legitimacy, the recourse is to instant and brutal proof to demonstrate what can be achieved no other way. The Western's traditional balance of education against bodily violence has shifted, as violence itself begins to take the place of "growing up." Indeed, it might well be said that the increasing brutality and accompanying impassiveness of '60s Westerns betrays a growing lack of faith that men can any longer actually *become* men. All that is possible is that they *be* men, or rather manly bodies (which, without hope of education, increasingly means taking the form of deadened corpses).

Yet if the problem of "growing up" seemed to have no clear solution in '50s Westerns, it was one still considered to be well worth addressing. Certainly, *Shane, Hondo,* and *High Noon* confront the problem in mutually exclusive ways, but they do so through an obsessive threshold imagery that reflects how much they shared a more general cultural panic. No consistent symbolic reading joins the three together, linking *Hondo's* self-enclosed nuclear family with *Shane's* alternative father figures, or either with *High Noon's* absence of fathers at all. It is that lack of unanimity, however, that itself confirms how central the problem was perceived to be: of adolescents growing into responsible adults, of boys becoming men and in turn fathers themselves. While fathers have always seemed to be a problem in the Western, the 1950s became the "classic" period of the genre by exploring its terms as never before.

8 VIOLENCE BEGETS

Our climate and scenery here has frequently raised the dead.
Owen Wister (1897)[1]

Show me a hero and I'll show you a villain with good excuses.
Robert C. Cumbow (1987)[2]

The Western's grip on our imaginations is due, so Robert Warshow claimed in 1954, to its "serious orientation to the problem of violence such as can be found almost nowhere else in our culture."[3] Warshow's choice of gangster films to pose against cinema Westerns confirmed how much weight he placed on the adjective "serious," how impatient he was with any genre unreflective about its violent disposition. The gangster film's upward-striving fable of social disruption, he claimed, simply pandered to a strain of postadolescent rebellion against the status quo. In contrast to that brutal genre ("anti-social, resting on fantasies of irresponsible freedom"), Warshow praised the Western's drama of self-restraint, where men opposed by seas of trouble refrained from arms until honorable means were exhausted. The question of what honor entailed—of what was required for its defense, or revealed it to others, or allowed it to remain itself in untoward circumstances—was for Warshow the distinguishing feature of violence in the Western.

Yet little more than a decade after this tribute to the Western hero's restraint, the genre had become as indiscriminately violent as any other—gangster, combat, and horror movies, detective and spy films, even science fiction. Explicit images proliferated everywhere in American life, encouraged by a general impatience with decorous standards of representation. If familiarity has always bred a certain contempt for such standards, never before had conventions for depicting violence (and sexual intimacy) evolved so rapidly. The usual explanation for this change involves a combination of political events and technological advances, with television broadcasting scenes of violence nightly into middle-class homes: the brutal repression of civil rights activists in Southern cities; the two Kennedy and the King assassinations; the chain of major urban riots in Northern ghettos; and most incessantly, the escalating carnage in Vietnam. Yet the issue (once again) is never so simple as art reflecting life by offering allegories of events. Different as '60s Westerns are from those preceding, they no more automatically reflect their culture than previous examples did.

Westerns became more violent not because America did but because taboos against depicting violence were suddenly dislodged, allowing violent events to be contemplated now with a more open eye. And for a genre centrally concerned with gauging "the value of violence," this easing of prohibitions against barbarous acts could now be played out in plots that seemed to advocate those acts. The change was a remarkable one for a genre devoted to testing the legitimacy of violence—whose standard scenes of lynchings and shoot-outs enacted the failure of restraint, the need at last to capitulate to deadly action if honor were to be maintained. Yet by the end of the 1960s, Westerns seemed no less *grand guignol* than other popular genres, depicting violence as always brutal, never redemptive, warranted simply by virtue of superior force.

Remaking Westerns

The two most influential directors of '60s Westerns, Sergio Leone and Sam Peckinpah, turned the genre familiar to Warshow inside out, offering "spaghetti" and X-rated films that form a frontal assault on the viewer.[4] Not only did violence no longer offer moral resolution, it also served only marginally as closure to Western plots now loosely defined. Indeed, it is as if Cooper's practice of absorbing plot through landscape description had been executed in a minor key, replaced by violent outbursts that likewise disable narrative progression. Landscape continues as much a part of '60s Westerns as in those preceding, but instead of audiences distracted by settings into moments of timeless arrest, the effect of stasis is achieved through bloody set pieces. Whereas Cooper had established a rhythm in which that effect was enforced by landscape descriptions (interrupted by violent action legitimated by aimless glances over landscape), Westerns now give the sense that violent action itself *is* stasis. And perhaps unsurprisingly, the person responsible for this was Leone, whose operatic Westerns borrow heavily from Italian opera seria, in which narratively pointless arias likewise halt stage time in order to allow meditative expansion along some other line.

While the explicit violence of '60s Westerns served extramoral, even extradramatic, ends, then, most viewers nonetheless responded in conventional moral terms, educated by the genre itself to the virtues of restraint. The new heroes therefore seemed merely professionals doing a job, possessed of traditional gunslinging skills but committed to little else. A diminished legacy of Natty Bumppo's hectoring expert, these men formed a degraded version of the stalwartly moral Westerner whose vision now extended no further than his own well-being. The various misfits, loners, bullies, mavericks, and sociopaths of films like John Sturges's *The Magnificent Seven* (1960), Richard Brooks's *The Professionals* (1966), Ted Post's *Hang 'Em High* (1968), and Henry Hathaway's *True Grit* (1969) possess merely the empty shell of an earlier expertise. And in some cases, even that expertise has eroded, to be counted on no more than a man's moral code. "The heroes are now professional fighters," Will Wright has observed; "men willing to defend society only as a job they accept for pay or for love of fighting, not from commitment to ideas of law and justice."[5]

However apt this characterization, it does little to explain the achievement of the decade's most remarkable "professional" films: Leone's first effort, *Per un pugno di dollari* (1964, released in 1967 as *A Fistful of Dollars*), and Peckinpah's acknowledged masterwork, *The Wild Bunch* (1969). Before turning to them, we need to sketch out the shared generic context from which they emerged. Leone's film heralded the advent of the "spaghetti Western," a subgenre of cheaply produced Italian films whose extraordinary popularity altered the shape of the Hollywood Western. Following the 1958 peak of the genre's classic period (when fifty-four feature Westerns were released), the number dipped to eleven in 1963; by 1965, however, after the advent of the spaghetti Western, production had doubled to twenty-two Hollywood films.[6] The key to this market transformation was *A Fistful of Dollars,* the plot of which Leone stole from Akira Kurosawa's samurai film, *Yojimbo* (1961), and which led immediately to two sequels—*For a Few Dollars More* (1965) and *The Good, the Bad and the Ugly* (1966).[7] All three films, moreover, set the stage for Sam Peckinpah, who responded to the challenge of Leone's parodic perspective by once again making the standard Hollywood film into an "authentic" Western myth.

Despite flagrant differences in cinematic vision, in plots and *mise-en-scènes,* the two directors shared a similar fascination with the genre and its construction of masculinity. Parodically, Leone resurrected certain standard personalities, self-consciously breathing life into characters long since become caricatures. By focusing on glaring eyes, mean faces, and lean bodies, all in a flamboyant style that diverts attention from the motion of plot itself, he humorously succeeds in undercutting the idea of any moral code—if only by treating such codes as little more than a physical reflex. Leone's characters seem mere empty shells, and issues of right and wrong, appropriate behavior, and honorable acts are either disregarded or self-mockingly reduced to questions of skill, puncturing the 1950s ideal of the high-minded man with a gun. By contrast, Peckinpah so insistently stresses a personal code that the concept transcends any immediate social concerns—concerns represented in dense detail in a variety of Anglo and His-panic contexts. Even so, despite the intensity with which his characters express a moral sensibility, they respond unthinkingly, out of ingrained habit, nullifying the idea they are energetically espousing. While Peckin-pah's characters seem at first glance more humane, less cartoonish than Leone's, they are merely less obvious versions of the mechanical hero who expresses a code irrelevant to his actions, and whose semblance of bour-geois humanity is thereby revealed as his most automatic feature.

Leone and Peckinpah reinvigorate the Western, that is, with an oddly similar effect from angles diametrically opposed: Leone, from the premise of amusing the viewer about the Western's tired conventions; Peckinpah, under the assumption that those conventions still pertain, even if ideals for action do not. Leone's spoof of the genre's baroque disposition to violence paradoxically reinforces the conventions he spoofs, while Peckinpah's stress on the casualness of everyday violence has the effect of disguising generic demands that nonetheless structure his film. Differences aside, what the two men most share is a joint sense of belatedness, of needing to revive the Western at a moment when it had come to seem exhausted as a form. If that is an old story for the genre, felt equally by each generation of writers and directors—indeed, perhaps itself a sign of creative self-consciousness *in* a genre—it is significant that both men shared with predecessors the self-conscious determination to cast their films more "realistically" than those preceding (both, in fact, achieving notoriety in the search for actors who resembled the faces they had researched in archives). As well, however, they both turned away from fixed generic assumptions, most prominently by turning the Western itself to a Mexican context, placing Anglo-American characters in a culturally alien setting rather than loose in wilderness space. The shift south of the border contributed to the overall process by which the genre was further defamiliarized, diverting attention yet again from plot to questions of character.

This effort to force the Western back to a set of traditional preoccupa-tions corresponded to larger social and political uncertainties during the 1960s about the legitimate uses of violence. At least in part, the invective as well as acclaim that greeted each director can be understood in terms of an ongoing debate about directions the nation was taking both domestically and abroad—registered through the separate crises that defined the Civil Rights movement and the Vietnam War. Again, as with earlier Westerns, the unique appeal of *A Fistful of Dollars* and *The Wild Bunch* hinged on their curiously Janus-faced structures—their deft incorporation of mutually ex-clusive ideologies about the individual and his (invariably masculine) capacity for restraint and violence. And again, they achieved this almost entirely through idiosyncratic styles.

Facescapes

Not the least striking feature of Leone's first Western is that it still retains the power to shock. Especially for first-time viewers, the desolate setting and improbable plot of *A Fistful of Dollars* are as disorienting today as its bizarre soundtrack and slightly garish color matching. And to these one can add, as Robert C. Cumbow does in listing the film's innovations:

the mercenary bounty-killer haunted by unspecified ghosts from his past; the uneasy partnerships created by the gunman for his own profit; double- and triple-crosses; pervasive death imagery; breathtaking, rule-breaking use of the wide-screen; a near-fetishist devotion to the close-up; cryptic dialogue and quirky plotting that have nothing to do with motivation or logic; an unprecedented marriage of music and image; and, the relentless pace of mythic storytelling.[8]

The masterful combination of these features, which recur throughout Leone's films, prompt a viewer to ask if the whole is to be taken straight or tongue-in-cheek.[9] The question is never resolved, since each film balances precariously on the border between interpretive frames—self-consciously flamboyant in every detail while true to the genre in overall effect.

Yet even Cumbow's list of structural innovations in *A Fistful of Dollars* hardly suggests the impact of more specific parodic twists: Clint Eastwood's cigarillo tirelessly clenched in his teeth, his worn serape, sheepskin vest, and designer stubble; the elaborate, interminable, shifting stares among adversaries, and even among family and friends; the farce of vicious Benito Rojo (Antonia Prieto) declaring, "I want law and order in this place"; the one-sided duels in which no one besides the hero gets off a round; the film's central scene, when No Name rescues Marisol (Marianne Koch) by killing six men with five shots, or, more magically, when he finally kills six Rojos with a loaded .45, then releases the bound innkeeper with a miraculous seventh shot. That seventh bullet is a neat touch, inserting No Name into a line of mythic marksmen like the famous Freischütz, whose pact with the devil guides his bullets magically to their target. As the innkeeper, Silvanito (Pepe Calvo), remarks to No Name while they spy on the army ambush: "It's like playing cowboys and Indians." Altogether, this mocking inflation of staple materials recasts the genre by altering our understanding of its standard images, settings, and sounds, finally precluding us from seeing the classic Western ever the same again (and lending an irony to Leone's reliance on Stevens's *Shane* as one of his primary models).

A careful student of the genre, Leone's most trenchant idea involved reimagining the central pairing of landscape and code—and not simply by modifying these intertwined concepts (as writers and directors since Cooper had done) but radically reconfiguring their relation. Refusing to imagine his hero in a wilderness milieu living by a self-defined code, he transformed the landscape (the "West") into a vague topography that might be almost anywhere and the western code into mere capitalist excess at its most ruthless. The flat, emptied-out sweep of his desert is utterly alien and undistinguished, as if the mythically resonant Far West had been reduced to sandy terrain to be found on any of several continents. Additionally, the "code" of the hero has been eviscerated and recast as simple thievery—the knight of the prairies now stripped to ignoble essentials, become a mere bandit for selfish ends.

The actual appearance of *A Fistful of Dollars* signaled the advent of a working man's Western, an unembellished version (made on the cheap) in which costly extras appear as townsfolk in only two brief scenes. Such economizing has the effect of clearing out Leone's western village, converting it into a ghost town void of signs of traffic, industry, or commerce, with no domestic life or buzz of social engagement, indeed, with only the most minimal traces of citizenry (innkeeper, coffin maker, bell ringer)—leaving the professional heroes and villains to operate in an uncanny social vacuum. While the emptying out of San Miguel may have resulted from immediate production constraints, that imposed "civic vision" corresponds to Leone's larger mythic sensibility, expressed in his most distinctive revision of the Hollywood Western: the draining of any life at all from the landscape, clearing it of animation so entirely as to seem to define death itself. This cynical eye is strong enough to suggest not only Leone's dismissal of the big-screen Western's fascination with scenery but his demythologizing of a tradition that extends back to Cooper, of American wilderness as setting for moral regeneration. Leone's West is merely an empty arena for haphazard violation and death—a conclusion reinforced by the film's odd cinematography and editing: "the comic-book colors," as Robert C. Cumbow has remarked, "the sharp depth, the exotic angles, the sweaty-close flesh landscapes, and the slow-paced kinetics of Leone's Techniscope world."[10]

The oddness of such stark empty landscape is compounded by the set Leone creates in San Miguel. Its line of empty adobe houses look like nothing other than "fronts," hastily erected, cheaply finished, with a single ludicrous Moorish church capped by a bell tower at the end of the street, next to a grotesque mansion built in Spanish modernist style. From the beginning, San Miguel is conceived allegorically, as a cityscape of death where even women are professedly not women but "only widows." Silvanito complains that "we spend our time here between funerals and burials," eliciting from No Name the dry confirmation that he "never saw a town as dead as this one." So extreme is the antiludic impulse embodied by the town that all nonlethal activity seems excluded: "No one ever comes here to play." Even the central premise of Marisol's abduction by Ramon Rojo (Gian Maria Volonté)—that her husband, Julio, had "cheated at cards"—seems patently absurd, since the last thing anyone would do in this town is to spend time playing a game, cards or any other. It is "a world irredeemably condemned to immobility, somnolence, to the lack of all resource and development."[11]

Town and landscape, in other words, collapse here into a single depressing symbolic entity, controverting the genre's traditional split between nature and culture, West and East, the wild and the civilized. And though Leone's setting is generic—instantly recognizable as such, like the dark forests of fairy tales, *Batman's* Gotham City, immigrant neighborhoods in gangster films—it remains dull in a strangely non-Western fashion, drained of redeeming significances projected into it by nearly every other writer and director. Even so, the parched, ominous, patently fake quality of this setting still holds a fascination for the viewer—in part, because it seems the antithesis of human, even animate desires; in larger part, paradoxically, because it seems nonetheless *as* landscape to embody Leone's conception of the human and personal so vividly. The leathery, lizard-like look of his characters combined with their automaton-like behavior makes them seem products of their environment, as if just emerged from the desolate waste. The film's climactic moment when No Name magically appears from a cloud of dust to confront the Rojos serves not only to break plot suspense, then, but even more importantly to confirm the lingering sense we have had all along that he is functionally part of the landscape, shaped Antaeus-like by its imperatives.

What emerges as never before in the Western is a landscape so lifeless and inert that it can no longer even be anthropomorphized. The implication for character is that men simply fall back on themselves (with interestingly sad results), since the landscape no longer preaches, enforces, provides clues, or otherwise resonates with moral significance. But the implication for that most habitual descriptive gesture of the Western—of allowing the eye to pause over topography—is just as radical. The aimless glance that Cooper offers of landscape becomes for Leone, in the absence of animate terrain (and in a different medium), a lingering over a visual "landscape" best construed as the terrain of character—or what, given his intense concentration on the contours of physiognomy, might better be termed "facescapes." The appeal of supposedly authentic faces led Leone to research eye-witness accounts and historical photographs for his first two films, leading to an inimitable ugliness in his casting only surpassed in his own later films (Klaus Kinski, as it were, trumping Mario Brega). Such strains of historical realism have always been curiously central to the Western, extending back through the archival efforts of George Stevens and Stanley Kramer, from L'Amour and Wister to Cooper, all anxious to confirm in footnotes the authenticity of their visions.

Yet this casting of "realistic" faces serves an end other than naive realism, suggested by the fact that no major director has used close-ups so often, so lingeringly, in such diverse combinations. Only after his first film would Leone recognize the implications of that technique, which he later explored by directing the camera to selected parts of the face, finally experimenting with long shots that cropped all but the eyes. A Fistful of Dollars, however, registers this cinematic style in seminal form with an attendant concentration less on turns of plot than points of character. Events seem disconnected, occurring with an arbitrary and random abandon, while a violent series of face-offs are injected as the means of settling haphazard accounts. The rationale behind these conflicts matters less than the conflicts themselves—the animosity, hostility, and belligerence that wells up all but inexplicably.

Living Dead

Yet character is not really the issue either for Leone, as it becomes clear that his prolonged close-ups serve a formal, structural purpose far more than the customary emotional one. That is, the camera follows faces not to probe psychology but simply to register the impossibility of any greater knowledge of character than one has at first glance—as if our interest in the mask of a face lay simply in recognizing it *as* a mask, realizing how unrevealing it can be, how little affect a supposedly animate being can have. Or, to adapt Gilles Deleuze's reading of the facial close-up, how minimal it is possible to make "micro-movements on an immobilised plate of nerve."[12] This pattern is notably different from the landscape contemplation of earlier Westerns, where the terrain was always replete with clues and ready to be read in contemporary moral terms—whether it was Grey displacing anxieties about women's status onto purple sage, or Cooper assigning democratic principles onto Adirondack brush. For Leone, the object of contemplation renders nothing except itself. Faces no longer offer signs of meanings that lie behind a set of features; instead, they represent only non-sense, the ultimate thwarting of interpretive effort.

230   In this, Leone suggests a foreboding as great as any physical violence,

something more troubling than anything implied in earlier Westerns. For if violence is often little more than an unbuttoned reaction to violence—an equation far older than the Western but central to its mechanics—the real terror is that the object of contemplation can no longer be decoded, defying clarification altogether. However intensely brutal it is possible for films to become (Leone suggests), as long as violence can be decoded comfort can still be found. The great fear is that the object of our contemplation—landscapes, facescapes—will no longer speak back to us and that we therefore will not understand bloody deeds that can no longer be read as a sign.

Paradoxically, one condition that might help negate Leone's concentration on impenetrable masks is the notorious anonymity of Clint Eastwood's "man with no name." For anonymity is normally an interpretive irritant, encouraging us to wonder about the question of character—something the Western has long known in a tradition that extends back through Wister's unnamed Virginian, through Crane's storied figures, back to Cooper's Natty Bumppo, whose given name is rendered irrelevant by nicknames and sobriquets. Unlike Cooper and Wister, however, Leone ignores the normal psychological effects of anonymity, shunning the process of interesting us in the idea of character abstracted from history. After first impressions, the presence or absence of a name clarifies nothing of identity (as Ramon Rojo confirms when, in response to No Name's greeting that "everybody talks about Ramon," he avers, "And many speak of you too").

The completeness with which Eastwood's character is rendered anonymous—not simply his lack of a name but his lack of a past or of future intentions, of glib conversation or ready emotion, of facial expression altogether—suggests that Leone is less interested in *using* the mysterious hero than in killing it by parodying it *as* a convention. Other writers have created anonymous heroes because they are interested in "what a man is like when divested of the things by which we normally recognise him," as Christopher Frayling observes, "such as his name, his past, his conversation, even his complexity."[13] By contrast, Leone seems interested in the *form* of the Western hero's personality as a series of gestures signaling little other than sheer absence, psychological lack, emotional diminishment.

Much of this alienation effect is achieved through the sound track, through a splitting of visual from aural effects, enforced both by the bizarre musical score and by the patchwork of lip-synching necessary to dub a film made in several languages. Ennio Morricone's score offered a surprising innovation, functioning in a way that music rarely had before in Western films by giving acoustic definition to personalities who seem visually two-dimensional. Compensating, as it were, for the silence of characters, the 231 music offers an external, sonic expression to attitudes left otherwise unexpressed, even unfelt. And where the plot occasionally fails to press narrative interest along, Morricone's music singularly succeeds—a phenomenon partially explained by the fact that Leone often directed scenes to match music already composed, fitting images to the sound track in what is a complete reversal of conventional scoring of films.[14]

That sound track differs entirely from the kind of music traditionally associated with the Western, as Robert C. Cumbow observes: "To scenes of primal violence, Leone and Morricone were lending not only music but, astonishingly, *melody*, haunting and lovely, a kind of melody worlds away from the neo-Wagnerian 'mood music' and Coplandesque American folksong variations that even in its best incarnations (in the hands of Dmitri Tiomkin and Elmer Bernstein) had, until then, typified the Hollywood western score."[15] Morricone's unlocalizable electronic whirr at moments of emotional tension, or (as a narrative link) a flute in a declining five-note trill, or minimalist oboes and low piano beats: all end up defining an emotional range greater than any that No Name himself expresses. Instead of following John Ford in using music to define a sense of community, or in shaping the viewer's response to landscape (as Peckinpah would masterfully do), Leone created a sound track to deflate any mysterious heroes, by counterpointing the uncanny silence of No Name with a busy but modernist sonic environment.

The hero's profound detachment and silence in *A Fistful of Dollars* thus seem the result of an emptying out of emotions *into* the world—emotions that infuse surrounding space in the form of strange musical sounds—giving the sense that emotions and world are in a kind of symbiotic relationship with one another. Surprisingly, this powerful condition of the film was an idea that developed only gradually. In fact, Clint Eastwood was "a late choice for the lead role," according to Leone, because "I looked at him and I didn't see any character . . . just a physical figure."[16] Or as Eastwood himself has wryly admitted of his acting style: "I don't just do something. I stand there." It was not simply his impassive manner that altered the characterization but his inability to speak Italian or even to smoke, forcing him to play the role of No Name in a self-described "fog" and contributing to the lack of self-expression that would become his habitual mode.[17] The inability to master Italian meant that considerable dialogue had to be cut from the original script, not only for him but for others in the international cast similarly handicapped.

Far from being a liability for the film, however, this linguisitic incompetence contributes to the odd overall effect by which character is defined, lending the cast something of a robotic aural penumbra in which no real person actually seems to be doing the speaking.[18] Because so many voices are clearly (even clumsily) dubbed, they appear to come from outside the costumed bodies they supposedly inhabit, resembling a ventriloquized dream where figures are not who they say they are since their voices are not their own. Bodies grumble, mutter, and snarl in monosyllabic tones, not as a means of authenticating their vitality but rather to verify that they are not what they seem: autonomous speaking subjects.

A more dramatic way to appreciate the effect of the *Dollars* trilogy is to see it pressing an analogy between character and landscape further than other Westerns. It is as if (in a grim acknowledgement of Cooper's conflation of personality and setting) Leone made one aware of how much one needed to become exactly like the deadened landscape to survive, in the process of which personality itself is evacuated, transmogrified into a series of caricatures of western types. The most obvious instance of this, of course, is No Name himself, whose stark elusiveness is heightened to form a clear parody of the genre's mysterious hero. So thoroughly, in fact, is animation erased from his features that he seems deprived of life altogether. As discussed in Chapter 6, others also appear as little other than walking dead who only finally become active and recognizably alive when they are shot, left twitching in pain, released at last into a realm where movement and vitality are once again feasible.

Repeatedly, Leone conveys through his hero's mechanical performance the sense of how formulaic the Western can be, not simply as a matter of parodying realistic conventions but of alerting us to the automaton-like behavior of figures more dead than alive—in a striking (if unintended) allusion to Cooper's tableaux in *The Last of the Mohicans* of people reduced to statuary. No Name's first encounter upon entering San Miguel is with a dead man made to seem alive, mounted on a horse with a sign on his back, "Adios Amigo"—vaguely suggesting he can still be made to speak, like a ventriloquist's doll. Similarly, the empty suit of feudal armor in the Rojas' possession, on which both Ramon and No Name practice their marksmanship, stands as an understated reminder of the mask-like state to which others seem to aspire. And the irony of the Rojas' jubilant cry at the end of the film when Ramon shoots No Name—"The Americano's dead!"—is that they are finally proclaiming what we have recognized all along. They are, that is, at once right and wrong, finally able to fathom No Name's inanimacy yet still oblivious to the fact that that means he cannot be killed.

This conceit of stripping character down to the status of walking dead is augmented through the film's reliance on a set of vertical and horizontal emphases, seeming to constrain human movement to predictable, undeviating, rectilineal dimensions. The long sequence of No Name's escape, 233 crawling under a series of boardwalks as pursuers step over his head, is only the most dramatic of these scenes where space is organized horizontally. All he can do, reduced so thoroughly, is inch slowly across the screen, apparently more dead than alive. Yet much of the mediate action of the film occurs likewise as a simple transition between two equivalent spaces—as when No Name rides cross-country with Silvanito to the cemetery; or races back and forth between the town and the house where Marisol is held hostage (magically taking short-cuts that seem in the process to defy any logic of setting, much as Venters does in *Riders of the Purple Sage*); or simply watches back and forth as Rojos and Baxters exchange prisoners on San Miguel's main street. Reinforcing this quickly alternating movement between spaces organized horizontally is the film's editing itself, rapidly cutting to and fro at various dramatic moments to give a sense of simultaneous action.

As if to withstand this flattening insistence on the horizontal, No Name frequently attempts to rise above the local scene, whether leaping at first from his runaway mule to hang from a pole outside Silvanito's saloon; or climbing stairs to examine the town ("Why are you going there? Hey?"); or scaling up and down the wall outside his room at the Rojos to hear their conversation. His sole expression of unguarded emotion in the film occurs as a rolling of eyes upward when he mistakenly hits Marisol—an expression that vividly contrasts with his normal squint-eyed shifting back and forth. Against the pressure of Western conventions to lay the inanimate individual low—a pressure discussed at greater length in Chapter 6—*A Fistful of Dollars* offers the contrast of figuratively arising from the dead, ascending above the horizontal.

Finally, the central scene in which No Name announces why "the dead can be very useful sometimes" becomes a description of the customary demeanor of the Western hero: so laconic and inexpressive in his later manifestations that he has to be "made to look alive," to act as if coming back from the dead (or at least, a dead cliché) in the process of reachieving his hold on our imaginations.[19] The only authentic protest against this use of overly familiar conventions occurs with Silvanito's disgruntled protest that the dead should be left alone, and certainly not reintroduced under false pretenses into our everyday world: "I would be unhappy if somebody living forces me to remain with the living." Here, he almost seems to remonstrate against the idea of genre itself, against the necessary reinscription of "dead" conventions that makes a genre continue to live.

Throughout *A Fistful of Dollars,* Leone invokes the idea of the living dead as automatons, as dolls or puppets that mimic the actions of living beings—an idea that always implies something invisible animating and standing behind (whether magician, puppeteer, or God). And in this, the first of his influential spaghetti Westerns, he reveals how past Westerns become the master puppeteers, breathing life into dead forms, lending the illusion once again (even as that illusion is being spoofed) that Western heros are ruggedly independent, self-motivating, self-reliant individuals. Antique conventions seem, however hackneyed, to develop a life of their own, even as Leone simultaneously reveals that that appearance of vitality is nothing more than an illusion—if one of the last now available to the Western.

Contradictions

Given how little Leone would seem to owe to Cooper, it is surprising to realize that his construction of character flows from assumptions instrumental in the creation of Natty Bumppo, whose moral code is based upon the performance of restraint. Performance, after all, has always been central to masculinity in the Western, beginning with Cooper's emptying out of morality to produce a figure who simply holds back, and finding its exemplum in the cowboy who offers a fetishized body as emblem of all he refuses to say and do, as symbol of silent restraint itself. By the appearance of Eastwood's No Name, we have come full circle from Hawkeye to a figure who performs the earnest restraint of his predecessors with a deathly perfection. At last, there is no need to invoke the slightest motivation in considering the plots of Leone's Westerns, since plot exists simply as a narrative frame to allow the hero an opportunity to perform—indeed, to show that he *is* performing.

So extreme is No Name's emotional *sangfroid* that he resembles nothing so much as death-in-life—a condition others aspire to throughout the *Dollars* trilogy but which none achieve so successfully as he. Indeed, unlike his heroic Western predecessors who acted in terms of a moral code, this behavioral tic comes close to being all that distinguishes No Name from everyone else, and notably from the villainous Baxters and Rojos, who are alternately consumed by rage, lust, envy, hatred, disgust, and other violent extremes of emotion. In a world with no consistent vision of future or of past, with a commitment neither to the prospect of progress nor to the claims of history, all rules seem irrelevant, and the only code is one of meticulous accuracy, defined by No Name's wry apology to the coffin maker for having killed four men rather than the three he promised. That understated precision sets the pattern for the film's ideal of behavior.

In contrast to the model of mute exactitude perfected in Eastwood's performance, the Rojo brothers (Benito, Esteban, Ramon) seem strangely excessive, even flamboyant in their behavior. In part, this is simply due to casting, especially of the well-known Italian actor, Gian Maria Volonté, as Ramon Rojo. For as Robert C. Cumbow has stated, Volonté is

a bad guy of such emotional intensity that he brings a pitiable sense of inner torment to even the most irredeemable, reprehensible, villainous roles. Volonté is one of those *busy* actors. Every part of him is working all the time; he makes you uneasy just watching him. . . . His larger-than-life style was perfectly suited to Leone's purpose of creating stark, almost comic stereotypes, then of plunging into them as if they were full-blown characters.[20]

In *For a Few Dollars More*, the baroque sequel to *A Fistful of Dollars*, Volonté plays the villainous El Indio even more "over the top," as a self-destructive, dope-smoking sadist haunted by the image of a beautiful woman he has killed. Leone establishes, in other words, the sharpest of contrasts between Eastwood and Volonté, and does so for reasons that seem to be linked to certain ideals of cultural style. Hispanic characters in these films are played (by Italian and German actors) as hot-blooded, expressive, gaudy, even ostentatious types, while the American mode is represented as restrained, imperturbable, inflexible, with ice water in the veins.

This raises an interesting question of why such a distinct contrast in national stereotypes should have succeeded so well with the Italian audiences for whom the film was intended—of why the repressed Anglo-American hero should have generated enthusiasm in Italy, in contrast to the supposedly Hispanic villains who are represented more vibrantly and robustly. Leone, that is, establishes moral discriminations in terms of ethnic differences: between an apparently puritanical Anglo-American mode of restraint and an assumed Hispanic vitality. To press the observation further, the *Dollars* trilogy suggests that the operatically extravagant Hispanic characters are evil because they come ostentatiously alive, and that No Name conversely signifies moral redemption through a species of terminal inaction, as the heroic emblem of walking death. Virtue resides not, as Milton would have it, in engagement with life's vicissitudes but rather through a certain inert immobility. And that helps explain the prolonged scene of torture at the hands of the Rojos, when No Name is reduced to bloody insensibility and yet acts little different from before. The scene confirms the film's central theme: that the conventional Western hero is simply a caricature disguised as a character, essentially "dead" before and after he has been resuscitated, laudable simply by virtue of an ability not to respond.

One of the film's most striking moments is thus of No Name's escape from the Roja gang in an unfinished coffin: a living corpse who has at last found its appropriate berth in a genre given up (as no other genre) to celebrating funerals and burials. Borrowing the logic of Poe's "The Purloined Letter," Leone places No Name in the one obvious hiding place no one thinks to examine, wheeled openly through the streets as killers frantically set fire to San Miguel in search of their man. Leone also situates the viewer with No Name through a long subjective shot, forcing us into the coffin of living dead in order to survey the action from that singular perspective, with coffin lid slightly ajar. The sole other moment akin to this cinematic co-option occurs in the death of Ramon Rojo, when the camera adopts his fatally wounded view, spins as he does in the throes of death, and seems to lose focus as his consciousness fades—all, again, in the attempt to make the viewer identify with the moment of death.

When morality is simply performance of restraint, and performance becomes so stylized that it is indistinguishable from death, questions of motivation can be reduced to a minimum. Certainly, there is no need to worry over Leone's choice of a bounty hunter (as various critics have done), since "wanting money" and "sacrificing money" are neither more than performed behaviors. As if to prove the point, the money so strenuously acquired by No Name in all three of the *Dollars* trilogy is never spent nor does its acquisition help to explain the most important events of the films. Odd as this may seem, it follows from a central tenet of the genre: "there is no poverty in Western movies," Robert Warshow has explained, "and really no wealth either: those great cattle domains and shipments of gold which figure so largely in the plots are moral and not material quantities, not the objects of contention but only its occasion. Possessions too are irrelevant."[21] The accumulation of capital in *A Fistful of Dollars* is at once everyone's exclusive goal (the sole reason for being in San Miguel) and merely the occasion for exhibiting certain attitudes and skills. The moment No Name arrives, the theme is underscored by the bell ringer Juan de Dios, who repeatedly intones, "You want to get rich, heh?" No Name soon announces, to no one in particular, "I don't work cheap," and, in the ensuing conflict between gun-running Baxters and liquor-selling Rojos, he persistently explains that the only reason he is trading information is for dollars. As Consuela Baxter (Margherita Lozano) says: "Very soon, you're going to be rich," to which he responds, "Yeah, it's not gonna break my heart."

This money-grubbing impatience for the "almighty dollar" might be explained as a Marxist critique of American capitalism, especially given Leone's acknowledgment elsewhere of how little faith he shares in civic ideals: "I see the history of the West as really the reign of violence by violence."[22] Nowhere is this Hobbesian view expressed more succinctly than in the epigraph to *For a Few Dollars More:* "Where life had no value, death, sometimes, had its price. That is why the bounty-killers appeared." Throughout

237

the trilogy, No Name values only the price he can extract for his efforts, explaining his refusal to accompany the Rojos on an expedition by saying, "When a man's got money in his pocket, he begins to appreciate peace." Yet this statement is repeatedly belied in the trilogy, where money is never spent and only fleetingly possessed, suggesting how fully Warshow's claim for earlier Westerns persists ("material quantities [are] not the objects of contention but only its occasion"). Indeed, the emphasis in *A Fistful of Dollars* on working solely for money is at odds with altruistic acts that defy any mercenary logic. No Name rescues Marisol from the Rojos and gives her and her husband a roll of bills before encouraging them to flee, all because "I knew someone like you once. There was no one there to help."[23] Likewise, at the end he willingly relinquishes to the Mexican government the gold he has so strenuously acquired.

In a film that so resolutely rejects moral attributes, in which unscrupulousness and ruthless stratagems are slyly admired, these gestures might be considered romantically retrograde, as if No Name were being redeemed to a set of older, generic virtues. What belies this interpretation and contributes to the film's parodic vision, however, is that even such circumscribed altruism emerges from a living dead man and seems as automatic, as mechanical, as anything else he does. A predictable requirement of the genre is displayed once again, undercutting both the hero's mercenary and altruistic behavior. Like Peckinpah's "wild bunch," whose insistent moral reflections seem unrelated to their behavior, No Name is revealed as someone only capable of acting as he is programmed to act.

Leone and Peckinpah

The deeply divided response to American ideology that lies at the heart of the spaghetti Western is, as it happens, most poignantly conveyed by Leone's own recollection of encountering American soldiers in World War II:

In my childhood, America was like a religion. Throughout my childhood and adolescence . . . I dreamed of the wide open spaces of America. The great expanses of desert. The extraordinary "melting-pot," the first nation made up of people from all over the world. The long, straight roads—which begin nowhere, and end nowhere—for their function is to cross the whole continent. Then real-life Americans abruptly entered my life—in jeeps—and upset all my dreams. They had come to liberate me! I found them very energetic, but also very deceptive. They were no longer the Americans of the West. They were soldiers like any others, with the sole difference that they were victorious soldiers. Men who were materialist, possessive, keen on pleasures and earthly goods. In the GIs who chased after our women, and sold their cigarettes on the black market, I could see nothing that I had seen in Hemingway, Dos Passos, or

Chandler. Nor even in Mandrake, the magician with the outsized heart, or Flash Gordon. Nothing—or almost nothing—of the great prairies, or of the demi-gods of my childhood.[24]

It would be hard to find a better description of what occurred to the '60s Western than this, right down to the disillusioned stationing of demigods in a diminished landscape. Decades after experiencing so radical a sense of disruption that it "upset all my dreams," Leone responded with a series of films that pay homage to the traditional genre by eviscerating it. His stark parodies clearly spoof the classic Hollywood Western, but through the indirect, impudent route of recasting Japanese samurai films (themselves second-generation Westerns) as serape swashbucklers. The hoary dictates of the genre provided Leone with a recognizable structure that freed him to express a surreal sense of dismay *at* the genre, with its historically irrelevant yet mythically compelling terms.

Leone had a strong if unacknowledged influence on Peckinpah, attested in part through innovations introduced by the Italian that became the American's cinematic signature: the Southwestern *mise-en-scène;* the propensity for close-ups of faces; the manipulation of the sound track (and self-conscious use of music); and a wandering, even aimless plot given over to the theme of pursuit (of money and people). Yet Peckinpah's Western films seem worlds from the *Dollars* trilogy produced in the same period: whether *Ride the High Country* (1962) or *Major Dundee* (1964), *The Wild Bunch* or *The Ballad of Cable Hogue* (1970). The high seriousness with which Peckinpah avoids parodic gestures, the stark intensity of his actors' performances, simply the additional cinematic possibilities represented in the expense of a major Hollywood production (of costly sets, wide-screen cinematography, sophisticated soundtrack, complicated second unit scenes, and hundreds of paid extras): all contribute to a more comprehensive, more polished series of films than any of the *Dollars* trilogy. Though Peckinpah shares Leone's inclination to eviscerate Westerns while honoring them, he refuses to explode surrealistically the logic behind that tradition, choosing instead a sympathetic view that measures the genre's present inadequacy in terms of belatedness. A once-honorable set of ideals associated with the Western no longer have a place, except as the measure of how far we have fallen.

Where the two directors seriously differ lies in three controversial areas, each accentuating the contrast between Leone's wry mockery and Peckinpah's earnest address. The first involves the question of realistic *mise-en-scène,* of whether the setting is meant to be accurate, geographically or historically—a question Leone sardonically dismisses and Peckinpah forthrightly engages. The second area of contention involves the genre's traditional moral code, which elicits jointly dismissive yet strangely diverse responses from both directors. The third, most critical difference rests in separate responses to Warshow's "value of violence." Both directors expressed a significant debt to George Stevens's *Shane,* among other things as the first Western to show (in Leone's words) "what really happens when a bullet hits someone."[25] Leone responded to that knowledge by creating characters as walking dead whose further death is thereby cinematically devalued in any exchange of gunfire. The violence of his films thus involves beatings and bludgeonings, not fatal shootings, since characters have invariably to show how they can reconstitute themselves. Peckinpah endeavored on the contrary to show fatal violence as more gruesome than one might have imagined, especially if all one had seen were earlier Westerns (including Leone's films).

Both directors shared a sophisticated knowledge of the history of cinema Westerns, even though they invoke that history's materials and conventions to different ends: Leone, to make us self-consciously aware of the Western *as* artifice—bizarre, arbitrary, excessive, unreal—even as he delights in satisfying the most basic of generic expectations; Peckinpah, to challenge those expectations, to disrupt the desire for the genre's conventional moves, and in the process to convince us (in a fashion as familiar as the genre itself) that his narrative is, because unformulaic, thereby somehow authentic. Leone allows us to believe that the West can be momentarily envisaged his surreal way, even if such depictions have little to do with a verifiable historical record. Peckinpah, by contrast, encourages us to think that the West was actually once as the Western elsewhere imagines it, and that the hero's celebrated ideals were in fact part of an everyday ethos—even though that storied West exists only in Peckinpah as a distant memory, inaccessible, no longer relevant.

This golden age has, of course, as little to do with reality as Leone's outlandish vision. Quite the contrary, the unfallen world recalled by Peckinpah's characters, where restraint was routine and heroics habitual, is even more an imaginative tic than the dauntlessness of Leone's No Name. The fundamentally automaton-like behavior of *The Wild Bunch* is simply better disguised, more rarely belied—whether in the final grim walk-down to slaughter Mapachi's men, or by the hysterical laughter that is significantly reprised in the closing credits. Peckinpah's vision seems minute by minute more authentic because less cartoonish, but the evidence of his characters' mechanical bearing is finally more frightening than Leone's. Differences aside, however, both directors succeed as never before in puncturing the belief in traditional Western virtues (the ideal of honor, the legitimacy of violence, and so on), which itself forms the most troubling conclusion to be drawn from the '60s Western.

Belatedness, Nostalgia, *The Wild Bunch*

Right from its opening sequence of color images frozen into black-and-white stills, *The Wild Bunch* self-consciously registers the problem of memory and historical accuracy. Already, long before we know what they mean, the images of uniformed riders are made to anticipate their own timely passage into closeted recollection. The cinematic marking of this transition from present to past, the quick to the dead, occurs before we can absorb its full implications, as if lithographs had been taken from aging news accounts and inserted into a living story to provide the viewer with an authentic sense of historical setting: Madero's 1913 revolution against Diaz in northern Mexico. In the most striking of contrasts to Leone's broad, comic-book strokes—the rudimentary, parodic gestures of his characters, the haphazard sets, the geographical imprecision—Peckinpah opens his film with an offhand salute to John Ford, and specifically to Ford's obsession with historical fact (one of the reasons Peckinpah liked to be known as "John Ford's bastard son").[26] We are placed in a specific border town (Starbuck, Texas) at a precise historical moment (the summer of 1913) with the weight of historical consciousness bearing firmly down, as it will throughout.

The reason such consciousness weighs so heavily is because we are made to feel the present is already too late—too clearly the tag end of an era gone by, whose values resonate more deeply because so ineffectively. That sense of belatedness is defined both internally and externally: both in terms of narrative chronology (set thirty years after the 1880s, the period of American history in which the Western was classically imagined) and in terms of the film's own production (fifteen years after the classic moment for Western film production in the mid–1950s). "We got to start thinking beyond our guns," Pike Bishop (William Holden) observes after the failed bank robbery in Starbuck; "Those days are closing fast." And throughout, that apprehension is made explicit: of it being the "last job" for Lyle Gorch (Warren Oates) or of Dutch Engstrom (Ernest Borgnine) wondering how they can retire after "just one more good score": "Back off to what?"

Casting itself reinforces more visibly this notion of time lamentably past, raising the question of what it is that visible physical age accomplishes in film Westerns. Peckinpah was obsessed by the interlinked issues Ford had addressed in *Liberty Valance,* of lost youth, a spiritless present, and nostalgia for a vital past, though he treats them less theatrically, more directly, finally more sentimentally because uninterested in exposing the 241 mythic past as a dream. Where Ford reveals the memories of aging characters as anxious wish fulfillment, the strained projection of present desires onto the stage set of the past, Peckinpah seems instead to cherish the myth and to lament its passing. As in his earlier *Ride the High Country* (1962), the appeal of earlier times grows stronger precisely because that West is never seen, only heard about through survivors appalled by a world that has passed them by. In this regard, at least, Peckinpah's vision is more timid, less incisive than Ford's.

What Peckinpah achieves through the presence of such aging actors as Strother Martin, Edmund O'Brien, and Emilio Fernandez, William Holden, and Robert Ryan is a resurrection of the myth of a heroic West through a sort of mediated desire (their desire to see it again creating a similar desire in us). All define through wrinkled eyes, sagging skin, bulging midriffs, and tired movements the sense that we as well have arrived too late and that their best years (and films) are well behind them. Indeed, costuming itself lends a hint that the Western mode is now inadequate, with Pike Bishop made to look more a gangster than cowboy: white shirt and business suit, rifle with telescopic sights and high-powered binoculars, a late-model U.S. army Colt .45 automatic concealed under his vest rather than worn openly on his hip. Further compounding the sense of tired belatedness is the postromantic view of behavior and gestures: of squabbling gang members and crudely selfish townsfolk; of children tormenting insects or Sykes defecating in the desert; of even the characters' monosyllabic names—Pike, Dutch, Deke, Sykes, and Lyle and Tector Gorch—as if in a gutteral attempt at some asocial, prelinguistic environment.

Against this vision of aging ineptness, personal inadequacy, and social breakdown (a scenario common to '60s Westerns), Peckinpah fosters a fierce strain of nostalgia for that earlier time "just like it used to be," before the era of cars, airplanes, automatic weapons, scientific management, and industrial waste registered a transformation in modern American life. The alternative to this nightmare of Progressive bureaucracy (with its anticipation of the social engineering in Lyndon Johnson's Great Society) is the self-sufficient, wholly integrated, rural culture of Peckinpah's Mexican villagers. Tector Gorch (Ben Johnson) may be oblivious to the vitality of this alternative vision—"Just more of Texas as far as I'm concerned"—but that is because, as Angel (Jaime Sanchez) intones, "you have only eyes and no heart." This rather easy, overly sentimental split between the Gorch brothers and Angel is elaborated in the film's persistent division between present and past, anomie and moral coherence, the heartlessness of modern America and the coherent vitality of Mexican life. Against the venal motives of the bounty hunters relentlessly pursuing the Bunch, Peckinpah presents the heroic (and maudlin) scene of peasant warriors mutely securing their guns, or the gang's departure from Angel's town drowned out by the strains of "La Golondrina," or the suggestive encounter entirely in Spanish between Angel and his former lover, Teresa. What the film repeatedly declares, however, is that race and culture preclude the gang themselves from ever achieving this yearning vision of social integrity—except *as* a lost vision, a revelation of what no longer counts in American culture, perhaps never did.

This self-conscious belatedness reflects Peckinpah's own serious, somewhat rueful devotion to a genre that has always celebrated native landscape, indigenous history, and masculine ideals but that no longer feels confident about the merits of such celebration. Leone's insouciant vision marked how far Westerns could swerve and still remain Westerns, and it became a delicate test to make Westerns that did not simply repeat that achievement (including Leone's own later films), or become self-mocking (Elliot Silverstein's *Cat Ballou* [1965], Mel Brooks's *Blazing Saddles* [1974]), or cloyingly romantic (Henry Hathaway's *True Grit* [1969], George Roy Hills's *Butch Cassidy and the Sundance Kid* [1969]). The sense, however mistaken, that the 1950s was a period of confident achievement—whether in the nation's domestic life or in its major cinema Westerns—helped reinforce a contrast with the 1960s, in which even a perception of unanimity of opinion about common ideals had been rudely shattered.

For Peckinpah, the urge to revive the appeal of the Western meant invoking certain filmic conventions, which explains why the adulation for an earlier era represented *in The Wild Bunch* can be taken as a reflection of the profound esteem of the film *for* earlier Westerns. The gang's past heroism (and by extension, the heroics accomplished in earlier Westerns by the actors who play gang members) is expressed repeatedly by Robert Ryan's Deke Thornton, who even in deadly pursuit of his former cohort describes Pike Bishop as "the best." Deke's contempt for the scavenging bounty hunters he leads is portioned out invidiously as praise for the memory of his erstwhile confederate. Ironically, the final process of reclaiming the past will be enacted in the looting of Bishop's dead body, as the vulpine Coffer (Strother Martin) exclaims: "T.C. it's *him*. It's *Pike*. You ain't so damn much now, are you, Mr. Pike?"

More specific influences from the Western tradition are quoted less directly—most notably, the references to John Ford's celebration of communal life in his 1940s cavalry trilogy, through the Mexican village sequences and the triumphal ride through Agua Verde. Peckinpah likewise borrows whole scenes from John Huston's *Treasure of the Sierra Madre* (1948), emphasizing the special emotional tenor brought to that film by   243

Walter Huston, repeating his performance in Edmond O'Brien's craggy characterization of Freddy Sykes. Yet despite the obvious affection embodied in his backward-turning glance—the valuing of a simpler time when moral dynamics seemed less complicated—Peckinpah shares with Leone the sharp recognition that the past and its uncommon resources are no longer accessible.

Moral Codes

As if in defiance of that recognition, *The Wild Bunch* celebrates the ideal of a moral code so exorbitantly as to remind the Western enthusiast of nothing less than Cooper's hectoring on proper behavior. The code is repeatedly invoked by characters who give it explicit elaboration, claiming for it loyalty, fidelity, restraint, veracity, a commitment to underdogs: all qualities invoked by Wister and Grey in envisioning their own heroic encounters. Thus, against the common centrifugal impulse to pull selfishly away on one's own, or the centripetal tendency to turn rancorously on one another, Pike and Dutch Engstrom stress the twin goals of self-control and mutual fidelity. The most eloquent expression of this is contained in Pike's rebuke to Tector Gorch, who is angered that Syke's horse has forced them all to tumble down a dune: "You're not gonna get rid of anyone. We're gonna stick together, just like it used to be; when you side a man you stay with him, and if you can't do that, you're like some animal; you're finished—we're finished—*all* of us." Or as he later reiterates, confirming the ideal of group solidarity: "We started together, we'll stay together."

Yet Pike's very emphasis on a code and his attribution of moral distinctiveness to the Bunch helps draw into question that attribution. After all, Tector Gorch must be rebuked by Pike for not sharing this common vision, and much of the rest of the film shows how little the ideal is manifest in action. Even the discipline touted as a feature distinguishing them from Harrigan's bounty hunters is evident only in spurts. And Deke Thornton's command of the vulturous bounty hunters seems at least as inspired as Pike Bishop's leadership, further suggesting the absence of any real distinction between the groups. More to the point, Pike's self-heroizing stance is repeatedly belied by the film, which exposes how frequently he is mistaken, or misleads others, or falls short of his own moral claims. The ambush in Starbuck, for instance, then allowing Angel to take guns to Mapache—like his past assurances to his partner, Deke, that they were "safe" right before Thornton is captured ("Damn sure is my business")—involve miscalculations so flagrant as to put into doubt his qualifications to lead. Less pardonable than errors in judgment, however, are actual lapses in his self-defined

244

"code" ("when you side a man you stay with him"). After all, he is the one to abandon Crazy Lee Stringfellow (Bo Hopkins) in the failed Starbuck robbery, and moments later he summarily executes Buck because he is blinded, unable to ride. Later, he leaves behind both a wounded Sykes and a tortured Angel—just as years before he had deserted Thornton after confidently assuring him he never would.

The film significantly makes a fetish of the idea of a code of loyalty—as if Peckinpah were actually reinstituting a possibility that Leone had parodically abandoned—only to reveal that code as honored more in the breach than in practice. The isolated legitimate instance, in fact, of hewing to the code is the final act of returning for Angel that will clearly end in destroying them all. So quixotic is that gesture, moreover, that it seems motivated by nothing so much as the impulse to validate a code that otherwise has no lived meaning in the film. For in contrast to this single, sentimentally noble but thoroughly futile gesture, the rest of the film exposes the self-serving logic by which everyone ordinarily behaves. Dutch openly claims the moral low ground in quarreling with Pike's expressed ideal of "giving one's word"—"That ain't what counts," he retorts; "it's who you give it *to!*" And even this circumscribed understanding seems largely irrelevant to the actions and events of the film. Indeed, reiterated ethical distinctions fail to convince the viewer of little more than the Bunch's continuing self-deception: "We ain't nothing like him," Dutch protests of a comparison with Mapache; "We don't *hang* nobody." Yet, on the contrary, the Bunch comes to seem much like Mapache, and all that separates their greed from his—their lack of concern for the common citizens of Starbuck during the opening bank robbery, as his for Mexican peasants—is the desperate belief that they share a redeeming code of behavior.

In vivid contrast to Pike's declared moral discriminations, the film underscores a sense of ubiquitous amorality, of modern aimlessness, of the absence of anything larger than the self and its fleeting desires. Leone had been willing simply to accept the terms of this debased vision, renegotiating generic conventions in order to explore where the Western might go from there. By contrast, Peckinpah rails against such a diminished conception, unwilling to accept the loss of a moral idealism that had always been central to the genre, yet from a modern perspective unable realistically to imagine what a fixed code might mean, if in part because resistant to the idea of allowing conventions to seem fixed at all. His reinvigoration of the Western, therefore, corresponds to his view of everyday life: unstructured, undirected, impulsive. And it is entirely apt that the most common exchange among characters in *The Wild Bunch* should be simply "Let's go" and "Why not?"—serving as the loosest rationale for behavior as well as for plot. The 245 words attest to the absurd gratuitousness in doing anything whatsoever, with the only reason invoked for a course of action simply the fact that it is there to do—suggesting again how little separates the "criminal society" of Harrigan from the Bunch.

Reign of Violence

Peckinpah's shrewdest insight lay in recognizing how essential to the Western a form of moral self-deception has always been, with roots that extend back past Wister's Virginian to Leatherstocking's Jesuitical discrimination between "natur' and gifts," his earnest avowal of tenets from which he himself impulsively lapses. What had first appeared as Peckinpah's flagrant breach of expectations, then, can more accurately be seen as an exposure of the powerful confusion central to the genre's dynamic—a confusion between the restraint we initially desire and the violence that finally seems necessary—which has always lent the Western such a strong visceral appeal. The genuine originality of Peckinpah's film rests in this revision of the viewer's sanction of a need for violence, and of what that presumed need is narratively meant to serve.

Part of the answer has to do with the fact that the Western's landscape at last no longer served its traditional role, as a "book" of nature imbued with moral lessons an expert can read. Ever since Cooper (as noted above in the discussion of Leone's facescapes), scenery had conventionally been overcoded, sodden with significances that helped identify terms in which violence might be understood, even countenanced. By the 1960s, however, this way of reading landscape seemed neither useful nor true. Leone dramatically emptied out scenery to reinforce a conception of mechanical character, and other Westerns offered little hope that terrain might assist in grasping ethical significances. Violence simply occurred, gratuitously, irrationally, unjustifiably; and it occurred in the '60s in popular culture everywhere more explicitly than it had before.

If pondering the landscape no longer helped explain how to respond to violence, then all that was left for the Western was to ponder scenes of gratuitous violence themselves. As discussed above, arias of violence first became for Leone the stasis one is meant to contemplate, and that metonymic logic of transferring the gaze from landscape to bloody scenes helps explain much about Peckinpah's style. On the one hand, his film nullifies generic conventions in its narrative content, through the venal motives of his "heroes," their vulgar behavior, and so on; on the other hand, it revives the genre's formal preoccupation with sheer description. Because that description is no longer displaced onto landscape, however, the effect is to raise a series of questions about what the Western has always meant. More to the point, this revival of traditional form allows Peckinpah to challenge the Western's persistent obfuscation of issues it has always engaged, by exposing the bad-faith gesture in the genre's conventional solicitation of violence.

This challenge to generic expectations is made in the very opening moments of *The Wild Bunch,* in the visual irony that allows the viewer to assume the Bunch are genuine American troops. In contrast to Leone's unproblematic identification of the viewer with No Name in *A Fistful of Dollars*—making the character's first uninformed view of San Miguel the audience's own, and establishing familiar moral coordinates through Chico's (Mario Brega's) mistreatment of the boy, Jesus—Peckinpah maintains a curious moral deception well into his initial scene, right until Pike Bishop barks a command at the end of the opening credits: "If they move, kill 'em." That eerily unofficial tone confounds our projected sympathy, as does his subsequent order about a railroad official caught in the bank: "When I kick him out, blast 'em. We'll make a run for it." The ensuing massacre—in which a woman is trampled, a sousaphone player killed, and innocent citizens wounded and maimed—disorients us, arresting the process of identification. And the rest of the scene compounds that perplexity in the squalid brutality of everyone else, whether callous bounty hunters gratuitously killing whoever happens to move, or a ruthless official ordering the massacre with no thought to public safety, or arrogant townspeople lured into a dangerous voyeurism. The later discovery that the whole was an ambush planned by the railroad official, Harrigan, and that the Bunch had succeeded in stealing nothing more than bags of washers, only underscores the scene's ghastly futility.

In contrast to the gently parodic tone of Leone's opening, Peckinpah mounts a violent assault on the viewer, with psychological mayhem expressed through a combination of deep focus long shots, telephoto close-ups, slow motion sequences, and flash cuts lasting less than a second. As discussed in Chapter 6, *The Wild Bunch* has more "edits" than any other Hollywood film ever made, with 3,642 individual cuts in the original uncut version, some of only three and four frames (compared to 600 cuts for the average two-hour film of the period).[27] Editing is keyed not to physical events but to viewers' emotions, with a heartbeat pounding through the sound-track, swelling gradually louder as the pulse speeds up. Especially at peak moments of violence, Peckinpah orchestrates fragments of scenes, intercutting them to suggest an incoherent immediacy—as in the slow-motion fall of an outlaw through a window, interrupted by nine other shots of random violence before he hits the ground. This "ballet of death" pro-

247

vides a curious correlative to the pattern devised by Cooper; now, however, instead of narrative yielding to landscape descriptions, it is suspended in favor of an acute concentration on the topography of violence. Moral significance is eliminated, but the aimless glance that authenticates narrative still functions much as it always has, if with considerably more intensity. And that is Peckinpah's point: to clarify how fully the Western's secret desire has always been for violence—justified if possible but violence nonetheless.

This point is rendered explicit by the forceful placement of the initial scene, assaulting the viewer as much by that opening status as by its studied choreography of violence. Here, Peckinpah radically inverts one of the genre's oldest conventions, which dictates that even necessary violence be a last resort, deferred long enough to allow peaceful alternatives to be imagined. And the reason for breaching that rule of deferral is to expose the rule's actual effect, which is less to encourage the impulse toward pacifism than to grant time to savor the imminence of violence that everyone knows will come. Philip French has noted this effect as it operates in even more pacific Westerns:

Incipient violence, too, determines the structure of *High Noon*. As the clock ticks inexorably towards the final encounter, the actual scenes of physical confrontation—one fistfight, one shootout—occupy about five minutes of the picture. This very sparing use of action is dramatically admirable, and possibly socially responsible, yet it has the effect . . . of almost making the audience *will* the violence upon the characters involved.[28]

This narrative pattern emerges repeatedly in the most successful texts, making it difficult for modern audiences to watch such classics as *Stagecoach* and *Shane* in their steady deferral of the violence they solicit (as discussed in Chapter 7 above). Walter Van Tilburgh Clark most notably anticipated the technique in *The Ox-Bow Incident* (1940), where long conversations postpone action, encouraging the reader to yearn for the violent solution being condemned—all as a means of projecting a sense of how virulent mob psychology can be, and how irrepressible.

While the unusual level of Peckinpah's cinematic violence has frequently been remarked, then, as important to its significance is that it comes so soon, flouting expectations for how violence should be unleashed in the Western. Not even Leone quite did this, though the possibility is acknowledged in *For a Few Dollars More,* when a distant, whistling rider is inexplicably shot from his horse as part of the precredit sequence. Peckinpah's films raised the stakes of that agenda, by imaginatively engaging a question usually relegated to narrative need: of how often, how explicitly, how creatively cinematic violence should be invoked, and to what thematic end. When, that is, was violence merely gratuitous and when essential to issues at the heart of the genre?

The answer to this question is hardly clear, with further confusion generated by Peckinpah's own impulse to give conflicting responses in interviews. What is clear is that *The Wild Bunch* challenges assumptions and defies conventions without drawing attention to its iconoclastic mode, keeping the viewer ever distanced and off balance. Peckinpah's notably "nervous" cinematic technique serves a similar end, whether alternating between slow-motion and standard footage, or between romantic and realistic styles, detached and immediate perspectives. So persistent is this nervous fracturing of cinematic modes that by the closing massacre the rules have long been firmly broken, with the effect of making the logic of that massacre less compelling. Following the opening's breach of convention, Peckinpah continues disrupting expectations so as to shift responsibility for the narrative back onto the viewer, to make us aware of our own resistant narrative desire. If, as Henry James claimed, the intelligent reader does "quite half the labor," helping create a text through a set of coded expectations, then the experience was just as appropriate in film, for which Peckinpah likewise wanted to involve the viewer: "I hate an audience that just sits there," he once sourly exclaimed.[29]

One way in which the viewer discovers complicity with the film lies in scenes that seem eminently formulaic, that elicit the most conventional of moral responses and yet reveal themselves as only stronger versions of an iconoclastic agenda. In *A Fistful of Dollars,* that unexpected scene is No Name's generosity to Marisol—a gesture of seemingly simple nostalgia that seems at first unlikely, only to emerge as a further expression of his mechanical moral character. In *The Wild Bunch,* even more powerfully, Peckinpah introduces the nostalgic ideal of Angel's devotion to "my people, my village, Mexico." His commitment extends to a willingness to sacrifice self-interest for the common good, to give up his share of stolen gold for a case of guns, and later to refuse to betray the Bunch to Mapache. As Dutch observes, he "had guts," and that becomes the "inspiration" for the final massacre. That scene supposedly differs from the opening mayhem forced on the Bunch because it is chosen and not a mechanical repetition: "We've done it right this time." And in the slow heightening of the sound track, the gradual crescendo of martial music, the tightening of narrative tension all in the image of four men walking to certain death, the viewer is also impelled to desire that end as the sole solution capable of granting their aimlessness a focus and direction.

The climax of the film's violence in Mapache's slashing of Angel's throat is followed by a long, dramatic pause after the Bunch shoots Mapache, realizing they have "done it." When Pike Bishop then opens fire on the German advisor, the anticlimax of the massacre commences, as individuals are decimated by machine-gun fire, slit by sabers, riddled by bullets. It was this scene that led to the awarding of the first R-rating for a Western and yet, as David A. Cook has written, the issue was less one of violence per se than its vivid representation. Peckinpah was for the first time in the Western simply being self-conscious about what was at stake:

As with *Bonnie and Clyde,* the violence of *The Wild Bunch was* revolutionary, *was* excessive for its time. . . . Their films introduced conventions for the depiction of violence and carnage which others exploited *ad nauseum* in the seventies. But both directors insisted for the first time in American cinema that the human body is made of real flesh and blood; that arterial blood spurts rather than drips demurely; that bullet wounds leave not trim little pin-pricks but big, gaping holes; and, in general, that violence has painful, unpretty, humanly destructive consequences.[30]

Lucian Ballard's extraordinary photography of the final scene, with multiple cameras running at different speeds, edited by Peckinpah even more intricately than the opening massacre, assaults the viewer accustomed to sanitized and straightforward representations of violence. Even today, the film elicits an intense visceral response.[31]

Yet few have thought to question not simply the explicitness of the violence or its cinematic "aestheticizing" by Ballard—topics that have clearly influenced imitators and viewers ever since—but the way in which the larger framing structure of *The Wild Bunch* itself compels a reconsideration of "the value of violence" in the Western. After the unsettling logic of the opening scene is clear, in other words—that those on either side of the law are equally callow and brutal—then any genuine moral distinctions among Harrigan, Mapache, the bounty hunters, or the Bunch seem simply invidious. We may "side" with the Bunch against the "they" ironically invoked by Freddy Sykes—"Who the hell is *they?*"—but that is only for lack of any other figures with whom to identify.[32] The world seems askew, in this and other films of the 1960s, and not only does no imagined social structure seem capable of setting it right but individual morality is clearly deficient. The Western as a form appears incapable of coping with the social problems it is asked to resolve, and one of its central premises—that violence is legitimate in certain circumstances where all else fails—is gradually undone through its own excess.

Sixties Sociology

Among various reasons for the popularity of *A Fistful of Dollars* and *The Wild Bunch*—films that share little in conception or execution—are their separate engagements with the Western's celebration of beatings, knifings, and death by explosions of gunfire. At a time in American history when the state itself was seen as excessively violent—not only in response to foreign policy in Southeast Asia but to integrationist and antiwar activities at home—these films were among the few to confront the issue of legitimate violence directly. And although Warshow first pointed out how the Western characteristically inquires into the legitimate ends of violence, these two "anti-Westerns" also raise the problem of beginnings, doing so more directly and intensely than any previous generic example. Among the questions they implicitly address are: Where does violence originate? Is physical aggression part of a natural cycle, innate to the human species, or somehow culturally conditioned and therefore only learned? In this conflict of Hobbes with Rousseau, are men evil because of nature or nurture?[33]

The questions are hardly framed in this manner, of course, nor are answers pursued with a straightforward logic. Apart from other objections, that would defy the premise behind each of the preceding chapters: that a text's popularity depends on an ability to satisfy mutually conflicting interpretations of what contemporaries feel are unresolved social dilemmas. The sharp ideological conflict between inherited traits and environmental training, however, has been a persistent one in the popular culture of this century, as revealed in versions of that debate already discussed in Chapters 4 and 5. Leone and Peckinpah explore two sides of the national conflict of the 1960s, in which liberal policy was prominently pitted against conservative detractors on the issue of social inequity. Lyndon Johnson's commitment to a Great Society—of federally funded projects that assisted the disabled and disadvantaged—aroused tremendous controversy, with forceful advocates arguing for the expenditure of billions that opponents contended were dollars ill-spent.

Dividing these groups was the premise of social welfare itself: whether federally supported programs could ever provide a permanent remedy for social ills. The liberal position was that people suffered unfairly because of social inequities and that arbitrary handicaps resulting from discriminations of race, class, age, and gender, of sexual preference and medical ill fortune (among others) could be erased through a well-conceived program of remedial social services. If suffering, however, resulted instead not from social discrimination but from innate inequalities, then the best that any radically egalitarian society could hope to do was not interfere. Taxation or policing constraints that might be placed upon private enterprise only permit an inefficient public bureaucracy to squander national resources and thereby to obstruct the possibility of true social progress.

Within this charged context, it can be seen how sharply *A Fistful of*   251

Dollars differs in its implicit social agenda from *The Wild Bunch*—a difference that emerges from their directors' disagreement over the way in which suffering should be alleviated and more generally from their disparate assumptions about the sources of evil. Leone adopts (as one might have imagined from an Italian leftist) a fiercely liberal position, which presumes that children are born innocent and must somehow be taught to be cruel; training and environment, from this perspective, are both responsible for forming individual morality. Among the three families represented in his first spaghetti Western, Marisol's son, Jesus, stands as an emblem of virtuous filial devotion, in stark contrast to the sons in both the Baxter and Rojas clans. Consuelo Baxter has created a psychopathic brood through years of brutal effort, deliberately instilling cruelty in them, infecting them with her own impassioned malignity. And although the Rojas have no parents, the brothers' sadistic alliance suggests again that personal experience and family training have been at fault.

In sharp contrast to this vision of dysfunctional families, Peckinpah suggests that evil is born, not made, and that children come into the world already brutal and remorseless creatures before personal influences shape them. That harsh judgment is established immediately in the notorious opening scene of *The Wild Bunch,* when the Bunch ride by a circle of children gleefully tormenting two scorpions with killer ants. Throughout the massacre in Starbuck, the memory lingers of children at malicious play, and, as the escaping gang leaves town, they again ride by the children now setting fire to the ants.[34] This scabrous vision of childhood is confirmed in the scene of Mexican tots merrily chasing after the tortured body of Angel, dragged by an automobile. And the theme is reiterated when a boy later shoots Pike Bishop in the back. Each of these chilling moments gives the lie to the Mexican village elder, who declares: "We all dream of being children again, even the worst of us—perhaps the worst most of all." Alone among the characters, Angel offers an exception to the general rule (at least in relationship to his own people), and even his altruism seems to confirm Peckinpah's larger premise: that good and evil are not achievable states but simple givens, inexplicable, unpremeditated. No book can teach us how to act.

Indeed, Peckinpah here defies a key motif of the Western, of self-transformation achieved through education, of learning how to become a man. Ever since Cooper, the prospect of personal change has presented itself insistently, with older generations taking time to instruct youth in gender roles. The "lesson" Peckinpah ironically offers is just the other way around, however, of children teaching their elders a certain amoral sado-masochistic delight (though elders hardly need to learn the lesson). In fact, nobody really changes now or even has the expectation, and the ideal of conduct books seems somehow not even humorous, merely arcane. In a world where faces are no longer readable, where landscape can no longer be decoded, where people are what they were without hope that they may become better or different, the Western itself begins to fall victim to its own deepest assumptions and contradictions.

Leone's and Peckinpah's antithetical visions do not prepare for the irony that both directors shift attention from the full implications of their social positions. Leone's characters, for instance, never advert to ethical or moral concerns, even though the film implies that behavior should be attributed to upbringing and environment. The kinds of questions so common in other versions of the genre—of what kind of environment is preferable; of how one should act, or why; of what behavior is appropriate for boys, and girls—are simply irrelevant to the film. Peckinpah's characters, on the other hand, obsessively dispute proper behavior, argue appropriate codes, and throughout are given to considering the implications of morally reputable acts—even though the film suggests that individuals are innately flawed, with nothing in their pasts that might have altered them one way or the other. Leone thus implies that nurture transforms one for better or worse, even as he ignores what any such transformation must involve; Peckinpah conversely dramatizes the absence of any genuine moral realm (since behavior is all more or less equivalent, and in any case innate), and yet his characters repeatedly stress what moral considerations might look like.[35]

Compounding these separate paradoxes, however, is the fact that both films seem in the final analysis strikingly akin in their social politics. Leone's environmentalism, for all its parodic excess, bears a notable resemblance to Peckinpah's Hobbesian vision, starkly unaccommodating as it is. While each film's rationale for behavior appears at once well-defined and antithetical, then, various factors obscure those characteristics to render the films indistinguishable, at least morally speaking. Their relative lack of plot tends to orient the viewer to the issue of character, which quickly means that we lose sight of why individuals act as they do (nature? nurture?) to focus instead on simple behavior. And other contradictions in both films help to blur any clear distinctions. Eastwood's performance as No Name, for instance, is one of inexpressive mysteriousness—of tightly clipped words, impassive face, economical gestures—that make it seem as if he were less a person than simply a body, with accompanying traits that are innate, not developed—this, in flat defiance of what seems the film's underlying agenda. Conversely, the Wild Bunch frequently discuss the past with regret, even remorse, giving the sense that they feel events might have been different had they only acted differently—and that they therefore have the power through changed behavior to alter the future.

In short, neither nature nor nurture seems more determinative than the other, though the viewer is alternately encouraged to think of each as a primary cause. What succeeds instead in motivating sinister behavior and keeping evil alive are the conventional narrative patterns of the genre, played out in a series of imaginative revisions and inversions. In both these innovative films, '60s viewers who stood on opposite sides of the political spectrum could discover a narrative logic that seemed to support their agendas and that justified contradictory appeals—either to the individual or to social structures. Notably as well, these films reveal their directors' strong reading of earlier Westerns—a sense of generic tradition that looms as powerfully as does any immediate pressing issue.

Both Leone and Peckinpah, moreover, share a fundamental ambivalence about that tradition, which emerges in the self-consciousness of their films *as* Western films. Peckinpah's extraordinary editing contributes a powerful effect of narrative disjunction—something that Leone achieves through (among other things) facial closeups, eery music, eccentric acting. Yet energetically as both films succeed on their own terms, they also speak to the end of an era, making it difficult to know how the genre might in turn be renegotiated and revived. In both, violence has been so split off from its traditional function as a legitimate "value"—with action reduced to little more than a passing *frisson*—that it is hard to imagine successors able to have a similar striking effect, moving imaginatively beyond these directors in reinventing (rather than simply repeating) a newly revived genre.

As always, there is little way to gauge the actual effect of these films on those who first saw them, although both succeeded not only in transforming the Western but in influencing other popular genres. During the late 1960s, a tremendous resurgence took place in both literary and cinematic Westerns that would last for more than a decade—prompted at first by Leone's success, then spurred on by Peckinpah. And that success helped spawn the development of related genres—action-adventure films, vigilante movies, science fiction, and so on—whose success in turn would explain the temporary demise of the Western in the 1980s.

Even as *A Fistful of Dollars* and *The Wild Bunch* transformed the Western through the use of innovative cinematic and narrative techniques, they also succeeded by deftly falling back on a central motif from the genre tradition, of the robber-bandit committed to restoring the *status quo ante*. That motif is certainly much older than the Western and is central to other popular genres as well, but that is a reason in conclusion to recall the stark force of that tradition, as described by its best historian, Eric Hobsbawm:

Insofar as bandits have a "programme," it is the defence or restoration of the traditional order of things "as it should be" (which in traditional societies means as it is believed to have been in some real or mythical past). They right wrongs, they correct and avenge cases of injustice, and in doing so apply a more general criterion of just and fair relations between men in general, and especially between the rich and the poor, the strong and the weak.[36]

Such a description, loose as it is, points to the central struggle in both films, which suggests how much Leone and Peckinpah relied on a folk ideal in transforming the Western. What distinguishes their treatment is the melancholy recognition that that ideal, however seductive, is finally no longer appropriate.

9 LAST RITES

I want you to round up every vicious criminal and gunslinger in the West. Take this down. I want rustlers, cutthroats, murderers, bounty-hunters, desperadoes, mugs, pugs, thugs, nitwits, half-wits, dim-wits, vipers, snipers, con-men, Indian agents, Mexican bandits, muggers, buggerers, bushwackers, horn-swogglers, horse thieves, bull dykes, train robbers, bank robbers, ass kickers, shit kickers, and Methodists.

Hedley Lamarr, *Blazing Saddles* (1972)

Every hero becomes a bore at last.

Ralph Waldo Emerson (1845)[1]

Almost the moment the Western emerged, critics hastened to pronounce the last rites, as if a melancholy nostalgia that would come to permeate the genre was also part of its reception. The very year that Wister turned the romantic cowboy into a best-selling hero, Arthur Chapman anticipated countless readers in hoping that "some keen-eyed genius, who recognizes the theatrical untruth of the accepted school, will catch the interest phases of actuality. Then we shall get some capital stories of . . . the ranch, minus the cowboy and the roundup."[2] Barely a decade later, the producer Thomas Ince informed the soon-to-be famous cowboy star William S. Hart that "he was too late; every company was making Westerns because they were cheap to make, the movie houses were surfeited with them, and besides, they were on the way out."[3] That prediction has been sounded nearly every decade since, always to be silenced by a spate of new Westerns that revive a floundering industry. Pauline Kael's famous funeral oration in a 1974 New Yorker essay preceded the explosion two years later of a dozen major films. And following the debacle of Michael Cimino's Heaven's Gate (1980), Will Wright lauded the "space epic" as the film Western's successor because it had no link to a verifiable historical past.[4]

Yet the space epic already seems like something of a relic, a '70s costume drama, while the Western has, amazingly, renewed itself once again. Perhaps we yearn for links to history, however mythologized, after all. Kevin Costner's Dances with Wolves (1990) and Clint Eastwood's Unforgiven (1992) have had the same galvanizing effect on the industry as did James Cruze's 1923 epic The Covered Wagon or Leone's spaghetti Westerns in the 1960s.[5] The resurgence in the genre includes half-a-dozen black Westerns, led by Mario Van Peebles's Posse (1993); feminist Westerns like John Duigan's Outlaws (1994), Maggie Greenwald's Ballad of Little Jo (1994), Sam Raimi's The Quick and the Dead (1994), with Sharon Stone playing a hair-trigger gunwoman, and Jonathan Kaplan's *Bad Girls* (1994), in which Madeleine Stowe is whipped and convalesces through the mediation of a male helpmate; and pro-Native American films like Walter Hill's *Geronimo: An American Legend* (1994). By late 1993, two dozen Westerns were in production, and more were being planned.

Trade publishing has experienced a comparable explosion, with "new Westerns" (also known as "vigilante Westerns") given over to exoticized violence and sexual explicitness.[6] Alongside these have been more serious, experimental efforts like Ishmael Reed's postmodern African-American Western, *Yellow Back Radio Broke-Down* (1969), and Richard Brautigan's *The Hawkline Monster: A Gothic Western* (1974). The success of Larry McMurtry's *Lonesome Dove* (1989) encouraged the first of a number of television miniseries, and even a decline in production of Western films does not necessarily mean that popularity suffers. The year Will Wright lamented the death of the genre, for instance, Westerns were the second most popular item in the video market.[7]

Just because this pattern of resurgence sounds so familiar, however, is no reason in itself to assume the genre will always continue to thrive. Recent efforts may indeed represent the Western's heralded last stand, especially since by certain measures the level of interest today hardly compares with peak years of the genre. Only a single Western series is currently being aired on television *(Dr. Quinn, Medicine Woman)*, and the industry more generally can be gauged by a decline from 1956, when more than 700 horse wranglers supplied livestock to Hollywood productions, to only 35 wranglers in business by 1993.[8] Tellingly, the celebrated Marlboro Man is no longer a Western cowboy, and in the process "the world's most familiar, and powerful, advertising image" has become merely the icon of a past era of masculine self-creation.[9]

Whether the Western has actually taken its final bullet will become clear only in the decades to come, but one consequence of this recurrent history of decline and resurgence is that anyone writing about the genre has always needed to consider the possibility that it is on its way out. Some of these critics believe that the Western is an intrinsically fragile form, dependent on those with a living memory of the untrammeled West itself. Others (like Wright), prone to a catastrophist theory of evolution, cite the financial disaster of *Heaven's Gate,* which scared Hollywood away from the Western for years. Still others note the familiar truth of the inevitable aging of Western stars to explain why audiences prefer younger actors in newer genres. A larger explanation for the Western's decline lies in the recent diminished appeal of strict genres themselves, as popular culture turns from conventionally identifiable plots.[10]

This last development is well worth keeping in mind: genres must regularly transform themselves, imaginatively manipulating classic givens, if they are to maintain a compelling hold over their audiences. The transition from Wister to Grey, from Ford and L'Amour to Leone and Peckinpah, has been a series of dramatic revisions of generic materials focused invariably on the process of manhood, and on the violent ways in which that process needs to be exposed and secured in a landscape where the moral issues at stake can be reproduced. The present problem of reviving the Western is that there seems little room for either customary violence or familiar landscape to be further revised. By the late 1960s, the most imaginative authors and directors had exhausted these generic staples, denying any redemptive virtue to either violence itself or the allure of landscape. All that was left was a repetition of plots, visual fetishes, character types. And while the Western is always an elegy for something dead before we began (as the Introduction claimed), even elegies have to invoke belief that conventions can be brought alive somehow. That moment is wonderfully captured at the conclusion of Mel Brooks's *Blazing Saddles* (1974), when the barroom brawl at Rock Ridge spills over into a Busby Berkeleyish musical being directed on the adjoining sound stage, and then flows over into the commissary. As the escaping villain Hedley Lamarr (Harvey Korman) says to a passing cabbie, "Drive me off this picture." Sheriff Bart (Cleavon Little) pursues him on his palomino, galloping after the taxi to a screening of "Blazing Saddles," where the final shoot-out occurs in a postmodernist scene that ends with Bart leaving town because it is becoming "too dull around here."

When Westerns themselves become too worn or stylized, tiredly incapable of renewing themselves, other ideas charge in, eager to take over everything worth recycling, fashioning fragments and fetishes into new structures. And the irony is that those who have wanted to liven up the genre just as often dismantle it, translating its parts into alien forms and distant contexts that bear no resemblnce to the genre (or as Leon Uris, one of the '70s' most popular authors, unwittingly described this phenomenon, "You can write westerns in any part of the world").[11] George Miller baldly steals from Western visual conventions in his *Mad Max* trilogy (*Mad Max* [1979], *The Road Warrior* [1981], and *Mad Max beyond Thunderdome* [1985]), starring Mel Gibson as an isolated hero who prevails against evil, bearded characters in a postnuclear, Australian wasteland. With a more consistent sense of generic progression, Clint Eastwood evolved from the "Man with No Name" to "Dirty Harry," transforming the '60s Western hero into an '80s action-adventure icon, the figure newly heroized in such popular films as Sylvester Stallone's Rambo series (beginning with Ted Kotcheff's *First Blood* [1982]), Ridley Scott's *Blade Runner* (1982), and James Cameron's

Terminator (1984). All these examples usurp the Western's role in assuaging a dominant culture's local anxieties, while at the same time keeping its aesthetic habits (its rhythm of landscape and narrative adventure; its concentration on a male body, beaten and convalescent; its investigation of the fragile balance between restraint and violence).

The question, then, has less to do with why the Western may be dying out than how it has continued to be reborn so often, and what it is that other genres might learn from this pattern. For if the action-adventure format is to maintain the hold it has newly gained, it will have to find increasingly elaborate ways to represent those issues so successfully engaged by the Western. The anxieties described in preceding chapters—over family authority, moral codes, social justice, the value of violence, and especially masculine self-construction—will once again need to be addressed through fictions and films that are imaginatively dense, offering sites of contention where the most pressing of contemporary dilemmas can seem to be resolved. As well, any new genre will need to take up masculinity where the Western left off, offering constructions of manhood that satisfy a somewhat bewildered '90s sensibility, caught between Robert Bly's tribal chest thumpings and Hugh Grant's stumblingly sensitive domestic partner.

Recently, Eastwood's *Unforgiven* has aroused speculation that the Western has other lives to live, and in the pages remaining I want to test that assumption by looking at some of the film's innovations. Critics have noted how deftly the film debunks the myth of a heroic past, beginning with the thoroughly unglamorous scene of the gunfighter-turned-farmer, William Munny (Eastwood), scrambling in a muddy pen to separate healthy from sick hogs. Thereafter, Munny is represented as a man whose body repeatedly fails him, who consistently has trouble mounting his horse (or then staying on it), who suffers from debilitating fever chills and horrifying memories of a wayward youth.[12] Early on, he practices shooting in front of his scornful children, able to hit a can on a stump only at last with a shotgun. Subsequent scenes reinforce this view of diminished male skills and prosaic body: of a cowboy murdered as he defecates in an outhouse; of Ned Logan (Morgan Freeman) crudely inquiring into Munny's current celibacy ("You just use your hand?"); of the tedious incompetence of the sheriff, Little Bill (Gene Hackman), as a carpenter; even of Munny's reform at the hands of a dead wife whose iron rule still keeps him domesticated. This unmasking of masculine achievement is made explicit through the subplot of the dime novelist, W. W. Beauchamp (Saul Rubinek), who concocts with the help of English Bob (Richard Harris) an inflated past of masculine valor. His book, *Duke of Death,* offers Little Bill the occasion to mock such nostalgic heroics, as he explains how English Bob, the "duck of death," was merely a sloppy drunk lucky enough to shoot an unarmed man.

This dismantling of mythic claims may have elated viewers of *Unforgiven,* but it was hardly a new tack, forming perhaps the most prevalent feature of earlier revisionist Westerns, and best represented by *The Man Who Shot Liberty Valance.* Unlike Ford, however, who exposed how fully legend and fact create one another, Eastwood relies on a more conventional transition from initial debunking to mythic restoration. After the opening sequences of heroism rudely deflated, of Munny reduced by his sagging body, the film then turns back on itself to confirm the truth of the mythic vision it unmasks. The Schofield Kid (Jaimz Woolvett) wonders aloud about a notorious episode of Munny "shooting your way out of a scrape," with two deputies pointing pistols at him, and Munny's mute response seems to confirm Little Bill's disdain for such mythic heroics. But shortly after, Ned reverses this judgment, recalling (as an eyewitness) that the experience involved not two, but three deputies, thereby lending Munny even greater mythic status. More bizarre, Munny's metamorphosis into a gunfighter able single-handedly to defeat a roomful of armed men follows just weeks upon his sorry display of marksmanship for his children. Only later do we realize that Little Bill's deflationary narrative of the misfire of Two-Gun Corcoran's Walker Colt ("a failing common to that model") anticipates the intrepid behavior of Munny when his own shotgun misfires, corroborating in the process Little Bill's accent on the need for "coolness," not speed.

If "it's not easy killing a man," as Ned points out to Munny (anticipating his own later anguished response), the conclusion of the film proves just the opposite, with Munny taking on the aura of a Freischütz whose bullets never miss. And the Schofield Kid's adolescent enthusiasm is meant to anticipate the audience's own delight—"Was that what it was like in the old days, Will? Everybody riding out and shooting, smoke all over the place, folks yelling and bullets whizzing by?" The film itself is structured to redeem, not condemn, that view of electrifying violence—to vindicate for the audience what Munny's own mother-in-law cannot understand. The importance of that vindication is stressed at the film's beginning and end, as both opening and closing credits roll past the same scene of Munny standing over his wife's grave while a short passage describes his mother-in-law's "heartbreak" at Claudia's marriage: "there was nothing on the marker to explain to Mrs. Feather why her only daughter had married a known thief and murderer, a man of notoriously vicious and intemperate disposition." That ironic, bracketing description of Munny, repeated nearly word for word, affirms for the viewer the heroic stature of a man portrayed as a brutal killer.[13]

Yet *Unforgiven* is not as radical or unsettling as this description suggests, and less for reasons of plot than of conventional cinematography, music, lighting, and other syntactic elements. The supposedly genuine tone of the opening segment at the farm is offset immediately when Munny rides to meet Ned Logan, filmed against the stunning autumnal scenery of Alberta—a sequence recapitulated when he, Ned, and the Schofield Kid start for Big Whiskey, as gentle string music swells through the sound track and aerial shots of fall foliage are intercut with images of beautiful horses splashing through water. The sentimentality of such scenes is compounded by the banal melodrama of other moments: of thunderclaps punctuating the gesture of English Bob given a gun in his cell; or of Munny deciding to avenge Ned's death, as the sound track shifts to dark chords and thunderclaps, as rain drives down, and low-angle shots of his horse's legs on the way to town are intersected by a whiskey bottle thrown into the street. The whole finale magically transforms Munny from incompetent hog farmer into dazzling exemplar of gunfighter heroism, able single-handedly to kill five gun-toting deputies.

The film itself borrows heavily from Western tropes described in chapters above, without offering the innovative inversions of those tropes characteristic of earlier films. The male body's mutilation forms an exaggerated theme, as Little Bill elaborately stages not one but a series of public beatings, of Munny, of Ned, and of English Bob, in the process exposing Richard Harris's lacerated face and Morgan Freeman's muscled back. The beating of Eastwood quotes directly from his first film, *A Fistful of Dollars,* where (as here) he painfully crawls from a saloon along a wooden boardwalk to the street. And his recovery predictably ensues with the help of the disfigured whore Delilah Fitzgerald (Anna Thomson), who represents an overtly scarred double of himself ("we both got scars"). Among the film's elaborate scenes of violence, that is the one innovation (as in *Ballad of Little Jo*): to allow the woman to be slashed.

Likewise, the film confirms the genre's obsession with proper burial, thematized in the open display of Ned's corpse, which prompts Munny's vengeance on the town and his fierce final oath: "You better bury Ned right. You better not cut out of it or I'll come back and kill every one of you sons of bitches." Perhaps the most embellished trope of the film, however, is its concentration on education, with the middle-aged dime novelist patronizingly characterized as a youth: "Look son," Little Bill tells the wide-eyed W. W. Beauchamp in explaining the advantage to a gunman of being cool-headed rather than quick on the draw. And thereafter the film follows the conventional Western paradigm of a "teach in," as Beauchamp learns how to load and cock a gun, how to maintain his resolve, indeed learns that the past lives on as both legend and fact in the body of William Munny.

Unforgiven is less revisionist than its 1990s audience assumed, adding little to the cinematic innovations introduced by Leone and Peckinpah a generation before (or by Ford, a generation earlier in turn). While it addresses familiar issues linked to masculine self-construction (including self-presentation, education, convalescence, and moral codes), it stages these rituals in stock ways that fail to transform a genre or to resolve the conflicting ideologies that the genre entertains. Nor does it ever clarify a confusion about its own generic materials (Is Beauchamp's dime novel accurate or not? Does masculinity consist in self-restraint or violence? Is competence a matter of luck or effort?). Instead, the film traces an untroubled transition from pacifism to brutal intervention and then delights in the conventional violence that Munny is obliged to perform. By contrast, a director like Peckinpah had wanted to evoke a completely different response: to "take the facade of movie violence and open it up, get people involved . . . and then twist it so that it's not fun anymore, just a wave of sickness in the gut. It's not fun and games and cowboys and Indians. It's a terrible, ugly thing."[14]

Part of the appeal of *Unforgiven* is attributable to its realist deflation of the male body conjoined with that body's mythic transcendence of a brutal social dynamics. And that conjunction helps explain why critics have read the film as an allegory of American foreign policy in a rudderless, post-Communist era, an era during which old assumptions no longer avail.[15] Once again, however, the two-dimensional reading flattens innovative details and silences narrative syntax: gestures of reduction that fail to explain the film's appeal. Thinly disguised political allegories do not in themselves gain popular favor; *Unforgiven* cannot be reduced to so weak a brew. By the same token, Eastwood's film remains ephemeral because it never quite succeeds in confronting its own confusion. It well may be that a full generation after Leone and Peckinpah transformed the "syntax" of the Western, little room exists for further development or revision.[16] Yet the very recurrence of that suspicion, voiced so often in the decades before, paradoxically gives hope that the genre will not peter out into endless variations of romanticized shoot-outs and beaten men but evolve instead into Westerns able to appeal to diverse publics by consistently transforming the materials available. Perilously thin as those materials have worn after more than a century, they make the challenge of finding new solutions to their creative integration all the greater.

A genre that began in the masculinizing fantasies of Jacksonian America, that took uncertain shape in the nationalizing period following 263 the Civil War, that reached its characteristic form in the midst of the suffragette movement, and that soon was identified as America's most distinctive narrative form: the Western has featured a long history of creative efforts at dissecting some of the nation's most compelling crises. No other genre has come close in purity of form or simplicity of materials to its ability to engage issues that have a compelling contemporary resonance. And precisely as past Westerns continue to haunt us with narratives of foregone cultural crises, the possibility persists that writers and directors will once again find in the image of a man with a gun, sitting astride a horse, silhouetted against an empty landscape, the figure capable of engaging us in the midst of anxieties yet unimagined. Certainly, the dilemma of masculinity is no less urgent in a world far more urban, bureaucratic, and technological than ever imagined (or feared) a century ago. And just as certainly, in a world where the cultural construction of identity has become a hackneyed expression, it is easy to see reasons for our continuing fascination in the West's characteristic landscape of renewal, and even more in the Western's far from characteristic process of making the man.

notes

Epigraph

1. Cited by Philip French, *Westerns: Aspects of a Movie Genre* (London: Secker & Warburg, 1973), p. 6.

2. Cited by Darryl Ponicsan, *Tom Mix Died for Your Sins: A Novel Based on His Life* (New York: Delacorte Press, 1975), p. 135.

3. Roland Barthes, "Myth Today," in *Mythologies*, trans. Annette Lavers (New York: Hill & Wang, 1972), p. 112.

Acknowledgments

1. Rick Altman, *The American Film Musical* (Bloomington: Indiana University Press, 1987), p. 45.

Introduction

1. Oriana Fallaci, *Interview with History* (Boston: Houghton Mifflin, 1976), p. 41.

2. Philip French, *Westerns: Aspects of a Movie Genre* (London: Secker & Warburg, 1973), p. 24.

3. For an account of this transformation, see Kent Ladd Steckmesser, *The Western Hero in History and Legend* (Norman: University of Oklahoma Press, 1965).

4. Henry Nash Smith, *Virgin Land: The American West as Symbol and Myth* (Cambridge, MA: Harvard University Press, 1950), pp. 91–92.

5. Tony Bennett and Janet Woolacott, *Bond and Beyond* (New York: Methuen, 1987), p. 20.

6. So exemplary has the Western seemed as a form that those interested in the structural constraints of other genres turn first for comparison to it. Mary Ann Doane contrasts the Western with melodrama in *The Desire to Desire: The Woman's Film of the 1940s* (Bloomington: Indiana University Press, 1987), pp. 171–72; as does Geoffrey Nowell-Smith, "Dossier on Melodrama," *Screen* 18, no. 2 (Summer 1977): 115. Philip French argues instead for the musical as "the feminine counterpart" to the Western (*Westerns*, p. 66). Marshall McLuhan defines the differences between "Horse Opera and Soap Opera," in *The Mechanical Bride: Folklore of Industrial Man* (Boston: Beacon Press, 1951), pp. 154–57. Lucy Fischer observes that "as a general rule, women are

portrayed as 'mystery' within the *film noir* genre"—a placement inverted by the Western's concentration on the mysterious hero, in *Shot/Countershot: Film Tradition and Women's Cinema* (Princeton: Princeton University Press, 1989), p. 36. Discussing horror films, Carol J. Clover claims "that westerns are really horror 'underneath' . . . and that each enables the other to be told," in *Men, Women, and Chain Saws: Gender in the Modern Horror Film* (Princeton: Princeton University Press, 1992), p. 165.

7. See Christine Bold, *Selling the Wild West: Popular Western Fiction, 1860–1960* (Bloomington: Indiana University Press, 1987), pp. 10–18, 40–43; and Henry Nash Smith, *Virgin Land,* pp. 67–70, 98–102. For those who agree that Cooper was "the father" of the Western, see *The BFI Companion to the Western,* ed. Edward Buscombe (New York: Atheneum, 1988), pp. 97, 173; Douglas Pye, "The Western (Genre and Movies)," in *Film Genre Reader,* ed. Barry Keith Grant (Austin: University of Texas Press, 1986), p. 147; and Henry Nash Smith, "Consciousness and Order: The Theme of Transcendence in the Leatherstocking Tales," *Western American Literature* 5 (Fall 1970): 180.

8. Among critics who believe the Western can only be cinematic (paradoxically supporting my argument for the genre's theatrical bent), Kim Newman has made the starkest claim: "the Western proper was not possible before the invention of the cinema. Unlike such genres as the thriller, the musical, the comedy or the horror story, the Western is uniquely of the cinema." See *Wild West Movies: How the West Was Found, Won, Lost, Lied about, Filmed and Forgotten* (London: Bloomsbury, 1990), pp. xv–xvi; also George N. Fenin and William K. Everson, *The Western: From Silents to Seventies* (1973; rev. ed. Harmondsworth: Penguin, 1977), p. 9.

9. Perry Miller discusses the period's obsession with nature, in "The Romantic Dilemma in American Nationalism and the Concept of Nature," in *Nature's Nation* (Cambridge, MA: Harvard University Press, 1967), pp. 197–207.

10. On Porter's invention of a "truly cinematic narrative language" with this, the most widely distributed film prior to D. W. Griffith's *The Birth of a Nation* (1915), see David A. Cook, *A History of Narrative Film* (New York: W. W. Norton, 1981), pp. 24–25. Westerns of a sort had anticipated this feature film by a full decade: Annie Oakley appeared in films beginning in 1894, the year Edison produced such short subjects as *Sioux Indian Ghost Dance, Indian War Council,* and *Bucking Bronco.* "So popular were westerns during narrative cinema's formative years (1903–1911)," Tag Gallagher has facetiously remarked "that it may well be that, rather than the cinema having invented the western, it was the western, already long existent in popular culture, that invented the cinema. Picturesque scenery, archetypal characters, dialectical story construction, long shots, close-ups, parallel editing, confrontational cross-cutting, montaged chases—all were explicit in the western before the Lumières cranked their first camera. By 1909, and during the next six years, there were probably more westerns released *each* month than during the entire decade of the 1930s." See "Shoot-Out at the Genre Corral: Problems in the 'Evolution' of the Western," in *Film Genre Reader,* ed. Barry Keith Grant (Austin: University of Texas Press, 1986), p. 204.

11. For figures on film production, see Phil Hardy, *The Western* (London: Aurum Press, 1983), pp. 365–71.

12. Robert Warshow, "Movie Chronicle: The Westerner" (1954); rptd. in *The Immediate Experience: Movies, Comics, Theatre, and Other Aspects of Popular Culture* (Garden City, NY: Doubleday, 1962), pp. 135–54. For other astute early critics, see André Bazin, "The Evolution of the Western," in *What Is Cinema?* vol. 2, trans. Hugh Gray

(Berkeley: University of California Press, 1971), pp. 149–57; and *Cahiers du Cinéma, The 1950s: Neo-Realism, Hollywood, New Wave*, ed. Jim Hillier (Cambridge, MA: Harvard University Press, 1985), esp. pp. 169–70; Bernard DeVoto, "The Easy Chair: Birth of an Art," *Harper's Magazine* 211 (December 1955): 8–9, 12, 14, 16; and "The Easy Chair: Phaethon on Gunsmoke Trail," *Harper's Magazine* 209 (December 1954): 10–11, 14, 16; and Marshall McLuhan, "Horse Opera and Soap Opera," in *The Mechanical Bride*, pp. 154–57.

Steve Neale observes: "Eric Partridge dates the first colloquial use of the term 'Western' in anything other than an adjectival sense to around 1910. The first use of the term cited in the *Oxford English Dictionary* with reference to a film dates from 1912." Yet even without the specific term, the genre "had been around for some time" ("Questions of Genre," *Screen* 31, no. 1 [Spring 1990]: 52–55). Cynthia S. Hamilton likewise observes that Westerns were not generically fixed until relatively late, and that Zane Grey's novels were touted before 1920 as "love storys" (*Western and Hard-Boiled Detective Fiction in America: From High Noon to Midnight* [London: Macmillan, 1987], pp. 60–61, and chap. 1n.14).

13. See John G. Cawelti, "Prolegomena to the Western," *Studies in Public Communication* 4 (Autumn 1962): 70–74; *The Six-Gun Mystique* (1973; 2d ed. Bowling Green, OH: Bowling Green Popular Press, 1984); *Adventure, Mystery, and Romance: Formula Stories as Art and Popular Culture* (Chicago: University of Chicago Press, 1976), esp. chap. 8, "The Western: A Look at the Evolution of a Formula," pp. 192–259; and "Trends in Recent American Genre Fiction," *Kansas Quarterly* 10 (Fall 1978): 5–18.

14. Fredric Jameson, "Ideology, Narrative Analysis, and Popular Culture," *Theory and Society* 4 (Winter 1977): 547. For another critique of Cawelti, see J. Fred MacDonald, *Who Shot the Sheriff? The Rise and Fall of the Television Western* (New York: Praeger, 1987), p. 6. Cawelti rarely assesses texts in the terms he endorses, and his tendency to invoke "psychological needs" to explain the Western's continuing popularity renders his generic conclusions unpersuasive (*Adventure, Mystery, Romance*, p. 7).

15. Will Wright, *Six Guns and Society: A Structural Study of the Western* (Berkeley: University of California Press, 1975). For critiques, see Janey Place, "Structured Cowboys," review of *Six-Guns and Society*, in *Jump Cut* 18 (1978): 26–28; and Christopher Frayling, *Spaghetti Westerns*, pp. 43–51.

16. Jane Tompkins, *West of Everything: The Inner Life of Westerns* (New York: Oxford University Press, 1992), p. 39.

17. Allegorical interpretations (based on "reflection theory") treat texts as simple expressions of an attitude imputed to viewers, as in Richard Slotkin's assumption that "increasing emphasis on military displays in Wild West scenarios . . . suggests that the readiest way to modernize the frontier hero was to militarize him." See *Gunfighter Nation: The Myth of the Frontier in Twentieth-Century America* (New York: Atheneum, 1992), p. 88; also pp. 183, 207. Walter Benn Michaels attributes a similar fixed attitude to all contemporary instances of the genre, in "The Contracted Heart," *New Literary History* 21 (Spring 1990): esp. pp. 515–17.

18. Fredric Jameson, *The Political Unconscious: Narrative as a Socially Symbolic Act* (Ithaca: Cornell University Press, 1981), p. 102.

Chapter One

1. *The Last of the Mohicans*, in *The Leatherstocking Tales* (New York: Library of America, 1985), 1:798.

2. Marshall McLuhan, *The Mechanical Bride: Folklore of Industrial Man* (Boston: Beacon Press, 1951), p. 156.

3. F. Scott Fitzgerald, *The Great Gatsby* (New York: Charles Scribner's Sons, 1925), p. 174.

4. Texts are sometimes criticized as confused by critics who fail to recognize how such confusion can contribute to their success. See Philip Wander, "The Aesthetics of Fascism," *Journal of Communication* 33, no. 2 (1983): 70–78; Robert Entman and Francis Seymour, "Close Encounters with the Third Reich," *Jump Cut* 18 (1978): 3–6; and Dan Rubey, "*Star Wars:* Not So Far Away," *Jump Cut* 18 (1978): 9–14. On the need for contradiction in popular texts, see *American Media and Mass Culture,* ed. Donald Lazere (Berkeley: University of California Press, 1987), p. 234; and Tania Modleski, "The Search for Tomorrow in Today's Soap Operas," in *American Media and Mass Culture,* p. 276 (taken from her *Loving with a Vengeance: Mass-Produced Fantasies for Women* [Hamden, CT: Archon Books, 1982]).

5. Further study needs to be done on audiences for Westerns to determine distributions of gender, ethnicity, race, class, age groups, and sexual preference. For partial attempts, see John A. Dinan, *The Pulp Western: A Popular History of the Western Fiction Magazine in America* (San Bernardino, CA: Borgo Press, 1983), esp. p. 8; and Fred Mac-Donald, *Who Shot the Sheriff? The Rise and Fall of the Television Western* (New York: Praeger, 1987), esp. pp. 10–22.

On film audiences, Garth S. Jowett has noted the "difficulty in creating categories of films which will provide meaningful data. 'Westerns,' as an example, may be cheap $100,000 class 'B' pictures, or an expensive $3 million Technicolor extravaganza, yet both stories come under the heading *western*" ("Giving Them What They Want: Movie Audience Research before 1950," in *Current Research in Film: Audience, Economics, and Law,* vol. 1, ed. Bruce A. Austin, [Norwood, NJ: Ablex Publishing Corp., 1985], p. 32). For conflicting readings of the audience for Westerns, see Steve Neale, "Questions of Genre," *Screen* 31, no. 1 (Spring 1990): 64; and Robert Sklar, *Movie-Made America: A Social History of American Movies* (New York: Random House, 1975), p. 271. Carol J. Clover points out that film audiences have been far less analyzed than television audiences and that at present there is no way to study video rental audiences, in *Men, Women, and Chain Saws: Gender in the Modern Horror Film* (Princeton: Princeton University Press, 1992), p. 6.

More generally, David Morley is the most significant figure now working on audience response and popular texts, applying "an ethnographic approach to media audiences" and cautious about confusing real readers with constructed ones, in *Television Audiences and Cultural Studies* (London: Routledge, 1992), p. 13; also *The "Nationwide" Audience: Structure and Decoding* (London: British Film Institute, 1980). For further discussions, see Robert C. Allen, "From Exhibition to Reception: Reflections on the Audience in Film History," *Screen* 31, no. 4 (Winter 1990): 347–56; Bruce A. Austin, *The Film Audience: An International Bibliography of Research* (Metuchen, NJ: Scarecrow Press, 1983), esp. "The Motion Picture Audience: A Neglected Aspect of Film Research," pp. xvii–xlii; Michael Denning, *Mechanic Accents: Dime Novels and Working-Class Culture in America* (London: Verso, 1987), esp. chap. 3, "'The Unknown Public': Dime Novels and Working Class Readers," pp. 27–46; and Janice A. Radway, *Reading the Romance: Woman, Patriarchy and Popular Literature* (Chapel Hill: University of North Carolina Press, 1984); also her "Introduction: Writing *Reading the Romance*" to the 1991 ed., pp. 1–18; and her "Reception Study: Ethnography and the Problems of

Dispersed Audiences and Nomadic Subjects," *Cultural Studies* 2, no. 3 (1988): 359–76. For a critique of Radway, see Tania Modleski, "Some Functions of Feminist Criticism; or The Scandal of the Mute Body," *October* 49 (1989): 3–24; repeated in *Feminism without Women: Culture and Criticism in a "Postfeminist" Age* (New York: Routledge, 1991), pp. 41–44.

6. Geoffrey O'Brien, "The Ghost Opera," review essay, *New York Review of Books* 38, May 30, 1991, p. 10.

7. Miriam Hansen has pointed out that 60 percent of the patronage of an 1897 fight film were women (counter to the all-male clientele of live prize fights)—raising questions about what women wanted to see (*Babel and Babylon: Spectatorship in American Silent Film* [Cambridge, MA: Harvard University Press, 1991], p. 1). There is an eavesdropping effect—women spying upon male worlds, men upon women's—that is facilitated by literature and film and that may make for surprises in any investigation of typical reading and viewing publics.

8. Alice Payne Hackett addresses the difficulty of gaining an adequate reading of sales in *Seventy Years of Best Sellers: 1895–1965* (New York: R. R. Bowker Co., 1967). As she points out, best-seller lists are only prepared for bookstore outlets and do not include sales by book clubs or in paperbound reprint editions. Still, the most popular Westerns have regularly sold considerably less than books in the "Crime and Suspense" category, averaging only 2 million overall sales versus 5 million for "crimis."

9. John Sutherland, *Bestsellers: Popular fiction of the 1970s* (London: Routledge & Kegan Paul, 1981), pp. 35, 155.

10. Clement Greenberg, "Avant-Garde and Kitsch" (1939); rptd. in *Art and Culture: Critical Essays* (Boston: Beacon Press, 1961), p. 10. Van Wyck Brooks had addressed these issues earlier in *America's Coming-of-Age* (1915; Garden City, NY: Doubleday, 1958), esp. chap. 1, "'Highbrow' and 'Lowbrow,'" pp. 1–19.

11. For Theodor W. Adorno's view that the Western itself was the most obvious example of culture industry control, see "Culture Industry Reconsidered" (1967), in *New German Critique* 6 (Fall 1975): 14; also Max Horkheimer and Theodor W. Adorno, "The Culture Industry: Enlightenment as Mass Deception," in *Dialect of Enlightenment,* trans. John Cumming (1944; New York: Herder & Herder, 1972), pp. 120–67; and "Art and Mass Culture," in *Critical Theory* (New York: Herder & Herder, 1972), pp. 273–90; and Herbert Marcuse, "Repressive Tolerance," in Robert Paul Wolff, Barrington Moore, Jr., and Herbert Marcuse, *A Critique of Pure Tolerance* (Boston: Beacon Press, 1969), p. 83. For overviews of the Frankfurt School, see Martin Jay, *The Dialectical Imagination: A History of the Frankfurt School and the Institute of Social Research, 1923–1950* (Boston: Little, Brown, 1973), esp. pp. 173–218; and Patrick Brantlinger, *Bread and Circuses: Theories of Mass Culture as Social Decay* (Ithaca: Cornell University Press, 1983).

12. For further discussion, see my "Henry Nash Smith's Myth of the West," in *Writing Western History: Essays on Major Western Historians,* ed. Richard W. Etulain (Albuquerque: University of New Mexico Press, 1991), pp. 247–75.

13. Peter Burke, "The Discovery of Popular Culture," in *People's History and Socialist Theory,* ed. Raphael Samuel (London: Routledge & Kegan Paul, 1981), pp. 219–20, 225.

14. Anthony C. Hilfer, "Inversion and Excess: Texts of Bliss in Popular Culture," *Texas Studies in Literature and Language* 22, no. 2 (Summer 1980): 124.

15. Stuart Hall, "Notes on Deconstructing 'The Popular,'" in *People's History and*

Socialist Theory, ed. Raphael Samuel (London: Routledge & Kegan Paul, 1981): 232, 228, 233. Denis McQuail's review of "macro-approaches" to mass society—including the Marxist, Frankfurt, and Birmingham Schools—reveals how "much work has been done over a period of forty years to show that audiences can and do describe their media experience in functional (that is, problem-solving or 'need-meeting') terms." The problem, as he concludes, is to find evidence that the audience "is indeed 'active' and that a causal process is at work, beginning in the experience of the viewer, listener or reader. There is so much 'noise' in the system, so much unmotivated and casual attention to media that the answer to the fundamental question is unlikely to be reached" (*Mass Communication Theory: An Introduction* [London: Sage, 1983], pp. 163–64).

16. Fredric Jameson, "Reification and Utopia in Mass Culture," *Social Text* 1 (1979): 141.

17. Ariel Dorfman and Armand Mattelart, *How to Read Donald Duck,* trans. David Kunzle (New York: International General, 1975).

18. See "Taking Tarzan Seriously," chap. 2 of Marianna Torgovnick's *Gone Primitive: Savage Intellect, Modern Lives* (Chicago: University of Chicago Press, 1990), esp. p. 62; and Eric Cheyfitz, *"Tarzan of the Apes:* U.S. Foreign Policy in the Twentieth Century," *American Literary History* 1 (1989): 339–60.

19. Catherine Belsey *Critical Practice* (London: Methuen, 1980), p. 114. For comparable studies, see Thomas Andrae, "From Menace to Messiah: The Prehistory of the Superman in Science Fiction Literature," *Discourse* 2 (Summer 1980): 84–107; Ariel Dorfman, *The Empire's Old Clothes: What the Lone Ranger, Babar, and Other Innocent Heroes Do to Our Minds* (New York: Pantheon, 1983); Charles Eckert, "Shirley Temple and the House of Rockefeller," rptd. in *American Media and Mass Culture,* pp. 164–77; and Umberto Eco, "The Myth of Superman," *Diacritics* 2, no. 1 (Spring 1972): 14–22.

20. Tony Bennett and Janet Woolacott address "the problem of reading Bond's readers" in chap. 3, "Reading Bond," *Bond and Beyond* (New York: Methuen, 1987), pp. 44–80. Reacting against Umberto Eco's a priori assumption of an undifferentiated "mass audience," they point out that "those 'vertical' divisions produced by the operation of such factors as race, gender, nation and region" may be more important than class determinations: "It would be equally plausible to argue that gender divisions produce a clustering and patterning of reading practices which both cut across and are socially and culturally more consequential than those produced by the sophisticated/average reader distinction" (78).

21. *Stephen Crane: Prose and Poetry,* ed. J. C. Levenson (New York: Library of America, 1984), p. 732. Subsequent references to Crane's stories appear parenthetically in the text.

22. See Tag Gallagher *John Ford: The Man and His Films* (Berkeley: University of California Press, 1986), p. 253; and Robert Ray, *A Certain Tendency of the Hollywood Cinema, 1930–1980* (Princeton: Princeton University Press, 1985), pp. 216–40. Ray observes that the frame shoot-out defies the usual contract with an audience over the convention of shot-reverse shot, creating a "formal rupture": "Doniphon's confession undermined the invisible style itself, exposing the guarantee on which its most fundamental figure rested as a mere cinematic convention" (231).

23. Tag Gallagher, *John Ford,* p. 385.

24. For histories of this period, see Lewis Atherton, *The Cattle Kings* (Bloomington: Indiana University Press, 1961); Gene M. Gressley, *Bankers and Cattlemen* (New

York: Alfred A. Knopf, 1966); and William W. Savage, Jr., *The Cowboy Hero: His Image in American History & Culture* (Norman: University of Oklahoma Press, 1979).

25. See Don D. Walker, "Freedom and Individualism on the Range: Ideological Images of the Cowboy and Cattleman," in *Clio's Cowboys: Studies in the Historiography of the Cattle Trade* (Lincoln: University of Nebraska Press, 1981), pp. 76–92.

26. Richard Irving Dodge, *Our Wild Indians: Thirty-three Years' Personal Experience among the Red Men of the Great West* (Hartford, CT: Worthington, 1882), p. 611.

27. Theodore Roosevelt, *Ranch Life and the Hunting-Trail* (1888; New York: Century, 1899), p. 6. For further discussion of this "splendid set of men," see Roosevelt's *The Rough Riders* (New York: Charles Scribner's Sons, 1899), esp. pp. 15–19, 27–29.

28. Alfred Henry Lewis, *Wolfville Nights* (New York: Frederick A. Stokes, 1902), p. 10.

29. Theodore Roosevelt, *Ranch Life and the Hunting-Trail*, p. 6. The influence of Roosevelt's socially conservative vision should not be underestimated: his dislike of immigrants, resistance to commercialism, outspoken contempt for the new bureaucracy, and renewed concern with "Americanism" as "the antithesis of what is unwholesome and undesirable." See "True Americanism" (1894), rptd. in *American Ideals: The Strenuous Life; Realizable Ideals* (New York: Charles Scribner's Sons, 1926), p. 15.

30. Richard White, *"It's Your Misfortune and None of My Own": A History of the American West* (Norman: University of Oklahoma Press, 1991), p. 621.

31. Marshall McLuhan, *Mechanical Bride,* p. 156. McLuhan continues: "Again, under complex conditions of rapid change, the family unit is subject to special strain. Men flounder in such times. The male role in society, always abstract, tenuous, and precarious compared with the biological assurance of the female, becomes obscured. Man the provider, man the codifier of laws and ritual, loses his confidence. For millions of such men horse opera presents a reassuringly simple and nondomestic world in which there are no economic problems" (*Mechanical Bride,* p. 156). See also Eric Hobsbawm's description of "the noble robber," in *Bandits* (1969; 2d ed. Harmondsworth: Penguin, 1985), p. 56.

According to Blake Allmendinger, "to be a 'real' cowboy, a man had to orphan himself, at least metaphorically." See *The Cowboy: Representations of Labor in an American Work Culture* (New York: Oxford University Press, 1992), p. 123.

32. Martin Pumphrey, "Masculinity," in *The BFI Companion to the Western,* ed. Edward Buscombe, p. 181.

Chapter Two

1. "Fenimore Cooper's Literary Offenses," in *The Portable Mark Twain,* ed. Bernard DeVoto (New York: Viking, 1968), pp. 541–42.

2. D. H. Lawrence, *Studies in Classic American Literature* (New York: Thomas Seltzer, 1923), p. 81.

3. Interview with Cynthis Grenier, "Pastalong Cassidy Always Wears Black," *Oui* 2 (April 1973): 88.

4. *The Pathfinder,* in *James Fenimore Cooper: The Leatherstocking Tales* (New York: Library of America, 1985), 2:175. Subsequent references to all five novels of the series are to this edition and included parenthetically. Few need be reminded that the series' order of publication consists of *The Pioneers* (1823), *The Last of the Mohicans* (1826),

The Prairie (1827), *The Pathfinder* (1840), and *The Deerslayer* (1841). Or that the chronological order of the series' central figure, Natty Bumppo, begins with *The Deerslayer* (set in 1740, with Natty aged 23–24), extending then through *The Last of the Mohicans* (set in 1757, with Natty aged 36–37), *The Pathfinder* (set 2 years later), *The Pioneers* (set in 1793, with Natty 71–73), and *The Prairie* (set in October 1805, with Natty identified alternately as 80, 86, 87, and "over ninety"). See also Allen M. Axelrad, "The Order of the Leatherstocking Tales: D. H. Lawrence, David Noble, and the Iron Trap of History," *American Literature* 54 (1982): 189–211. For an analysis of the transformations in the character of Leatherstocking, see Renata R. Mautner Wasserman, "The Reception of Cooper's Work and the Image of America," *ESQ: A Journal of the American Renaissance* 32, no. 3 (1986): 190–91.

5. For discussion of this point, see John Fairbanks Lynen, *The Design of the Present: Essays on Time and Form in American Literature* (New Haven: Yale University Press, 1969), esp. pp. 188, 203. The centrality of this trait to the Western can be measured by the fact that inadequate men frequently have faulty vision. The most flagrant example is the character actor Jack Elam, whose sightless left eye creates a sinister atmosphere exploited in villainous roles in numerous films of the 1950s and 1960s.

6. James D. Wallace declares: "The importance of Cooper's protracted grappling with the problem of audience cannot be overestimated. Quite simply, Cooper created the community of readers whose taste would dominate the market for fiction in America (and for American fiction abroad) throughout the nineteenth century" (*Early Cooper and His Audience* [New York: Columbia University Press, 1986], p. 171; also pp. 163 ff., for discussion of the "major cultural event" caused by publication of *The Pioneers,* with its "new approach to the representation of the American landscape" [179]). For a still convincing analysis of "Cooper's professional rise and decline," see William Charvat, *Literary Publishing in America, 1790–1850* (1959; Amherst: University of Massachusetts Press, 1993), esp. pp. 54–56.

7. George Dekker, *James Fenimore Cooper: The Novelist* (London: Routledge & Kegan Paul, 1967), p. 65. In his study of Cooper's publisher, David Kaser claims the novel "sold so well that both author and publisher profited greatly from it. Cooper stayed with the firm for some twelve years thereafter and was paid more than $40,000 for the rights to his books during that period, unprecedented earnings by an American author" ("Carey & Lea," in *Publishers for Mass Entertainment in Nineteenth-Century America,* ed. Madeleine B. Stern [Boston: G. K. Hall, 1980], p. 76). William Charvat claims it was "possibly the most popular novel in the world," in "Introduction," *The Last of the Mohicans* (Boston: Houghton Mifflin, 1958), p. v. Dorothy Waples notes that "a list in a newspaper of the fads and fashions of 1826 named this novel among the other popular crazes," in *The Whig Myth of James Fenimore Cooper* (New Haven: Yale University Press, 1938), p. 64. Alice Payne Hackett lists both *The Last of the Mohicans* and *The Deerslayer* as "Early Best Sellers" and includes only one other novel by Cooper on that list: *The Spy* (*Seventy Years of Best Sellers: 1895–1965* [New York: R. R. Bowker Co., 1967], p. 235).

Waples and Dekker describe an asymmetry in the period between the response of critics and reviewers on the one hand and the sales of books on the other, with even *The Last of the Mohicans* receiving bad notices (see also James D. Wallace, *Early Cooper,* pp. 173–74). A concern for reviews, however, helps explain the 1850 "Preface" to the collected series, in which Cooper tried to understand "why the later books of the series should be overlooked" (2:490). In fact, this observation misrepresents the sales of both volumes and Cooper's own delighted response with their success, as confirmed by *The Letters and Journals of James Fenimore Cooper,* ed. James Franklin Beard (Cambridge, MA: Harvard University Press, 1964), 4:34, 174, 345; and James Franklin Beard, "Historical Introduction," pp. xlvi–li.

8. Among the more famous of these authors, who published at least thirty "Westerns" apiece, were Mayne Reid and Percy St. John in England; Gustave Aimard and Gabriel Ferry in France; Emilio Salgari in Italy; Charles Sealsfield, Friedrich Armand Strubberg, Friedrich Gerstäcker, Balduin Möllhausen, and Karl May in Germany. May's 70 books sold over 30 million copies in more than 20 languages, and were read by over 300 million people (among them Einstein and Hitler, for whom he was a favorite author). See Ray Allen Billington, *America's Frontier Culture: Three Essays* (College Station: Texas A & M University Press, 1977), pp. 78–80; and for a comprehensive discussion of Cooper's influence in Europe, see chap. 2, "The Image-Makers: Land of Savagery," in *Land of Savagery, Land of Promise: The European Image of the American Frontier in the Nineteenth Century* (New York: W. W. Norton, 1981), pp. 29–57. See also Richard H. Cracroft, "World Westerns: The European Writer and the American West," *A Literary History of the American West* (Fort Worth: Texas Christian University Press, 1987), pp. 159–79; and Cracroft, "The American West of Karl May," *American Quarterly* 19 (Summer 1967): 247–58.

9. For exemplary representatives of these positions, see George Dekker, *Cooper,* esp. chap. 2, "An American Scott," pp. 20–42; James D. Wallace, *Early Cooper,* pp. 176–77; and David Leverenz, "The Last Real Man in America: From Natty Bumppo to Batman," *American Literary History* 3 (Winter 1991): 760.

10. D. H. Lawrence, *Studies,* p. 80.

11. James Franklin Beard, Jr., has claimed that "all of the more prominent painters of Cooper's time turned directly to his fiction for subjects; and if the records were complete, they might show that almost every major scene in his early novels was transferred to canvas" ("Cooper and His Artistic Contemporaries," *New York History* 35 [1954]: 484, 490). For other studies of Cooper's pictorialism, see Howard Mumford Jones, "Prose and Pictures: James Fenimore Cooper," *History and the Contemporary: Essays in Nineteenth-Century Literature* (Madison: University of Wisconsin Press, 1964), pp. 61–83; Blake Nevius, *Cooper's Landscapes: An Essay on the Picturesque Vision* (Berkeley: University of California Press, 1976); H. Daniel Peck, *A World by Itself: The Pastoral Moment in Cooper's Fiction* (New Haven: Yale University Press, 1977); Donald A. Ringe, *The Pictorial Mode: Space and Time in the Art of Bryant, Irving and Cooper* (Lexington: University Press of Kentucky, 1971). For more on Cooper's anxiety to record wilderness scenes, see my *Witnesses to a Vanishing America: The Nineteenth-Century Response* (Princeton: Princeton University Press, 1981), pp. 43–47.

12. Cited in *Fenimore Cooper: The Critical Heritage,* ed. George Dekker and John P. McWilliams (London: Routledge & Kegan Paul, 1973), p. 197.

13. Cited in *Critical Heritage,* p. 129. Cooper himself anticipated this response, nervously writing to his publisher before the novel appeared: "I had announced the work as a 'descriptive tale' but perhaps have confined myself too much to describing the scenes of my own youth—I know that the present taste is for action and strong excitement, and in this respect am compelled to acknowledge that the two first volumes are deficient" (*Letters and Journals,* 1:85).

14. Umberto Eco, "Narrative Structures in Fleming," in *The Role of the Reader: Explorations in the Semiotics of Texts* (Bloomington: Indiana University Press, 1970), pp.

165, 167. See also Roland Barthes's discussion of the need for "useless details" in narrative, in "The Reality Effect," in *French Literary Theory Today,* ed. Tzvetan Todorov (New York: Cambridge University Press, 1982): 11–17.

15. Ibid., pp. 166, 165, 167.

16. Cited in *Critical Heritage,* pp. 157–58. Tony Tanner has more recently remarked on the "colonizing eye" in Cooper's suspension of narrative for scenic evocation, and on the narrative having had no effect on Glimmerglass history: "The scene is, temporarily, stronger than the sign." See the title essay in *Scenes of Nature, Signs of Men* (Cambridge: Cambridge University Press, 1987), pp. 2, 7.

17. D. H. Lawrence, *Studies,* p. 74.

18. W. H. Gardiner, review of *The Pioneers* and *The Last of the Mohicans,* in *North American Review* 23 (July 1826): 154, 175.

19. David Simpson observes of Cooper's "positive coding of silence" that "silence speaks for an integrated rather than an aggressive relation of man to nature (although nature itself may contain a principle of aggression). It is the (a)linguistic analogue of a kind of ecological tact in Cooper's heroes; they leave no trace behind them, and create no disturbance" (*The Politics of American English, 1776–1850* [New York: Oxford University Press, 1986], pp. 196–97).

20. Gérard Genette observes that "description might be conceived independently of narration, but in fact it is never found in a so to speak free state; narration cannot exist without description, but this dependence does not prevent it from constantly playing the major role. Description is quite naturally *ancilla narrationis,* the ever-necessary, ever-submissive, never emancipated slave" ("Frontiers of Narrative," in *Figures of Literary Discourse,* trans. Alan Sheridan [New York: Columbia University Press, 1982], p. 134). See also "Flaubert's Silences," pp. 182–202, where Genette argues that Flaubert indulges a "love of contemplation" in "moments when the narrative seems to fall silent and become frozen under what Sartre was to call 'the great petrifying gaze of things'" (192, 194).

21. As Thomas Philbrick declares: "Between the pulsations of violent action, the characteristic attitude of Cooper's figures is one of intent listening." See "Sounds of Discord," *American Literature* 43 (March 1971): 36.

22. An analogous if more brutal scene occurs in *The Pathfinder,* when the Iroquois create a deceptive tableau of corpses to lure rescuers into thinking they are still alive (2:375).

23. As in *The Last of the Mohicans,* one character stands apart, serving as social misfit even as she allegorizes the novel's thematic concerns. Hetty Hutter is less self-conscious than anyone else in succumbing to this spiritual inclination "to mingle with the universe." Part of the reason is that she is constitutionally incapable of self-preservation, a stranger to common sense—or as the novel intones, "feeble minded" (2:643). Like David Gamut, the eccentric who acts out the earlier novel's motif of voice versus silence, Hetty personifies the more radical experience delineated in *The Deerslayer* by melding her idiosyncratic character with an impersonal landscape, suggesting the virtual consolidation of narrative and description. That self-submersion is most notably enacted in chapter 10, with her nighttime excursion into the dangerous, "intensely dark" woods, leading her to feel the "sublimity of her solitude" (2:649). The chapter both focuses on Hetty and ellides her, defining her sympathies yet reducing her to a passive reflector of landscape, absorbed as subjective self by the confluence of

lakeside topography, forest sounds, and wildlife activity—unlike Natty, whose identification with landscape confirms a staunch independence.

Cooper would not have agreed with this description. As he wrote in 1842: "I confess Hetty is my own favorite . . . but I find no one of my own way of thinking" (*Letters and Journals*, 4:308–9; also 345).

24. George Dekker, *Cooper*, p. 190. Apropos this comment, Gérard Genette points out that description, "because it lingers on objects and beings considered in their simultaneity, and because it considers the processes themselves as spectacles, seems to suspend the course of time and to contribute to spreading the narrative in space" ("Frontiers," p. 136).

25. Natty offers the most cogent elaboration of this pairing in response to Judith Hutter's questioning: "'A natur' is the creatur' itself; its wishes, wants, idees and feelin's, as all are born in him. This natur' never can be changed, in the main, though it may undergo some increase, or lessening. Now, gifts come of sarcumstances. Thus, if you put a man in a town, he gets town gifts; in a settlement, settlement gifts; in a forest, gifts of the woods. A soldier has soldierly gifts, and a missionary preaching gifts. All these increase and strengthen, until they get to fortify natur', as it might be, and excuse a thousand acts and idees. Still the creatur' is the same at the bottom" (2:921).

The asymmetry in this binary opposition is only compounded by the addition of racial distinctions ("each race [has] its gifts," 2:528)—especially since the distribution of qualities is clearly racist: "Revenge is an Injin gift, and forgiveness a white-man's" (2:566). Throughout the series, "color" becomes a floating signifier, identified sometimes as "gifts," at others as "natur'." And two questions left unanswered by this "philosophy" are: Why should race be deeper than culture, color more severe than gifts? and, Why is it that Natty stops at the color line, not the culture line? For discussion of the theory of racial "gifts" current in Cooper's time, see Robert E. Beider, "Anthropology and History of the American Indian," *American Quarterly* 33 (1981): 309–26.

26. Marius Bewley claims that "this episode is the key to the significance of Deerslayer's life" (*The Eccentric Design: Form in the Classic American Novel* [New York: Columbia University Press, 1963], p. 99). The power of Natty's gesture can be measured by how often it is repeated in later Westerns, including Louis L'Amour's *Hondo* (1953; New York: Bantam, 1981), where the hero refuses to help the army because he "gave my word I wouldn't" to the Apache chief, Vittoro (165). Sam Peckinpah invokes the gesture in *The Wild Bunch* (1969), only to critique it. Twice, the viewer is reminded that Deke Thornton "gave his word" to the railroad official, Harrigan. In response to Pike Bishop's rhetorical question, "What would you do in his place? He gave his word," Dutch Engstrom angrily responds "Gave his word to a railroad." Pike retorts, "It's his word!" to which Dutch rejoins, "That ain't what counts. It's who you give it to."

27. Robert Warshow anticipates this claim in his review of the formula Western, emphasizing the "style" of the Western hero as the basis of his morality: "good or bad is more a matter of personal bearing than of social consequences." He makes an even larger claim, however: "The truth is that the Westerner comes into the field of serious art only when his moral code, without ceasing to be compelling, is seen also to be imperfect" ("Movie Chronicle: The Westerner" [1954]; rptd. in *The Immediate Experience: Movies, Comics, Theatre, and Other Aspects of Popular Culture* [Garden City, NY: Doubleday, 1962], pp. 146, 142). Thomas Philbrook observes how much critics disagree about Natty's code ("Sounds of Discord," pp. 25–26). The most dismissive treatment is

Henry Nash Smith's, who views Natty's morality as "merely eccentric" in "Conscious-ness and Social Order: The Theme of Transcendence in the Leatherstocking Tales," *Western American Literature* 5 (Fall 1970): 187. The strongest defense of Natty's moral development is James Franklin Beard, "Historical Introduction," *The Deerslayer: or, The First War-Path,* ed. James Franklin Beard, The Writings of James Fenimore Cooper (Albany: State University of New York Press, 1987), pp. xxxiv–xxxvii.

28. Susan Cooper, Introduction to *The Deerslayer,* Household Edition (New York: Houghton Mifflin & Co., 1876), p. xxxiii.

29. George Dekker has noted of Cooper's hidden political agenda that "hatred of the Whigs is scattered throughout his later novels (*Cooper,* p. 159). See also James Franklin Beard, Jr., "Historical Introduction," pp. xxvi, xxix.

30. Sean Wilentz describes the disappearance of an artisan republic and develop-ment of a working class in the 1820s: the cost of the new productivity was a "collapse of the crafts and their replacement with a network of competition, underbidding, and undisguised exploitation" (*Chants Democratic: New York City and the Rise of the Ameri-can Working Class, 1788–1850* [New York: Oxford University Press, 1984], p. 128).

For opposing views of the 1820s as the "age of Egalitarianism," see Lee Benson, *The Concept of Jacksonian Democracy: New York as a Test Case* (Princeton: Princeton Uni-versity Press, 1961), p. 18; Edward Pessen, "The Egalitarian Myth and the American Social Reality: Wealth, Mobility, and Equality in the 'Era of the Common Man,'" in *The Many-Faceted Jacksonian Era: New Interpretations,* ed. Edward Pessen (Westport, CT: Greenwood Press, 1977), pp. 19, 28; also his *Jacksonian America: Society, Personality, and Politics* (Homewood, IL: Dorsey Press, 1969, esp. chap. 3, "The Less than Egalitar-ian Society," pp. 39–58; and Douglas T. Miller, *Jacksonian Aristocracy: Class and Democ-racy in New York, 1830–1860* (New York: Oxford University Press, 1967). Sean Wilentz warns against any facile political division of the period, since "both major parties were led by established and emerging elites and their professional allies, usually lawyers"; by 1829, "party service was now the measure of political virtue" (*Chants,* pp. 7, 174).

31. Sean Wilentz, *Chants,* p. 110. See also Angela Miller, *The Empire of the Eye: Landscape Representation and American Cultural Politics, 1825–1875* (Ithaca: Cornell Uni-versity Press, 1993), p. 12.

32. In *Fathers and Children: Andrew Jackson and the Subjugation of the American In-dian* (New York: Alfred A. Knopf, 1975), Rogin points out that "fear of debt was wide-spread in Jacksonian America. Tied for Jackson to loss of control over his children, this fear may also have had roots in anxieties over bodily control" (285). One of the more popular selections in the McGuffey "Readers" for the period was "An Ironical El-egy on Debt," which made its warning through a mock-ironic presentation: "There is no certainty but in instant enjoyment. Look at schoolboys sharing a plum-cake. The knowing ones eat, as for a race; but a *stupid* fellow *saves his* portion; just nibbles a bit, and 'keeps the rest for another time.' Most provident blockhead!" This 1855 selection is cited in *Ideology and Power in the Age of Jackson,* ed. Edwin C. Rozwenc (New York: New York University Press, 1964), p. 140. Fred Somkin adumbrates this theme in the period, proving that speakers were regularly concerned to show that "the problem of freedom was the problem of the internalization of order, and not simply a reliance upon documentary guarantees" (*Unquiet Eagle: Memory and Desire in the Idea of Ameri-can Freedom, 1815–1860* [Ithaca: Cornell University Press, 1967], p. 53).

33. Mrs. Margaret Bayard Smith, wife of the Maryland senator, in a March 11, 1829 letter, collected in *The Age of Jackson,* ed. Robert V. Remini (Columbia: University

of South Carolina Press, 1972), p. 16. See also, for fuller description, Remini, *The Election of Andrew Jackson* (Philadelphia: J. B. Lippincott Co., 1963), pp. 200–202; and *Andrew Jackson and the Course of American Freedom, 1822–1832* (New York: Harper & Row, 1981), pp. 177–79.

34. Cited by James Parton, *The Presidency of Andrew Jackson* (1860; New York: Harper & Row, 1967), p. 2.

35. Ibid., p. 1.

36. Senator James Hamilton, Jr., cited by Robert V. Remini, *Andrew Jackson,* p. 178.

37. *The Prose Works of Ralph Waldo Emerson* (Boston, 1870), 1:154.

38. Henry Forster Burder, *Mental Discipline; or, Hints on the Cultivation of Intellectual and Moral Habits* (Andover, MA: Flagg & Gould, 1827). An anonymous author a decade earlier illustrated the height of Christian faith as a matter of forebearance under serious illness, facing death without fear, fully silent. See *The Friendly Instructor . . . Very Suitable for Sunday Schools* (n.p.: Lincoln & Edmands, 1818).

For general backgound on conduct books, see Jacques Carre, *The Crisis of Courtesy: Studies in the Conduct-Book in Britain, 1600–1900* (New York: E. J. Brill, 1994). The most popular schoolbooks in the nineteenth century were the McGuffey Readers, which first appeared in 1836 as a response to "the excesses of Jacksonian democracy with its plea for universal suffrage." According to Dolores P. Sullivan, these books were based on the premise that "the development of a strong moral character was the only safeguard of republican institutions" (*William Holmes McGuffey: Schoolmaster to the Nation* [Rutherford, NJ: Fairleigh Dickinson University Press, 1994], p. 154). For discussion of virtues extolled in these primers similar to those in conduct books, and the differences between the 1836 and 1879 editions, see John H. Westerhoff III, *McGuffey and His Readers: Piety, Morality, and Education in Nineteenth-Century America* (Nashville, TN: Abingdon, 1978), pp. 94–95, 104–7.

39. George W. Burnap, *Lectures to Young Men on the Cultivation of the Mind, the Formation of Character, and the Conduct of Life* (Baltimore: John Murphy, 1840), pp. 27, 65, 70.

40. Francis Lieber, *The Character of the Gentleman* (1846; Philadelphia: J. B. Lippincott & Co., 1864), pp. 18, 89.

41. More than half of James Burgh's argument is devoted to the religious basis for conduct, in *The Dignity of Human Nature; or A Brief Account of the Certain and Established Means for Attaining the True End of Our Existence* (Hartford, CN: Oliver D. Cooke, 1802), esp. pp. 22, 62–63. See also Lewis Cornaro, Dr. Franklin, and Dr. Scott, *The Immortal Menton* (Philadelphia: Francis & Robert Bailey, 1796), p. 9; John Mason, *Self-Knowledge: A Treatise Showing the Nature and Benefit of That Important Science and the Way to Attain It* (Wilmington, DE: Bonsal & Niles, 1801), pp. 5–6, 97; and Laban Thurber, *Young Ladies' and Gentleman's Preceptor* (Warren, RI: n.p., 1797), pp. 50–52.

William Burkitt's *The Poor Man's Help, and Young Man's Guide* (1693) was still popular a century later, appearing in its thirtieth ed. (New York: Robert Hodge, 1788). Burkitt emphasizes Christian belief as the inspiration for proper conduct and counsels silence and self-restraint because God is watching (12). He advises "to compose the frame of your mind, and to regulate the behaviour of your body, whilst you are attending upon Almighty God in his public ordinances, often remember the several eyes that are upon you, and taking notice of you; namely, the all-seeing eye of God, the observing eye of conscience, the vigilant eye of the world, and the malignant eye of Satan" (36). Restraint exists not for its own sake but because the entire universe is watching.

42. For a still later example, Samuel Smiles claimed that "self-control is only courage under another form. It may almost be regarded as the primary essence of character. It is in virtue of this quality that Shakespeare defines man as being 'looking before and after.' It forms the chief distinction between man and the mere animal; and, indeed, there can be no true manhood without it. Self-control is at the root of all virtues." Restraint has by now become an end in itself, the "root" of virtue rather than a means to it. See *Character* (New York: Harper, c. 1880), p. 165.

Richard Butsch states, "After the 1830s, respectability was measured in terms of outward expressions of civility, which became increasingly important as a standard of middle-class deportment for both men and women. . . . The subdued qualities that ruled middle-class behavior from 1830 to 1850 insisted on a separation from coarseness, rowdiness, and other forms of emotional outlet that characterized the lower classes. Colorful male dress gave way to drab black and gray suits. Body management called for proper posture and gesture, even control of one's gaze and walk. Spitting was prohibited. Emotional control was also part of this elaborate etiquette. Anger and conflict were to be avoided; even laughter was restrained" ("Bowery B'hoys and Matinee Ladies: The Re-Gendering of Nineteenth-Century American Theater Audiences," *American Quarterly* 46 [September 1994]: 385).

43. *The Young Man's Own Book: A Manual of Politeness, Intellectual Improvement, and Moral Deportment* (Philadelphia: Key, Mielke & Biddle, 1832), pp. 30, 32.

44. See Wayne Franklin, *New World,* pp. 72, 107; and "Wilderness of Words," p. 42; also James F. Beard, "Historical Introduction" to *The Deerslayer,* p. xxvi–xxvii; Marvin Meyers, *The Jacksonian Persuasion: Politics and Belief* (1957; Stanford, CA: Stanford University Press, 1960), p. 59; and Warren Motley, *The American Abraham: James Fenimore Cooper and the Frontier Patriarch* (New York: Cambridge University Press, 1987), p. 5.

45. See Fred Somkin, *Unquiet Eagle,* p. 161.

46. Cited in *Critical Heritage,* p. 196.

47. Marvin Meyers, *Jacksonian Persuasion,* p. 12. See also Sean Wilentz, *Chants,* p. 189.

48. Michael Paul Rogin, *Fathers and Children,* p. 288.

49. Cited by George Forgie, *Patricide in the House Divided: A Psychological Interpretation of Lincoln and His Age* (New York: W. W. Norton, 1979), p. 77. Robert Remini describes the Farewell Address as an incitement of the people to constant vigilance against narrow self-interest and corrupt parties, in *Andrew Jackson and the Course of American Democracy, 1833–1845* (New York: Harper & Row, 1984), pp. 416–17.

Chapter Three

1. Cited by Clarence King, *Mountaineering in the Sierra Nevada* (1874; Harmondsworth: Penguin, 1989), pp. 179–80.

2. *The Letters of Bret Harte,* ed. Geoffrey Bret Harte (London: Hodder & Stoughton, 1930), p. 154.

3. Cited by Gordon Hendricks, *Albert Bierstadt: Painter of the American West* (New York: Harry N. Abrams, Inc, 1972), p. 140.

4. *Mark Twain in Eruption,* ed. Bernard DeVoto (New York: Grosset & Dunlap, 1940), p. 265.

5. Cited by Gary Scharnhorst, *Bret Harte* (New York: Twayne, 1992), p. ix. For evidence of the shift his career took, see the descriptive bibliography of all reviews of Harte's publications in Linda Diz Barnett, *Bret Harte: A Reference Guide* (Boston: G. K. Hall & Co., 1980). For discussion of Bierstadt's popularity, see William H. Truettner, "Ideology and Image: Justifying Westward Expansion," in *The West as America: Reinterpreting Images of the Frontier* (Washington, DC: Smithsonian Institution Press, 1991), pp. 37, 119–20.

6. Michael Brenson, "He Painted the West That America Wanted," *New York Times*, February 8, 1991, p. C22.

7. Gordon Hendricks, *Bierstadt*, p. 10. Matthew Baigall agrees: "Of the most famous painters of large canvases in the late nineteenth century . . . Bierstadt had the worst, even an angry, press" (*Albert Bierstadt* [New York: Watson-Guptill, 1981], p. 8).

8. This 1879 criticism by George W. Sheldon is cited by Patricia Trenton and Peter N. Hassrick, *The Rocky Mountains: A Vision for Artists in the Nineteenth Century* (Norman: University of Oklahoma Press, 1983), p. 126.

9. Cited by Gordon Hendricks, *Bierstadt,* p. 164. For assessments of the Düsseldorf "school," see Peter C. Marzio, *The Democratic Art: Pictures for a 19th-Century America: Chromolithography 1840–1900* (Boston: David R. Godine, 1979); and the essays collected in *The Düsseldorf Academy and the Americans,* ed. Donelson F. Hoopes (Atlanta: High Museum of Art, 1972), esp. Wend von Kalnein, "The Düsseldorf Academy," pp. 13–18, and Donelson F. Hoopes, "The Düsseldorf Academy and the Americans," pp. 19–34.

10. Wolfgang Born, *American Landscape Painting: An Interpretation* (New Haven: Yale University Press, 1948), p. 106. Criticism clearly disturbed Bierstadt, who at the height of his popularity in 1870 felt compelled to disown earlier efforts. According to Gordon Hendricks, his "action seems almost desperate, as though he had had enough of disparaging remarks from the critics and had decided to escape more" (*Bierstadt,* pp. 189–93).

11. Wallace Stegner, "Introduction" to Bret Harte, *The Outcasts of Poker Flat* (New York: New American Library, 1961), p. vii.

12. Donald E. Glover, "The Later Literary Career of Bret Harte, 1880–1902," Ph.D. dissertation (University of Virginia, 1965), p. 174.

13. These are Harte's own words, angered at the imputation (*Letters,* pp. 25–26). Twain's rumpled look allowed him more easily to fulfill Eastern expectations, as Margaret Duckett has noted in *Mark Twain and Bret Harte* (Norman: University of Oklahoma Press, 1964), p. 90.

14. See Gordon Hendricks, *Bierstadt,* p. 8; also pp. 30, 97, 179, 207, 241; and Matthew Baigell *Bierstadt,* p. 8. Linda Ferber thinks Bierstadt was unfairly punished by critics for his entrepreneurial style, in "Albert Bierstadt: The History of a Reputation," in *Albert Bierstadt: Art and Enterprise,* ed. Linda S. Ferber (New York: Brooklyn Museum, 1990), pp. 21–68.

15. Linda Ferber admits to difficulty organizing a 1991 exhibition because owners refused to part with large canvases for more than a year: "'By virtue of their scale, these works occupied important positions in their homes,' said Dr. Ferber. 'Some people were intensely reluctant to let them go.'" *New York Times,* February 6, 1991, p. C13.

16. Gordon Hendricks, *Bierstadt,* p. 233.

17. Cited in William H. and William N. Goetzmann, *The West of the Imagination* (New York: W. W. Norton, 1986), p. 166.

18. For fuller investigation of reasons for Mark Twain's success, see my "Verbally *Roughing It*: The West of Words," *Nineteenth-Century Literature* 44 (June 1989): 67–92; and "Naming the West and Making a Name: The Reputations of Bierstadt and Twain," *Prospects* 14 (1989): 93–123.

19. See Matthew Baigell, *Bierstadt*, pp. 9–10. For other historical explanations of Bierstadt's decline, see Edward Buscombe, "Inventing Monument Valley: Nineteenth-Century Landscape Photography and the Western Film," in *Fugitive Images: From Photography to Video*, ed. Patrice Petro (Bloomington: Indiana University Press, 1995), pp. 87–108; and Linda Ferber, "Reputation," pp. 31, 49, 60–61.

20. Matthew Baigell believes the painter saw Carleton E. Watkins's photos in New York City as early as 1863, before heading West for his second trip (*Bierstadt*, p. 13). Moreover, he claims that Watkins's mammoth photos, taken on plates as large as 22 × 25 inches, may have affected Bierstadt's sense of artistic scale and even determined him to go West again (28, 38). Whether true or not, Baigell offers convincing analyses of certain paintings in terms of photographic influences, including "Thunderstorm in the Rocky Mountains" (1858), pp. 36 ff.

21. James Jackson Jarves, *The Art-Idea*, ed. Benjamin Rowland, Jr. (1864; Cambridge, MA: Harvard University Press, 1960), pp. 191–92. What Jarves assumes is a liability for Bierstadt—his impulse to make "two pictures in one, from different points of view"—encapsulates the more general plight of the American artist as Barbara Novak has described it. Her definition of "luminism" fits Jarves's critique: an inability to sacrifice the clarity of realistic detail to the demands of Impressionist light, yet nonetheless a fascination with light itself as a vehicle for the transcendence of a merely local perspective. See *American Painting of the Nineteenth Century: Realism, Idealism, and the American Experience* (New York: Harper & Row, 1979), esp. chap. 5, pp. 92–109. For Novak's view of this painting as panorama, see *Nature and Culture: American Landscape and Painting, 1825–1875* (New York: Oxford University Press, 1980), pp. 24–28. Patricia Trenton and Peter N. Hassrick offer a contrasting interpretation in *Rocky Mountains*, p. 139.

22. *The Confidence-Man: His Masquerade*, CEAA Edition, ed. Harrison Hayford, Hershel Parker, G. Thomas Tanselle (1857; Evanston, IL: Northwestern University Press, 1984), pp. 182–83.

23. Howard Mumford Jones has made an assertion that corresponds to much of the following discussion: "If one tried to isolate significant components in the delineation of Western landscape in paint or words, one would find, I think, at least five leading elements: (1) astonishment; (2) plenitude; (3) vastness; (4) incongruity; and (5) melancholy." He mentions Bierstadt only in relation to the third point, but all five can be appropriately invoked to explain the painter's achievement. See *O Strange New World—American Culture: The Formative Years* (New York: Viking Press, 1964), p. 379.

24. Henry T. Tuckerman, "Albert Bierstadt," *The Galaxy* 1 (August 15, 1866): 680. Reproduced in the Archives of American Art, roll N.Y. 59-11, frames 614–17. For a useful discussion of this painting, see Nancy K. Anderson, "'Invention,'" pp. 88–89.

25. Cited by Wolfgang Born, *Landscape Painting*, p. 149. According to Matthew Baigell, "The Rocky Mountains" was "the first popular panoramic western scene" (*Bierstadt*, p. 36). For precise corrections of Bierstadt's landscape geography by an experienced mountaineer, see Patricia Trenton and Peter N. Hassrick, *Rocky Mountains*, pp. 362–63nn.58–60.

26. Nancy K. Anderson, "'Invention,'" p. 89. See also Wolfgang Born, *Landscape Painting*, p. 86.

27. Michael Rogin, "'Make My Day!': Spectacle as Amnesia in Imperial Politics," *Representations* 29 (Winter 1990): 106.

28. Ray Allen Billington, *Land of Savagery, Land of Promise: The European Image of the American Frontier in the Nineteenth Century* (New York: W. W. Norton, 1981), p. 98.

29. In some cinematic efforts, this transmogrification of the landscape can be disorienting. Henry Hathaway's "Garden of Evil" (1954) offers a plot largely based on a weirdly convoluted Mexican landscape, of palm trees, desert sand, pine forest, volcanic talus, ocean cliffs, and mesa outcroppings—all crossed over sequentially in the week-long ride that Leah Fuller (Susan Hayword) organizes to an abandoned gold mine. It is as if Bierstadt's principle of unrelated landscape elements were projected over time, unscrolled as background to the emotional conflicts aroused by that pastiche of landscape itself.

30. For Bierstadt's major influence on western photography and cinematography, see Anne Hollander, *Moving Pictures* (New York: Alfred A. Knopf, 1989), p. 357.

31. *San Francisco News Letter and California Advertiser,* September 4, 1869. Cited by Nancy K. Anderson in "'Invention,'" p. 87.

32. Bret Harte, *The Luck of Roaring Camp,* vol. 7 of the Argonaut Edition of the Works of Bret Harte (New York: P. F. Collier & Son, 1914), pp. 22–23. Subsequent references to this widely available edition appear parenthetically.

33. As an English reviewer noted of one of Bierstadt's paintings: "It strikes you at once as a work of art, not a literal reproduction of nature; indeed, the artifices used are sometimes too evident. But in an age when some hold the theory that art may be dispensed with, and that mere copyism is enough, we welcome a man like Bierstadt, who, though as devoted a lover of the grandest scenes in nature as any painter who ever lived, is at the same time given to plotting and planning for purely artistic ends. . . . The excess of his effort after these things may be repugnant to some critics, because it is so obvious, and seems incompatible with the simplicity and self-oblivion of the highest artistic natures. We believe, however, that in art of this kind, where the object is to produce a powerful impression of overwhelming natural grandeur, a painter must employ all the resources possible to him" (*Saturday Review,* London, June 15, 1867, p. 754 [cited by Nancy K. Anderson, "'Invention,'" p. 92]).

34. *Bret Harte's Stories of the Old West,* ed. Wilhelmina Harper and Aimée M. Peters (Boston: Houghton Mifflin Co., 1940), pp. 92–93. Harte's first story, "M'Liss," appeared in two versions, making it a particularly revelatory example of Harte's compositional habits (described in 1873): "In 1860, I wrote the 'Story of M'Liss,' as it appears in 'The Luck,' etc. for the 'Golden Era,' a weekly San Francisco paper, with which I was connected. Three years after (1863), . . . I attempted to create a longer story or novel out of it, but after writing nine or ten chapters I wound it up in disgust. As I always preferred my first conception, I adopted *that* when I put it in 'The Luck'" (*Letters,* p. 23). The three paragraphs quoted here are from the revised version published in 1863, following the separation of "the master" and Melissa. The original differs substantially, not only in point of view but in the brevity of description and diction, as the master accompanies Melissa to Smith's corpse: "The walls of the cavern were partly propped by decaying timbers. The child pointed to what appeared to be some ragged, cast-off clothes left in the hole by the late occupant. The master approached nearer with his flaming dip, and bent over them. It was Smith, already cold,

with a pistol in his hand and a bullet in his heart, lying beside his empty pocket" (*The Luck,* vol. 5).

35. Van Wyck Brooks was the first to overstate Harte's influence on the Western in *The Times of Melville and Whitman* (New York: E. P. Dutton & Co., 1947), p. 281. Jay Hyams more accurately notes that Prentiss Ingraham and Ned Buntline created characters in dime novels who would appear in later Westerns, in *The Life and Times of the Western Movie* (New York: W. H. Smith, 1983), pp. 12, 20.

36. "Introduction," p. ix. According to Linda Diz Barnett, Harte's use of "paradoxical natures" was frequently observed by contemporary readers (*Reference Guide,* p. viii).

37. Cited by Donald E. Glover, "Career," p. 144. Kevin Starr has documented the romanticizing effect of Harte's stories upon contemporary Californians and their historians in *Americans and the California Dream, 1850–1915* (New York: Oxford University Press, 1973), pp. 49–50, 120–21, 156, 168–69.

38. Philip French, *Westerns: Aspects of a Movie Genre* (1973; rev. ed. London: Secker & Warburg, 1977), p. 129. French goes on to add: "There is perhaps an analogy between poker and the Western movie: one could say that it forms a microcosm or more accurately a paradigm of the form. In addition to the aspects already mentioned, the game might be seen as a steady progression, in which courses of action are undisclosed, towards a final confrontation between two men, the more circumspect and fainthearted (usually identified as the married, the marginally secure and the weak) having dropped out on the way and thrown in their hand. Even when not playing poker, Westerners . . . resort to its terminology: the showdown, the four-flusher, calling someone's bluff, keeping a poker face" (130).

39. Peter Brooks, *The Melodramatic Imagination: Balzac, Henry James, Melodrama, and the Mode of Excess* (New Haven: Yale University Press, 1976), pp. 40–41.

40. Ibid., p. 53.

41. Peter Brooks refers to this as melodrama's "aesthetics of astonishment" (ibid., p. 54).

42. Matthew Baigell, *Bierstadt,* p. 9.

43. Michael Brenson, "He Painted the West," p. C22.

44. Gail Hamilton, "Bierstadt's Picture of the Rocky Mountains," *Congregationalist,* May 15, 1863, p. 1. Cited by Nancy K. Anderson, "'Invention,'" p. 94.

45. Cited by Nancy K. Anderson, "'Invention,'" p. 91.

46. Twain most pointedly parodied "The Outcasts of Poker Flat" (1869) in *Roughing It,* vol. 2 of the Works of Mark Twain, ed. Franklin R. Rogers and Paul Baender (Berkeley: University of California Press, 1972), p. 221. See also Margaret Duckett, *Mark Twain and Bret Harte,* pp. 54, 59–61.

47. Harte would continue to lament his lost public, as in this 1896 letter from England: "When Max Nordau . . . lately wrote that I was the 'Columbus of American fiction' (whatever that may mean?), and that my own countrymen did not appreciate me sufficiently, I thought it might strike some echo in America—but, alas! I have not seen even an allusion to it in my American publishers' *advertisements!*—while here it is copied largely and discussed!" (*Letters,* pp. 433–34). For a damning critique of how Harte "became the prisoner of his own success," see Richard O'Connor, *Bret Harte: A Biography* (Boston: Little, Brown, 1966), p. 104.

48. Donald E. Glover has stated: "How much Harte's sudden success was the product of conditions beyond his control can be attested by the overwhelming re-

sponse to 'Plain Language from Truthful James,' which appeared in the *Overland* in September, 1870. What in different times would have been a mediocre piece of dialect poetry became a national poetic favorite" ("Career," p. 73). See also Glover, "A Reconsideration of Bret Harte's Later Work," *Western American Literature* 8 (Fall 1973): 143–51. For Bierstadt, see Patricia Trenton and Peter N. Hassrick, *Rocky Mountains,* p. 117.

49. On the importance of *Stagecoach,* see Edward Buscombe, *Stagecoach* (London: British Film Institute, 1992); and Tag Gallagher, *John Ford: The Man and His Films* (Berkeley: University of California Press, 1986), pp. 145–62. Orson Welles claimed that in creating *Citizen Kane* "John Ford was my teacher. My own style has nothing to do with him, but *Stagecoach* was my movie text-book. I ran it over forty times." Cited by Peter Cowie, *The Cinema of Orson Welles* (New York: A. S. Barnes, 1965), p. 27.

50. The genius of the film is hardly limited to these innovations. As Tag Gallagher notes, *Stagecoach* "is a virtual anthology of gags, motifs, conventions, scenes, situations, tricks, and characters drawn from past westerns, but each one pushed toward fresh intensities of mythic extremism, thus consciously revisiting not only the old West but old westerns as well, and reinterpreting at the same time these elements for modern minds." See "Shoot-Out at the Genre Corral: Problems in the 'Evolution' of the Western," in *Film Genre Reader,* ed. Barry Keith Grant (Austin: University of Texas Press, 1986), p. 208.

Chapter Four

1. Cited in *Owen Wister Out West: His Journals and Letters,* ed. Fanny Kemble Wister (Chicago: University of Chicago Press, 1958), p. 17.

2. Vladimir Nabokov, *Lolita* (New York: Vintage, 1989), p. 170.

3. The play, coauthored with Kirk La Shelle, opened in New York City on January 1, 1904, ran for four months, and then went on the road for ten years. For a discussion of Wister's problems with "writer's block" during this period, see John L. Cobbs, *Owen Wister,* pp. 25–26; and more generally, Darwin Payne, *Owen Wister: Chronicler of the West, Gentleman of the East* (Dallas: Southern Methodist University Press, 1985), pp. 216–17, 220–26.

4. G. Edward White has described the growth of an Eastern social elite that defined itself in terms of the American West, in *The Eastern Establishment and the Western Experience: The West of Frederic Remington, Theodore Roosevelt, and Owen Wister* (New Haven: Yale University Press, 1968). As White points out, the Social Register appeared in 1887 just as the cowboy emerged as a national symbol of egalitarian masculinity (50–51). Christine Bold assesses the political consequences of this fascination with the cowboy in "The Rough Riders at Home and Abroad: Cody, Roosevelt, Remington, and the Imperialist Hero," *Canadian Review of American Studies* 18 (Fall 1987): 321–50; and Richard Slotkin offers a discussion of Roosevelt's thesis in *Gunfighter Nation: The Myth of the Frontier in Twentieth-Century America* (New York: Atheneum, 1992), pp. 39–65.

5. On the success of "Buffalo Bill's Wild West" show, see Richard Slotkin, *Gunfighter Nation,* pp. 66–87. The cowboy made his first appearance in a dime novel by Prentice Ingraham in 1887 (*Buck Taylor, King of the Cowboys*), and became instantly popular. For more on the influence of Cody's show and the "flood" of "Buffalo Bill" dime novels that inundated Europe during this period, as well as on Buck Taylor's emergence as the first popular cowboy in the 1880s, see Ray Allen Billington, *Land of Savagery, Land of Promise: The European Image of the American Frontier in the Nineteenth*

Century (New York: W. W. Norton, 1981), pp. 48–50, 170; Christine Bold, *Selling the Wild West: Popular Western Fiction, 1860 to 1960* (Bloomington: Indiana University Press, 1987), pp. 1–36; and Stephen Tatum, "Dime Novels," in *The BFI Companion to the Western,* ed. Edward Buscombe (New York: Atheneum, 1988), pp. 109–11.

For a discussion of the enthusiasm for historical romance in the 1890s, see T. J. Jackson Lears, *No Place of Grace: Antimodernism and the Transformation of American Culture, 1880–1920* (New York: Pantheon, 1981), esp. pp. 103–7. On the dime novel's decline, see Michael Denning, *Mechanic Accents: Dime Novels and Working-Class Culture in America* (London: Verso, 1987), pp. 201–2; and Russel Nye, "The Dime Novel Tradition," in *The Unembarrassed Muse: The Popular Arts in America* (New York: Dial Press, 1970), pp. 200–215.

6. See G. Edward White, *Eastern Establishment,* esp. chap. 9, "Roosevelt, Remington, Wister: Consensus and the West," pp. 184–202. According to Darwin Payne, Wister was commissioned by *Harper's Monthly* in June 1893 to write eight western stories with Remington as illustrator, to be later compiled in a book. Henry Mills Alden stipulated that "we wish in this series to portray certain features of Western life which are now rapidly disappearing with the progress of civilization" (138). In fact, Wister had already absorbed this sense of an ephemeral West, as revealed in *Owen Wister Out West,* pp. 114, 158–59. As Wister's narrator says in *Lin McLean* (1897; New York: A. L. Burt Co., 1907), p. 188: "From this point of the evening on, I think of our doings—their doings—with a sort of unchanging homesickness. Nothing like them can ever happen again, I know; for it's all gone—settled, sobered, and gone. And whatever wholesomer prose of good-fortune waits in our cup, how I thank my luck for this swallow of frontier poetry which I came in time for!" In fact, little of Wister's comprehensive knowledge of the cowboy appeared in his novels.

7. As Wister wrote to his mother in September 1893, after meeting Remington in Yellowstone Park: "he thinks as I do about the disgrace of our politics and the present asphyxiation of all real love of country. He used almost the same words that have of late been in my head, that this continent does not hold a nation any longer but is merely a strip of land on which a crowd is struggling for riches" (*Owen Wister Out West,* pp. 181–82).

8. As Ben Merchant Vorpahl notes, reviewers offended Wister by comparing his early stories to Harte's (*My Dear Wister,* p. 39).

9. Owen Wister, *The Virginian: A Horseman of the Plains* (New York: MacMillan, 1902), p. viii. Subsequent references appear parenthetically in the text.

10. Cited by Ben Merchant Vorpahl, *My Dear Wister,* p. 92.

11. G. Edward White has noted that "in virtually all of Wister's western fiction, which began after his fifth journey to Wyoming in 1891, a tenderfoot narrator serves as both a recounter of various anecdotes and an interpreter of them from a somewhat alien perspective. The use of this persona, who is as much a butt of his own jokes as a chorus to the action, gave Wister a mode of narration with which he felt comfortable, just as he took delight in his acknowledged success at being a 'brilliant listener' who could remain 'passive in the clutches' of his colorful native confidants" (*Eastern Establishment,* p. 125).

12. For a discussion of the decade-long genesis of the novel, see Darwin Payne, *Owen Wister,* pp. 131–37, 193; and Robert Murray Davis, *Playing Cowboys: Low Culture and High Art in the Western* (Norman: University of Oklahoma Press, 1992), p. 11.

13. There is some interest, then, in the fact that the novel began with the story

of Balaam's beating of his horse and the Virginian's response, based on Wister's frustration with Robert Tisdale's cruel blinding of his horse in 1891, while Wister stood helplessly by. Restraint, that is, as intentional self-control rather than simple fear, incompetence, or slow-wittedness, is central to Wister's vision. See *Out West,* pp. 107–12.

14. Words, that is, gain power only when they can be enforced, and defeating another verbally succeeds in the Western only when one has gunslinger skills. Otherwise, those with "smart mouths" are simply throttled or destroyed. This explains why violence always in the end asserts itself. A good example of this pattern is George Marshall's *Destry Rides Again* (1939), with "No Gun Destry" (James Stewart) finally forced to exhibit his sharpshooting skills before his words can achieve their effect.

15. *Owen Wister Out West,* p. 31. Notably, Yellowstone Park reminded Wister "of certain of the most beautiful passages in Wagner's trilogy—those moments when the whole orchestra seems to break into silver fragments of magic—sounds of harps and the violins all away up somewhere sustaining some theme you have heard before" (*Out West,* p. 128).

16. Cited by Ben Merchant Vorpahl, who goes on to claim that for Wister "the land had an existence of its own, apart from men or politics. Remington painted the action of its conquest—that process through which it acquired a political identification—but Wister indulged a preference for those qualities of the land that he thought of as somehow eternal" (*My Dear Wister,* p. 226). See also John L. Cobbs, *Owen Wister,* p. 65; and Christine Bold, *Selling,* pp. 64–66.

17. Christine Bold describes Remington's lack of landscape consciousness in "The Rough Riders at Home and Abroad," p. 339; and more fully in *Selling,* pp. 52–64. For Remington's preference for a "vacant land," see Ben Merchant Vorpahl, *My Dear Wister,* pp. 228, 258–59. And for a critique of Remington's realism, see Alex Nemerov, "'Doing the "Old America,"': The Image of the American West, 1880–1920," *The West as America: Reinterpreting Images of the Frontier,* ed. William H. Truettner (Washington, DC: Smithsonian Institution Press, 1991), pp. 284–343.

18. The opening of *Lin McLean,* for instance, describes how "the long range of the mountains lifted clear in the air. They slanted from the purple folds and furrows of the pines that richly cloaked them, upward into rock and grassy bareness until they broke remotely into bright peaks, and filmed into the distant lavender of the north and the south . . . " (2; see also 17). For prominent examples in *The Virginian,* see pp. 405, 407–8, 422.

19. Self-conscious about keeping his hero nameless, Wister wrote to Richard Harding Davis: "he was meant by me to be just my whole American creed in flesh and blood. . . . It was by design he continued nameless because I desired to draw a sort of heroic circle about him, almost a legendary circle and thus if possible create an illusion of remoteness" (cited by John L. Cobbs, *Owen Wister,* p. 82; also pp. 63–67).

20. This scene was always repeated in stage and cinematic versions of *The Virginian,* suggesting something about the ongoing anxiety of this particular social construction.

21. On Wister's contempt for western small towns, see *Owen Wister Out West,* p. 116. Wister's 1895 essay, "The Evolution of the Cow-Puncher," lays out the inchoate assumptions he shared with Roosevelt and Remington. As Robert Murray Davis notes, his thesis sounds like social Darwinism, "but, looked at closely, the essay in fact denies evolutionary process because 'the slumbering untamed Saxon' persists through various successive conditions. And only the Saxon is able to survive on the plains be-

cause of superior wildness. . . . The emotional confusion is even more pervasive than the intellectual confusion" (*Owen Wister's West: Selected Articles,* ed. Robert Murray Davis [Albuquerque: University of New Mexico Press, 1987], p. 33). The essay is reprinted on pp. 33–53. See also Ben Merchant Vorpahl, *My Dear Wister—the Frederick Remington–Owen Wister Letters* (Palo Alto, CA: American West Publishing Co., 1972), pp. 62, 76; and Darwin Payne, *Owen Wister,* pp. 204–5.

22. Ben Merchant Vorpahl, *My Dear Wister,* p. 278.

23. Later, the reason given for the fact that Trampas is not arrested is because "he helped elect the sheriff in that county" (447). William S. Hart, the star and director who supposedly introduced realism into the Western, had acted in the stage version of the novel in 1907–8 and complained to Wister that the novel was unrealistic: "In the first place, the foreman would have refused flat-footed to trail his friend, and the ranchers would have respected him for so refusing. In the next place, if he had led the posse he would have led them in the wrong direction and the ranchers would have expected him to do so, and again, respected him for it." Cited by Jon Tuska, *The Filming of the West* (Garden City, NY: Doubleday, 1976), p. 188.

24. Although the Virginian concedes the achievement of *The Mill on the Floss,* he is not excited by it: "A fine book. But it will keep up its talkin'. Don't let you alone" (140). When Molly corrects him about its authorship, he exclaims: "A woman did! Well, then, o' course she talks too much." As his own behavior proves, however, he resists not the amount of talk but the kind of discursive control such "talk" implies. The second novel he dislikes is identified only as a "detective story" with an unknown "murderer" (139), which might suggest Dickens's *The Mystery of Edwin Drood* (1870) or perhaps *Our Mutual Friend* (1865), Wilkie Collins's *The Woman in White* (1860) or a story by Poe. None of these possibilities are suggestive for issues raised by the novel.

25. For fuller discussion of this letter and Wister's response, see Darwin Payne, *Owen Wister,* pp. 201–2. As one anonymous reviewer stated: "Throughout the tale, Molly Wood is never quite good enough for the pains and persistence with which the Virginian woos her" (*Nation* 75, October 23, 1902, p. 331).

26. In his prefatory "To the Reader," Wister announced: "Any narrative which presents faithfully a day and a generation is of necessity historical; and this one presents Wyoming between 1874 and 1890" (viii). As other chapters show, this desire for historical authenticity is common to the formula, extending from Cooper through Peckinpah.

27. Contemporary reviews suggest that more than a few readers approved of the novel in antifeminist terms. The anonymous (presumably male) reviewer for the *Nation* made his feelings explicit: "Heroes of fiction, being scrutinized, so seldom turn out to be men, that the highest praise bestowed by authority on *Tom Jones* is, 'This is not a book, but a man.' Presumably, women novelists can not draw a real man, and men are afraid to. Owen Wister's *The Virginian* is a 'sure-enough' man, a male being, whom the most earnest female advocates of equality of the sexes could never convert into a thing like unto themselves" (331).

Other reviewers tacitly revealed a similar bias, including one who admired the plot romance and concluded that "Mr. Wister's cowboy is a fine specimen of manhood, quick-witted, audacious, and masterful" ("A Horseman of the Plains," *Outlook* 10, August 30, 1902, p. 131). Lucy Monroe likewise identified the "alert and masterful" hero as "a real man," and asserted that the novel formed "a gracious picture of a fine, chivalrous type—a type that conquers and compels" ("*The Virginian* Wins East and West," *Book Buyer* 41 [October 1902]: 358). H. W. Boynton admired the fact that "the Virginian wins his successes fairly by force of character," and allowed that Molly was "fit to be grafted upon this wild offshoot of a good Southern stock" (*Atlantic Monthly* 90 [August 1902]: 277–78.

28. Peter Gabriel Filene, *Him/Her/Self: Sex Roles in Modern America* (2d ed.; Baltimore: Johns Hopkins University Press, 1986), p. 38. For fuller discussion, see pp. 16–42; Paula Baker, "The Domestication of Politics: Women and American Political Society, 1780–1902," *American Historical Review* 89 (June 1984): 620–44; and Sandra L. Myres, "Suffering for Suffrage: Western Women and the Struggle for Political, Legal, and Economic Rights," in *Westering Women and the Frontier Experience, 1800–1915* (Albuquerque: University of New Mexico Press, 1982), pp. 213–37.

29. Gail Bederman describes the Men and Religion Forward Movement, "the only widespread religious revival in American history which explicitly excluded women," and which made a claim for the need for more men in Protestantism, given the church's "excessive feminization." Moreover, "scattered evidence suggests most women approved" of this movement. See "'The Women Have Had Charge of the Church Work Long Enough': The Men and Religion Forward Movement of 1911–1912 and the Masculinization of Middle-Class Protestantism." *American Quarterly* 41 (1989): 452.

Patricia Searles and Janet Mickish analyze stories in twelve 1905 issues of *Ladies Home Journal* and find a clear emphasis on the idea of innate differences between the sexes: "The traditional, good-hearted, self-sacrificing woman who embraces her 'natural' role as wife and mother is central to this fiction" ("'A Thoroughbred Girl': Images of Female Gender Role in Turn-of-the-Century Mass Media," *Women's Studies* 10 [1984]: 263).

30. Mark C. Carnes asserts that secret fraternal ritual dominated life in the late nineteenth century, making it the "Golden Age of Fraternity," with some 70,000 fraternal lodges. The reason for this popularity was "that fraternal ritual provided solace and psychological guidance during young men's troubled passage to manhood in Victorian America," which "entailed the acquisition of a wide range of roles and statuses." Moreover, he describes the increasing involvement of fathers in child rearing: "The emotionally detached and distant fathers of the mid-nineteenth century were separated from the nurturing family men of the early twentieth by a cultural chasm" (*Secret Ritual and Manhood in Victorian America* [New Haven: Yale University Press, 1989], pp. 14, 155). See also T. J. Jackson Lears, *No Place of Grace,* esp. pp. 98–139.

31. See Darwin Payne, *Owen Wister,* p. 171.

32. The bill did not even have this effect, in part because eastern suffragists stayed put in order to win enfranchisement in their own states. Among female residents in Wyoming during this period, a handful created a stir by serving on juries and as justices of the peace but with only a short-lived effect on public behavior, only in certain local constituencies. For a history of western suffrage, see Carl Degler, *At Odds: Women and the Family in America from the Revolution to the Present* (New York: Oxford University Press, 1980), pp. 334–49; Alan P. Grimes, *The Puritan Ethic and Woman Suffrage* (New York: Oxford University Press, 1967), pp. 47–77; and T. A. Larson, "Woman Suffrage in America," *Utah Historical Quarterly* 38 (Winter 1970): 17–19.

33. It may be no more than a nice coincidence that William H. Bright, the legislator who introduced the suffrage bill in 1869, was himself a Virginian. T. A. Larson has observed of Bright: "In later life when queried, he explained that he had intro-

duced the suffrage bill because he thought it right and just and because he thought that if Negroes had the right to vote, as they did, women 'like my wife and mother' should also have the franchise. . . . For twenty years after the event, contemporaries agreed that Bright deserved major credit for placing Wyoming at the head of the women suffrage parade, but thereafter he was almost forgotten" ("Woman Suffrage," p. 12). Wister would have heard of Bright, perhaps even have met him, during trips to Wyoming.

34. Molly Haskell points out that this is often "the highest tribute" film heroes can pay the heroine—"to tell her she has performed like a man (Bogey's 'You're good, you're awfully good')"—and then adds: "isn't that, at least partly, what the American woman has always wanted to be told? Hasn't she always wanted to join the action, to be appreciated for her achievements rather than for her sex?" (*From Reverence to Rape: The Treatment of Women in the Movies* [New York: Holt, Rinehart & Winston, 1974], p. 211).

35. On August 7, 1902, James wrote to his good friend, "My dear Owen," confessing his thoroughgoing admiration: "The point is that the argument of the thing so appealed to me, interested me, convinced me." Identifying that argument as "the exhibition, to the last intimacy, of the man's character," James then admitted that his one reservation emerged from this admiration: "I find myself desiring all sorts of poetic justice to hang about him, & I am willing to throw out, even though you don't ask me, that nothing would have induced me to unite him to the little Vermont person, or to dedicate him in fact to achieved parentage, prosperity, maturity, at all—which is mere *prosaic* justice, & rather grim at that. I thirst for his blood. I wouldn't have let him live & be happy; I should have made him perish in his flower and in some splendid and somber way." Cited by Carl Bode, "Henry James and Owen Wister," *American Literature* 26 (May 1954): 251–52. For confirmation of James's admiration of Wister, see Hamlin Garland's reminiscence, in *Henry James: Interviews and Recollections,* ed. Norman Page (New York: St. Martin's Press, 1984), p. 92.

36. This preface is reprinted in Wister, *The Virginian* (New York: New American Library, 1979), p. vii.

37. Ben Merchant Vorpahl, *My Dear Wister,* p. 300. Darwin Payne characterizes Wister's increasing conservatism as the "curmudgeon" period of his life, marked by his selection as vice-president of the Immigration Restriction League and his openly contemptuous letters to editors about labor organizers (*Owen Wister,* p. 229–31). Vorpahl claims that "riots, strikes, and Populism eroded Wister's faith in the West's transforming possibilities until little was left but sentiment" (257). For a reading of Remington's paintings in terms of political conservatism, see Alex Nemerov, "Doing the 'Old America,'" pp. 284–343.

Chapter Five

1. Robert J. Moorehead, *Fighting the Devil's Tripple Demons—the Traffic in Innocent Girls—Rum's Ruinous Ruin—the Sins of Society: Three Books in One* (Philadelphia: National Book Publishing Co., 1911), p. 49.

2. Zane Grey, *Riders of the Purple Sage* (New York: Oxford University Press, 1995), p. 109. Subsequent references appear parenthetically in the text.

3. Arthur Conan Doyle, *A Study in Scarlet,* ed. Owen Dudley Edwards (Oxford: Oxford University Press, 1993), p. 130.

4. Even Mormon readers were not immune to the novel's appeal. The Church-

owned *Deseret Evening News* announced the novel's publication but did not print a review. The other major newspaper, the *Salt Lake Tribune,* was a vehemently anti-Mormon instrument that characteristically praised the way in which "the dominance of the Mormon ecclesiastics, the cruelty of their men, the self-abnegation, hardships, and oppressions of their women, are strikingly brought out." As well, after emphasizing the conflicts between Mormons and Gentiles (which reflected contemporary disagreements), the reviewer noted: "It is a vivid, faithful, realistic picture of the types, characterized so realistically and strongly in this powerful novel" (*Salt Lake Tribune,* vol. 84, no. 113, February 4, 1912, p. 20).

5. Before Grey, other writers had tried to imitate Wister's success, without becoming best-sellers. William MacLeod Raine began in 1905 to write what would become more than a hundred novels over the next fifty years, but his books had only modest sales. Clarence E. Mulford published *Bar 20* (1907) to considerable acclaim, as did Bertha M. Bower with her *Chip of the Flying U* stories. See Frank Gruber, *Zane Grey: A Biography* (New York: World Publishing Co., 1970), p. 107.

6. Altogether, Grey wrote seventy-eight books (at an average of two per year, totaling somewhere near a million words), of which fifty-eight were about the West. Even after his death, Harper's Brothers continued to publish a new novel every year until 1963. By 1955, 27 million copies had been sold in the United States and 4 million more abroad, translated into nearly every language. The best estimate of total readers is well over a quarter-billion, with at least another quarter-billion having seen the forty-one film adaptations of his novels. See Jay Hyams, *The Life and Times of the Western Movie* (New York: W. H. Smith, 1983), p. 22; Kenneth W. Scott, *Zane Grey: Born to the West: A Reference Guide* (Boston: G. K. Hall, 1979), p. vii; and *The BFI Companion to the Western,* ed. Edward Buscombe, p. 131. For further assessments of the novel's popularity, see Carleton Jackson, *Zane Grey* (1973; rev. ed. Boston: Twayne, 1989), pp. 38, 51, 56. And for assessments of Grey's career success, see Alice Payne Hackett, *Seventy Years of Best Sellers: 1895–1965* (New York: R. R. Bowker Co., 1967), p. 7.

7. For useful introductions to the genre, see Richard VanDerBeets, *The Indian Captivity Narrative: An American Genre* (Lanham, MD.: University Press of America, 1984); Alden T. Vaughan and Edward W. Clark, "Cups of Common Calamity: Puritan Captivity Narratives as Literature and History," in *Puritans among the Indians: Accounts of Captivity and Redemption, 1676–1724* (Cambridge, MA: Harvard University Press, 1981), pp. 1–28. James Axtell's *The Invasion Within: The Contest of Cultures in Colonial North America* (New York: Oxford University Press, 1985) offers a revisionist history of actual colonial captivities in chap. 13, "The White Indians," pp. 302–27. See also Richard Drinnon, *Facing West: The Metaphysics of Indian-Hating and Empire-Building* (Minneapolis: University of Minnesota Press, 1980); and Richard Slotkin, *Regeneration through Violence: The Mythology of the American Frontier, 1600–1860* (Middletown, CT: Wesleyan University Press, 1973), esp. chaps. 4–6, pp. 94–179.

8. The choice of Mormons as villains would have been simple in a period when plural marriage was considered *the* great evil. As Thomas G. Alexander suggests, many readers were also suspicious of the Church's political influence over its members. Although polygamy was officially declared illegal in 1890, the practice persisted and intense anti-Mormon publicity erupted in 1910, when charges were made that the Church was importing young women for the purpose of polygamy. Mormons had already mounted a countercampaign in 1905 that lasted for fifteen years, supporting the publication of positive books and articles and (beginning in 1912) using the new

technology of motion pictures. See *Mormonism in Transition: A History of the Latter-Day Saints, 1890–1930* (Urbana: University of Illinois Press, 1986), pp. 67–70, 239–57; and Klaus Hansen, *Mormonism and the American Experience.* Interestingly, as Jim Hitt points out, all four film versions of the novel drop any reference to Mormonism (*The American West from Fiction [1823–1976] into Film [1909–1986]* [Jefferson, NC: McFarland & Co., 1990], p. 131).

9. Richard Hofstadter, "The Paranoid Style in American Politics," in *"The Paranoid Style in American Politics" and Other Essays* (New York: Alfred A. Knopf, 1965), p. 14.

10. Christine Bold, *Selling the Wild West: Popular Western Fiction, 1860–1960* (Bloomington: Indiana University Press, 1987), p. 87; see also pp. 213–14. A significant exception to Bold's thesis involves the conflicting revelations of Oldring's death and his uncertain status as Bess's putative father (discussed below).

11. Only one passing allusion to the major event of the 1860s occurs in the novel, when Lassiter explains: "Gun-packin' in the West since the Civil War has growed into a kind of moral law" (128).

12. As noted above, Grey's novels were frequently adapted to the screen (sometimes six and seven times per novel). *The Riders of the Purple Sage* appeared in four versions altogether, all produced by Fox: two silent (1918, 1925), and two sound (1931, 1941). See Jim Hitt, *The American West,* pp. 131–32.

13. "By the nineties the whole character of tourism in Western America, so recently established, was clearly in flux." Earl Pomeroy goes on to claim that "appreciation of the wilderness by the early years of the century was more than a mood; it was becoming a movement [and] . . . was on the way to becoming institutionalized" (*In Search of the Golden West: The Tourist in Western America* [1957; rptd. Lincoln: University of Nebraska Press, 1990], pp. 145, 152). Grey's other novels of this period offer similarly lengthy descriptions of western landscapes, elaborating flora and fauna, self-consciously educating the reader. *Desert Gold* (1913; Roslyn, NY: Walter J. Black, 1941) presents a Yaqui guide who enumerates invisible signs of the Arizona desert in leading the central party to safety; *The Lone Star Ranger* (1914) follows the wounded hero through a maze of thickets, mesquite, and quicksand along the Rio Grande; *The Light of Western Stars* (1914; New York: Grosset & Dunlap, 1942) offers extended depictions of mountain groves and New Mexican mesas.

14. In the same period as the Swiss lithographer Escher and Grey, Franz Kafka created architectural sites that, as Slavoj Zizek points out, "are characterized by the fact that what appears from the outside a modest house changes miraculously into a endless maze of staircases and halls once we enter it" (*Looking Awry: An Introduction to Jacques Lacan through Popular Culture* [Cambridge, MA: MIT Press, 1991], p. 15). Grey's mystification of space may have helped establish one strong strain in the Western, provocatively identified by Geoffrey O'Brien: "The classic Western is customarily less epic than it is a study in claustrophobia and repetition, offering not wide open spaces but dead ends, the canyons and defiles of ambush, the mesa beyond which there's nowhere else to hide, the alleys and stables where men on the run are cornered. 'They've got this whole town boxed up.' Open space being lyrical rather than dramatic, the Western's formal problem becomes one of making space ever tighter and narrower" ("Killing Time," *New York Review of Books* 39, March 5, 1992, p. 40).

15. Jean Louis Comolli, "Machines of the Visible," in *The Cinematic Apparatus,*

ed. Teresa De Lauretis and Stephen Heath (New York: St. Martin's Press, 1980), pp. 122–23.

16. For more on the frequency of this sort of passage in Grey, see William Bloodworth, "Zane Grey's Western Eroticism," *South Dakota Review* 23 (Autumn 1985): 5–14.

17. Roland Barthes, *S/Z,* trans. Richard Howard (New York: Hill & Wang, 1974), p. 19.

18. Leslie Fiedler, *The Return of the Vanishing American* (New York: Stein & Day, 1968), p. 21.

19. Cited by Werner Sollers, *Beyond Ethnicity: Consent and Descent in American Culture* (New York: Oxford University Press, 1986), p. 3.

20. Stuart Byron has observed the almost obsessional impact of John Ford's *The Searchers* (1956) on recent directors and screenwriters: Steven Spielberg, *Close Encounters of the Third Kind* (1977); George Lucas, *Star Wars* (1977); Michael Cimino, *The Deer Hunter* (1978); Martin Scorcese, *Mean Streets* (1973) and *Taxi Driver* (1976); Paul Schrader, *Hardcore* (1979); and John Milius, *Dillinger* (1973) and *The Wind and the Lion* (1975). In each, "an obsessed man searches for someone—a woman, a child, a best friend—who has fallen into the clutches of an alien people. But when found, the sought one doesn't want to be rescued" ("*The Searchers:* Cult Movie of the New Hollywood," *New York Magazine,* March 5, 1979, p. 45). See also Brian Henderson, "*The Searchers:* An American Dilemma," *Film Quarterly* 34 (Winter 1980–81): 9–23.

21. Alvar Nuñez Cabéza de Vaca, *The Journey of Alvar Nuñez Cabéza de Vaca,* trans. Fanny Bandelier (New York: Allerton Book Co.), 1922. As he notes, "So we found ourselves in the same plight as before" (46). The most useful fictional evocation of this journey's transformation of the man is still Haniel Long's *Interliner to Cabéza de Vaca,* first published in 1936 and available in many later editions.

22. *The Sovereignty and Goodness of God . . . a Narrative of the Captivity . . . of Mrs. Mary Rowlandson,* Journeys in New Worlds: Early American Women's Narratives, ed. William L. Andrews et al. (Madison: University of Wisconsin Press, 1990), p. 64.

23. Earlier, Beth is described: "the rider's costume did not contradict, as it had done at first, his feeling of her feminity. She might be the famous Masked Rider of the uplands, she might resemble a boy; but her outline, her little hands and feet, her hair, her big eyes and tremulous lips, and especially a something that Venters felt as a subtle essence rather than what he saw, proclaimed her sex" (100). For further discussion, see John D. Nesbitt, "Uncertain Sex in the Sagebrush," *South Dakota Review* 23 (Autumn 1985): 15–27; and William Bloodworth, "Western Eroticism," pp. 5–14.

24. Mark Thomas Connelly, *The Response to Prostitution in the Progressive Era* (Chapel Hill: University of North Carolina Press, 1980), p. 6. See also T. J. Jackson Lears, *No Place of Grace: Antimodernism and the Transformation of American Culture, 1880–1920* (New York: Pantheon, 1981); Alan Trachtenberg, *The Incorporation of America: Culture and Society in the Gilded Age* (New York: Hill & Wang, 1982); and Robert Wiebe, *The Search for Order, 1877–1920* (New York: Hill & Wang, 1967).

25. The best account of the transition from the model of the demure Victorian lady to the aggressive, college-educated New Woman is Peter Gabriel Filene, *Him/Her/Self: Sex Roles in Modern America* (2d ed.; Baltimore: Johns Hopkins University Press, 1986). Filene identifies a new "nervousness" at the turn of the century that "betrayed a profound, unarticulated discontent among many middle-class women" (18).

293

26. In *Cheap Amusements: Working Women and Leisure in Turn-of-the-Century New York* (Philadelphia: Temple University Press, 1986), Kathy Peiss reveals that these women dominated the work force from 1880 to 1920, and that unprecedented leisure and income led to a shift in standards of dating, marked by new expressions of female desire and permissible male pressures. Peiss's evidence for a "homosocial world of working-class amusements" includes the existence of "widespread prostitution" (11–33). Peter Filene has observed, "Between 1880 and 1900 the number of employed adult women more than doubled; between 1900 and 1910 it increased by another 50 per cent, approximately twice the male rate" (*Him/Her/Self*, p. 29).

27. Carl N. Degler, *At Odds: Women and the Family in America from the Revolution to the Present* (New York: Oxford University Press, 1980), p. 281. See also David J. Pivar, *Purity Crusade, Sexual Morality and Social Control 1868–1900* (Westport, CT: Greenwood Press, 1973).

28. "The Social Evil," *Outlook* 101 (1912): 246; and Sprague Carleton, "The Prostitute," *Hahnemannian Monthly* 43 (1908): 824. Both cited by Mark Thomas Connelly, *Response*, p. 18. According to one minister in 1913, "True marriage means love between mate and mate—nothing more and nothing else. Where love is there is marriage—where love is not, there is prostitution." Cited by Walter Benn Michaels, "The Contracted Heart," *New Literary History* 21 (Spring 1990): 506.

29. "Wages and Sin," *Literary Digest* 46 (1913): 621. In 1915, according to official reports, only 23 percent of working women could live on the wages they earned, and a theory developed linking low wages with sin. Paul Boyer points out that organized prostitution was often ironically noted as a "stabilizing and conservative urban social force" in contemporary writing, and that the reasons women gave for going into prostitution were "varied, personal, and unpredictable. . . . Time and again in these interviews one encounters real-life parallels to David Graham Phillips's Susan Lenox—spirited women who have chosen prostitution in preference to boring, demeaning, or otherwise intolerable situations." As he notes, crusaders invoked white slavery as the cause of prostitution, but prostitutes themselves saw their choice as "a liberating *escape* from bondage" (*Urban Masses*, pp. 202–4). The prostitute was deplored, as Mark Thomas Connelly states, "because her life-style, attitudes, and behavior were ominous signs of change in the feminine ideal, which would ultimately influence the behavior of all women. The problematical woman would become the new woman" (*Response*, p. 47).

30. In *Response*, Mark Thomas Connelly holds a skeptical view of the influence of any actual white slavers or of widespread physical coercion of women (see esp. pp. 129–30). Ruth Rosen is more sympathetic to the idea that white slavery existed, but her logic is unpersuasive (at one point, she asserts "the actual existence of white slavery, as opposed to merely a widespread belief in it, is supported by abundant records of criminal convictions. For example, from June 1910 to January 1915, 1,057 persons were convicted of white slavery in the United States"). Still, Rosen aptly describes the ambivalence of reformers, whose own sexual repressions contributed to their desire to "save" women from prostitution. The appeal of the white slavery explanation was that it "emphasized women's passivity. With their own class presumption of women's supposed sexual purity, many middle-class Americans could not imagine a woman voluntarily entering prostitution." See *The Lost Sisterhood: Prostitution in America, 1900–1918* (Baltimore: Johns Hopkins University Press, 1982), pp. 118, 133; also Paul Boyer, *Urban Masses and Moral Order in America, 1820–1920* (Cambridge, MA: Harvard Univer-

sity Press, 1978), esp. chaps. 13 and 14, pp. 191–220; Egal Feldman, "Prostitution, the Alien Woman and the Progressive Imagination, 1910–1915," *American Quarterly* 19 (Summer 1967): 192–206; Daniel J. Leab, "Women and the Mann Act," *Amerikastudien/American Studies* 21, no. 1 (1976): 53–65; Thomas C. Mackey, *Red Lights Out: A Legal History of Prostitution, Disorderly Houses, and Vice Districts, 1870–1917* (New York: Garland Publishing, 1987); and Judith Walkowitz, *Prostitution and Victorian Society: Women, Class and the State* (Cambridge: Cambridge University Press, 1980).

31. In fact, most prostitutes were not young immigrant women, but fears of an "excess" immigrant population were rampant in the period, evidenced in the succession of increasingly restrictive Immigration Acts (of 1903, 1907, and 1910). As Charles W. Eliot, ex-president of Harvard, stated of prostitution in 1913: "We have got to remove this evil, or this country will not be ruled by the race that is now here. The family life of the white race is at stake in its purity, in its healthfulness, and in its fertility" ("New Methods of Grappling with the Social Evil," *Current Opinion* 54 [April 1913]: 308–9). Notably, the Mann Act could be used to hound individuals politically or socially anathema, as notoriously in the cases of Jack Johnson and Frank Lloyd Wright.

32. Garth Jowett, *Film: The Democratic Art* (Boston: Little Brown, 1976), p. 63. For further examples of commission reports and tracts, see U.S. Congress, Senate, *Importing Women for Immoral Purposes,* S. Doc. 196, 61st Cong., 2d sess., 1909; rptd. in Francesco Cordasco, *The White Slave Trade and the Immigrants: A Chapter in American Social History* (Detroit: Blaine Ethridge Books, 1981), pp. 47–109; *Woman and Children First,* ed. David J. Rothman and Sheila M. Rothman, series on Social Reform Movements to Protect America's Vulnerable 1830–1940 (New York: Garland Publishing, 1987), which includes white slavery tracts. *The Prostitute and the Social Reformer: Commercial Vice in the Progressive Era,* Sex, Marriage and Society Series, ed. Charles Rosenberg and Carroll Smith-Rosenberg (New York: Arno Press, 1974), which contains two Vice Commission Reports, from Minneapolis (1911) and Philadelphia (1913). The most notorious instance of these tracts is Clifford G. Roe, *The Great War on White Slavery; or, Fighting for the Protection of Our Girls* (1911; rptd. New York: Garland, 1979). For a discussion of white slavery films, see Kay Sloan, *The Loud Silents: Origins of the Social Problem Film* (Urbana: University of Illinois Press, 1988), pp. 80–86, 94. See also Mark Thomas Connelly's excellent bibliography in *Response,* pp. 211–52.

33. Ironically, Mormons themselves were accused of forced immigration of young women, eliciting strong protests from the Church. O. A. Snow wrote a letter to the *New York Times,* printed on January 8, 1912, in which he denied that white slavery had ever been associated with Mormonism: "Every one who knows the slightest thing about 'Mormon' polygamy in the days when it was permitted knows that it was a thing not in the remotest degree connected with the question of immigration." Snow cites "an insinuation that young girls are 'imported'" by Mormons, made by *Everybody's Magazine,* and invokes immigration figures to support his own conclusion. The letter was reprinted in the *Deseret Evening News* 62, January 20, 1912, p. 4.

34. Richard Hofstadter first defined this historical strain in "The Paranoid Style in American Politics," pp. 3–40 (see n.9). Among other studies, see Richard O. Curry and Thomas M. Brown, eds., *Conspiracy—the Fear of Subversion in American History* (New York: Holt, Rinehart & Winston, 1972); David Brian Davis, ed., *The Fear of Conspiracy: Images of UnAmerican Subversion from the Revolution to the Present* (Ithaca: Cornell University Press, 1971); William W. Frehling, "Paranoia and American History,"

New York Review of Books 17, September 23, 1971, pp. 36–39; Robert Levine, *Conspiracy and Romance: Studies in Brockden Brown, Cooper, Hawthorne, and Melville* (New York: Cambridge University Press, 1989); and Michael Paul Rogin, *Ronald Reagan, the Movie: And Other Episodes in Political Demonology* (Berkeley: University of California Press, 1987), pp. 272–300.

35. Grey's other novels of the period obsessively recapitulate this structural pattern. *Desert Gold* (1913) presents the Mexican bandit Rojas, who nearly succeeds in kidnapping and raping the Mexican heiress Mercedes Castaneda. Later, she is repeatedly asked to describe her tormented feelings, giving one character "some sinister, ghastly joy. But to humor him Mercedes racked her soul with the sensations she had suffered when Rojas hounded her out on the ledge" (261). *The Light of Western Stars* (1914) depicts Gene Stewart's repeated rescue of Madeline Hammond from Don Carlos, who wants to abduct her to Mexico. Even the tall tales exchanged in the novel involve recovering women from abductors. *The Border Legion* (1916; New York: Grosset & Dunlap, 1944) involves the abduction of Joan Randle by the lascivious outlaw Jack Kells. She fends him off repeatedly, until he finally kisses her in a passage worth quoting in full to show what Grey had learned from the success of *Riders of the Purple Sage:*

> Then she let herself go. He crushed her to him. He bent her backward—tilted her face with hard and eager hand. Like a madman, with hot working lips, he kissed her. She felt blinded—scorched. But her purpose was as swift and sure and wonderful as his passion was wild. The first reach of her groping hand found his gun-belt. Swift as light her hand slipped down. Her fingers touched the cold gun—grasped with thrill on thrill—slipped farther down, strong and sure to raise the hammer. Then with a leaping, strong intensity that matched his own she drew the gun. She raised it while her eyes were shut. . . . It was a moment in which she met his primitive fury of possession with a woman's primitive fury of profanation. She pressed the gun against his side and pulled the trigger. (56)

Later, Kells's control of the outlaw Border Legion declines, although its ubiquitous power remains: "It operated all over the country at the same time, and must have been composed of numerous smaller bands, impossible to detect" (240).

Even in *The Lone Star Ranger* (1914), from which the pattern is largely absent, the novel's opening section describes the hero Buck Duane's infiltration of the Bland gang to rescue Jennie, stolen by Bland and his wife when she was only fourteen. As she exclaims, "Maybe you're the man to save me—to take me away before it's too late!" (68). Succeeding in their escape, Jennie is kidnapped by another gang and dies in captivity some years later. Only then does the plot proper begin.

36. Grey complicates this premise in later novels, further developing its ambivalent resonances. In *The Border Legion* (1916), the abductor Kells forces Joan Randle to cross-dress as a bandit, in a fancy black outfit with pearl-handled guns and a mask. "Her shame was singular, inasmuch as it consisted of a burning hateful consciousness that she had not been able to repress a thrill of delight at her appearance, and that this costume strangely magnified every curve and swell of her body, betraying her femininity as nothing had ever done" (121). With the mask, however, "she was no longer Joan Randle. Her identity had been absolutely lost." Later, she becomes upset that her "charms" have visibly impressed Jim Cleves: "Joan's agony lay not in the circumstance of his being as mistaken in her character as he had been in her identity, but that she,

of all women, had to be the one who made him answer, like Kells and Gulden and all those ruffians, to the instincts of a beast" (148). Revealing herself to Cleves, she then kisses him in a long, passionate scene.

37. While the pattern of novels Grey published in the teens remains the same, their plot semantics and thematic implications are transformed in the 1920s—playing out implications anticipated in the Venters-Beth plot of *Riders of the Purple Sage*. The structure of the captivity narrative is repeated, that is, but now the abductors are future husbands. In *Code of the West* (1923; New York: Harper & Row, 1962), the "flirt" Georgiana Stockwell is finally kidnapped by Cal Thurman, and she lives together with him in unconsummated marriage as she learns to forgo her reckless ways. Similarly, *Lost Pueblo* (New York: Harper & Brothers, 1927) presents Philip Randolph advised by Janey Endicott's father to kidnap her, which he does, taking her to his mountain hideaway: "She began to discover hidden depths in herself" (107). Having overheard the original conversation, she accedes to the plan even though it involves an occasional spanking when she has been too forward. The novel ends with a formal marriage and her ironic kidnapping of him.

38. When Venters returns after two months away, Jane is amazed at his appearance: "Wild, rugged, unshorn—yet how splendid! He had gone away a boy—he had returned a man. He appeared taller, wider of shoulder, deeper-chested, more powerfully built. . . . His eyes—were they keener, more flashing than before?—met hers with clear, frank, warm regard. . . . 'Look at me long as you like,' he said, with a laugh'" (164). This theme of the handsome man is reiterated in *The Lone Star Ranger* (New York: Harper & Brothers, 1915), p. 333; *The Vanishing American* (1922–23, in *Ladies' Home Journal*) (New York: Harper & Row, 1925), pp. 17, 277, 280); *Lost Pueblo* (New York: Harper & Brothers, 1927), p. 47; and *Stairs of Sand* (New York: P. F. Collier & Son, 1928), pp. 13, 40, 134. For fuller discussion, see Chap. 6.

39. More of this national mood is suggested in Henry F. May's appropriately titled book *The End of American Innocence: A Study of the First Years of Our Own Time, 1912–1917* (New York: Alfred A. Knopf, 1959), esp. 166–68 (for American prewar attitudes toward Europe).

Chapter Six

1. Constance Rourke, "American Art: A Possible Future," in *The Roots of American Culture and Other Essays,* ed. Van Wyck Brooks (New York: Harcourt, Brace, 1942), p. 290.

2. Cited by Georgina Howell, "Cool Clint," *Vogue* (February 1992): 222.

3. Peter Gabriel Filene, *Him/Her/Self: Sex Roles in Modern America* (2d ed.; Baltimore: Johns Hopkins University Press, 1986), pp. 77, 91, 92.

4. Cited by Joseph H. Pleck, "The Theory of Male Sex-Role Identity: Its Rise and Fall, 1936 to the Present," in *The Making of Masculinities: The New Men's Studies,* ed. Harry Brod (Boston: Allen & Unwin, 1987), p. 22. See also, in this collection, Michael S. Kimmel, "The Contemporary 'Crisis' of Masculinity in Historical Perspective," pp. 121–53; and Peter Gabriel Filene, *Him/Her/Self,* pp. 198, 200–201.

In his cross-cultural study of *machismo,* David D. Gilmore claims that "there is a constantly recurring notion that real manhood is different from simple anatomical maleness, that it is not a natural condition that comes about spontaneously through biological maturation but rather is a precarious or artificial state that boys must win against powerful odds. This recurrent notion that manhood is problematic, a critical threshold that boys must pass through testing, is found at all levels of sociocultural development regardless of what other alternative roles are recognized. It is found among the simplest hunters and fishermen, among peasants and sophisticated urbanized peoples; it is found in all continents and environments." By contrast, femininity "rarely involves tests or proofs of action, or confrontations with dangerous foes. . . . Rather than a critical threshold passed by traumatic testing, an either/or condition, femininity is more often construed as a biological given that is culturally refined or augmented" (*Manhood in the Making: Cultural Concepts of Masculinity* [New Haven: Yale University Press, 1989], pp. 11–12).

5. One sign of this obsession lies simply in the characteristic invocation of "man" in Western film titles, unlike any other genre. A few examples: *Man in the Saddle* (1951), *The Man from the Alamo* (1953), *A Man Alone* (1955), *The Man from Laramie* (1955), *Man without a Star* (1955), *Man of the West* (1958), *The Man Who Shot Liberty Valance* (1962), and *A Man Called Horse* (1970).

6. Carol J. Clover, *Men, Women, and Chain Saws: Gender in the Modern Horror Film* (Princeton: Princeton University Press, 1992), p. 13; also p. 160.

7. Owen Wister, *The Virginian: A Horseman of the Plains* (New York: Macmillan, 1902), p. 4. Future references appear parenthetically in the text.

8. As the director, Anthony Mann, said more directly: "Something in those eyes tells you fantastic things. . . . They are at once electric, honest, devastating. And he knows how to look through them. . . . No one can so graphically reveal his thoughts by the look on his face." Cited by Richard Schickel, "Introduction," *Gary Cooper* (Boston: Little, Brown, 1985), xvii.

9. Cited by Tom Ryall, *The BFI Companion to the Western,* ed. Edward Buscombe, p. 288.

10. So extraordinary was Wayne's appeal that he alone escaped from class "B" Westerns to feature films, as Phil Hardy has noted: "The gap between the series Western and the A Western seemed unbridgeable; John Wayne was the only exception" (*The Western* [London: Aurum Press, 1983], p. xv).

Part of the explanation for Wayne's unusual stature as Western hero is that his career took so long to get going. His performance in Raoul Walsh's *The Big Trail* (1930) failed to save the picture, and most of his 1930s movies were "B" Westerns. His major second chance, as the Ringo Kid in *Stagecoach,* turned out successfully, but he still did not receive top billing in films through the 1940s until Hawks's *Red River* (1948), when he played an older Tom Dunson (and was already himself in his forties). By 1949, when he first appeared on the Top Ten list of Hollywood stars, he was being cast as an aging patriarch. Emanuel Levy discusses this career pattern in *John Wayne: Prophet of the American Way of Life* (Metuchen, NJ: Scarecrow Press, 1988), pp. 61–73 (see also chap. 6, "Wayne's Sex Image: A Tough Gentleman," pp. 131–61). For other attempts to account for Wayne's appeal, see Richard D. McGhee, *John Wayne: Actor, Artist, Hero* (Jefferson, NC: McFarland & Co., 1990), p. 40; and Joan Didion, "John Wayne: A Love Song," in *Slouching Towards Bethlehem* (New York: Farrar, Straus & Giroux), pp. 29–41.

11. See Steve Neale, *Genre* (London: British Film Institute, 1980), p. 57; and his further argument in "Masculinity as Spectacle: Reflections on Men and Mainstream Cinema," *Screen* 24, no. 6 (1983): 2–16.

12. Laura Mulvey, "Visual Pleasure and Narrative Cinema," in *Visual and Other Pleasures* (Bloomington: Indiana University Press, 1989), p. 19. See as well, "After-

thoughts on 'Visual Pleasure and Narrative Cinema' inspired by *Duel in the Sun*," pp. 29–38.

13. Ibid., p. 20.

14. Christine Gledhill, "Recent Developments in Feminist Criticism," *Film Theory and Criticism: Introductory Readings,* ed. Gerald Mast and Marshall Cohen (3d ed.; New York: Oxford University Press, 1985), p. 839. Pam Cook and Claire Johnson claim that "woman is not only a sign in a system of exchange, but an empty sign," in *Feminism and Film Theory,* ed. Constance Penley (New York: Routledge, 1988), p. 27.

15. See Janet Bergstrom, "Alternation, Segmentation, Hypnosis: Interview with Raymond Bellour—an Excerpt," in *Feminism,* ed. Constance Penley, p. 192; also Raymond Bellour, "Femme (théogonie)" in *Le Western: Approches, Mythologies, Auteurs-Acteurs, Filmographies* (2d ed.; Paris, Union Générale d'Éditions, 1966), pp. 146–59.

16. Mary Ann Doane, *The Desire to Desire: The Woman's Film of the 1940s* (Bloomington: Indiana University Press, 1987); E. Ann Kaplan, *Women and Film: Both Sides of the Camera* (London: Methuen, 1983); Teresa de Lauretis, *Alice Doesn't: Feminism, Semiotics, Cinema* (Bloomington: Indiana University Press, 1984); and Tania Modleski, *The Women Who Knew Too Much: Hitchcock and Feminist Theory* (New York: Methuen, 1988); and *Feminism without Women: Culture and Criticism in a "Postfeminist" Age* (New York: Routledge, 1991); and D. N. Rodowick, *The Difficulty of Difference: Psychoanalysis, Sexual Difference, and Film Theory* (New York: Routledge, 1991). See also Lucy Fischer, *Shot/Countershot: Film Tradition and Women's Cinema* (Princeton: Princeton University Press, 1989); Janet Walker, "Psychoanalysis and Feminist Film Theory: The Problem of Sexual Difference and Identity," *Wide Angle* 6, no. 3 (1984): 16–23; and Marcia Pointon, *Naked Authority: The Body in Western Painting, 1930–1980* (New York: Cambridge University Press, 1990).

17. Carol J. Clover, *Chain Saws,* p. 46; see also chap. 4, "The Eye of Horror" (166–230), in which Clover stresses her thesis that "each of the horror genres in its own way collapses male and female to the point of inextricability," making it impossible to ask "really" a male or "really" a female (217). Linda Williams, *Hard Core: Power, Pleasure, and the "Frenzy of the Visible"* (Berkeley: University of California Press, 1989), p. 205. Williams offers a good review of recent film theorists in terms of their ability to distance themselves from Mulvey (pp. 204–15). For similar discussions, see Tony Bennett and Janet Woolacott, *Bond and Beyond* (New York: Methuen, 1987), esp. chap. 7, "Pleasure and the Bond Films," pp. 204–30; John Ellis, *Visible Fictions—Cinema, Television, Video* (London: Routledge & Kegan Paul, 1982), pp. 43–44; and Gaylyn Studlar, *In the Realm of Pleasure: Von Sternberg, Dietrich, and the Masochistic Aesthetic* (Urbana: University of Illinois Press, 1988), esp. pp. 32, 192.

18. Williams, *Hard Core,* p. 114. For a particularly prominent example of this binary logic applied to gender in films, see Teresa de Lauretis, "The Violence of Rhetoric: Considerations on Representation and Gender," in *Technologies of Gender: Essays on Theory, Film, and Fiction* (Bloomington: Indiana University Press, 1987), pp. 31–50.

19. Only recently, E. Ann Kaplan argues, have male stars like John Travolta and Robert Redford been made objects of woman's gaze (*Women and Film,* p. 29). Miriam Hansen, however, powerfully counters this assertion in her discussion of Valentino's appeal in the 1920s, arguing for "the ambivalent constitution of scopic pleasure, the potential reversibility and reciprocity of roles." Indeed, it was Valentino's inability to break out of what Hansen terms a male double bind, of not being considered manly because of his physical attractiveness, that "called into question the very idea of a

stable sexual identity" (*Babel and Babylon: Spectatorship in American Silent Film* [Cambridge, MA: Harvard University Press, 1991], pp. 277, 268). For another strong counterexample, see Steven Cohan, "Masquerading as the American Male in the Fifties: *Picnic,* William Holden and the Spectacle of Masculinity in Hollywood Film," *Camera Obscura* 25–26 (January/May 1991): 43–74.

20. This is Grey's early description of the Indian hero, Nophaie, in *The Vanishing American* (1922–23, in *Ladies' Home Journal;* New York: Harper & Row, 1925), p. 17. See chap 5n.38 for further examples from Grey's novels. Andy Warhol spoofs this aestheticizing impulse in *Lonesome Cowboys* (1968), when Ramona Alvarez (Viva) remarks about cowboys entering town, "They're not bad looking," to which a man responds, "They sure ride tall in the saddle. Oh, Ramona, that one. I think he's got mascara on." She responds: "I think he's got false eyelashes. I wonder where he got them around here." Much of the rest of the film is concerned with charges about mutual staring, wondering where one should get one's hair cut, what styles are best suited, how to shrink jeans for the best tight look, doing exercises to build up thighs, the need for squatting exercises: "It puts meat on the buns, all that bending and everything. You can do knee bends tonight."

21. John Ellis, *Visible Fictions,* pp. 47–48. Linda Williams offers an effective counterexample to this reading of the fetishizing gaze, using Eadward Muybridge's photographs: "Men's naked bodies appear natural in action: they act and do; women's must be explained and situated: they act and appear in minidramas that perpetually circle about the question of their femininity. In other words, in Muybridge's case fetishization seems to *call* for narrative, not to retard it" (*Hard Core,* p. 43).

22. Richard Harding Davis, *The West from a Car-Window* (1892; rptd. New York: Harper & Brothers, 1903), p. 140.

23. Charles M. Russell, *Trails Plowed Under* (1927; rptd. New York: Garden City Publishing Co., 1941), p. 3. Douglas Kent Hall agrees that the cowboy's "visual image" is still "a fiercely guarded commodity," in *Working Cowboys* (New York: Holt, Rinehart & Winston, 1984), pp. 11–12. Leslie Fiedler discusses how "the real cowpuncher begins to emulate his Hollywood version," watching his screen idol in an effort to find out how to behave, in "Montana; or the End of Jean-Jacques Rousseau," in *An End to Innocence: Essays on Culture and Politics* (Boston: Beacon Press, 1955), p. 136.

24. Owen Wister, *The Virginian,* p. 114. In *Lin McLean* (1897; rev. ed. New York: A. L. Burt Co., 1907), Wister had described the effect of his handsome hero's careful morning toilet: "'Bugged up to kill!' exclaimed one, perceiving Lin's careful dress" (3). That effect is further detailed on his railroad trip east: "There were ladies in that blue plush car for Boston who looked at Lin for thirty miles at a stretch; and by the time Albany was reached the next day one or two of them commented that he was the most attractive-looking man they had ever seen! Whereas, beyond his tallness, and wide-open, jocular eyes, eyes that seemed those of a not highly conscientious wild animal, there was nothing remarkable about young Lin except stage effect" (32). For an even more prominent instance, see pp. 53–54.

Darwin Payne points out that this obsession may have begun with Wister's own experience in the mid–1880s, when he hired the proficient guide and cook George West: "Wister was attracted especially to the confident and proficient West, whom he described as 'much better looking than any of us'" (*Owen Wister: Chronicler of the West, Gentleman of the East* [Dallas, TX: Southern Methodist University Press, 1985], p.

101).

25. Since the cowboy is so distinctly a fetishized figure, it is worth recalling Freud's claim that "the fetish is a substitute for the woman's (the mother's) penis that the little boy once believed in and—for reasons familiar to us—does not want to give up." He adds, "an aversion, which is never absent in any fetishist, to the real female genitals remains a *stigma indelebile* of the repression that has taken place" and all fetish items are therefore "substitutes for the absent female phallus." See "Fetishism," 1927; *Standard Edition* 21, pp. 152, 154–55. As Kaja Silverman points out, "However, Lacan throws a wrench into both of these arguments by insisting that the penis itself can assume the status of a fetish—by maintaining, that is, that the ostensible referent or base-term within the fetishistic scenario may be no more than a supplement or prop disguising a lack which is no longer conceived in strictly anatomical terms." Female fetishism, in other words, is equally possible. See *Male Subjectivity at the Margins* (New York: Routledge, 1992), p. 118.

26. Richard Schickel notes that Gary Cooper was "famous for freezing on camera—especially in the early stages of his career. These moments, people noticed, always occurred when he was required to speak of high emotions, lofty sentiments. His whole system simply balked at directly expressing them" ("Introduction" to *The Virginian*, p. xvii).

27. According to Linda Williams, the introduction of sound into film in the 1920s had the effect not only of placing more cinematic emphasis on people talking but of altering the construction of character itself; theorists "have emphasized the way these uses of sound create the illusion of the viewing subject's unity" (*Hard Core*, p. 122). By contrast, the cowboy hero's silence registers a potential lack of unity, always needing to be constructed in the process of exerting self-restraint.

28. Jane Gaines, "Costume," in *BFI*, p. 99.

29. Parker Tyler, "The Horse: Totem Animal of Male Power," in *Sex Psyche Etcetera in the Film* (1969; Harmondsworth: Penguin, 1971), p. 31. For the implications of a mounted man outlined against an empty horizon, see Tyler's entire essay (pp. 29–38).

30. Robert Warshow, "Movie Chronicle: The Westerner" (1954); rptd. in *The Immediate Experience: Movies, Comics, Theatre, and Other Aspects of Popular Culture* (Garden City, NY: Doubleday, 1962), pp. 151–52.

31. Tony Tanner's description of "the devices of Puritan punishment" notes how bodies are "deformed to register their inner faults or contraventions of Puritan law. . . . [I]n various ways the body has been mutilated to carry the sign of the victim's deviance or transgression; the body is treated as a script on which can be inscribed or imprinted the 'letter' of the law. . . . Thus the whole community lived in an atmosphere of sadistic semiology, everybody looking for the bad signs in everybody else. Once discerned, these could be translated into more enduring, more visible, signs, tokens, badges: as it were, extracting the sin *out* of the body and making it into a concrete sign which could be imposed *on* the body." See the title essay of *Scenes of Nature, Signs of Men* (Cambridge: Cambridge University Press, 1987), p. 11.

32. Zane Grey, *Code of the West* (1923; New York: Grosset & Dunlap, 1962), pp. 283–90.

33. Deleuze specifically remarks, "The close-up does not divide one individual, any more than it reunites two: it suspends individuation. . . . The facial close-up is both the face and its effacement. Bergman has pushed the nihilism of the face the furthest, that is, its relationship in fear to the void or the absence, the fear of the face con-

fronted with its nothingness" (*Cinema 1: The Movement-Image,* trans. Hugh Tomlinson and Barbara Habberjam [Minneapolis: University of Minnesota Press, 1986], p. 100).

34. Ted Post's *Hang 'Em High* (1968) opens with a perfect instance of this logic: Jedidiah Cooper (Clint Eastwood) is mistakenly condemned by vigilantes, who drag him behind a horse to a hanging tree, then punch him repeatedly, cutting up his face. At the question, "Are we gonna hang him, or beat him to death?" they put a noose around his neck, leaving his body to swing under the limb as the film's title and credits go by. The plot then depicts his revivification and revenge—as he repeatedly shows others his scarred neck, with closeups of his slowly healing face—before he is again shot from behind and recovers with the help of Rachel Warren (Inger Stevens).

35. Slavoj Zizek, *Looking Awry: An Introduction to Jacques Lacan through Popular Culture* (Cambridge, MA: MIT Press, 1991), pp. 22–23. Another notable instance of this self-conscious impulse occurs in George Marshall's *Destry Rides Again,* when Frenchy responds to praise of the original hero by claiming "But Destry is dead!" eliciting the retorts "That makes him the right man for the job!" and "Saves us a lotta trouble."

36. While the funeral sequence from Cooper's *The Last of the Mohicans* stands at the head of this tradition, Bret Harte confirmed the centrality of the theme to the genre in, among other stories, "Tennessee's Partner," "The Luck of Roaring Camp," "The Outcasts of Poker Flat," and "M'liss: An Idyll of Red Mountain." One of the strangest burials occurs in Wister's *Lin McLean,* when the hero must bury his ex-wife in the cemetery at the evil town of Drybone, in a coffin once used by another corpse, in a grave that now holds another body.

Some representative cinematic examples are Charles Swickard's *Hell's Hinges* (1916), which ends with a long scene of Blaze Tracey (William S. Hart) and his new fiancée standing over the grave of her brother; Hawks's *Red River* (1947) and the funeral for Dan Lattimere, the cowboy victim of the cattle stampede; Stevens's *Shane* (1953) and the burying of "Stonewall" Torrey; Ford's *She Wore a Yellow Ribbon* (1949), as John Wayne communes with his dead wife; Ford's *The Searchers* (1956), with Ethan Edward's (John Wayne) impatience at the funeral—"Put an Amen to it, there's no more time"; the opening of John Sturges's *The Magnificent Seven* (1960), with Yul Brynner and Steve McQueen battling a town to drive an Indian corpse to the cemetery; Leone's spaghetti Westerns, where gold is buried in coffins and corpses are costumed; Peckinpah's *Ride the High Country* (1962), in which a corpse is posed as if in prayer; Ford's *The Man Who Shot Liberty Valance* (1960), in which John Wayne's coffin centers the entire movie. By the time of Peckinpah's *The Wild Bunch* (1969), the motif can only be dealt with contemptuously. Pike Bishop asks sarcastically, after shooting the fatally wounded Butch in order to facilitate their escape, "You boys want to move on, or give him a decent burial?" And when the Gorch brothers persist in asking to remain, Dutch Engstrom mockingly remarks: "I think the boys are right. Say a few words, and perhaps a few hymns are in order, followed by a church supper, with a choir." For further discussion, see Philip French, *Westerns: Aspects of a Movie Genre* (1973; rev. ed. New York: Oxford University Press, 1977), pp. 123–26; and *BFI,* pp. 84–85, 231.

37. This stark version of the process has a long pedigree in cultural discourse, with Jesus Christ filling the bill as the first Western hero (as Dean May observed to me in discussion): beaten, tortured, and crucified, then having his body ministered to by Mary Magdelene and the Virgin Mary; rising erect to Heaven after three days to be-

come what he has always been; later reappearing in the flesh to others as he physically once was.

38. Recent gender studies in America suggest that this is also true of the general population's belief. See Michael and Diane Ruble, "Beliefs about Males," *Journal of Social Issues* 34 (1978): 6–7, 11; and David D. Gilmore, *Manhood in the Making*, p. 224. The strongest period of bipolar sex-role identification coincides with the Western's "classic" era, the 1950s. Talcott Parsons first lent authority to the idea of "roles" in gender construction, which had declined by the 1970s as research failed to support the notion that absent fathers influenced boys' sex typing, school performance, or delinquency. See Joseph H. Pleck, "The Theory of Male Sex-Role Identity: Its Rise and Fall, 1936 to the Present," in *The Making of Masculinities: The New Men's Studies*, ed. Harry Brod, pp. 21–38.

39. Steve Neale, "Masculinity as Spectacle," p. 8. See also Paul Willemen, "Anthony Mann: Looking at the Male," *Framework* 15/16/17 (Summer 1981): 16; and "Voyeurism, the Look, and Dwoskin," in *After Theory Reader*, ed. Philip Rosen (New York: Columbia University Press, 1986), pp. 212–13.

40. Sigmund Freud's 1919 essay, "A Child Is Being Beaten: A Contribution to the Study of the Origin of Sexual Perversions," suggests that the process of identification (especially with images of torture and beating) are both complex and flexible, and that male and female roles, passive and active drives, are not disposed of in predictable ways. See *The Standard Edition of the Complete Psychological Works of Sigmund Freud*, vol. 17, ed. and trans. James Strachey (London: Hogarth Press, 1958), pp. 179–204. For discussions of this essay, see D. N. Rodowick, "The Difficulty of Difference," *Wide Angle* 5, no. 1 (1982): 4–15; and Constance Penley, "Introduction: The Lady Doesn't Vanish," *Feminism and Film Theory* (New York: Routledge, 1988), p. 22. Carol J. Clover powerfully counters Laura Mulvey (as well as Christian Metz) on the scopophilic power of the gaze in her claim that gazing always contributes to powerlessness in the horror film. As she points out, Freud "makes the argument in 'A Child is Being Beaten' to the effect that all children, male and female, are subject to the unconscious fantasy that they are being beaten—that is, 'loved'—by the *father*. Whereas the girl's fantasy is 'straight' (at least in Freud's reading), the boy's involves a gender complication: to be beaten/loved by his father requires the adoption of a position coded as 'feminine' or receptively homosexual. Thus 'feminine masochism' refers not to masochism in women, but to the essence of masochistic perversion in *men*" (*Chainsaws*, p. 215).

Miriam Hansen adds to this: "Freud's analysis of the sadomasochistic fantasy suggests that we distinguish between the sadistic appeal articulated in point-of-view structure, on the one hand, and the masochistic pleasure in the identification with the object, on the other. Transexual identification, instead of being confined to simple cross-dressing, relies as much on the feminine qualities of the male protagonist as on residual ambiguity in the female spectator" (*Babel and Babylon*, p. 287). For further discussion, see Parveen Adams, "Of Female Bondage," in *Between Feminism and Psychoanalysis*, ed. Teresa Brennan (New York: Routledge, 1990), pp. 247–65; and Kaja Silverman, *Male Subjectivity at the Margins* (New York: Routledge, 1992), esp. chap. 5, "Masochism and Male Subjectivity," pp. 185–213.

41. For an account of the painting and the context within which it was received, see Samuel Y. Edgerton, Jr., "The Murder of Jane McCrea: The Tragedy of an American *Tableau d'Histoire*," *Art Bulletin* 47 (1965): 481–92.

42. Ray Allen Billington, *Land of Savagery, Land of Promise: The European Image of the American Frontier in the Nineteenth Century* (New York: W. W. Norton, 1981), p. 122. From one perspective, it is supremely important that fictional Indians were often the sources of torture. But for our purposes, this litany has less to do with torturer than victim, and with the ways in which the exposed body becomes a source of self-betrayal and self-transformation.

43. Zane Grey, *The Heritage of the Desert* (New York: Grosset & Dunlap, 1910), p. 60.

44. Zane Grey, *The Lone Star Ranger* (New York: Harper & Brothers, 1915), p. 366. See also, for prior quotations, pp. 114, 130, 180.

45. See, for example, Arnold M. Cooper, "What Men Fear: The Facade of Castration Anxiety," in *The Psychology of Men: New Psychoanalytic Perspectives*, ed. Gerald I. Fogel, Frederick M. Lane, and Robert S. Liebert (New York: Basic Books, 1986), p. 113.

46. The quoted phrase is part of Martin Pumphrey's argument in "Masculinity," in *BFI*, p. 181. Tony Bennett and Janet Woolacott take a different tack, in claiming that "romances play with a phallic castration of the hero which can take a number of forms. The wounding, mutilation or blinding of the hero, tends to be a signal for the heroine to fall in love and take over the active male role" (*Bond and Beyond*, p. 225). One might indeed conceive the beating scenario in Oedipal and Lacanian terms: that the hero's wounds serve as a metonymy for the feared wound of castration; that we watch the assault upon him so as to assuage fears of assault on the phallus; that the female figure who nurses him back to health serves as a mother-figure offering a second birth again into wholeness. The erect hero, in other words, images the uncastrated figure whom we all fantasize. Since neither male nor female *is* the phallus, both men and women can look at it desiringly—that is, at that impossible body which ever figures for us our desire. In this context, Lacan's reading of Sade is instructive: that the victim needs to be beaten to death but cannot die (see "Kant avec Sade," in *Écrits 2* [Paris: Éditions du Sevil, 1971], pp. 119–48).

47. Cited by Raymond Bellour in interview with Janet Bergstrom, *Camera Obscura* 3/4 (Summer 1979): 87.

48. Louis L'Amour, *Hondo* (New York: Bantam, 1983), p. 124. Subsequent references appear parenthetically.

49. As J. A. Place remarks of Ford's contrasts of verticals and horizontals, Stewart maintains a consistently horizontal posture through the film, seeming "to possess a collapsible body," walking in crouched position, almost falling over, looked down upon even by Hallie: "He towers over Tom's coffin only in the first scene, and even then his upright position represents not a real strength, but an assumed one" (*The Western Films of John Ford* [Secaucus, NJ: Citadel Press, 1974], p. 218).

50. Elaine Scarry, *The Body in Pain: The Making and Unmaking of the World* (New York: Oxford University Press, 1985), p. 4. Subsequent references appear parenthetically.

Chapter Seven

1. Philip French, *Westerns: Aspects of a Movie Genre* (1973; rev. ed. New York: Oxford University Press, 1977), pp. 69–70.

2. Benjamin Spock, *The Common Sense Book of Baby and Child Care* (New York: Duell, Sloan & Pearce, 1946), p. 3. The paperback edition (originally priced at twenty-five cents) appeared under the title of *The Pocket Book of Baby and Child Care*

(New York: Pocket Books, 1946). Subsequent references to the original hardcover edition appear parenthetically in the text.

3. Cited from the television series "Happy Days" by Jay Hyams, *The Life and Times of the Western Movie* (New York: W. H. Smith, 1983), p. 115.

4. *The Deerslayer,* in *The Leatherstocking Tales* (New York: Library of America, 1985), 2:500.

5. Alice Payne Hackett claimed that Spock had sold 19 million copies of his book by 1967, placing him finally at the top of the all-time best-seller list. See *Seventy Years of Best Sellers: 1895–1965* (New York: R. R. Bowker Co., 1967), p. 12. Since that time, sales have risen to an excess of 40 million copies.

6. Mark Twain, "Fenimore Cooper's Literary Offenses," in *The Portable Mark Twain,* ed. Bernard DeVoto (New York: Viking, 1968), pp. 541–56.

7. "I fear I cannot claim," Bret Harte announced in the preface to *The Luck of Roaring Camp,* "any higher motive than to illustrate an era of which Californian history has preserved the incidents more often than the character of the actors." See vol. 7 of the "Argonaut Edition" of the Works of Bret Harte (New York: P. F. Collier & Son, 1914), p. vi. That motive was incorporated even more earnestly in *The Virginian,* where Owen Wister adopts the footnotes and prefatory testimonials that Cooper and Twain had invoked to justify his own text's authenticity. Film directors as well frequently followed this formulaic imperative, beginning with William S. Hart's silent ventures in the late teens and twenties as testament to his firm belief in authenticity (see Jay Hyams, *Life and Times,* pp. 25–30). For discussion of Louis L'Amour's exaggeration of this formulaic strain, see Christine Bold, *Selling the Wild West: Popular Western Fiction, 1860–1960* (Bloomington: Indiana University Press, 1987), pp. 146–47; also pp. 131–33. By contrast, Franco Moretti has claimed of the detective story that "one reads only with the purpose of remaining as one already is: innocent. Detective fiction owes its success to the fact that it teaches nothing" (*Signs Taken for Wonders: Essays in the Sociology of Literary Forms,* trans. Susan Fischer et al. [rev. ed.; London: Verso, 1988], p. 138).

8. Foreman, among American cinema's leading New Wave writers, had a subpoena awaiting him while writing *High Noon* and was blacklisted immediately after shooting ended. For an account of HUAC and its effect on Hollywood, see Robert Sklar, *Movie-Made America: A Social History of American Movies* (New York: Random House, 1975), pp. 256 ff. For Foreman's parodic spoof of political correctness (as well as of Leone and Peckinpah) in the gesture of a remake "twenty years after," see "*High Noon* Revisited," *Punch,* April 5, 1972, pp. 448–50.

9. See John H. Lenihan, *Showdown: Confronting Modern America in the Western Film* (Urbana: University of Illinois Press, 1980), p. 120; and Stephen Tatum, "The Classic Westerner: Gary Cooper," in *Shooting Stars,* ed. Archie P. McDonald (Bloomington: Indiana University Press, 1987), p. 79.

10. Pauline Kael's phrase for *Shane,* in *Kiss Kiss Bang Bang* (London: Calder & Boyars, 1970), p. 347.

11. Robert Warshow, "Movie Chronicle: The Westerner" (1954); rptd. in *The Immediate Experience: Movies, Comics, Theatre, and Other Aspects of Popular Culture* (Garden City, NY: Doubleday, 1962), p. 149; and Slavoj Zizek, *Looking Awry: An Introduction to Jacques Lacan through Popular Culture* (Cambridge, MA: MIT Press, 1991), p. 113.

12. For further discussion of this cinematic conceit, see Will Wright, *Sixguns and*

Society: A Structural Study of the Western (Berkeley: University of California Press, 1975), p. 58.

13. "To emphasize the terrible power of gunshots," Jay Hyams claims, "Stevens had the two main victims—Elisha Cook, Jr., and Jack Palance—rigged so that they could be jerked backward when shot. Stevens achieved the effect of violence—so much that it thrilled and delighted both audiences and filmmakers. Gentle, poetic *Shane* marks the beginning of graphic violence in westerns. As Sam Peckinpah has been quoted as saying, 'When Jack Palance shot Elisha Cook, Jr., in *Shane,* things started to change'" (*Life and Times,* p. 115).

14. If that perspective contributed to the film's popular success, it also led to a mixed reception among Western fans, who missed the stylized action characteristic of the genre. As an anonymous writer for *Variety Film Reviews,* April 15, 1953, wrote: "This measured, deliberate handling in many of the sequences may seem too slow for the tastes of the more regular run of audiences, and does account for the picture taking up nearly two hours of footage, but when the plot demands action [Stevens] deals it out in such rugged doses that even the most avid fan of violence will be satisfied." Penelope Houston similarly noted that "the build-up to a climax of action seems a little drawn out," in "*Shane* and George Stevens," *Sight and Sound* 23 (October–December 1953): 72.

15. Louis L'Amour, *Hondo* (New York: Bantam, 1983), p. 67. Subsequent references appear parenthetically.

16. Steven Mintz and Susan Kellogg have noted how pervasive the problem of proper sex-role identification was perceived to be in the 1950s, especially for boys: "the underlying source of the anxiety pervading child-rearing manuals during the postwar era lay in the fact that mothers were raising their children with an exclusivity and in an isolation without parallel in American history" (*Domestic Revolutions: A Social History of American Family Life* [New York: Free Press, 1988], p. 190). In 1957, the psychologist Helen Mayer Hacker addressed this issue directly, focusing instead on the conflicting demands placed upon men. As she claimed of the problems of learning gendered behavior, "masculinity is more important to men than femininity is to women," since "If a man is not masculine, not a 'real man,' he is nothing. But a woman can be unfeminine, and still be a person. There is a neuter category for women, but not for men" ("The New Burdens of Masculinity," *Marriage and Family Living* 19 [August 1957]: 231).

17. L'Amour's good fortune was to have arrived at the beginning of the cheap paperback revolution in the 1940s, which allowed him to transform the pulp Western into a major one-man industry. On paperback industry pressures, see Christine Bold, *Selling,* pp. 143–44. On L'Amour's self-merchandising, see John Tuska, "Louis L'Amour's Western Fiction," in *A Variable Harvest: Essays and Reviews of Film and Literature* (Jefferson, NC: McFarland & Co., 1976), p. 333. For figures on L'Amour's sales, see Dennis E. Showalter, "Blazing a New Trail," *Publisher's Weekly,* January 11, 1993, p. 3.

18. John Tuska, "L'Amour's Western Fiction," pp. 331–32. See also John D. Nesbitt, "Change of Purpose in the Novels of Louis L'Amour," in William T. Pilkington, *Critical Essays on the Western American Novel* (Boston: G. K. Hall, 1980), pp. 150–63. That L'Amour dated the beginning of his career from *Hondo* is clear in the self-aggrandizing biography attached to Bantam paperbacks, in which the novel is identified as his "first full-length" production (180).

19. For discussion of L'Amour's need to clear a space for his productions, see Christine Bold, *Selling,* pp. 151–52.

20. In the final chapter (entitled "To Both Their Own") of her 1949 study of sexuality, Margaret Mead warned that "our tendency at present is to minimize all these differences in learning, in rhythm, in type and timing of rewards, and at most to try to obliterate particular differences that are seen as handicaps on one sex. . . . [E]very adjustment that minimizes a difference, a vulnerability, in one sex, a differential strength in the other, diminishes their possibility of complementing each other." Or as she added, in a sentiment underlying many scenes in 1950s Westerns: "If we once accept the premise that we can build a better world by using the different gifts of each sex, we shall have two kinds of freedom, freedom to use untapped gifts of each sex, and freedom to admit freely and cultivate in each sex their special superiorities" (*Male and Female: A Study of the Sexes in a Changing World* [New York: Morrow, 1949], pp. 371, 382).

21. Brandon French has pointed out "the curious fact that Joey—with his straight blond hair and blue eyes—looks very much like Shane (and almost nothing like his curly-haired brunet, brown-eyed father), confirming at a deep spectatorial level the adulterous link between Marianne and Shane" ("The Amiable Spouse: *Shane,*" in *On the Verge of Revolt: Women in American Films of the Fifties* [New York: Ungar, 1978], p. 43).

22. Philip French, *Westerns,* p. 61. Robert Warshow had earlier commented on Alan Ladd as an unparalleled "'aesthetic' object": "his special quality is in his physical smoothness and serenity, unworldly and yet not innocent, but suggesting that no experience can really touch him" ("Movie Chronicle," p. 149).

23. Described by an anonymous reviewer of the film for *Variety Film Reviews* 8, April 15, 1953, n.p.

24. Cited by Geoffrey O'Brien, "Killing Time," *New York Review of Books* 39, March 5, 1992, p. 38. Gary Cooper was the number one male box-office star through the 1930s, prompted by the success of Victor Fleming's *The Virginian* (1929). Cooper's "often evasive yet penetrating glances," Stephen Tatum claims, "his casual lean in the saddle, his slight eyebrow movement or pursing of the lips, his calculated shift in weight, his at times halting delivery suddenly exuding firm confidence—these and other aspects of Cooper's subtle performance command the camera's attention" ("Classic Westerner," p. 69). By 1950, however, before the success of *High Noon,* he was considered a has-been.

25. Steven Mintz and Susan Kellogg, *Domestic Revolutions,* p. 185. See more generally chap. 6, "The Rise of the Companionate Family, 1900–1930," pp. 107–31, and chap. 9, "The Golden Age: Families of the 1950s," pp. 177–201; also Mary Jo Bane, *Here to Stay: American Families in the Twentieth Century* (New York: Basic Books, 1976); Peter Gabriel Filene, *Him/Her/Self: Sex Roles in Modern America* (2d ed. Baltimore: Johns Hopkins University Press, 1986), p. 189; and Christopher Lasch, *Haven in a Heartless World: The Family Besieged* (New York: Basic Books, 1977), esp. chap. 5, "Doctors to a Sick Society," pp. 97–110, on "the new gospel of marriage and parenthood" (107). For contemporary documents, see *Culture and Commitment, 1929–1945,* ed. Warren Susman (New York: George Braziller, 1973), esp. sec. 16, "The Home, the Family, the Child," pp. 201–19; and sec. 18, "The Young," pp. 235–45.

26. Margaret Mead, *Male and Female,* p. 3. Five years later, she noted the confu-

sion facing newly married men and women: "Although we are now entering a new era in which fathers take a great deal of care of young children, the present working generation grew up in a period when child care was woman's work" ("Theoretical Setting—1954," in *Childhood in Contemporary Culture,* ed. Margaret Mead and Martha Wolfenstein [Chicago: University of Chicago Press, 1955], p. 5). As Peter Filene notes, "By 1954 *Life* magazine was announcing 'the domestication of the American male'" (*Him/Her/Self,* pp. 197–98).

27. Prominent examples include Erik Erikson, *Childhood and Society* (1950); David Riesman, *The Lonely Crowd: A Study of the Changing American Character* (1953); Edgar Friedenberg, *The Vanishing Adolescent* (1959); Paul Goodman, *Growing Up Absurd: Problems of Youth in the Organized System* (1960); Kennith Keniston, *The Uncommitted: Alienated Youth in American Society* (1965).

28. Joseph F. Kett, *Rites of Passage: Adolescence in America, 1790 to the Present* (New York: Basic Books, 1977), p. 243. For background to this development, see Lee Soltow and Edward Stevens, *The Rise of Literacy and the Common School in the United States: A Socioeconomic Analysis to 1870* (Chicago: University of Chicago Press, 1981). G. Stanley Hall's mammoth study, *Adolescence: Its Psychology and Its Relations to Physiology, Anthropology, Sociology, Sex, Crime, Religion and Education* (1904), coincided with a transformation in professional thinking about American patterns of upbringing.

29. This is part of the legacy left by G. Stanley Hall, as Dorothy Ross describes it: "With real sensitivity to adolescent experience, Hall described alternating periods of overactivity and inertness; of strong self-feeling and distrust of self." She elaborates in terms that anticipate my discussion of Spock: "Hall's concept of adolescence, then, was founded on a basic ambivalence—on a desire for wide freedom of self-expression and development of potential coupled with the wish to control and direct that development into respectable, ethical forms" (*G. Stanley Hall: The Psychologist as Prophet* [Chicago: University of Chicago Press, 1972], pp. 327, 332). For more on evolving attitudes about adolescence, see John Modell, *Into One's Own: From Youth to Adulthood in the United States, 1920–1975* (Berkeley: University of California Press, 1989), esp. chap. 5, "War and Its Aftermath," pp. 162–212; John Demos, *Past, Present, and Personal: The Family and the Life Course in American History* (New York: Oxford University Press, 1986), esp. chap. 3, "The Changing Faces of Fatherhood," pp. 41–67, and chap. 5, "The Rise and Fall of Adolescence," pp. 92–111; and Judith Sealander, "Families, World War II, and the Baby Boom (1940–1955)," in *American Families: A Research Guide and Historical Handbook,* ed. Joseph M. Hawes and Elizabeth I. Nybakken (Westport, CT: Greenwood Press, 1991), pp. 157–81.

30. James Gilbert claims that "quite simply, the parallel growth of mass media and delinquency after World War II appeared to have a causal relationship," and that "modern mass culture, in particular, radio, the movies, and comic books, was inciting children everywhere to delinquent acts" (*A Cycle of Outrage: America's Reaction to the Juvenile Delinquent in the 1950s* [New York: Oxford University Press, 1986], pp. 80, 77). For further studies of the 1950s' obsession with juvenile delinquency, see Peter Biskind, *Seeing Is Believing* (New York: Pantheon, 1983), esp. chap. 4, "Wild in the Streets: Juvenile Delinquency," pp. 194–227. A symptom of this anxiety was manifested in Dr. Frederick Wertham's hysterical attack on horror comic books as the prime cause of delinquency: "Comic books and life are connected. A bank robbery is easily translated into the rifling of a candy store. Delinquencies formerly restricted to adults are increasingly committed by young people and children." Such reading leads

as well to other forms of psychopathology, as in his claim that "the Batman stories are psychologically homosexual. Our research confirms this entirely. . . . [A] subtle atmosphere of homoeroticism . . . pervades the adventures of the mature 'Batman' and his young friend 'Robin'" (*Seduction of the Innocent* [New York: Rinehart, 1954], pp. 25, 189). Wertham's fears were taken seriously enough for him to be asked to testify before Senator Estes Kefauver's Subcommittee on Juvenile Delinquency where, according to James Gilbert, he claimed that "mass culture could cut through the loving bonds of family to ensnare any child. It could cancel the ties of social, cultural and moral order. Mass culture alone, he suggested, could be more potent than family, social class, tradition or history acting together. This argument, in various forms, echoed throughout the late 1940s and early 1950s, not only because of Wertham's energetic expression, but because, in fact, he spoke to already existing fears about the effects of mass media on children" (*Cycle of Outrage,* pp. 3, 9; for further discussion of Wertham's "crusade," see pp. 91 ff.).

Robert Warshow points out that "*Seduction of the Innocent* is a kind of crime comic book for parents, as its lurid title alone would lead one to expect. There is the same simple conception of motives, the same sense of overhanging doom, the same melodramatic emphasis on pathology, the same direct and immediate relation between cause and effect. If a juvenile criminal is found in possession of comic books, the comic books produced the crime. If a publisher of comic books, alarmed by attacks on the industry, retains a psychiatrist to advise him on suitable content for his publications, it follows *necessarily* that the arrangement is a dishonest one" ("Paul, the Horror Comics, and Dr. Wertham," in *Immediate Experience,* p. 98).

31. Nora Sayre discusses a new focus on "the interior life of the young" in screenplays of the early '50s, especially in terms of "troubled family relationships." As she states, "Clearly, the emphasis on 'craziness' reflects the period's fixation on delinquents—who were laden with lines like 'I'll never get close to anybody' or 'Nobody can help me'" (*Running Time: Films of the Cold War* [New York: Dial Press, 1982], pp. 28, 112–14).

32. The best account of the precipitous decline in movie attendance is contained in Robert Sklar's *Movie-Made,* esp. chap. 16, "The Disappearing Audience and the Television Crisis," pp. 269–85. See also Lawrence Alloway, *Violent America: The Movies 1946–1964* (New York: The Museum of Modern Art, 1971), esp. pp. 21–22; Charles Champlin, *The Flicks: Or Whatever Became of Andy Hardy?* (Pasadena, CA: Ward Ritchie, 1977), pp. 21–23; Garth Jowett, *Film: The Democratic Art* (Boston: Little, Brown, 1976), pp. 333–58; Fredric Stuart, *The Effects of Television on the Motion Picture and Radio Industries* (New York: Arno Press, 1976), p. 10; and for statistics on gross profits of films, see William R. Meyer, *The Making of the Great Westerns* (New Rochelle, NY: Arlington House, 1979), p. 154.

Not until 1935 were Westerns more than 25 percent of feature films (with 1926 offering a sole exception of 28 percent). See Thomas H. Pauly, "The Cold War Western," *Western Humanities Review* 33 (Summer 1979): 257–73; "Westerns as a Proportion of all Features Produced 1926–67," in *The BFI Companion to the Western,* ed. Edward Buscombe, (New York: Atheneum, 1988), p. 427; Phil Hardy, *The Western* (London: Aurum Press, 1983), pp. xv, 188; Garth Jowett, *Film,* p. 369; and Richard White, *"It's Your Misfortune and None of My Own": A History of the American West* (Norman: University of Oklahoma Press, 1991), p. 613.

33. See Thomas H. Pauly, "Cold War Western," p. 257. The number of people

who saw *High Noon* when it first appeared—over 4 million—was an extremely high number for black-and-white films in 1952. Phil Hardy claims that it was one of "the two most influential (and imitated) Westerns of the fifties" (*Western*, p. 188). At $9 million, *Shane* is the eighth top money-making Western ever. See Cobbett S. Steinberg, *Film Facts* (New York: Facts on File, 1980), p. 12.

34. According to *BFI*, p. 427, Western television series began to be aired in 1949, with ten series in 1950 growing to a peak of forty-eight in 1959, and shrinking back to eleven in 1970. Donald H. Kirkley, Jr., claimed in 1979: "Since the emergence of television as a dominant medium of entertainment, no program type has been offered in such abundance as the Western." According to him, the peak period of 1959–60 had 28 series for a total of 570 hours of film footage, equal to 450 75-minute Western feature films. See *A Descriptive Study of the Network Television Western during the Seasons 1955–56—1962–63* (New York: Arno Press, 1979), pp. 1, 111; also Michael Barson, "The TV Western," in Brian G. Rose, ed., *TV Genres* (Westport, CT: Greenwood Press, 1985); John W. Evans, "Modern Man and the Cowboy," *Television Quarterly* 1, no. 2 (May 1962): 31–41; and J. Fred MacDonald, *Who Shot the Sheriff? The Rise and Fall of the Television Western* (New York: Praeger, 1987).

35. For interpretations of Dr. Spock and comparisons of various editions of his book, see William G. Bach, "The Influence of Psychoanalytic Thought on Benjamin Spock's *Baby and Child Care*," *Journal of the History of the Behavioral Sciences* 10, no. 1 (January 1974): 91–94; Lynn Z. Bloom, *Doctor Spock: Biography of a Conservative Radical* (New York: Bobbs-Merrill Co., 1972), esp. chap. 6, "*Baby and Child Care:* Impact and Reaction," pp. 121–49; Nancy Pottishman Weiss, "Mother, the Invention of Necessity: Dr. Benjamin Spock's *Baby and Child Care*," *American Quarterly* 29 (1977): 519–46; and Michael Zuckerman, "Dr. Spock: The Confidence Man," in Charles E. Rosenberg, ed., *The Family in History* (Philadelphia: University of Pennsylvania Press, 1975), pp. 179–207. Bach in particular emphasizes that Spock contends with the rivalry between adolescents and parents in his advice about 4–6-year-olds.

36. John B. Watson, *The Psychological Care of Infant and Child* (New York: W. W. Norton, 1928), p. 12. The statement, italicized by the extremely influential Watson, was preceded by an appeal to "the modern mother who is beginning to find that the rearing of children is the most difficult of all professions, more difficult than engineering, than law, or even than medicine itself." Steven Mintz and Susan Kellogg describe this postwar shift to "scientific mothering" in the work of such behaviorists as Watson, which spurred the counterefforts of Dewey, Montessori, and Gesell (*Domestic Revolutions*, p. 122).

In 1954, Margaret Mead argued an "extreme transformation" in pediatric assumptions since 1914: "At the earlier date, the infant appeared to be endowed with strong and dangerous impulses. . . . In contrast to this we find in 1942–45 that the baby has been transformed into almost complete harmlessness. The intense and concentrated impulses of the past have disappeared." She then adds: "Formerly, giving in to impulse was the way to encourage its growing beyond control. The baby who was picked up when he cried, held and rocked when he wanted it, soon grew into a tyrant. This has now been strikingly reversed" ("Fun Morality: An Analysis of Recent American Child-Training Literature," in *Childhood in Contemporary Culture*, pp. 169–71). Yet, as David Riesman notes of "the tasks of defining the goals for modern children," in this same volume of essays, "These goals are no longer clear-cut" ("'Tootle': A Modern Cautionary Tale," p. 237).

37. Spock followed Dewey in trusting to natural development, controverting his most important predecessor, John Watson, who had declared that "children are made not born" and that "there are no instincts. We build in at an early age everything that is later to appear" (*Psychological Care*, pp. 7, 38). Some sense for the standard advice before Spock can be gained from a brief survey of Watson's ideas, for instance, "on the dangers lurking in the mother's kiss" ("There are serious rocks ahead for the over-kissed child"), on "over-coddling," on discouraging thumb sucking "during the first few days of infancy" with gloves, on masturbation ("Their hands should be watched"), and on instilling continence by isolating the eight-month-old in a bathroom strapped to a toilet seat (pp. 70, 78, 136, 174, 121). "There is a sensible way of treating children. Treat them as though they were young adults. . . . Let your behavior always be objective and kindly firm. Never hug and kiss them, never let them sit in your lap. If you must, kiss them once on the forehead when they say good night. Shake hands with them in the morning. Give them a pat on the head if they have made an extraordinarily good job of a difficult task. Try it out. In a week's time you will find how easy it is to be perfectly objective with your child and at the same time kindly. You will be utterly ashamed of the mawkish, sentimental way you have been handling it" (81).

Nancy Pottishman Weiss discusses the context within which Watson developed his Pavlovian ideas, and his distance from the Freudian Spock, only to add: "But viewed more closely, the two manuals have more in common than meets the eye" ("Mother," p. 531).

38. Unlike Michael Zuckerman, who asserts the Spock baby is instinctually amiable, William Graebner claims: "At the center of this unstable world was an unstable infant and child—fearful, frustrated, insecure, and potentially destructive in his aggressive tendencies" ("The Unstable World of Benjamin Spock: Social Engineering in a Democratic Culture, 1917–1950," *Journal of American History* 67, no. 3 [December 1980]: 612–13). For a more laudatory reading of Spock, see A. Michael Sulman, "The Humanization of the American Child: Benjamin Spock as a Popularizer of Psychoanalytic Thought," *Journal of the History of the Behavioral Sciences* 9 (1973): 258–65.

39. Benjamin Spock, *Common Sense Book,* p. 193. See also pp. 144, 20, 147, 352. Spock's conventional emphasis on the masculine pronoun (which continued until editorial changes in 1960 editions) is less significant than the disproportionate concern with male activities—something reflected in other analysts of child development as well. Ruth Benedict opens her own 1954 investigation of childhood by focusing on "three such contrasts that occur in our culture between the individual's role as child and as father." See "Continuities and Discontinuities in Cultural Conditioning," in *Childhood in Contemporary Culture,* p. 23. For an account of Spock's revisions in the 1957, 1968, and 1976 editions of his book, see Nancy Pottishman Weiss, "Mother," passim.

40. Nancy Pottishman Weiss notes that Spock's "Freudian world is . . . scrubbed of seething ids, constraining and punishing superegos, and fixations in oral, anal, and genital stages," and concludes that "this world of rearing the young is free of dissonance or conflict, or the recognition of poverty or cultural difference" ("Mother," pp. 539, 546). As Steven Mintz and Susan Kellogg observe, however, "Despite Dr. Spock's warm and comforting language, child care manuals of the 1950s were characterized by an undercurrent of anxiety. No previous generation of child care books had ever expressed so much anxiety and fear about children's health, safety, and happiness" (*Domestic Revolutions,* p. 188). See also Dorothy Ross, *Hall,* p. 332.

41. This contrast is made explicit when Marian tries on clothes, dressed in Joey's funny hat, followed immediately by the stunning sight of Shane with his guns. Martin Pumphrey notes that only Joey and Marian Starrett are allowed to gaze ("Masculinity," *BFI*, p. 183).

42. The immense popularity of Tiomkin's ballad led to theme- and title-songs as a requirement in subsequent films. For an account of Tiomkin's musical innovations in the film, see Christopher Palmer, *The Composer in Hollywood* (London: Marian Boyers, 1993), pp. 142–43; and Tony Thomas, *Music for the Movies* (London: Tantivy Press, 1973), pp. 64–74; "Dmitri Tiomkin on Film Music," in *Film Score: The View from the Podium,* ed. Tony Thomas (New York: A. S. Barnes & Co., 1979), pp. 98–99. For a discussion of film music as the "hypnotist's voice," see Claudia Gorbman, *Unheard Melodies: Narrative Film Music* (Bloomington: Indiana University Press, 1987), p. 6.

43. For the suggestion that the film's success owed to a self-conscious invocation of television requirements, as if the "high noon" countdown posed a critique of half-hour programming, see Rose K. Goldsen, *The Show and Tell Machine: How Television Works and Works You Over* (New York: Dial Press, 1977), pp. 250, 350.

44. In a section cut from the screenplay, it is clear that Amy Kane's family does not understand her: "Back home they think I'm very strange. I'm a feminist. You know, women's rights—things like that." As well, Amy is partially identified with Harvey Pell, in Kane's repetition to them both of the line, "If you don't know, there's no use of me telling you." While Harvey wants a job and Amy wants an explanation, the logic of Kane's silence in both cases remains the same.

45. Don Graham, *"High Noon" (1952)*, in *Western Movies,* ed. William T. Pilkington and Don Graham (Albuquerque: University of New Mexico Press, 1979), pp. 57–58.

Chapter Eight

1. Owen Wister, *Lin McLean* (1897; rev. ed. New York: A. L. Burt Co., 1907), p. 56.

2. Robert C. Cumbow, *Once upon a Time: The Films of Sergio Leone* (Metuchen, NJ: Scarecrow Press, 1987), p. 155.

3. Robert Warshow, "Movie Chronicle: The Westerner," in *The Immediate Experience: Movies, Comics, Theatre, and Other Aspects of Popular Culture* (Garden City, NY: Doubleday, 1962), p. 151.

4. Peckinpah's enthusiasm for cinematic violence seemed to many a self-conscious commentary on America's belligerence in Southeast Asia. See David A. Cook, *A History of Narrative Film* (New York: W. W. Norton, 1981), p. 631; and Jay Hyams, *The Life and Times of the Western Movie* (New York: W. H. Smith, 1983), pp. 134 ff.

5. Will Wright, *Sixguns and Society: A Structural Study of the Western* (Berkeley: University of California Press, 1975), p. 85.

6. "Spaghetti Westerns" consisted of some 300-odd films released in Italy between 1963 and 1969—a genre created by Italian directors shooting in Spanish locations with international casts sometimes speaking five languages. Shooting schedules were short; *A Fistful of Dollars* was written in three weeks and shot in seven more. For further discussion, see Christopher Frayling, *Spaghetti Westerns: Cowboys and Europeans from Karl May to Sergio Leone* (London: Routledge & Kegan Paul, 1981); and Rob-

ert C. Cumbow, *Once upon a Time*. For further statistics, see *The BFI Companion to the Western*, ed. Edward Buscombe, (New York: Atheneum, 1988), pp. 426–27.

7. Copyright violations precluded the film from being released in the United States until 1967 and explain why Leone agreed to give Kurosawa 15 percent of international profits. For discussion of Kurosawa's influence on Leone and *Shane's* influence on both directors, see Robert C. Cumbow *Once upon a Time*, p. 2; Christopher Frayling, *Spaghetti Westerns*, pp. 147–53; and Stuart Kaminsky, "Comparative Forms: The Samurai Film and the Western," in *American Film Genres: Approaches to a Critical Theory of Popular Film* (n.p.: Pflaum, 1974), pp. 33–42.

Fistful was budgeted at only $200,000; *For a Few Dollars More* was given $600,000; *The Good, the Bad and the Ugly* cost $1.2 million. Each grossed $8.5 million, which exceeded any other Italian film in the 1960s. Leone's critically acclaimed fourth film was far less popular: *Once upon a Time in the West* (1968), written by Bernardo Bertolucci. Another sign of success was the turn in Clint Eastwood's career: he started in the television series, "Rawhide," in 1958–66; was offered $15,000 for Leone's first film; $50,000 for the second; and $250,000 plus 10 percent of the profits for the third. See Christopher Frayling, *Spaghetti Westerns*, p. 169.

8. Robert C. Cumbow, *Once upon a Time*, p. 2.

9. In 1972, Simone de Beauvoir admitted "some adventure films have kept me in suspense—some westerns, for example, including films made by the Italians such as *The Good, the Bad and the Ugly*. Stories that I should think ludicrous if they were written down can enchant me on the screen. . . . There is an odd shift, a difference of phase, between the immediate evidence of one's eyes (the indestructible illusion of reality) and the unlikelihood of the facts. If a director uses this shift intelligently, he can make it produce the most delightful effects. That is the basis of the humour of the Italian westerns. But it has to be used intelligently" (cited by Christopher Frayling, *Spaghetti Westerns*, p. 129).

10. Robert C. Cumbow, *Once upon a Time*, p. 144.

11. Franco Ferrini, cited by Christopher Frayling, *Spaghetti Westerns*, p. 188.

12. Deleuze's analysis of Eisenstein's facial close-ups is based on "an example which is *not* a face: a clock which is presented to us in close-up several times. On the one hand it has hands moved by micro-movements, at least virtual ones. . . . On the other hand it has a face as receptive immobile surface, receptive plate of inscription, impassive suspense: it is a *reflecting and reflected unity.*

"The Bergonsian definition of the affect rested on these two very characteristics: a motor tendency on a sensitive nerve. In other words, a series of micro-movements on an immobilised plate of nerve. . . . But is this not the same as a Face itself? The face is this organ-carrying plate of nerves which has sacrificed most of its global mobility and which gathers or expresses in a free way all kinds of tiny local movements which the rest of the body usually keeps hidden. Each time we discover these two poles in something—reflecting surface and intensive micro-movements—we can say that this thing has been treated as a face [*visage*]: it has been 'envisaged' or rather 'faceified' [*visagei-fiée*], and in turn it stares at us [*dévisage*], it looks at us . . . even if it does not resemble a face" (*Cinema 1: The Movement-Image*, trans. Hugh Tomlinson and Barbara Habberjam [Minneapolis: University of Minnesota Press, 1986], p. 87). See also his refutation of both psychoanalysis and linguistics in their claims that the close-up represents a partial object (castration, synechdoche) rather than the entity abstracted "from all spatio-temporal co-ordinates" (95).

13. While Frayling here in fact is describing what he takes to be Leone's concern (*Spaghetti Westerns*, p. 171), Robert C. Cumbow seems to me closer to the truth when he claims: "Anonymity is central to heroism in Leone's world. Throughout the *oeuvre*, nicknames, generic names, pseudonyms, and anonyms are more common than given names and surnames. It's all part of Leone's notion of silence—his development of the prototypical silent stranger of the Hollywood western paradigm: The survivor is he who says the least, reveals the least about himself; doing that, he is the least vulnerable" (*Once upon a Time*, p. 165).

14. See Jay Hyams, *Life and Times*, p. 165; and Christopher Frayling, *Spaghetti Westerns*, pp. 167–68. Alan Williams notes a correlation between cinematography and sound, with both close-ups and distinctive sound tracks making events seem closer, more intense, in a way that Leone can be seen to have coordinated. See "Is Sound Recording Like a Language?" *Cinema/Sound*, a special issue of *Yale French Studies* 60 (1980): 51–66.

15. Robert C. Cumbow, *Once upon a Time*, p. 199. Cumbow also points out that Dmitri Tiomkin, who composed the music for *High Noon*, had the "strongest influence on Morricone" (202).

16. Cited by Robert C. Cumbow, *Once upon a Time*, p. 155.

17. Leone claimed of Eastwood that "before the second film, he said to me 'Listen, Sergio, I'll do everything you want, except smoke!'—but this was impossible, since the protagonist was the same" (cited by Christopher Frayling, *Spaghetti Westerns*, p. 146).

18. Slavoj Zizek borrows from Michel Chion the notion of "la voix acousmatique" to discuss this experience of identifying an "errant voice" with an object: "Insofar as it is not anchored to a specific source, localized in a specific place, the *voix acousmatique* functions as a threat that lurks everywhere" (*Looking Awry: An Introduction to Jacques Lacan through Popular Culture* [Cambridge, MA: MIT Press, 1991], pp. 126–27).

19. This scene is itself a repetition of Ramon Rojas's ploy in posing the corpses of Mexican and U.S. government forces to look as if they had annihilated each other. Although Leone otherwise borrowed almost shot for shot from Kurosawa's *Yojimbo*, the two scenes that have no analogue in that film are this and the later sequence in the cemetery where No Name arranges the corpses (see Robert C. Cumbow, *Once upon a Time*, pp. 4–5).

20. Robert C. Cumbow, *Once upon a Time*, p. 162.

21. Robert Warshow, "Movie Chronicle," pp. 137–38.

22. Cited by Christopher Frayling, *Spaghetti Westerns*, p. 135.

23. In another instance of Eastwood's linguistic inability affecting the plot, Georgina Howell claims that he drew "a line through three pages of dialogue" and himself substituted the first sentence here ("Cool Clint," p. 222). Christopher Frayling declares that the help No Name "offers the 'holy family' is almost inseparable from his intention to escalate the Baxter-Rojo rivalry," suggesting another motive as well (*Spaghetti Westerns*, p. 183).

24. Cited by Christopher Frayling, *Spaghetti Westerns*, p. 65.

25. Cited in ibid., p. 126. Rick Altman poses the question in generic terms: "Why is it that the western, from the fifties on, becomes fascinated with the very violence that earlier constituted its unquestioned appeal?" His answer is that the "generic

syntax" of the Western "establishes violent confrontation as a method of punishing the unjust," even though it "removes consideration of violence itself from the realm of western signification," and that this "repressed" consideration returns in later versions (*The American Film Musical* [Bloomington: Indiana University Press, 1987], pp. 117–18).

26. Jim Kitses, *Horizons West—Anthony West, Budd Boetticher, Sam Peckinpah: Studies of Authorship within the Western* (London: Thames & Hudson, 1969), p. 169.

27. For an account of the making of the movie, see Garner Simmons, *Peckinpah: A Portrait in Montage* (Austin: University of Texas Press, 1976), esp. pp. 101 ff. The prerelease version of the film was 190 minutes, and in a sneak preview in Kansas City thirty-odd people walked out, some physically ill. The original release time was 143 minutes, while the American version was 135 minutes (8 minutes cut by Warner Brothers). See Doug McKinney, *Sam Peckinpah* (Boston: Twayne, 1979), pp. 85–89; and Paul Seydor, *Peckinpah: The Western Films* (Urbana: University of Illinois Press, 1980), pp. 78–79.

28. Philip French, *Westerns: Aspects of a Movie Genre* (London: Secker & Warburg, 1973), p. 115.

29. Cited by John Cutts, "Shoot!" *Films and Filming* 16 (October 1969): 8. For the quote from Henry James, see "The Novels of George Eliot," *Atlantic Monthly* 28 (1866): 485.

30. David A. Cook, *Narrative Film*, pp. 631–32. See also Brian Garfield, *Western Films: A Complete Guide* (New York: Rawson Associates, 1982), p. 59, for an account of the film's innovations.

31. For two critics outraged by the film when it first appeared, see Stanley Kauffman, *Figures of Light: Film Criticism and Comment* (New York: Harper, 1971), p. 182; and Paul Seydor, *Peckinpah*, p. 116.

32. Peckinpah himself remarked on this "strange" sense of identification: "I wasn't trying to make an epic, I was trying to tell a simple story about bad men in changing times" (cited by Paul Seydor, *Peckinpah*, p. 77).

33. In *Welcome to Hard Times* (New York: Random House, 1960), E. L. Doctorow addresses this question as the central issue of the Western, suggesting through the cyclical character of his plot two competing claims for the origins of evil: violence is at once part of a natural cycle and a social effect. The novel raises the question of whether Bad Men from Bodie are produced by nature or nurture. The narrator, Blue, identifies these evil figures as natural forces, who "came with the land, and you could no more cope with them than you could with dust or hailstones" (7). Yet the process of the novel is also to show, through Jimmy Fee's upbringing, how such men are created and given names.

34. To complicate the issue (in Peckinpah's inimitably self-contradictory way), he also claimed, "I believe in the complete innocence of children. They have no idea of good and evil. It's an acquired taste" (Richard Whitehall, "Talking with Peckinpah," *Sight and Sound* 38 [Autumn 1969]: 175). See also Jim Kitses, *Horizons West*, p. 161; and Philip French, *Westerns*, p. 32.

35. For alternative views, see Robert C. Cumbow: "The question, 'What would they have done if things had happened differently?' doesn't arise in watching a Leone film. . . . [W]e see Leone's films do not feature character interaction in response to a situation or an environment (conventional narrative cinema does that). Things happen

the way they do in Leone's films because they cannot happen otherwise" (*Once upon a Time,* p. 57). And Jim Kitses, who claims that *"The Wild Bunch* is nothing if not moral" (*Horizons West,* p. 168).

36. Eric Hobsbawm, *Bandits* (1969; 2d ed. Harmondsworth: Penguin, 1985), p. 26.

Chapter Nine

1. *Representative Men: Seven Lectures,* The Collected Works of Ralph Waldo Emerson, vol. 4 (Cambridge, MA: Harvard University Press, 1987), p. 16.

2. Cited from 1902 journal by Don D. Walker, "Criticism of the Cowboy Novel: Retrospect and Reflections," *Western American Literature* 11 (February 1977): 277–78.

3. Cited from 1913 by Rita Parks, *The Western Hero in Film and Television: Mass Media Mythology* (Ann Arbor, MI: UMI Research Press, 1982), p. 155.

4. Will Wright, "The Empire Bites the Dust," *Social Text* (Fall 1982): 120. See also Richard Slotkin, *Gunfighter Nation: The Myth of the Frontier in Twentieth-Century America* (New York: Atheneum, 1992), pp. 627–34.

5. Prior to the Oscar triumphs of *Dances with Wolves* and *Unforgiven,* only one other Western had gained an award for Best Picture: *Cimarron* in 1930–31. For the effect of Cruze's film on the industry, see Jay Hyams, *The Life and Times of the Western Movie* (New York: W. H. Smith, 1983), p. 33; also p. 44.

6. John Sutherland describes a transformation that took place in marketing popular books, in *Bestsellers: Popular fiction of the 1970s* (London: Routledge & Kegan Paul, 1981), esp. pp. 33–37. See also his chapters on *"Death Wish:* From Stetson to Hard Hat" and "The 'New Western' and the Middle-Aged Reader," pp. 154–66.

7. See Phil Hardy, *The Western* (London: Aurum Press, 1983), p. viii.

8. Joel Engel, "Teachin' Ridin', Ropin' and Fallin' Outta the Durn Saddle," *New York Times,* December 26, 1993, sec. H, p. 25.

9. See Stuart Elliott, "The Marlboro Man Is Missing in Action in New Campaign," *New York Times,* October 23, 1992, sec. D, p. 16. For an account of the Leo Burnett advertising strategy that first developed the idea of "Marlboro Country" in 1963, see Andrew Jaffe, "They Came to Where the Money Was," *M* 9, no. 3 (December 1991): 59–62.

10. See *American Media and Mass Culture,* ed. Donald Lazere (Berkeley: University of California Press, 1987), p. 159; Carol J. Clover, *Men, Women, and Chain Saws: Gender in the Modern Horror Film* (Princeton: Princeton University Press, 1992), p. 236; and Richard Schickel, "Foreward," *The BFI Companion to the Western,* ed. Edward Buscombe (New York: Atheneum, 1988), p. 11, also pp. 53–54.

11. Cited by John Sutherland, *Bestsellers,* p. 203. On the vigilante film's indebtedness to the Western, see pp. 157–58; and also Philip French on the rise of "the police movie and the vigilante film," in *Westerns* (New York: Oxford University Press, 1977), p. 178–80.

12. Dennis Bingham has claimed that *"Unforgiven* finds Eastwood crossing over into the hysteria, masochism, and 'femininity' that emerge in the [James] Stewart performance style" (*Acting Male: Masculinities in the Films of James Stewart, Jack Nicholson, and Clint Eastwood* [New Brunswick, NJ: Rutgers University Press, 1994], p. 237).

13. As Paul Smith states, *"Unforgiven* suffers from being unable to criticize convincingly the very violence that it itself is involved in and that it does not shrink from re-representing" (*Clint Eastwood: A Cultural Production* [Minneapolis: University of Min-

nesota Press, 1993], p. 267). For an alternative view, see Susan Jeffords, *Hard Bodies: Hollywood Masculinity in the Reagan Era* (New Brunswick, NJ: Rutgers University Press, 1994), esp. pp. 180–86.

14. Cited by James Greenberg, "Western Canvas, Palette of Blood," *New York Times,* February 26, 1995, sec. 2, p. 19.

15. Frank Rich is one example: "Eastwood may have been a Republican poster boy, but this movie is a parable of the Clinton foreign policy the American public now wants: send the military on safe mercy missions to help victimized women and children . . . , but don't let Americans return to the perilous gulf combat role of Rambo" ("Clintonian Cinema," *New York Times Magazine,* March 21, 1993, p. 76).

16. Rick Altman observes that the Western from the 1950s onward became "fascinated with the very violence that earlier constituted its unquestioned appeal," and he goes on to show how that fascination finally exhausts itself in terms of "syntactic" variations. See *The American Film Musical* (Bloomington: Indiana University Press, 1987), pp. 117–18.

index

Adolescence: 8, 12, 204, 308nn.29 and 30; emergence of concept, 202–3; and family roles, 192, 196–97, 205–6, in film Westerns, 191–93, 199–204, 212–21. *See also* Education; Femininity; Gender; Juvenile delinquency; Maturation; Masculinity

Adorno, Theodor W., 18, 20, 271n.11. *See also* Frankfurt School

Advertising, use of western icons, 19, 25, 258. *See also* Popular culture; Television

African-Americans, in Westerns, 257–58

Aimard, Gustave, 275n.8

Aimless glance, as narrative technique, 33–35, 41–42, 53, 229. *See also* Landscape; Optic lawlessness; Spectacle

Alexander, Thomas G., 291n.8

Allmendinger, Blake, 273n.31

Altman, Rick, xvi, 314n.25, 317n.16

Andersen, Hans Christian, 68

Anderson, Bronco Billy, 140

Anderson, Nancy K., 68, 89

Anderson, Sherwood, 15

Anthony, Susan B., 115

Anti-Western, 7, 10, 98, 250–51. *See also* Spaghetti Western

Arthur, Jean, 200–201, 208 fig., 209

Audiences: 61–62, 236, 270n.5, 272n.20, 274nn.6 and 7; expectations of, 24–26, 258–60; and popular culture, 4, 16–17, 20–21, 259; as

shaped by Westerns, 15, 30, 198. *See also* Popular culture; Popular genres

Austen, Jane, 113

Baigell, Matthew, 282n.20

Ballard, Lucian, 250

Balzac, Honoré de, 31, 34, 52, 65

Barroom brawl. *See* Stock scenes

Barthes, Roland, vii, 12, 19, 134, 275n.14; *Mythologies*, 19

Bazin, André, 157, 268n.12

Beadle, Erasmus, 7

Beard, James Franklin, Jr., 275n.11, 277n.27

Beauvoir, Simone de, 15, 313n.9

Bederman, Gail, 289n.29

Beider, Robert E., 277n.25

Bellour, Raymond, 160

Bennett, Tony, 6, 272n.20, 304n.46

Bergman, Ingmar, 301n.33

Bernstein, Elmer, 232

Bertolucci, Bernardo, 313n.7

Bessie, Alvah, 191

Bettelheim, Bruno, 8

Bewley, Marius, 277n.26

Bierce, Ambrose, 72, 88

Bierstadt, Albert: 9, 56–93, 97, 103–4, 111, 119, 129, 130, 131, 148, 194; *Among the Sierra Nevada Mountains, California,* 76–77, 76 fig.; *The Domes of Yosemite,* 88–89, 88 fig.; *Mount Whitney,* 70, 71 fig.; *Night at Valley*   319